BEING MARRIED

BEING
MARRIED

by

EVELYN M. DUVALL, Ph.D.

REUBEN HILL, Ph.D.

With chapters in collaboration with

SYLVANUS M. DUVALL, Ph.D.

D. C. HEATH AND COMPANY *Boston*

For reproducing photographs grateful acknowledgment is made to the following sources: Photo Researchers Inc., pages 2, 30, 48, 120, 150, 272, 296, 336, 352, 374, 392; Monkmeyer, pages 70, 226; H. Armstrong Roberts, page 96; Ewing Galloway, page 134; J. R. Wood and Sons, Inc., page 170; Dr. Paul Wolff, page 194; A. Devaney, Inc., page 208; Magnum Photos Inc., page 248; Black Star, page 312; Three Lions, Inc., page 416.

The graphs were drawn by HARRISON B. GOODMAN.

Preface

Being married is exciting. But it is full of questions too. The questions that today's young people ask about marriage and family life are more mature, more sophisticated, and more urgent than those raised even a dozen years ago. Modern youth is encouraged to inquire into areas of life that used to be more severely censored. From childhood on they have been exposed to family life problems at home, in school, church, community groups, and through the mass media. So their questions reflect the spirit of inquiry as well as a rapidly increasing body of knowledge.

Being Married taps the accumulated findings of extensive recent research to meet the needs of the new generation. It draws upon published materials from scores of journals, periodicals and monographs. It utilizes unpublished findings reported at national and international conferences in the areas of dating, courtship, love, marriage, and family life. Despite this research orientation, the book is functional in its style and organization.

By functional education we mean the process of learning that begins with the interests, needs, and known readiness of the student, with the goal of helping him find answers to his questions. As his interests grow, so does the breadth of the coverage, in ever-widening circles. Functional education is clearly distinguished from the traditional academic approach which customarily starts with the historical backgrounds of the problem and focuses on theoretical concepts, only incidentally getting around to the student's concerns and interests—and usually late in the course sequence if at all.

Our philosophy expressed in this book is that love, marriage, and family life education does not need to be dull. We gear into the motivations that lie latent in the universal interests in men and women, their loves and problems, their interactions and plans in dating, courting, getting married, and raising a family. Each chapter, written around the human interest questions that introduce it, is reader-centered in design, readability, and focus.

Our debt to others who have blazed the trails we follow and who have encouraged us in our pioneering is too great to spell out in detail. We appreciate more than we can here enumerate the thousands of colleagues, friends, and students who have encouraged, assisted, and prodded us through the years.

We reaffirm our faith in the collaborative process—it is truly creative for those rugged enough to take it. The entire book has been thought through, worked over, written, and rewritten by both Duvalls and Hills. This, then, represents the active participation of two whole families who jointly dedicate this book to growing families everywhere.

EVELYN MILLIS DUVALL
REUBEN HILL

Contents

Part One: ANTICIPATING MARRIAGE

Part Two: BEING MARRIED

Part Three: BECOMING A FAMILY

ANTICIPATING MARRIAGE

1 Dating and Friendship Making

What do you get out of dating?

How do you get into the dating crowd?

How do you make friends?

What do you do on a date?

Who rates as a good date?

What are your dating aims and values?

Wher you marry, you marry someone you know. You are fortunate if you have become good friends over a period of time. Ideally you have had a variety of dates with each other in which you have discovered that it is good to be together. Hopefully, you have learned about each other, about yourself, and about your relationship through your association in dating. As a twentieth-century young American you have the privilege of finding your own friends, making your own dates, and eventually choosing from among them the one you will marry.

Until quite recently parents took a much greater responsibility for getting their children married through arranging and supervising their early associations, chaperoning their courtship, and deciding who would marry whom. In other countries, even today, a girl is sheltered from mixed association from puberty until the time her engagement is announced to the man her parents have selected for her. In such a culture, dating as we know it today is not necessary. Even in this country, dating is a fairly recent phenomenon, coming into its own within the last half century.

Dating today is a couple-arranged pairing off for a specific social occasion. A date is made by a boy and a girl, or a man and a woman, who agree to attend a social affair or to spend a period of time with each other, for the satisfaction of being together. The kind of satisfaction they get in their dating depends upon many complicated and interrelated factors.

What Do You Get Out of Dating?

Your dating depends upon a great many things—who you are, how you feel about yourself, your attitude toward the opposite sex, how ready you are to "get involved," and how socially expert you are in making friends, getting dates, and functioning in mixed groups and intimate associations.

Some dates are openly exploitative. The man is out for "what he can get" from the woman. The woman is frankly "using" the man for social, economic, or emotional purposes of her own. Some years ago Waller [1] described dating as characterized by competitive "rating." Since then, Margaret Mead and Geoffrey Gorer [2] in their general anthropological observations of our youth culture have both seen American dating patterns as largely exploitative and competitive.

More promising interpretations of dating have been made by sociologists studying campus life in recent years. Blood sees dating as preparing for marriage in several important ways: (1) gaining acquaintance with the other sex, (2) becoming acquainted with individual personalities, (3) trying out relationships, (4) acquiring skill in human interaction, (5) weaning emotionally from parents, and (6) finding the right person. [3]

Apart from its central service of preparing individuals for marriage dating is of value in itself. Whether or not anything comes of it, it can be pleasant recreation. It serves a real purpose in providing the means by which members of both sexes become socialized, learn how to behave in social situations, and to handle themselves smoothly in a wide variety of adult and near-adult circumstances. [4]

Dating is so well established in American communities that not to date is not to participate in many functions for youth. Having a date is

---

[1] Willard Waller, "The Rating and Dating Complex," *American Sociological Review*, October, 1937, No. 2, pp. 727–734.

[2] Margaret Mead, *Male and Female*, New York: Morrow, 1949, pp. 281–295; and Geoffrey Gorer, *The American People*, New York: Norton, 1948, pp. 106–132.

[3] Robert O. Blood, Jr., *Anticipating Your Marriage*, Glencoe, Illinois: Free Press, 1955, pp. 14–20.

[4] Samuel Harman Lowrie, "Dating Theories and Student Responses," *American Sociological Review*, June, 1951, Vol. 16, No. 3, pp. 334–340; and Evelyn Millis Duvall, *Facts of Life and Love*, New York: Association Press, 1956, pp. 109–221; further elaborated in Evelyn Millis Duvall, *The Art of Dating*, New York: Association Press, 1958.

so greatly emphasized that one feels left out and inadequate without one. Many a boy, many a girl wistfully wonders "What is the matter with me that I do not get dates?" From time to time a young person faces the searching questions, "How am I doing?" and "Where do I stand in my dating practice?"

How Do You Get into the Dating Crowd?

According to numerous recent studies most young people begin to have dates between 14 and 16 years of age.[5] By the time they reach college age the majority of both men and women are dating fairly regularly.[6] However, there are some young people who do not date at all through high school or college. One fourth of the girls (24 per cent) and 42 per cent of the boys, in a national sample of tenth- through twelfth-grade high school students, say they never or seldom have a date.[7] Smith's report of college dating reveals 12 per cent of the men and 3 per cent of the women who never have a date.[8] People who find it hard to get into the dating crowd in their home town face difficulties again when they reach college. Hill found both sexes reporting larger percentages of no dating at all in the first year of college than in the last year of high school (see Fig. 1).

It is safe to assume that in every residence hall there are girls who wait night after night for telephone calls that never come. Many a man throws himself into his work or his hobbies as a cover for his lack of skill with members of the opposite sex. With so much emphasis on being popular, the tendency is for members of both sexes to hide the lonely heart behind a brave smile and a pretense of other interests, rather than admit the insufficiency of their dates. Various reasons are

---

[5] Ruth Connor and Edith Flynn Hall, "The Dating Behavior of College Freshmen and Sophomores," *Journal of Home Economics*, Vol. 44, No. 4, April, 1952, p. 278; Samuel Harman Lowrie, "Sex Differences and Age of Initial Dating," *Social Forces*, Vol. 30, No. 4, May, 1952, pp. 456–461; Purdue Opinion Panel, Poll No. 43, *Male-Female Roles as Seen by Youth*, Lafayette, Indiana: Purdue University, February, 1956, pp. 2a and 3a; William M. Smith, Jr., "Rating and Dating: A Re-Study," *Marriage and Family Living*, Vol. XIV, No. 4, November, 1952, pp. 312–313; Survey Research Center, *A Study of Adolescent Boys*, Ann Arbor, Michigan: University of Michigan, 1957, p. 42; Survey Research Center, *Adolescent Girls: A Nation-wide Study of Girls between Eleven and Eighteen Years of Age*, Ann Arbor, Michigan: University of Michigan, 1957, p. 107; and other surveys and research studies summarized in Evelyn Millis Duvall, *The Art of Dating*, New York: Association Press, 1958.

[6] Connor and Hall, *op. cit.*, p. 278; Purdue Opinion Panel, No. 43, *op. cit.*, p. 4a; and Smith, *op. cit.*, p. 313.

[7] Purdue Opinion Panel, No. 43, *op. cit.*, p. 2a.

[8] Smith, *op. cit.*, p. 313.

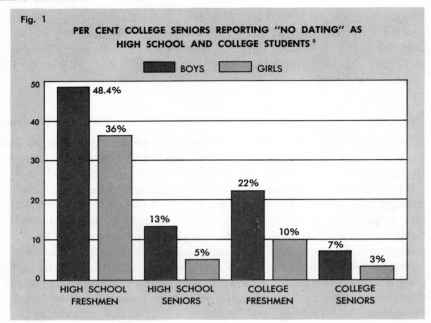

Fig. 1

PER CENT COLLEGE SENIORS REPORTING "NO DATING" AS HIGH SCHOOL AND COLLEGE STUDENTS [9]

■ BOYS   □ GIRLS

(chart values)
HIGH SCHOOL FRESHMEN — 48.4%, 36%
HIGH SCHOOL SENIORS — 13%, 5%
COLLEGE FRESHMEN — 22%, 10%
COLLEGE SENIORS — 7%, 3%

given for not dating. Connor and Hall report: "Several women gave 'No opportunity' as their reason for not dating, and almost equal proportions of both men and women stated that they were unable to attract persons who interested them." [10]

Students often complain of the lack of opportunities to meet members of the opposite sex. One study found 35 per cent of the men and 41 per cent of the women reporting that their opportunities for meeting members of the other sex were inadequate.[11] When one sex greatly outnumbers the other the problem is exaggerated. On one campus where the ratio was five men to one woman, the men experienced real difficulty in obtaining dates, especially during the beginning of their freshman year.[12] With time and experience the dating frequency increases, as is seen in Table 1, which compares freshmen, sophomore, junior, and senior men by their reports of dating more, less, or the same amount they did in high school.

[9] Reuben Hill, unpublished data collected at the University of North Carolina, Spring 1955.

[10] Connor and Hall, op. cit., p. 278.

[11] Clifford Kirkpatrick and Theodore Caplow, "Courtship in a Group of Minnesota Students," American Journal of Sociology, Vol. LI, 1945, p. 117.

[12] Roy H. Rodgers, "Effects of a High Sex Ratio on the Dating Behavior of Undergraduate Males," M.A. Thesis, University of North Carolina, Chapel Hill, N.C., 1957.

TABLE 1. *Dating Frequency on Campus as Compared with High School, as Reported by University Men* [13]

Relative Dating Frequency	1st Year	2nd Year	3rd Year	4th Year	Total
Date More	5	18	31	24	78
Date Same	19	20	19	22	80
Date Less	53	39	26	24	142
Totals	77	77	76	70	300

That some individuals consistently find it easier than others to get dates suggests that at least some of the lack lies within the person. In one study of senior high school boys and girls those who were successful in dating differed significantly from those who were not. The seniors who were not dating had (1) a lower estimation of themselves, (2) less wholesome family relationships, (3) parents who were less socially active (such as from non-English-speaking countries), and (4) less involvement in social activities as a whole.[14] This report recommends for incompetent daters:

1. Help in understanding the normality of their own bodies, their behavior, and feelings, in formulating standards and values, and in accepting their limitations as well as their assets
2. Help in understanding others and the society in which they live
3. Help in their social relations; for example, in finding a suitable opportunity to meet young people of similar interests under conditions which will put them at ease (These conditions include acceptable personal appearance and dress, competence in social skills.) . . .[15]

Most men and women have some social handicaps. All must somehow learn to live with what they have and are. If you are having trouble getting into the dating crowd, you are by no means alone. At any one time you have two alternatives in regard to your social inadequacies: (1) bemoan the lacks in the current situation and in your background, or (2) develop your social competence by learning the social attitudes and skills that you need. The answer to the question of this section is, "You get into the dating crowd by becoming more socially effective and learning how to make and enjoy friends."

---

[13] Rodgers, *op. cit.*
[14] Opal Powell Wolford, "How Early Background Affects Dating Behavior," *Journal of Home Economics*, Vol. 40, No. 9, November, 1948, p. 506.
[15] Wolford, *op. cit.*, p. 506.

How Do You Make Friends?

No one is born popular. Every person must learn to get along comfortably with others. This learning is a long process that begins in the cradle and continues through adulthood. Particularly through the adolescent and young adult years, there is a striving to become acceptable to others, to belong socially, to find friends and to become involved in the complex processes of dating, courtship, and marriage. Achieving satisfying social relationships with members of the other sex is a major task of the second decade of life.

Maturing social development that leads to marriage involves at least three requisites: (1) making a good first impression so that people will take a second look, (2) attaining the personality balance that leads to friendly, rewarding relationships, and (3) becoming emotionally indispensable to another person—the basis for love and marriage.[16]

Making a good first impression has become a multi million-dollar business in America. Sales of cosmetics outdistance those of textbooks year by year. The mass media literally bombard the eyes and ears of the public with the importance of "being sweet to be near." Clothes and grooming costs loom large in the spending of young people. For many an inadequate young person the advertisements suggest that all he (or more often she) has to do is to buy the right products and apply them to the right places to achieve overnight popularity. The millions who attempt the magic love potion path to romance eventually must realize that something more is needed to be desirable, to make friends, to have dates, to find a mate, and to prepare for marriage.

That something comes from within oneself. It is the quality that makes a plain girl attractive, and gives a homely man charm. This flowering of the human personality leads not only to marriage, but to satisfying relationships with others generally. With personal unfolding toward others comes release from self-conscious clumsiness and gradual expertness that makes a man or woman of any age socially smooth and self-confident.

Getting through to others

Developing social effectiveness involves first of all learning social skills and abilities, such as: introducing oneself into a group, making and acknowledging introductions easily, carrying on pleasant conversations at various levels of complexity, accepting invitations gracefully, and refusing unacceptable proposals effectively. One should be able

---

[16] Richard H. Klemer, informal communication from the American Institute of Family Relations, announcing a series of group and individual conferences on *Your Social Effectiveness . . . Developing Deeper Relationships with Other People,* October-November, 1957, p. 2.

competently to participate in sports played by one's group, dance, sing, drive a car, and travel in a variety of modes and situations; relate easily to members of one's own as well as older and younger generations; in short one should be able to do what is generally expected in ways that are considered appropriate.

Social skills are learned in action. Most young people develop their abilities to handle themselves smoothly in interaction with others through the years. As they acquire more and more experience in any of the required skills they become smooth in them in much the same way that any other proficiency is attained—by practice. A great many young people need and seek special help at various points in their social development where lacks and inadequacies in their present or past experience are especially evident. Classes in Social Arts; courses in Human Relations, Family Relationships, and Preparation for Marriage; panels on what each sex expects of the other in various situations; and practice in discerning the principles involved and playing out one's expected roles are of considerable help. Even without these special aids, most young people gain social competence by participating with others in a wide variety of settings. Those who have participated in projects, belonged to youth groups, sat on committees, and taken responsibilities with their peers for common enterprises learn a great deal in these generalized mixed group activities that makes for poise and social competence generally. Research findings indicate clearly that those who have many friends of both sexes, who have belonged to clubs and organizations within their school or college, church and community settings, are more apt to find mates, marry more happily, and to be better adjusted emotionally than the more socially isolated.[17]

An important factor in making meaningful friendships is being accessible to others. It involves being able to understand and being understood by others. It calls for the special sensitivity to others' feelings and points of view that is called *empathy*—the ability to put oneself in the other's place and sense how he feels about the situation in question.

It is entirely possible to acquire all the social skills of the drawing room dandy, or to become the belle of the ball, and yet be terribly lonely. Until one develops the self-confidence and the faith in others that allows him to be truly accessible to them, he may lack the ability to communicate in any but the most superficial ways. To become a real friend and true lover one needs somehow to feel safe with others— safe from ridicule, safe to reveal oneself, safe to give of oneself, safe to receive freely and to share widely.

---

[17] Ernest W. Burgess and Paul Wallin, *Engagement and Marriage*, Chicago: Lippincott, 1953, p. 148.

Intimate interaction cannot be a part of all relationships. Everyone finds that there are certain things that can be shared with strangers, others that are part of the association of acquaintances, still other levels of interaction that are possible with friends, and only the most intimate that are possible with close friends, lovers, and marriage partners. This brings us to the inevitable question—where do you find your friends?

Your potential friends

Take any collection of people—in a housing project, in a classroom, or in an assembly line—and try to predict which ones will become friends over a given period of time. This sounds like a well-nigh impossible assignment? Not at all. There have been numerous research studies that have pinpointed the factors involved in friendship making. One researcher organized the vast literature of theoretical and research material on friendship making and isolated two key factors involved in making friends. Then he predicted which girls in a college class first meeting together in September would be friends by December, three months later. He recognized that upon each girl of the ninety-two in his sample many forces were operating over which he had no control. Yet, because he knew that two factors are always at work in friendship making, he was able to report that "the degree to which the subjects did behave as predicted is certainly striking for this kind of material." [18] The two factors that have the most reliability in predicting friendship selection and maintenance are *accessibility* and *similarity*. The principle of accessibility holds that you make friends from among those persons with whom you have contact, who are accessible and available. The principle of similarity holds that you tend to select, and are selected by, friends who are in important ways your kind of person. Together these two established principles reliably predict that your potential friends are those with whom you have contact and who share at least some of your interests and values.

Implications of the principle of accessibility are many. Since you make friends only among those who are accessible, your efforts in friendship are more rewarding when applied to the actual people with whom you have real contact. This is why daydreaming about some noble creature you have never met is apt to be self-defeating. New friends are often found within the circle of acquaintances among persons already known superficially. The girl who is so quiet may prove to be pleasantly communicative on further acquaintance. The apparently conceited man may prove to be a loyal supporter whose ac-

[18] Carlfred B. Broderick, "Predicting Friendship Behavior: A Study of the Determinants of Friendship Selection and Maintenance in a College Population," Ph.D. Thesis, Cornell University, June, 1956, p. 231.

quaintance wears well. It is only when you explore your own small circle of availables that you have the chance to discover the potential friendships among them.

Furthermore, since your friends are to be found among those people with whom you have contact, your best hope of widening your friendship circles is to get into new groups and make yourself available to new persons. This is what a girl does who goes out for a part in a play, or what a man does who tries out for a place in the band, or what members of either sex do when they initiate overtures to persons in new situations.

Congeniality is double-barreled. It implies recognizing that your friends are likely to share your interests and values and ways of looking at life. It means also that many who in some ways seem uncongenial may in other ways be exceedingly compatible. It involves not only enjoying what you have in common but also in developing your interests and perspectives to include activities and projects that are meaningful to others. This can be seen in the way a girl learns about sports as she gets interested in boys, or in the way a boy becomes "domesticated" when he becomes fond of a girl. It is one respect in which friends are good for each other, in that they stretch each other's interests and horizons to include more of life in their common experience.

Friends affirm each other. Their support and loyalty provide what most persons need to find answers to their most haunting question: "Who am I?" If anyone should ask you the question "Who are you?" you probably would answer in terms of (1) your family ("I am the Joneses' son, John"), (2) your vocation ("I am a teacher in training"), or (3) your friends and friendship circles ("I am a frat man"). In this third sense your friends contribute to your sense of identity. They provide the social settings in which you find yourself, and they reaffirm you as a member in good standing in the circles with which you feel identified.

Identity, autonomy, and friendship

Establishing autonomy is another major accomplishment of young adulthood. Somehow each boy must become a mature man, capable of making his own decisions, standing on his own feet, and living his own life. If a girl is to mature, she must become an autonomous person who finds joy in freeing herself from too close dependence upon others. One astute observer has remarked that our friends teach us what we can expect of others. We learn the limits of loyalty on being "let down by" our friends. We find out that no one is perfect from firsthand experience with those we know best. We come to accept ourselves, with all our strengths and weaknesses, as human beings who need not fear being human. Friends, also, are important in reaffirming us when we have behaved badly, in continuing to accept us when we have failed them, or even in casting us out upon our own resources when we have gone beyond the limits they consider tolerable.

Your friends, like your parents, set limits, reward conformity, punish defections, express concern and interest in your welfare, and approve or disapprove your selections of friends, clubs, activities, vocations, clothes, limits, and even your eventual marriage partner.

Parental
controls of
dating
behavior

Normally, parental controls diminish with time. With young children, virtually every move is observed, supervised, and controlled. With adolescence, child training gives way to guidance, which optimally allows the young person to take responsibility for himself in ever-widening spheres of freedom. But parents are still in the picture during the dating days of most young people.

Kirkpatrick has pointed out that parents control the dating behavior of their sons and daughters by their approval or disapproval. He found that parental attitudes toward dating were not the same for girls as for boys, nor from fathers as from mothers, as is seen in Table 2.

TABLE 2. Attitudes of Fathers and Mothers toward First Dating [19]

Parental Attitude toward First Dating	Father's Attitude Reported by		Mother's Attitude Reported by	
	Male (N–141)	Female (N–258)	Male (N–141)	Female (N–258)
Prohibited or Disapproved	8.5%	18.0%	7.3%	9.5%
Indifferent	70.7	62.3	57.6	39.6
Encouraged	20.8	19.7	35.1	50.9
Total	100.0%	100.0%	100.0%	100.0%

These data suggest that there is a tendency for fathers to resist their daughters' dating more than their sons', while mothers tend to encourage their daughters' more than their sons' first dating experiences.

Koller's comparisons of three generations of women show that the tendency for parents to disapprove of the boys their daughters date has increased since grandmother (or mother) was a girl. Table 3, comparing attitudes of parents of young college-educated women with those reported by their own mothers and grandmothers, indicates clearly that while about the same number of all three generations are

[19] Adapted from Clifford Kirkpatrick, *The Family as Process and Institution,* New York: Ronald Press, 1955, p. 264.

TABLE 3. Parental Approval of Boys Dated in the Early Courtships of Three Generations of Married Women [20]

Parental Approval	Generations		
	First (Grandmothers)	Second (Mothers)	Third (Young Women)
Did Not Approve	62	91	109
Did Approve	104	89	69
Uncertain	25	20	22
Unknown	9	0	0
Total	200	200	200

uncertain about how their parents regarded the boys they dated, there is a straight-line trend toward more disapproval in recent decades.

Possible interpretations of these tendencies for increasing disapproval and decreasing approval include: (1) Changing courtship patterns that depart from the behavior of the older women in their girlhood; (2) Increasing opportunities for younger women to date men who are unknown or objectionable to their parents; and (3) Decreasing parental controls on choice of dating partners and dating behavior. Koller particularly supports the third interpretation because of the way each generation responded when they said they experienced parental disapproval. Twenty-three per cent of the grandmothers, but only 10 per cent of the young women, reported that they yielded to their parents' wishes when they differed about dating certain men. Practically half (49.5 per cent) of the young third-generation women in contrast to only 13 per cent of the grandmothers argued and tried to change their parents' negative attitudes about their boy friends.

Connor and Hall find that girls' parents, more than boys' parents, attempt to influence the type of person dated, their stipulations most often being that the individual dated must have a good reputation and be socially acceptable. This study indicates, too, some of the ways in which parents attempt to regulate the kinds of dating activities their college sons and daughters pursue. Most frequent parental regulations are "No bars and night clubs," "Be in at a specific time," "Call if unable to return at a specific hour," "Must not go far from city," and "No burlesque shows." The research evidence is that "large proportions of both the group of students living at the university and the group at-

[20] Marvin R. Koller, "Some Changes in Courtship Behavior in Three Generations of Ohio Women," *American Sociological Review*, Vol. 16, No. 3, p. 367.

tending the junior college said they usually follow their parents' regulations as to where they may date." [21]

What Do You Do on a Date?

What you do on a date depends on who your date is, the groups with whom you associate, the opportunities and limitations of your situation, and, most of all, who you are in terms of your maturity, interests, and values as a person. Modern communities and campuses offer a variety of dating possibilities, subject only to the limitations of what is considered appropriate and within the budget of the individual.

Cost of dates   Cost is one limiting factor in what you do on a date. While the money spent is by no means the only measure of the quality of a date, there is a wide range in the amount of expenditure for various kinds of dates. On one campus the range of cost is from less than $1 to $300, with routine dates costing $2 to $3, special dates averaging $5 or $6 to $20, and up to $35 for such special affairs as fraternity and sorority, class or "name band" dances, dinner dates, holidays and trips out of town.[22] On another campus the range of dating costs on informal evenings is estimated at from $1 to $20 depending on the activity, and formal dates are reported to cost from $5 to $37, varying with the affair and whether the girl was an import.[23]

It is customary for the man to bear the burden of the dating expenses. "Dutch dating," in which the girl shares the costs tends to be infrequent in this country. Smith found that practically half of his college men (56 per cent) and women (46 per cent) reported that they never "dutch treat" on dates, 42 per cent of the men and 52 per cent of the women say they sometimes do, and but 2 per cent of the men and 1 per cent of the women report they generally do. Two other investigators comparing practices on the campuses of the University of Wisconsin and the University of Oslo, Norway, find the sharing of dating costs with the girl significantly more frequent in Norway than in this country (see Fig. 2).

In this country it is generally recognized that women have costs in dating that may balance the men's outlay. American standards of grooming, clothing, and general appearance call for women's expenditures at the beauty parlor, the drugstore, the dress, shoe, and accessories shop for even the simplest party, while elaborate formal affairs

---

[21] Connor and Hall, *op. cit.*, p. 280.
[22] Connor and Hall, *op. cit.*, p. 279.
[23] Smith, *op. cit.*, p. 5.

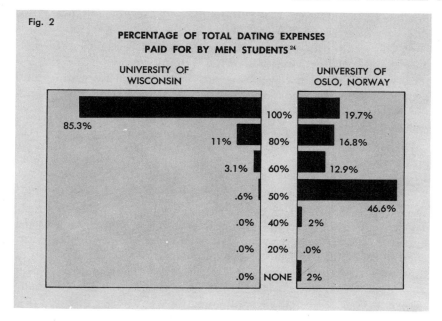

Fig. 2

PERCENTAGE OF TOTAL DATING EXPENSES
PAID FOR BY MEN STUDENTS [24]

UNIVERSITY OF WISCONSIN		UNIVERSITY OF OSLO, NORWAY
85.3%	100%	19.7%
11%	80%	16.8%
3.1%	60%	12.9%
.6%	50%	46.6%
.0%	40%	2%
.0%	20%	.0%
.0%	NONE	2%

can run the girl's costs up to or beyond what her date is paying for the evening.

American girls today find ways of reciprocating for the expenses of a date. Koller reports that while the grandmothers in his three-generation sample rarely gave gifts to their men before marriage, today's young women in many cases were giving more gifts to their sweethearts during courtship than they received in return.[25] Girls arrange for parties with their dates as their guests and they entertain boys in their homes as pleasant variations in dating activities.

"Going to the movies" is the most frequent dating activity reported in recent surveys of college dating practices. Smith found that 83 per cent of the 258 college women and 61 per cent of the 344 college men he studied went to the movies on dates.[26] Connor and Hall report that "movies, dances, and parties were the most frequently mentioned places for dating by all student groups." [27] Rodgers' data indicate the movies are the most frequently mentioned dating activity for inde-

Dating activities

[24] William Simenson and Gilbert Geis, "Courtship Patterns of Norwegian and American University Students," *Marriage and Family Living*, Vol. 18, No. 4, November, 1956, p. 336.

[25] Koller, *op. cit.*, p. 369.

[26] Smith, *op. cit.*, p. 313.

[27] Connor and Hall, *op. cit.*, p. 279.

pendent men; and second only to the fraternity party as the usual setting for a date by fraternity men.[28]

As one would expect, fraternity men generally center more of their dating and social activities within the fraternity program and the fraternity house, while independents rely more on general campus and community entertainment, sports events, and special interests. Smith points particularly to the influence of the fraternity on the dating activities mentioned by both sexes when he says,

> Formal dances were reported by 70 per cent of the women which is approximately the same percentage of women who had been dating fraternity men. The same activity was checked by 42 per cent of the men which is only slightly higher than the proportion of the men in this study who were fraternity members.[29]

Beyond the more obvious and visible dating activities, such as the movies and the fraternity party, lie a wide variety of personal interests enjoyed by members of both sexes on dates together. The tendency is for both men and women to find their dating activities and their dates in mutually enjoyable pursuits. For example, church-related young people of both sexes date in religious settings; musically oriented persons find enjoyment together in musical events; and socially sensitive men and women work and play together on their social concerns and projects. People generally find and enjoy those who like the things they like. These strong tendencies toward *homophily* (liking friends like oneself) carry over into marriage as *homogamy* (marrying a person like oneself) in ways that are reliably predictable (see Chapter 4— "Choosing Your Mate").

This brings you to the interesting question of the possible carry-over of dating activities and interests into marriage. Certain activities like team sports, fraternity house parties, and formal dances decrease sharply after marriage. Other interests, such as drama, music, hobbies, art, religion, literature, social problems, and domestic activities offer increasing scope and depth of enjoyment both before and after marriage.

The frequency of dating is not necessarily the best measure of its adequacy either in furthering the acquaintance of the dating pair or in preparing them for the kinds of recreational pursuits that continue on in marriage. The person who is obviously "popular" in the sense of being eagerly sought after at social events may not be laying as sound

[28] Rodgers, *op. cit.*, p. 51.
[29] William M. Smith, Jr., *Rating and Dating*, Research Publication No. 110, School of Home Economics, The Pennsylvania State College, June, 1952, pp. 4 and 5.

a foundation for marriage as is the person who enjoys dates and social activities that permit mutual sharing of interests and values.

The most controversial problem both between the sexes and between the older and younger generations is that of parking and petting. In grandmother's day a courting couple's behavior was much more closely supervised, if for no other reason than that it so much more often took place under the eyes and ears of the girl's family. Now there are fewer dates in the home while an ever increasing number are in automobiles where complete privacy and freedom from external controls are possible. This means that a dating couple's conduct is up to them; it is they who determine where they shall go, and how fast, when they shall stop, and how.

Parking and petting

Rodgers finds that parking is an important part of dating in the eyes of both independent and fraternity men.[30] More than 80 per cent of both men and women college students in the Connor and Hall samples indicate that they engage in necking and petting at least "sometimes."[31] The Kinsey reports, which define petting as including anything from "simple kissing and hugging" to the most passionate embraces, find that it is practically universal.[32]

Men and women do not see eye to eye on the necking and petting question. Smith reports that three times as many college men as women agree that a man must neck to be popular and seven times as many that he must pet to be popular. Similar differences between the sexes have been reported by Rockwood and Ford at Cornell and Christensen at the University of Wisconsin.[33]

A later sampling on the University of Wisconsin campus shows the same general discrepancy between the two sexes in their attitudes toward familiarities at various stages of dating involvement: 55 per cent of the men and 65 per cent of the women saying "no intimacy on the first date," 70 per cent of the men and 57 per cent of the women permitting necking by couples dating regularly, and 33 per cent of the men and 14 per cent of the women endorsing full sexual relations for engaged pairs. In contrast to Norwegian college students, Americans are more liberal at the beginning of courtship, and level off at necking

---

[30] Rodgers, *op. cit.*

[31] Connor and Hall, *op. cit.*, p. 279.

[32] Alfred C. Kinsey, Wardell B. Pomeroy, Clyde E. Martin, and Paul H. Gebhard, *Sexual Behavior in the Human Female*, Philadelphia: Saunders, 1953, Chapter 7.

[33] Smith, *Rating and Dating*, p. 9; Lemo D. Rockwood and Mary E. N. Ford, *Youth, Marriage and Parenthood*, New York: Wiley, 1945; Harold T. Christensen, "Courtship Conduct as Viewed by Youth," *Journal of Home Economics*, Vol. 40, April, 1948, pp. 187–188.

and petting, whereas Norwegians tend toward more restraint in early dating and to more complete sexual liberty during engagement, which lasts longer and is defined more formally in Norway than in the United States.[34]

Recent investigations at Indiana University indicate clearly that the two sexes tend to define dating situations differently in regard to intimacies expected on dates at various stages of involvement. In one study, 291 college girls reported more than one thousand (1,022) dating situations in which they had been offended by their date's aggressive sexual behavior. More than half (55.7) of the girls reported having been so offended at least once during the academic year, with 20.9 per cent offended by forceful attempts at intercourse (for additional data see Table 4).

TABLE 4.   Relationship Involvement and Erotic Intimacy Level at Which Offensiveness Occurs [35]

	Necking and Petting Above the Waist		Petting Below the Waist		Attempted Intercourse or Attempted Intercourse with Violence		
	No.	Per Cent	No.	Per Cent	No.	Per Cent	Total
Ride Home, First Date or Occasional Date	411	55.0	60	31.4	25	30.1	496 (48.5%)
Regular or Steady Date	295	39.4	104	54.5	43	51.8	442 (43.3%)
Pinned or Engaged	42	5.6	27	14.1	15	18.1	84 (8.2%)
Totals	748	100.0	191	100.0	83	100.0	1,022 (100.0%)

Several striking tendencies are apparent in these data: (1) Practically one half of the offensive episodes occurred very early in the relationship (ride home, first or occasional date). This suggests considerable misunderstanding between the sexes as to what is appropriate behavior. (2) Relatively few pinned or engaged girls (8.2 per cent) report offensive behavior on the part of their lovers. Can this be because they "love the guy" and are involved enough to submit to his urgencies; or is it perhaps because an engaged or pinned fellow respects his sweetheart's wishes and does not press the issue as he might with a casual date? (3) The highest incidence of episodes at advanced levels of intimacy are among the couples who are dating each other regularly

---

[34] Simenson and Geis, op. cit., pp. 336–338.
[35] Clifford Kirkpatrick and Eugene Kanin, "Male Sex Aggression on a University Campus," American Sociological Review, Vol. 22, No. 1, February, 1957, p. 55.

or going steady. More than half (54.5 per cent) of offensive behavior characterized by petting below the waist, and (51.8 per cent) of offensive behavior characterized by attempted intercourse are found in the going steady level of involvement. Does this suggest that men expect more sex liberties with their regular dates than their steadies define as suitable?

Granted that men are more aggressive sexually than their dates find acceptable, what is a girl to do? A follow-up study of 262 freshmen college girls asked to report on their difficulties with aggressive dates during their last year in high school and the summer before they came to the university, showed that girls but rarely call in the authorities to help them to fend off overly lusty males. Only 15.9 per cent of these girls said that they had appealed to parents or other adults for help in their sex-toned dating difficulties. One out of four (23 per cent) had kept the episode a secret. One out of three (31.2 per cent) had terminated the relationship with the boy in question, and another third (29.9 per cent) had used discussion—either with the boy or with the other girls— as her way of coping with the situation.[36]

Judson T. Landis asked over 200 girls how they handled situations in which it was necessary to control the extent of necking and petting and lists the methods reported from the most frequently to the least frequently mentioned in this rank order:

Be honest, say "No" sincerely
Keep talking, make interesting conversation
Avoid circumstances in which it is likely to happen
Plan dates thoroughly
Double- or group-date
Let boy know your attitude from the start
Set an early curfew
Plan after-date activities
Use reason
Start smoking; ask for a cigarette
Don't prompt it by your actions
Set point beyond which you *don't* go
Divert date's attention
Ask to be taken home
Keep attitude light and casual
Don't date fellows overinterested in necking and petting
Refrain from long good-nights
Pass off attempts as a joke.[37]

[36] Eugene J. Kanin, "Male Aggression in Dating-Courtship Relations," *American Journal of Sociology,* Vol. LXIII, No. 2, September, 1957, p. 203.

[37] Judson T. Landis and Mary G. Landis, *Youth and Marriage: A Student Manual,* New York: Prentice-Hall, 1957, p. 40.

"Talking" takes first and second place in girls' reported repertory in dealing with overly eager boy friends, implying that couples today discuss quite intimate questions in present-day dating and courtship. Evidence from high school girls' dating attitudes is that they are twice as likely to meet difficult personal problems (such as the boy's shifting interest from them to another girl) by talking it over with the boy than by any other approach.[38]

Young people of both sexes and of all age groups tend to rank conversational ability high on their lists of desirable qualities of a dating partner. Blood, for instance, found that "Is an intelligent conversationalist" was mentioned by all college men among characteristics they preferred in serious dates, and by 85.3 per cent of the qualities they mentioned as important in their casual dates.[39] Christensen finds that high school students of both sexes tend to criticize themselves for being shy, self-conscious, and ill at ease in dating situations more frequently by far than for any other fault.[40] This indicates that the ability to be poised and communicative ranks high in what members of both sexes expect of themselves and each other in dating situations.

What you can talk about on a date depends on you, your date, and the situation. Usually you talk about the things you know something about. When you have a number of common interests, you talk them over and are likely to learn a lot about each other as well as the topic of conversation. The more interests you have, the more you have to talk about. If you talk about the things that you are interested in and tell each other about the things you know something about there is no limit to discussable areas of conversation.

It is not so much what you talk about as the way you approach the subject that makes conversation on a date acceptable or not. There are some people who can make almost anything sound off-color and crude. Christensen, in the study reported above, found that being vulgar in speech or action was the most frequent criticism leveled against boys on dates both by boys and girls alike.[41] In contrast, the most intimate personal topics can be explored on a date in ways that are mutually acceptable. The difference is in the way in which the subjects are discussed. The man or the woman whose manner is self-respecting and

---

[38] Survey Research Center, *op. cit.*, p. 115.

[39] Robert O. Blood, Jr., "Uniformities and Diversities in Campus Dating and Preferences," *Marriage and Family Living*, Vol. XVIII, No. 1, February, 1956, p. 43.

[40] Harold T. Christensen, "Dating Behavior as Evaluated by High-School Students," *American Journal of Sociology*, Vol. LVII, No. 6, May, 1952, p. 584.

[41] *Ibid.*, p. 582.

appreciative of the other person can open up areas for discussion that would be closed to a less wholesome individual.

The motive in back of whatever is talked about sets the tone of the conversation. If one person is out to exploit the other, whatever his manner, or whatever topic of conversation he brings up is likely to reflect the underlying objective. This as the all too familiar phenomenon of the girl's "buttering up" the fellow when she wants something from him, or the boy's "sweet-talking" his date around to his way of thinking.

Sex can be discussed as a means of sex stimulation, or as a type of communication aimed at understanding the other person and the sex to which he or she belongs. The one approach "uses" the dating partner for personal gratification. The second approach develops between the two their sympathy for and understanding of the other, that is seen in their growing ability to feel *with* each other in an increasing variety of emotional climates. This is called *empathy*, which Vernon and Stewart suggest is a process that develops between two persons through their interaction with each other in given situations.[42]

The depth of interaction increases as the dating partners become better acquainted with each other. The range of their areas of communication depends primarily upon the extent of their separate and common interests. If food or sex is all they share interest in, their range of discussable topics is limited. If they stimulate each other to develop familiar interests and to open up new ones that might be jointly enjoyed, they broaden the base of their relationship immeasurably.

Dating and courting couples today discuss many more areas important for their future as married people than used to be the case. Koller's three-generation study finds that less than 5 per cent of the grandmothers, in contrast to half of the young married women, had talked over during courtship the various items important to their future marriage: handling money, having children, place to live, religion, wife working, husband's occupation, and so forth. Only 1.5 per cent of the young women failed to discuss any items suggested as possible problems in the future marriage.[43]

When dating is seen as an opportunity for two persons of opposite sex to become well acquainted with each other as two whole personalities, the problem of what to talk about on a date becomes minor, while their chances for enjoyment of each other and for long-term inter-

---

[42] Glenn M. Vernon and Robert L. Stewart, "Empathy as a Process in a Dating Situation," *American Sociological Review*, Vol. 22, No. 1, February, 1957, pp. 48–52.

[43] Koller, *op. cit.*, p. 369.

action as future married partners or as lifelong friends are greatly increased.

Who Rates as a Good Date?

Dating can be defined in two ways. The first is the stereotyped "catching a man" or "chasing a woman" that deals in artifices, poses, and pat prescriptions. The second is the opportunity to develop with a person of the other sex the art of becoming an interacting unity of kindred spirits. The first is exploitative and temporary. The second is mutually supportive and relatively permanent. The first is more common in the "playing around" type of casual date. The second is more characteristic of the serious date.

Arts and artifices in dating

There are certain general requisites for a dating partner that members of both sexes tend to agree upon. A good reputation, an attractive appearance, and intelligence equal to their own were the qualities both sexes specified in the freshmen and sophomore college student population studied by Connor and Hall.[44] The two top-ranking requisites for popularity of both men and women studied by Smith are: "Be smooth in appearance and manners," and "Know how to dance well." [45] The nationwide sample of high school students studied by Christensen listed items they considered most important in making or accepting a date in the following order:

> Is physically and mentally fit
> Is dependable, can be trusted
> Takes pride in personal appearance and manners
> Is clean in speech and action
> Has pleasant disposition and sense of humor
> Is considerate of me and others
> Acts own age, is not childish [46]

Out of related surveys on a number of campuses, as well as among American high schools, Christensen summarizes the qualities that each sex dislikes in the other as a dating partner in a way that might be even more discerningly helpful.

The girl that fellows dislike:

1. She is inconsiderate, selfish, conceited, self-centered, snobbish, overly critical, and possessive. She talks all the time about herself, or brags

---

[44] Connor and Hall, *op. cit.,* p. 279.
[45] Smith, *Rating and Dating,* p. 8.
[46] Christensen, *op. cit.,* p. 580.

about other dates, or flirts with other boys while she is out with me. She should be more sympathetic and helpful.

2. She is too forward in necking and petting, too free with kisses and caresses. She should make the fellow keep his place and shouldn't give in so readily in an attempt to hold him.

3. She is a "gold digger." She favors the boys who have money and cars, and she expects too many treats on the date. She should be more considerate of the fellow's pocketbook.

4. She lacks refinement, being too forward and loud around boys. She is boisterous, overtalkative, and flippant; she is sometimes slovenly and crude; she uses paint and perfume too freely and unskillfully; and she chews gum or puts on make-up or straightens her stockings in public. She should cultivate neatness in dress, graciousness in manner, and depth and interest in conversation.

5. She indulges in dishonest flattery, leads a fellow on, "strings him a line." She accepts dates when she doesn't care for the fellow or is dishonest or evasive in refusing. She tries to keep too many boys on the "string" at the same time, to have people fall for her, to be a woman of many loves. She should play the game fairly.

6. Miscellaneous criticisms are many, but these are among the most common: she drinks or smokes; she is overly dependent, and is too shy around boys; she is too emotional and romantic; and she pays too much attention to make-up.

The fellow that girls dislike:

1. He is egotistical and independent. He acts superior, often giving the impression that he thinks he is doing the girl a favor to go with her. He is boastful and argumentative. He shouldn't try to monopolize all the conversation or "try to explain the movies to us." He should be more thoughtful and attentive, and should show more consideration for our wishes and respect for our personalities.

2. He gives too much emphasis to necking and petting, making the girl feel indebted, and expecting intimacy as payment for the date. He is too abrupt and crude in his love-making, frequently making advances on the first date and occasionally in public. He should be more reserved and considerate in these things.

3. He is unfair in the way he asks for and carries out his dates. Sometimes he just drops in without even asking; often he doesn't tell her where they will be going so that she will know how to dress; and frequently he is late in calling. He should cultivate courage and poise and refinement in asking for dates, and should be more considerate of the girl's position.

4. He is often crude and ungentlemanly in both speech and action. He whistles and honks at girls; he swears, uses vulgar language, and tells dirty jokes; he is loud and boisterous in public, trying to show off and

be the life of the party; he uses poor English and is awkward in social etiquette; he is unclean and untidy in public. He should try to be more cultivated and refined.

5. Many of his compliments are insincere and even dishonest. He has a superficial politeness and engages in flattery and "a line" to make a girl feel good or to gain control. He plays with the girl's affections, pretending to be serious when he is not. In all fairness he should go with the kind of girl he will want to marry, and should be honest with her.

6. Among miscellaneous criticisms are the following: he hangs around at all hours and stays too late on dates; he is unwilling to associate with the girl's folks and is unnatural around them; he lacks vigor and initiative; and he sometimes coaxes the girl to smoke or drink.[47]

These lists of what men and women like and do not like in each other as dates suggest that neither sex is happy very long in a relationship that is based entirely upon the superficial artifices of "the chase." Both sexes distinguish between the qualities that would be all right in an occasional casual date and the characteristics they prefer in serious dates. Blood has studied these differences in dating preferences among college men and women in ways that point up sharply the difference between the "gay blade" and the "good Joe"; the "smart cookie" and "the swell gal." Note, for instance, in Table 5 that knowing how to dance well is significantly more often mentioned as preferred for casual than for serious dates, while being emotionally mature and dependable—universal requisites for serious dates—are significantly less often mentioned as qualities preferred in casual dating.

Hill summarizes his findings of substantially the same kind of distinctions made by students at Iowa State University:

Men especially differentiate between dating and courtship (mating), the one situation requiring a "good time girl" and the other calling for a quite different set of qualities. "A good date" is friendly, dresses well, is a good conversationalist, and has a sense of humor and a considerable amount of personal charm. Sex appeal is important but not indispensable. "A good mate" must above all be genuine and honest; second, a good companion; third, like children ("liking children" ranked twenty-fourth on a list of qualities desired in a date); and fourth, be friendly. Chastity came twenty-second on a list of requisites for a date and thirteenth in importance in selecting a mate. This last finding brought a response from one of the local ministers, who chided the men students in his congregation, pointing out that a high-grade prostitute could qualify as a desirable date according to

---

[47] Harold T. Christensen, *Marriage Analysis,* New York: Ronald Press, 1950, p. 217.

TABLE 5. *Different Characteristics Preferred in Casual and Serious Dating Partners, University of Michigan, 1953.*[48]

Characteristics Preferred in Dating Partners	Per Cent of College Men and Women Choosing Item as Personal Preferences	
	Casual Dates	Serious Dates
A. Discriminations Made by Both Sexes		
1. Is emotionally mature	84.2	100.0
2. Is dependable	87.8	99.3
3. Is a well-rounded person	84.6	98.5
4. Is affectionate	69.6	97.6
5. Is a good listener	88.3	97.4
6. Gets along with friends of own sex	80.6	96.4
7. Is ambitious and energetic	65.3	84.7
8. Person has my family's approval	24.5	72.1
9. Knows how to dance well	52.6	31.9
B. Discriminations Made by Men Students		
10. Has good sense, is intelligent	88.4	100.0
11. Is an intelligent conversationalist	85.3	100.0
12. Is honest, straightforward	80.0	96.8
13. Is willing to join a group	82.1	93.7
14. Has polished manners	66.3	81.1
15. Doesn't have a reputation for petting	38.9	74.7
16. Doesn't have a reputation for necking	34.7	67.4
17. Dates popular students only	9.5	3.2
C. Discriminations Made by Women Students		
18. Is willing to neck on occasion	34.3	67.7
19. Is willing to pet on occasion	8.2	32.1
20. Is good looking, attractive	61.2	45.5
21. Goes to popular places	38.8	22.6

their listing of qualities and that, whether they liked it or not, no man on the campus would marry a girl he hadn't first met as a date.[49]

What Are Your Dating Aims and Values?

Whether your date is for a night or a lifetime depends first of all upon your aims and values. If your dating is dalliance, the kind of per-

---

[48] Robert O. Blood, Jr., "Uniformities and Diversities in Campus Dating Preferences," *Marriage and Family Living*, Vol. XVIII, No. 1, February, 1956, p. 43.

[49] Reuben Hill, revision of Willard Waller, *The Family: A Dynamic Interpretation*, New York: Dryden Press, 1951, p. 156.

son you date, what you do on a date, and how you rate and are rated will be influenced by your goals for the evening. If you see your dating as a chance to get acquainted with one another, to make friendships, to become more socially at ease with others, to grow as a personality, or to become involved in the process that leads to marriage, then your choice of dating partners and your dating behavior will reflect your long-time objectives.

Efforts to be "popular" usually involve trying to acquire skills of a purely temporary kind. You may learn to dance well enough to get a reputation for being the best dancer on the floor, only to find that dancing has but a minor place in life outside of college. You may develop all the techniques of attracting and playing up to members of the other sex, only to find that such methods do not mix with marriage. You may spend everything you have on special clothes, only to find that they have little utility value beyond the immediate present. You may rate as a date and still not be a good risk as a prospective marriage partner.

Learning the arts of intimate interaction within dating has lasting values. As men and women learn to communicate with each other as whole personalities, they both are enriched—at the moment and for the years. As you learn to get acquainted with each other, as you develop the ability to get through to each other with sensitive understanding, you are growing as persons as well as friends. As you grow in your ability to love and be loved, you are developing an emotional repertory essential for the years ahead.

There is a place for temporary values in life. You can enjoy the "playing around" phases of dating, even if they do last but a little while. In fact, there is much to be said for feeling enough at home in the dating crowd so that you feel you belong. There are knowledges, skills, and attitudes to be acquired in dating that are important for present adjustment as well as for more permanent development. However, you should not pay a higher price for dating conformity than it is really worth to you.

You can test your present dating values as you ask yourself these questions:

1. Am I getting acquainted with members of both sexes near me?
2. Am I making real friends with both fellows and girls my own age?
3. Are we doing the things together that we mutually enjoy?
4. Do I get to some of the affairs that I would most like to attend?
5. Am I learning to take disappointments and disillusionments with my dates and my friends?

6. Is my emotional repertory enlarging in range and depth?
7. Are my methods and approaches realistic?
8. Is my dating rating-for-the-moment, or for a lifetime?

The ways of a man with a maid fill the thoughts of all of us. A girl dreams of being carried off by a prince in a red convertible. A man dreams of the girl who will be "so nice to come home to." Some of these dreams arise spontaneously out of the creative impulses that lie close to the surface of all men and women. Fulfilling them satisfyingly must be learned, within the realities of what is expected of us.

In the real world the girl is not usually swept off her feet by the handsome nobleman. Quite as often he is the shy, sweet boy at the next table. They do not start out together in a new-model car; more often than not they both save up for a down payment on a second-hand model. Their dating is not usually dancing cheek to cheek; far more often it is holding hands at a neighborhood movie. They do not dash off to be married after a few heavy dates, Hollywood style. In real life men and women gradually discover each other as potential marriage partners as they progress through successive stages of dating involvement.

READINGS

Bernard, Jessie, Helen E. Buchanan, and William M. Smith, Jr., *Dating, Mating, and Marriage.* Cleveland: Howard Allen, 1958, Chapter 3, "Dating."

Blood, Robert O., Jr., *Anticipating Your Marriage.* Glencoe, Illinois: Free Press, 1955, Chapter 1, "Dating."

Burgess, Ernest W., Paul Wallin, and Gladys Denny Shultz, *Courtship, Engagement and Marriage.* Philadelphia: Lippincott, 1954, Part 1, "Dating in the Modern Age."

Duvall, Evelyn Millis, *The Art of Dating.* New York: Association Press, 1958.

——, *Family Development.* Chicago: Lippincott, 1957, Chapters 11 and 12.

Ehrmann, Winston W., *Premarital Dating Behavior.* New York: Holt, 1959.

Hollingshead, August B., *Elmtown's Youth.* New York: Wiley, 1949.

Klemer, Richard H., *A Man for Every Woman.* New York: Macmillan, 1959.

Koos, Earl, *Marriage.* New York: Holt, 1953, Chapter 5, "Before Marriage: Dating."

LeMasters, E. E., *Modern Courtship and Marriage.* New York: Macmillan, 1957, Chapter 5, "Random Dating."

Magoun, F. Alexander, *Love and Marriage.* New York: Harper, 1956, Chapter 7, "Courtship."

Morgan, Mildred and William, *Thinking Together about Marriage and Family.* New York: Association Press, 1955, Chapter 7, "Social Relations of Men and Women—Dating."

Rutledge, Aaron L., ed., *Courtship and Marriage Readings.* New York: Harcourt, Brace, 1960.

Rutledge, Aaron L., *Responsible Marriage and Family Living: A Text with Adapted Readings*. New York: Harcourt, Brace, 1960, Part One, "Dating and Mating."

Stone, L. Joseph, and Joseph Church, *Childhood and Adolescence*. New York: Random House, 1957, Chapters 10, 11, and 12.

Taylor, Donald L., revision of Norman E. Himes, *Your Marriage*. New York: Rinehart, 1955, Chapter 2, "Courtship."

Winch, Robert F., and Robert McGinnis (eds.), *Selected Studies in Marriage and the Family*. New York: Holt, 1953, Chapter 14, "Dating and Courtship."

2 Becoming Involved

Is courtship so different now?

How involved are you?

What about going steady?

What does getting pinned mean?

How do you get in so deep?

How typical are you?

IT is a common stereotype that young men take pride in keeping free from entangling alliances while young women glory in their involvements. A girl is congratulated and envied by her friends when she succeeds in getting engaged, whereas a boy is teased for having "taken the bait." This version of the "battle of the sexes" is quite in contrast with the idea of romantic courtship where the swain uses all his persuasive powers to win and woo his fair but indifferent lady, who keeps him dangling to heighten his ardor.

Actually, neither picture accurately portrays the path of present-day involvements. With the increasing equality of the sexes there has developed also an increasing equality in courting relationships. As today's couples move from friendly dates into progressively greater stages of commitment, they are more frequently characterized by mutuality than by conflicts of interest.

Is Courtship So Different Now?

The finding of a mate and the details of arranging the betrothal were, until frontier days, the prerogatives of parents. In many countries this is still the pattern. Freedom of choice in this country dates

31

from the days when all the eligible men and all the eligible women were known by the entire community. Young ladies knew from childhood the men who might come "a-courting." Rarely would a stranger be permitted to compete for the hand of a local belle. Freedom of choice was limited to the local eligibles and was therefore safe enough.

In the more settled towns of the Atlantic seaboard, the problem was handled with prosaic formality. A formal introduction was followed by careful supervision of the relationship. A good girl refused to talk to any man who had not been first vouched for by a friend, and even then she consulted her parents for their approval. This system operated to limit the contacts of genteel young ladies to a relatively select group of eligible young men and discouraged social relations between ineligible women and men of good birth. Girls in those days had fewer opportunities to circulate, but the conditions under which they met men were conducive to the type of prolonged acquaintance necessary to judge men as potential marriage partners.

Today there is less likelihood of marrying one's first love, and somewhat greater opportunity for exploring the field to find what one's preferences are. Koller, in a study of three generations of women, has found some interesting changes in courtship patterns. The daughters had over four times as many dates per week as their grandmothers. They circulated more widely and considered more men seriously as spouses before settling on the man they finally married. The earlier generations averaged longer engagements (11 months, 9 months, and 6 months respectively), but did not have the statuses of "going steady" and "pinning" in which to explore each other's personalities. Moreover, the earlier generations covered considerably less territory in their premarital discussions and agreements.[1]

Under the contemporary system, if there are years of professional training ahead, it is possible to marry and go through the training together. It is also possible to maintain contact with the opposite sex through dating until marriage proves feasible, rather than to remain in the "not dating" category as so many did in previous generations. There is altogether a friendlier climate for today's young people seeking permanent attachments. This is apparent from the changes in courtship customs that have occurred from the turn of the century to the present time:

1. Dating and courtship begin at an earlier age
2. More frequent contact occurs between the sexes

[1] Marvin R. Koller, "Some Changes in Courtship Behavior in Three Generations of Ohio Women," *American Sociological Review*, Vol. 16, No. 3, June, 1951, pp. 366–370.

3. Dating and courtship last until later at night
4. There is more privacy for dating and courting pairs
5. There is less supervision and chaperonage
6. "Going steady" and "getting pinned" are accepted statuses
7. There is a wider range of patterns of intimacy and sex play
8. There are more discussable topics during dating and courtship
9. There is greater readiness for education in preparation for marriage
10. Courtship culminates earlier in engagement and marriage

How Involved Are You?

Although dating and courtship begin at an earlier age today, the period of meaningful involvements is concentrated in a relatively few years. It is important both to know how to involve others and to be able to yield some of your own autonomy if you wish the satisfactions of getting married. Fortunately, the statuses that intervene to mark your progress between casual date and marriage are well known, and the expectations of behavior appropriate to each stage can be described.

The stages of involvement from least to greatest commitment can be identified as: not dating, casual dating with different persons, frequent

Stages of involvement

Fig. 3

STAGES OF INVOLVEMENT

COMPLETELY COMMITTED

COMPLETELY UNATTACHED

FORMAL ENGAGEMENT

GOING STEADY, WITH PRIVATE UNDERSTANDING: INFORMAL ENGAGEMENT

GOING STEADY, FOR CONVENIENCE ONLY

CASUAL DATING ONLY

NOT DATING

dates with one person, going steady (for convenience or security), going steady with marriage as a possibility, informal engagement, formal engagement, and marriage. Couples move through these stages with many relationships breaking midway and return as individuals to begin again. Some individuals may be arrested at an intermediate stage and find it difficult to progress beyond that point, such as the uncoquettish female. Persons high on the popularity scale and those postponing the idea of marriage may wish to remain suspended in the less involved stages, keeping several affairs going concurrently.

TABLE 6. *Extent of Involvement Reported by 100 College Seniors* [2]

Stage of Involvement	High School								College							
	9th Grade		10th Grade		11th Grade		12th Grade		Freshmen		Sophomores		Juniors		Seniors	
	Boys %	Girls %	Boys %	Girls %	Boys %	Girls %	Boys %	Girls %	Boys %	Girls %	Boys %	Girls %	Boys %	Girls %	Boys %	Girls %
Not Dating Yet	33	17		9		3										
Group Dating	10	34	6	7		3										
Occasional Date	38	29	56	40	11	20	7	18	9	8	2	2				
Open-Field Dating	19	10	31	25	55	56	48	53	57	72	70	70	41	74	53	43
Going Steady:																
For Convenience		2	2	5	25	3	24		9	3	7	6	4	3		3
Feeling in Love		7	4	14	9	15	20	18	21	6	9	14	9	3		5
Marriage a Possibility							2	10	2	3	4	6	16	8	8	3
Pinned (Informal Engagement)									2	5	4		21	10	14	28
Formal Engagement										3	4	2	2	3	11	13
Married													7		14	5

Progress through these stages of involvement narrows the field down until one relationship takes precedence over all others. There are many variations, but the general pattern is for involvement with dating partners to accelerate in the second decade of life. This is evident in the data provided in Table 6, which is a profile of dating involvement of 100 college seniors as they recall their dating statuses for each of the eight previous years in high school and college.

[2] Unpublished data collected by Reuben Hill at the University of North Carolina, Spring, 1955. Percentages are rounded and so do not necessarily add up to 100 per cent in each column.

A number of observations are suggested by these data:

1. None of the boys, and few of the girls, recall being beyond open-field dating when they were freshmen in high school.

2. By the senior year in college, practically half of both men and women were seeing marriage as a possibility, were pinned, engaged, or already married.

3. More girls than men report being involved in dating year by year through high school and college.

4. More men than girls were already married as college seniors (14 and 5 per cent respectively), perhaps because more men than women continue their education after marriage.

5. Pinning and engagement cluster in the latter years of college, with few graduating seniors reporting being engaged before their last year in college. It is possible that those who had become engaged or married earlier in their academic lives had already dropped out of school and so do not appear in this sample.

6. Going steady in its less involved forms of being a matter of convenience or because of feeling in love, shows a wide scatter throughout high school and college days, while going steady with marriage as a possibility appears only among the older students.

Many studies have shown that there are great differences in social class and in level of aspiration between those who continue their education and those who drop out of school or college early to get married. Generally speaking, those from the higher socioeconomic brackets with plans for going into the professions and other occupations requiring advanced education delay formal involvement and marriage until fairly late in their college careers. Less ambitious young people, from less privileged backgrounds, more often get involved earlier and tend to drop out of school and to marry at younger ages.

Another factor interfering with the regular progression from casual dating through going steady, getting engaged, and finally married is that of the premature commitment that shortcuts the more gradual development of a relationship. The classic example is the "shotgun marriage"—the couple involved too soon, too fast, who must cut short their courtship in order to marry. The problem is not only that they "have to get married," but also that their relationship does not have the chance to develop gradually through the successive stages that normally lead to a true readiness for marriage.

In most heterosexual relationships there are powerful forces at work forging bonds of sentiment. Sex drives are always present in the relationships between the sexes. Pride in having and holding push for ever-

Random
dating

deeper ego involvement. Finally, shared work and play activities create binding ties. As these forces support one another in the interactions of day-to-day contact, the process of involvement builds up, carrying casual dating partners through to the very threshold of marriage.

"Just dating" which makes up the largest group in college assumes a minimum involvement. Coquetry and "the line" are frequently used and the skills of accosting, of quick contact, and smooth negotiation of a date are important techniques to master to get into and remain in this status. The abilities of the entertainer, a supply of stories and witticisms, and the capacity to hold one's own in repartee are prized. A good date is a good sport, follows the crowd's impulses, necks enough to be accepted, but knows how to keep the situation in hand. A good date does not wear his heart on his sleeve, nor is he possessive. These are reserved for later stages of involvement. "Just dating" as a status implies no commitments beyond the present date and is the status shared by newcomers to the game with veterans who are back in circulation after a love affair which didn't "work out."

What about Going Steady?

"Going steady" is less disapproved today than formerly (35 per cent disapproved in 1948 vs. 18 per cent in 1957) and is more widely practiced (42 per cent in 1948 vs. 50 per cent in 1957).[3] Herman found from the histories of University of Wisconsin students that "going steady" was the characteristic pattern of their last two years in high school, with random dating in second place.[4] There appear to be two patterns: the steady dating in high school which is not marriage oriented and. the going-steady-on-campus pattern which tends to be headed toward marriage. The first is really a form of "going steady for convenience" but doesn't move self-consciously toward marriage. Surveys of high school and college students find that 70 to 80 per cent have gone steady at one time or another and that about half are still dating the same person at graduation.[5]

Symbols of going steady are found in such forms as wearing each other's class rings, wearing matching pieces of clothing, significant deviations in the way wearing apparel is worn, such as the way buckles

---

[3] Purdue Opinion Panel, *Youth's Attitudes Toward Various Aspects of Their Lives*, Poll No. 49, April, 1957, p. 4.

[4] Robert D. Herman, "The Going Steady Complex: A Re-examination," *Marriage and Family Living*, Vol. 17, No. 1, February, 1955, pp. 36–40.

[5] Maureen Daly, *Profile of Youth*, Philadelphia: Lippincott, 1951, p. 30; Russell Smart, "Dating Patterns, 1957," *Journal of Home Economics*, December, 1957, p. 809; and Herman, *op. cit.*, p. 38.

are fastened or shoe laces are tied, as well as in characteristic hair styles and other grooming differentiations that distinguish the tied from the untied.

Statistical and clinical evidence indicates clearly that while there are real advantages in going steady under certain circumstances and among certain individuals, there are situations when going steady may not be wise for a given person at a particular time:

1. When you start too young, before you are ready to be tied down to one person.
2. When you are separated for long periods of time without enough significant security in your relationship with each other to tide you over.
3. When you get too involved, to the place where all other interests and growth are curtailed.
4. When you outgrow each other and find it hard to break off and get back into circulation.[6]

The disadvantages of going steady are recognized by young people themselves: (1) going steady prevents acquaintance with other eligible members of the other sex, (2) going steady is poor training for selecting a marriage partner, (3) going steady too often implies the intention to marry and socially commits a pair beyond their own readiness, (4) going steady "fences you in" and makes you miss too much fun, (5) going steady is generally frowned upon by parents and other adults, (6) going steady is too demanding and too often leads to being "taken for granted," (7) going steady is too often just a way of being sure of a date when you want one.[7]

Going steady in college, as contrasted with the pattern of high school steady dating, may move toward the informal engagement before graduation, and often does. LeMasters sees reasons for encouraging it. He lists advantages going steady has over random dating:

1. It reduces, at least temporarily, the competitive pressure in dating, thus producing a more relaxed dating atmosphere.
2. It assures the partners of a date at all times, reducing the insecurity prevalent in random dating.
3. It permits the partners to get to know each other much more realistically than random dating usually does.

---

[6] Taken in essence from Evelyn Millis Duvall, *Facts of Life and Love,* New York: Association Press, 1956, pp. 345–350.

[7] Drawn from the responses of 1,925 girls in the nationwide sample taken in 1956, Survey Research Center, *Adolescent Girls,* Institute for Social Research, University of Michigan, Ann Arbor, Michigan, 1957, pp. 108–109.

4. It provides some training in the norms required later in monogamous marriage: loyalty, faithfulness, honesty.[8]

Going steady as a status involves more commitment than random dating and introduces a new dimension into the relation. Going steady enables the pair to exclude others, to be alone more frequently, and to discover as well as to develop common interests; in short, to begin to build a separate pair identity with its own history and outlook. Whereas random dating tends to circumscribe the aspects of the self that are exposed to the partner and to delimit the obligations and intimacies, going steady is a status that encourages self-revelation and intimacies. Indeed, one of the dangers of going steady is that physical intimacies tend to outdistance personality exploration to the point of sexual exploitation. The whole question of premarital sexual experimentation is discussed in Chapter 8, "Sex Manners and Morals."

Getting a person to go steady is a subtle process of self-and-other involvement much like the strategy the young person must master to get engaged and to set a marriage date. Many otherwise marriageable girls never marry because they have not yet mastered the art of involving others into making firm commitments. Two theories may be cited to explain success in involving others. One appears highly manipulative but is undoubtedly descriptive of actual behavior of veteran campaigners. Waller describes the process as akin to hypnotism. There is a certain amount of deceit involved, but half-truths may be employed without conscious desire to deceive the other. Skillful campaigners go to great pains in order to avoid being categorized or fitted into any comfortable and established pattern in the mind of the other; they wish to be seen as entirely unique. They ask for the inane but deeply complimentary remark, "You're so different!" The enigmatic and mysterious character has an advantage, but it is necessary to remember that one need only seem mysterious to the illusioned and not very educated eyes of another. And often the character which is merely unformed can seem contradictory and mysterious.

. . . where a person is adventuring for the first time in the realm of emotional involvement, the unfathomed mysteries of the experience supply all that is needed of novelty and allurement. The other person seems strange and mysterious because one's attitude toward her is strange. It should be noted that after a prolonged courtship and engagement these mysterious qualities of the relationship slowly fade out.[9]

---

[8] Ersel LeMasters, *Modern Courtship and Marriage,* New York: Macmillan, 1957, p. 130.

[9] Willard Waller and Reuben Hill, *The Family: A Dynamic Interpretation,* New York: Dryden Press, 1951, p. 180.

Waller's views probably explain better the involvements of the starry-eyed couples who are "head over heels in love" than the more mature involvements reported by college students. The latter describe casual friendship deepening into an interdependent relation after a series of dates in which they have come to depend upon one another for response and recognition. Becoming "steadies" for them involves more of a mutual acknowledgment that going together has become a pleasant and rewarding "habit" which neither wishes to break for the moment and which holds promise for the future.

Getting a date to go steady, agreeing on the announcement of an engagement, or setting of the wedding date—all commitments of some moment—may seem the most natural next step to take for couples who welcome entangling alliances and are quite ready to yield the necessary personal autonomy to make them possible. For others, each added commitment appears to involve loss of freedom of action. As one enamored bachelor exclaimed to his eager sweetheart, "Why can't we go on like this forever without a care in the world!"

On many a college campus, senior coeds get what is called "senior panic" as they approach graduation without having achieved a permanent attachment which could grow into a marriage commitment. One such senior confided to her roommate, "Something always happens, first with Jim, then Bob, and finally Frank—I don't know what it is, but whenever we seem to be getting somewhere and I think we can begin to think we're going steady, I wake up and find he's moved on to some other gal. Going steady is one rut I would like to get into for a change!" How you involve others and get involved yourself is worthy of even more attention in the statuses of getting pinned and getting engaged.

What Does Getting Pinned Mean?

Fairly far along in the going steady period the couple seek some public recognition of their commitment to each other. This can take one of many forms, the most familiar of which is the "pinning" of the boy's fraternity pin on his girl. The term "being pinned" stands for the stage of commitment reached between going steady and formal engagement.

Pinning is a relative newcomer to the American courtship scene. Dating is at least fifty years old as a preliminary to serious courtship, "steady dating for convenience" is new, but "going steady with marriage as a goal" is not too different from the pattern of courting and "keeping steady company" of traditional courtship. Pinning, in contrast, arrives on the scene to take care of an obvious need for "trial engagements" in which the promise to marry is less important than the need to test the relationship for compatibility.

A real difficulty with pinning is its lack of uniformity and the variety of meanings ascribed to it. What does it mean to be pinned? Exclusive necking privileges? A steady date? A real engagement without the ring? A private understanding? Boys may use a pin to exploit girls sexually, girls assuming they are engaged and boys that they are just having fun. As pinning becomes more exclusively used as a "trial engagement," its usefulness will increase.

The pinning status is announced by the fraternity man's "planting his pin" on his sweetheart's sweater. On some campuses a girl carries the ring around her neck while "engaged to be engaged" and puts it on her finger when she is formally engaged. On other campuses the trial engagement of pinning moves into a new phase of formal commitment when the girl's pin and the boy's pin are joined with a chain—they are now *chained*, indicating that the wedding date has been set.

Being pinned usually occurs at the point in the involvement process when increasing intimacy, common interests, and quarrels have precipitated a more definitive love commitment. As the couple begin acting as if they were engaged, their friends begin treating them accordingly and urge a public announcement of their position.

Formal engagement

Because a full chapter is devoted to engagement, we shall be very brief in our discussion of it now. Engagement is best perceived as a period of compatibility testing, previewing and resolving some of the differences likely to arise in early marriage. This function is obviously more important for couples who become engaged after relatively short acquaintance than it is for engagements preceded by prolonged experiences of going steady and informal engagement.

The clear-cut advantages of the various statuses of commitment are perhaps obvious. By specifying what status you occupy as a couple, you can avoid misunderstanding and exploitation. A girl can legitimately ask "Where do we stand?" after a period of steady dating. If the answer is "Just dating" then she knows what her boy friend's intentions are, and can discount his line and his passes for what they are. If it's "Going steady" or "You have my pin, don't you?" the commitment may seem more binding. Girls worry, rightfully, that boys want "love" without giving up their freedom to play the field—their favorite song being "Don't Fence Me In"!

A steady boy friend who appears faithfully for months but never presses for marriage is another familiar problem. How can a graduating senior girl precipitate a proposal after two years of being pinned? Clearly these are problems that require open discussion, even at the risk of frightening the man away. More usually the involvement process moves both boy and girl forward imperceptibly by stages to the point of maximum commitment, requiring neither party to press the question "Where do we stand?"

How Do You Get in So Deep?

The involvement process [10] begins in dating, at which time there may be little serious intent, and ends in a climax of powerful emotional responses which are most evident in the engagement and honeymoon periods. Human beings act upon one another emotionally when they are thrown into intimate relationships. As emotions build up in one, they are communicated contagiously to the other. Unless there is opportunity for release, the climax which is attained may reach great proportions.

Courtship is a summatory process which builds up with many little experiences, some pleasant and some irritating, each affecting the other, and leaving the parties more involved than before. Each person becomes increasingly committed in his own eyes and in the eyes of the other. Once reaching a certain level of intensity, the process gets a movement of its own. It creates its own demands and needs, and each member finds himself more and more in need of the other to satisfy the new appetites which have been developed. The process tends to be irreversible after a certain momentum is reached, and the couple find they can't stop with being just good friends.

What are the specific components of the involvement process in this movement from casual dating to the emotional climax of engagement? When the brake is taken off a car on a hill, the car may start slowly enough at first, but there are the possibilities of excitement even at the beginning. The components of the courtship process are present in any dating period but are kept in leash by powerful inhibitions until the man, at least, is economically and psychologically ready to take full consequences of emotional involvement.

The involvement process begins with coquetry, behavior inviting   **Coquetry**
amorous adventure. It is seen in the toning up of the organism that occurs when boy and girl meet. The smile of the boy when he sees a

---

[10] We present the following discussion with acknowledgments to Willard Waller, who first developed the approach we are taking in his book, revised by Reuben Hill, *The Family: A Dynamic Interpretation*, New York: Dryden Press, 1951, pp. 175–190, and urge you to regard it as typical only of the middle-class courtships in America. No single courtship conforms in all details to the picture we present, but thousands approximate it in one or more ways.

pretty girl is automatic, and he takes her in with a glance which leaves nothing out. Her blush is evidence that she knows he sees her, and her own coquetry is expressed in her sparkling eyes and flashing smile.

Coquetry is found in all cultures and has been described beautifully in the literature of many peoples. Its tricks are legion. Small hints of interest are given, and hints of erotic possibilities with alternate advance and retreat; great interest is followed by mock modesty and by teasing. Teasing is one of the main techniques of coquetry by which tension is stimulated in the other person to a higher level; the impulse is to chase and be chased, but never quite to catch or be caught.

The line

In America a familiar accompaniment and expression of coquetry is "the line." The line is an exaggeration of feelings, as if the feelings exhibited in coquetry were not enough. It is used by both sexes and is called "handing her a line" or "laying it on." When you first meet a girl and you profess to be greatly impressed by her charms you don't expect to be taken too seriously or you will take flight. But you want to be taken somewhat seriously, and so does she. Neither knows how much is "line" and how much is sincerity.

The line covers up real emotional involvements by exaggeration. Under the soft words may be conflict, because each has the uneasy feeling that he is being tricked. Each avoids being caught by the loaded words of the other—each wishes, however, to dominate the fantasy of the other and to set him to dreaming.

Each tends to become involved in his own line, which he comes to believe in part, but each worries because the other doesn't reveal the extent to which he is sincere. This sense of insecurity which arises from not knowing just where they stand brings on the lovers' quarrel.

Lovers' quarrels

The line finally becomes so burdensome that it has to be broken through, and the crisis comes in a quarrel, followed by a release of tension. Each reveals in the process how much he truly cares for the other, and the pair come to take themselves more seriously. The quarrel tends to redefine the situation upward. Courtship quarrels are in contrast with divorce-directed quarrels, which tend to define the situation downward (see quarrels of alienation, pp. 321–322). The pair make up with a glorious sense of satisfaction and are more involved than before.

Quarrels leave the pair still using the line, but with more security and with a tenderness developing that was not there before. Each is surer of the other and both reach out to claim things which tie them together. Common interests further love involvements by giving the pair a common universe of discourse. The lovers can exclude the rest of the world and they feel a sense of superiority as they talk about things they understand better than anyone else.

Coquetry enhanced by the mutual interchange of lines and the build-up of common interests brings the pair increasingly together. The line encourages physical intimacy, and love gestures confirm the sincerity of the verbal "I love you." The other person becomes a bona fide love object to be reckoned with—not just another date, but a person with feelings. Feelings of tenderness develop, and the lover finds himself more sincere than before and impressed with his moral obligation to the other who believes in him so implicitly. *Increasing intimacy*

Another component of love involvement, which owes some of its development to the line, is idealization. In the line all the desirable characteristics of the other are stressed to the exclusion of the annoying or disturbing characteristics. It is not uncommon for young people to become so enamored of the loved one that they come to believe their own line. The lover forgets his sweetheart's crooked teeth, her so-so complexion, and her stringy hair, and remembers only her lovely eyes and regal carriage. Waller tells the story of a young man who was very conscious of a wart on his chin and went to the expense of an operation to remove it. After it had healed, he presented himself to his fiancée. "Notice anything different about my face?" The moment was embarrassing; she had never noticed the wart in the first place. *Idealization*

Idealization results in each replacing the other with an imaginary person to whom he reacts. Separation for brief periods tends to accentuate this process. Absence makes the heart grow fonder, because the real person's presence gives way to the imaginary one. Each feels troubled that his own weaknesses are not seen, but does not try too hard to expose them. Unfortunately for later adjustments, the greater the idealization, the greater is the disillusionment which must follow in the marriage period. But couples should remember it was their imagination which cheated them, not marriage.[11]

In the midst of this process, couple unity develops. Favored by the development of common interests which act to exclude the public and to give the pair a feeling of superiority, the couple reach out and seize upon evidences that they were "meant for each other." One couple in the course of their daily walk simultaneously focused their attention upon a certain mountain peak glittering in the sun and called it "our mountain." They took every opportunity thereafter to admire this sym- *Couple unity*

---

[11] For a description of idealization among couples separated by war, see W. Edgar Gregory, "The Idealization of the Absent," *American Journal of Sociology,* Vol. 50, No. 1, July, 1944, pp. 53–54. Ernest W. Burgess and Paul Wallin disagree with those who assign great weight to idealization as a mechanism of involvement, finding less evidence for it in their thousand engaged couples than they had anticipated, see their *Engagement and Marriage,* Chicago: Lippincott, 1953, Chapter 7.

bol of their unity. Years later they returned to the exact spot to get another view of the mountain which had come to mean so much to them during their courtship period.

Early in the development of unity, rings or other articles are exchanged to crystallize and render tangible that elusive "we feeling" which they sense but can't describe. As each leaves the other, he carries away a reminder of their growing unity. It is as if the exchanged articles could somehow summon the presence of the loved one, and the separation is thereby made more bearable.

Another development in this process is the growth of a special language between the two, which they alone can understand. They develop their own idioms, pet names, and inflections which tend to alienate any third person and make him realize that two is company but three is a crowd. Left more and more together, the pair build up a shorthand language which obviates the necessity of completing sentences. Conversation is speeded up tremendously. Their language may look and sound to the outsider like a combination of nudges, knowing winks, and half-finished sentences, with poorly repressed mirth at things the outsider doesn't think funny at all. The jokes are hardest of all for the intruder to understand. They can be fully appreciated and understood only by the couple themselves. The jokes grow funnier the more frequently they are repeated, because they develop unseen nuances and are attached to other associations of a pleasant nature in the relationship.

In summary, the process of developing pair unity is one of building a separate history and culture which the pair alone can understand. The relationship is stabilized in direct proportion to its success in throwing the pair on its own resources and in excluding, thereby, rivals and other members of the public.

The part friends play

All of these activities of the couple have not escaped the eyes of friends, who play a very important role in furthering love involvements. The self-restraint of friends in the early casual dating stage in not communicating their disapproval of a relationship facilitates love involvements, since at that stage the relationship is quite fragile. In one study of reticence of friends to interfere, only 15 per cent of the respondents said they would unequivocally share an adverse opinion of a friend's date with the object of breaking up the relationship; the balance either would say nothing or would do so only if asked their opinion.[12] Friends further love involvements by the self-restraint they

---

[12] John E. Mayer, "The Self-Restraint of Friends," *Social Forces*, Vol. 35, March, 1957, pp. 230–238.

show initially and by the subsequent treatment of the two as a "steady pair."

Whenever a young man and young woman appear together, even in the casual dating stage, they risk being identified as a likely marriage pair by well-wishers. Friendly gossip—"We hear that Bob and Mary are getting serious"—gets back to the ears of the participants. Gossip columns of community and campus newspapers are widely read and further the public's identification of the pair. There is something about being identified by the public which changes the relationship. The sense of moral obligation on the part of the man, particularly, is a function partly of what the public thinks of his affair. Yesterday he might have been asked by a relative of the girl what his intentions were; today his conscience asks him the same question and is quite as effective in furthering his feeling of obligation to clarify things.

People's talk acts as further pressure to drop the exaggerations of the line and become more sincere in the relationship. "People are saying we are going steady, but you haven't said a word about it. Margaret even asked me if we were engaged. The nerve. . . ." They quarrel, and in making up, many of the problems concerning their status which have given them the jitters are cleared up. The discussion and redefinition of the situation enables them to explain satisfactorily to themselves and to their friends where they stand.

The public plays its part in clarifying the situation by treating the two as a unit, arranging for them to be together, and inviting them to social affairs together. When a friend meets one member of the couple, he asks about the other member and expresses inferentially the hope that all is well between them. The pair come to feel that the public approves of the match and expects something to come of it. This sanctioning in itself has a pushing effect and changes the nature of the relationship subtly but effectively. Much of the exciting novelty of the relation is lost, but in its place comes a sense of responsibility and stability. If the pair are emotionally built up to a certain point, all it may take is a suggestion from a friend that they act as if they were engaged to crystallize the situation. It seems only natural and right to make a public announcement of their involvement, and a formal engagement takes place.

How Typical Are You?

No single courtship necessarily embodies all of the components described, and many courtships vary greatly from the pattern just presented. Young people who have taken courses in marriage and the family rarely use the line as seriously as described here, with the result that they build up fewer illusions about each other and indulge in relatively little idealization. Indeed, the courtship remains much more on the companionship level, and the emotions tend to be enjoyed on the spot rather than built up toward an explosive release at the honeymoon stage. These couples carry over into marriage few illusions about one another but nevertheless develop considerable fondness for each other as persons. They rarely build up ideas of the other as the incarnation of perfection so characteristic of those who have gone in for extreme idealization.

The courtship pattern followed by young people in a few very isolated rural areas may vary greatly from that of the middle-class urban couple described in the foregoing pages. Rural courtships may conform more closely to those of the last generation and move naturally and more easily from keeping company to serious courtship to engagement and marriage. Each step in the process is well marked. Moreover, the couple have probably known one another for so long that there is little possibility of extreme idealization. The line is not likely to take such exaggerated form and would not be taken seriously if it did.

A third variation is seen in the courtships of war and postwar couples who have telescoped the dating, courtship, and engagement periods into one undifferentiated stage of involvement which eventuates in immediate marriage.

Still a fourth variation is that of couples in middle age who after widowhood or divorce seek a second marriage partner. LeMasters describes their pattern as follows:

. . . there is a very brief random dating stage, usually not more than a month in length, during which the couple have about one date a week; this is followed by an intensive going steady period of perhaps six months, during which things become serious very rapidly, and this leads directly into marriage.[13]

Among middle-aged courting couples, Bernard estimates that the majority consummate the sexual relationship before marriage, a factor that may have something to do with their decision to skip the engagement stage.[14]

Finally, a fifth variation should be noted. The courtship pattern described above is largely a middle-class phenomenon. Lower-class young people make less use of pinning and engagement and are less

---

[13] LeMasters, *op. cit.*, p. 177.
[14] Jessie Bernard, *Remarriage*, New York: Dryden Press, 1956, pp. 154–155.

likely to dally in the premarital statuses. They marry after less variety in dating and fewer liaisons. They move into sexual intimacies earlier after fewer formalities and become parents earlier.[15]

This chapter has by no means told all about what is required to become involved in a satisfying relationship. Indeed, it has been hard to refrain from using the word "love" in treating the progressive involvements which lead to engagement and marriage. Love is, of course, the basic ingredient in bringing young people to mutual commitments, and as such it deserves separate attention. We turn now to a discussion of the facts and fictions about love, and the ways of distinguishing between love and infatuation.

READINGS

Baber, Ray E., *Marriage and the Family*. New York: McGraw-Hill, 1953, Chapter V, "Mate Selection and Courtship."

Becker, Howard, and Reuben Hill (eds.), *Family, Marriage and Parenthood*. Boston: Heath, 1955, Chapter VII, "Steps in Love and Courtship."

Blood, Robert O., Jr., "A Retest of Waller's Rating Complex," *Marriage and Family Living*, Vol. 17, February, 1955, pp. 41–47.

Burgess, Ernest W., and Paul Wallin, *Engagement and Marriage*. Chicago: Lippincott, 1953, Chapter IV, "Going Together."

Cavan, Ruth S., *American Marriage, A Way of Life*. New York: Crowell, 1959, Chapter 6, "Love as the Basis for Marriage."

Hill, Reuben, "Courtship in Puerto Rico: An Institution in Transition," *Marriage and Family Living*, Vol. 17, February, 1955, pp. 26–35.

Landis, Judson T., and Mary G. Landis, *Building a Successful Marriage*. Englewood Cliffs, New Jersey: Prentice-Hall, 1958, Chapter V, "Dating: a Growth Process."

LeMasters, E. E., *Modern Courtship and Marriage*. New York: Macmillan, 1957, Part II, "The American Courtship System."

Mead, Margaret, *Male and Female*. New York: Morrow, 1949, Chapter 14, "Pre-Courtship Behavior and Adult Sex Standards."

Waller, Willard, and Reuben Hill, *The Family: A Dynamic Interpretation*. New York: Dryden Press, 1951, Chapter 8, "The Social Contexts of Courtship."

---

[15] LeMasters, *op. cit.*, pp. 178–179, and A. B. Hollingshead, *Elmstown Youth*, New York: Wiley, 1949, pp. 414–436.

3 Is It Love or Infatuation?

What is wrong with romantic love?

What is love?

Who do you love—and how?

How do you learn to love?

What are the differences between love and infatuation?

How can you know your love will last?

Now that science has answers for so many of life's questions, it would be nice if there were a super computer by which any young person who wanted to know might discover just how long a particular love affair would last or could tell whether this were infatuation or the REAL thing. Unfortunately, the social sciences have no such kit of certainties to offer. As one research reviewer has succinctly put it, ". . . we do not know why 'A' falls in love with 'B' rather than with 'C' or 'D'; we are not sure what love is; and we don't know whether 'A' is any surer than we are." [1] Man may never unravel the mystery of love, but he can learn how to develop it, keep it alive, and enjoy it.

What Is Wrong with Romantic Love?

The romantic myth says that when you meet your "one and only" you will KNOW. The evidence to date indicates that you probably will *not* be sure of your choice, of yourself, or of your love, even when

---

[1] William M. Kephart, "Some Knowns and Unknowns in Family Research: A Sociological Critique," *Marriage and Family Living*, Vol. XIX, No. 1, February, 1957, p. 11.

you are at the threshold of marriage. After extensive research with hundreds of engaged couples who later married, Burgess and Wallin conclude that a large proportion of men and even more women have doubts and reservations about their choice of a marriage partner.[2]

The romantic myth says that love goes on forever. Yet the indications are that many persons find that what they thought was love did not last more than a few weeks. Ellis' study of the love lives of 500 college girls reports that less than one fourth of them were able to remain in love two years or more.[3] Kirkpatrick and Caplow's study of the courtship experience of students at the University of Minnesota found that among 141 college men, out of 314 love affairs 230 had been broken; while among 258 college women, 414 of their 582 love affairs had been broken.[4] Such experience is striking evidence of the fleeting, fragile quality of love in many of its manifestations known to young people.

Even more indicative of the potential damage in the romantic illusion is the evidence that a considerable number of both men and women feel trapped in love affairs that have become meaningless to them. When several hundred college men and women reporting broken love affairs were asked the question, "Did you continue the relation-

TABLE 7. Responses of College Students Reporting Broken Love Affairs to the Question "Did you continue the relationship after it ceased to be satisfactory?"[5]

Response	Men Students		Women Students	
	No.	%	No.	%
Yes		38.2		31.3
No		61.8		68.7
Replying	251		466	
Blank	63		116	
Total	314	100.0	582	100.0

[2] Ernest W. Burgess, Paul Wallin, and Gladys Denny Shultz, *Courtship, Engagement and Marriage.* Philadelphia: Lippincott, 1954, p. 136.

[3] Albert Ellis, "A Study of Human Love Relationships," *The Journal of Genetic Psychology,* Vol. 75, 1949, p. 67.

[4] Clifford Kirkpatrick and Theodore Caplow, "Emotional Trends in the Courtship Experience of College Students as Expressed by Graphs with Some Observations on Methodological Implications," *American Sociological Review,* Vol. X, No. 5, 1945, p. 619.

[5] From Clifford Kirkpatrick and Theodore Caplow, "Courtship in a Group of Minnesota Students," *American Journal of Sociology,* Vol. LI, 1945, p. 122.

ship after it ceased to be satisfactory?" more than a third of them reported that they had (see Table 7).

More men than women continue love affairs after they no longer are satisfactory. When asked the question directly, "Did you have a feeling of being trapped in the relationship?" considerably more men (30.2 per cent) than women (20.6 per cent) reported that they had either often or occasionally felt trapped in their love affairs.[6]

In many of its aspects romantic love is not particularly pleasant. College students have described how they felt in their love affairs by checking a long list of both positive and negative emotional states. Positive feelings such as love, tenderness, and inspiration were included as well as negative emotions such as hate, misery, and disgust. Not one in hundreds of reported love affairs had twice as many positive as negative feelings attributed to it by the lovers.[7]

In addition to the misery and uncertainty of romantic love, there are indications that even if you find your dream mate you may be in for more trouble. Dr. H. V. Dicks, discussing the findings of his studies at the Fifth International Congress on Mental Health, is reported to have said that the trouble with marrying a dream mate is that you do not marry a real person, but a distorted image of your inner fantasies projected onto your partner, so when your mate fails to measure up to your dream image, you suffer frustration and conflict.[8]

The overwhelming evidence to date is that romance alone is poor preparation for marriage or for life, and that romantic love is not to be trusted to provide more than a few thrills. It is certainly not "love enough to marry on."

What Is Love?

Love is many things to many people. It has become such an omnibus term that it has come to mean just about anything a given individual wants it to mean. One of the more comprehensive of recent attempts to define love is by Magoun:

Love is a passionate and abiding desire on the part of two or more people to produce together the conditions under which each can be and spontaneously express his real self; to produce together an intellectual soil and an emotional climate in which each can flourish, far superior to what either could achieve alone.[9]

---

[6] *Ibid.*, p. 121.

[7] *Ibid.*, pp. 123–124.

[8] John E. Gibson, "What's New about Love?" *This Week Magazine*, August 7, 1955, p. 20.

[9] F. Alexander Magoun, *Love and Marriage, Revised.* New York: Harper, 1956, p. 7.

Love can be seen as a complex of feelings, attitudes, and values associated with man's fundamental wish for response. Burgess and Locke see ten components of the love sentiment:

1. Sexual desire—the physiological component.
2. Physical attraction—social and personal discriminations of sex appeal.
3. Attachment—rapport through intimate association, mutual responsiveness.
4. Emotional interdependence—mutual fulfillment of basic personality needs.
5. Idealization—distortion of the other's image by lovers' dreams.
6. Companionship—common interests, mental interstimulation, and response.
7. Stimulation—adventure in new experiences together.
8. Freedom of communication and action—exchange of confidences, freedom to be oneself.
9. Emotional reassurance—mutual reaffirmation.
10. Status—pride of possession, mutual self-congratulation.[10]

It is possible to identify various aspects of the love sentiment as different combinations of these elements. The love of a young man for his twin sister maximizes components 3, 4, 6, 8, and 9 while suppressing components 1, 2, 5, 7, and 10. The "love at first sight" depicted in a Hollywood movie is based upon components 2, 5, 7, and possibly 1, but places little or no emphasis on the other components. Some students of the subject think adolescents' first loves lean more toward the romantic love components of physical attraction, attachment, idealization, and stimulation, while their love affairs in their twenties place more emphasis on emotional interdependence, companionship, and freedom of communication.[11] If this is true it may partly explain why teen-age marriages more frequently end in divorce than marriages among more mature persons.

Still another classification of love feelings has been formulated by Folsom who distinguishes four kinds by the parts of the body most obviously involved. (1) Sexual feelings are localized in the genital region with overtones throughout the body. (2) Tender feelings or "dermal love" involve sensations in the skin, particularly of the chest, face, lips, and inner surface of the arms. (3) Rapturous or ecstatic feelings or "cardiac-respiratory love" involve the chest, heart, and respiration. (4) Pleasant feelings seem not to be localized at all save perhaps in

---

[10] Ernest W. Burgess and Harvey J. Locke, *The Family from Institution to Companionship.* New York: American Book, 1953, pp. 322–326.

[11] Robert F. Winch. *The Modern Family.* New York: Holt, 1952, pp. 399–400.

laughter and smiling. These four types of love feelings can be roughly related to the kinds of contact between lovers. Sexual feelings arising from erotic urges seek expression in extensive or heavy bodily contact. Tender feelings arising from motives of affection call for light bodily contact when possible, though they also may be expressed at a distance. Rapturous feelings may be satisfied with little or no bodily contact. Joyful love feelings arising from motives of sociability or affection are usually expressed in face-to-face communication but require no bodily contact for satisfaction.[12]

Who Do You Love—and How?

Very few of us know exactly why we like the people to whom we are attracted because human likes and dislikes are so often irrational. The people we like are not necessarily the persons that a social scientist would recommend as our companions, either for a lifetime or for a few months. Yet these little-understood forces of personal attraction wield a mighty weight in the process of falling in love and getting married, and often overshadow more rational and sensible considerations in the choice of a wife or husband.

Some of the unconscious tendencies that determine our preferences for people are these:

Principles of attraction

1. We tend to like those who satisfy some particularly hungry spot in our make-up. Winch calls this the principle of mutual need gratification in mate selection.[13] The boy who has not had as much mother love as he needs may be strongly attracted to a mother type of girl. "I don't know why I love her. She just gives me all I need."

2. We tend to like the people and the things that remind us of pleasant and comfortable experiences in our past, many of which go way back into our early childhood and are forgotten except for the powerful, unconscious role they continue to play in our choices. "I loved him the minute I set eyes upon him."

3. We tend to be repulsed by the people and the things that are associated with uncomfortable and unpleasant experiences in our past. The original painful experience may be no longer remembered, but its influence continues to deflect us from anything and anybody that resembles some aspect of that unhappy situation. "Don't ask me why, I just don't like her."

[12] Joseph K. Folsom, *The Family in Democratic Society*. New York: Wiley, 1943, pp. 366–7.
[13] Robert F. Winch, *Mate Selection: A Study of Complementary Needs*. New York: Harper, 1958, pp. 88–89.

4. We tend to be attracted to those people who reassure us, do not make us feel less worthy or less able or attractive than we like to think we are. "She's just too smart to suit me," or "I can't stand him, he's always so *superior*," and "She makes me feel as though I am somebody."

5. We tend to seek the people who are considered attractive by those around us and to leave the unsought alone. "I want the kind of girl the other fellows will whistle at."

6. We tend both to reproduce and to repudiate the relationships in which we grew up. A boy may be attracted to anyone who reminds him of his mother and who can reproduce the feeling of the old parent-child relationships. A girl may be unable to tolerate anyone who even remotely reminds her of her father, a repudiation of the former parent-child relationships. "I want a girl just like the girl who married dear old dad," or "I can't stand her. Who does she think she is, my mother?"

Two well-known psychoanalysts tell of an interesting case that illustrates one of these principles well:

A student, walking past a building on the campus, noticed a girl in a blue dress standing on the steps. He had seen her before around the campus, but she was in none of his classes, he knew nothing about her, nor was she particularly pretty. Yet, looking up at her with the sunlight illuminating her golden hair, he was irresistibly attracted and instantly fell in love. The intensity of the emotion was incomprehensible to him. Only later, under different circumstances, did he realize that this golden-haired girl in the blue dress reminded him of another girl, one who had a similar appearance, of whom he had been very fond a number of years before; she had not acknowledged his shy advances and he had eventually forgotten all about her. When he saw the girl on campus he did not at the time remember the first girl, but the intense emotion connected with his earlier experience was instantly revived.[14]

The course of love affairs

Since it is well known that the course of love does not run smoothly let us look briefly at how love affairs begin and see what course they follow. The college girls that Ellis studied [15] reported that they first fell in love with, or became infatuated with, a man or boy when they were nearly twelve years old. They also indicated that between the ages of twelve and eighteen they each had been in love with, or infatuated with, more than six different men or boys. Although further research is needed in this area, general observation corroborates this finding that young people do tend to experience specific love feelings early and to

[14] Alexander Grinstein and Editha Sterba, *Understanding Your Family*. New York: Random House, 1957, p. 4.

[15] Albert Ellis, "Questionnaire Versus Interview Methods in the Study of Human Love Relationships. II, Uncategorized Responses," *American Sociological Review*, February, 1948, Vol. XIII, No. 1, pp. 62–64.

be attracted to a variety of members of the other sex throughout the entire second decade of life.[16]

Two other investigators show graphically that college students are able to plot the course of their love affairs on four levels of involvement: love, attraction, indifference, and dislike. The most frequently reported curve was regular, beginning with indifference, moving slowly or precipitately upward through attraction to love and then

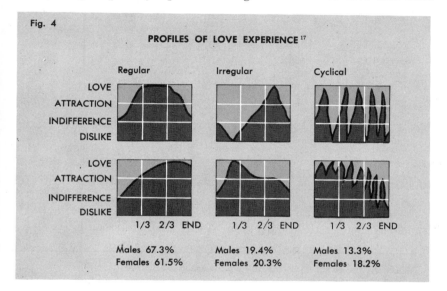

Fig. 4

PROFILES OF LOVE EXPERIENCE [17]

Regular   Irregular   Cyclical

LOVE
ATTRACTION
INDIFFERENCE
DISLIKE

LOVE
ATTRACTION
INDIFFERENCE
DISLIKE

1/3 2/3 END   1/3 2/3 END   1/3 2/3 END

Males 67.3%   Males 19.4%   Males 13.3%
Females 61.5%   Females 20.3%   Females 18.2%

(a) dropping again to indifference (indicating that the love had ended), or (b) remaining at a high level of love. About one fifth of the students, both male and female, reported an irregular course of love, while a somewhat smaller group showed their course of love to be vacillating or "cyclical" (see Fig. 4). Such findings reaffirm the importance of two other questions: (1) How does the capacity to love develop? and (2) How can you tell when you are in love?

The indications are that at any one time a majority of young people probably feel they are in love. When five hundred college girls on nineteen different campuses were asked if they were at that time in love or

Being in love is usual

[16] Evelyn Millis Duvall, *Facts of Life and Love*, New York: Association Press, 1956. Based on thousands of questions asked by teen-age young people of both sexes.

[17] Clifford Kirkpatrick and Theodore Caplow, "Emotional Trends in the Courtship Experience of College Students as Expressed by Graphs with Some Observations on Methodological Implications," *American Sociological Review*, October, 1945, X, No. 5, pp. 619–626.

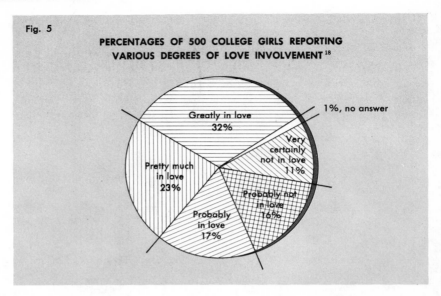

Fig. 5

**PERCENTAGES OF 500 COLLEGE GIRLS REPORTING
VARIOUS DEGREES OF LOVE INVOLVEMENT** [18]

Greatly in love
32%

1%, no answer

Very certainly not in love 11%

Pretty much in love 23%

Probably not in love 16%

Probably in love 17%

not, only 27 per cent said they probably or certainly were not (see Fig. 5).

More than half (55 per cent) of these girls were greatly or pretty much in love at the time of the study, while another 17 per cent

TABLE 8. *Emotional Reactions at the Breakup of Love Affairs* [19]

Reaction	Men (N-230)	Women (N-414)
Bitter	5.9%	4.4%
Hurt	10.0	14.3
Angry	3.3	3.5
Remorseful	6.6	6.7
Crushed	1.8	5.0
Indifferent	19.4	16.2
Relieved	15.2	16.8
Satisfied	11.5	8.5
Happy	4.4	3.5
Mixed Regret and Relief	21.9	21.1
Total	100.0%	100.0%

---

[18] Albert Ellis, "Love and Family Relationships of American College Girls," *The American Journal of Sociology*, Vol. LV, May, 1950, p. 554.

[19] Clifford Kirkpatrick and Theodore Caplow, "Courtship in a Group of Minnesota Students," *American Journal of Sociology*, Vol. LI, 1945, p. 124.

thought they probably were then in love. Fully one third (33 per cent) could reply only with the qualifying "probably" they were or they were not in love, which goes to show that it is sometimes difficult for young people to be sure whether they are in love or not. The 11 per cent who replied vehemently that they "very certainly" were *not* in love possibly represent in part those whose love affairs had recently broken leaving them with hurt, angry, or bitter feelings.

In spite of all the "blues" of song and spirit, getting over a broken love affair is not always painful. Two social scientists who studied the question on a college campus find that in the majority of cases love affairs "just faded away." Being hurt is only one of many feelings in losing a loved one (see Table 8). *[Broken love affairs]*

This same study shows reasons why less than 20 per cent of either the men or the women were hurt or bitter over the breakup of their love affairs. Getting interested in another person was reported by 15.1 per cent of the men and twice as many (32.2 per cent) women; while partner's interest in another person bore out the implied tendency for more women than men to want to change partners: 29.7 per cent of the men and 15.3 per cent of the women saying in effect that they had been "jilted." [20] The most frequent reason for breakups was found to be "mutual loss of interest" with 46.9 per cent of the men and 38.1 per cent of the women so reporting.

How long does it take to recover from a broken love affair? Practically half of both men and women, in the study above, said that it took no time at all for them to adjust after a breakup. Another third of the men and a fifth of the women said it took several weeks for them to recover; 8 per cent of the men and 20 per cent of the women had a re-adjustment period of several months; while the rest, 7 per cent of the men and 12 per cent of the women, said they were one or more years getting over their loss. "Carrying a torch" for a lost lover may be a familiar theme in popular songs, but actually it is done in only a minority of cases. How is it that so many recover so quickly and with so little pain? What do people do to get over a broken affair? Table 9 lists recovery patterns. *[Getting over a broken heart]*

One point that neither the men nor the women mention is perhaps taken for granted. That is the courage to pick oneself up after an emotional crisis and get going again. It is easy to feel sorry for oneself, to punish oneself with recriminations, or to blame the other or someone else for the situations that led to the broken romance. A broken love affair is most tragic to a person who thinks he can love only once and

---

[20] *Ibid.*, p. 123.

TABLE 9. *Behavior in Adjusting to Broken Love Affairs* [21]

Behavior	Men (N-230)	Women (N-414)
Frequenting Places with Common Associations	11.3%	10.0%
Avoiding Places with Common Associations	2.9	3.4
Avoiding Meetings	4.7	5.1
Attempting Meetings	5.9	4.3
Remembering Only Unpleasant Things	2.3	3.9
Remembering Only Pleasant Things	15.6	15.8
Dreaming about Partner	15.5	11.2
Daydreaming	14.3	11.4
Imagining Recognition	6.4	7.9
Liking or Disliking People Because of Resemblance	5.5	5.4
Imitating Mannerisms	1.8	2.1
Preserving Keepsakes	7.0	10.8
Reading Over Old Letters	6.8	8.7
Total	100.0%	100.0%

will never love again. This is far from true. In a person's growing up there are many loves. One learns to love in childhood and by adulthood has loved many persons.

How Do You Learn to Love?

You develop the capacity to love gradually through years of interaction with other people. You learn to love just as you learn to eat, to walk, and to read. You were born with native tendencies and potentialities for loving and being loved. Given favorable opportunities, these capacities develop and flower; and as in all learning, first experiences set the stage for later responses. To trace the development of the ability to love and to be loved, we must go back to the early days of infancy.

Developing the capacity to love

In his mother's arms the baby receives his first lessons in learning to love. As she holds him close in nursing, he feels the comfort of her supporting arms, the warmth of her body, the gratification of the satisfying milk, and the pleasure of the sucking process itself. Before long his eyes focus on her face, he sees her smile and soon manages one of his own in return. He coos back to her as she talks and sings to him. The glow of comfort he feels in her presence quickly becomes associated

---

[21] *Ibid.*, p. 125.

with the mother herself, as the baby learns that these highly pleasurable experiences arrive wrapped in the sound and the smell and the feel and the sight of his mother. Associated with all his fundamental satisfactions, this first mother-love establishes the pattern for further responses to others.

Winch [22] develops in some detail the process by which the child effects this transfer of affection from the parents, more usually the mother, to successive substitutes until he settles on an age mate with whom he experiences "companionship love." Winch explains the process as maturation of the capacity to love without "leaning" dependently on another. From the extremely dependent love of the infant for the mother, based on the infant's complete dependence on her for the gratification of his needs, the child develops self-dependence in many areas of his life, diffuses his "needs-meeting" among many individuals outside the family, and eventually does not need to have all his needs met through one all-consuming love. By means of trial-and-error, he discovers persons whose needs to gratify others complement his needs to be gratified. His parents become alternates in his love life, and companionship love of an interdependence-of-peers sort is experienced with one or more age mates. In marriage, this love, based on complementary needs, becomes a solidifying factor, particularly if the love patterns keep abreast of the changing needs of the partners throughout their marriage.

If the child is frustrated in his first important relationships, he may come to feel that he is living in a hostile world in which he must fight for what he needs; or if the outlook is too discouraging, he may lapse into the listless lethargy described so vividly by Ribble.[23] If he is neglected, handled harshly, or fed too little, the unfortunate child develops irritability instead of the glow of the happy child. He feels frustration in continued hunger, and he misses the cuddling support and warmth of the mother. He whimpers his discontent, lashes about in his discomfort, cries out in distress, and if no relief is forthcoming he may lapse into troubled, discouraged apathy.

The neglected child has been deprived of the first opportunities of feeling and responding warmly to another. Years later as an adult he may attempt to compensate for his childhood deprivations by excesses and undue personal demands upon others. His early protests may con-

---

[22] Robert F. Winch, *The Modern Family*, New York: Holt, 1952, especially pp. 396–400.

[23] Margaret A. Ribble, *The Rights of Infants*, New York: Columbia University Press, 1943.

tinue into marriage in the form of unpredictable, little-understood aggressions toward his wife and children.

The child . . . becomes lovable . . . only if he learns to curb the hostile emotions that inevitably arise toward the parent. Instead of going into temper tantrums when he is thwarted, he learns to accept delays in the gratification of his wishes. He abandons his imperious attitude toward the world and learns not to make impossible demands. Gradually he realizes that he must offer love to his parents in return for theirs. In substance, a "good" child is one who *gives up hate as a means of getting what he wants in life.*

The secret of true loveability lies in the combined virtues derived from this reciprocal pattern of exchange. All of us throughout life constantly search for substitutes to replace the good parents of our infancy. We find them in employer and business associates who help provide us with our livelihood; in the wife or husband who gives us love, comfort and protection . . .[24]

Diffusion of love to others

Mother may be the first love, but she is not the last. Father often enters into the affectional set-up very early. As he helps bathe and dress the child, as he comes in for a frolic before bedtime, as he tucks the infant under the covers, he too becomes an object of the child's love. Soon his voice and his step are awaited with eagerness, and his presence brings peculiarly satisfying meanings to the child. The child now responds to both father and mother with love.

The baby learns still another type of love response from children. Their play with the child is less tender; their laughter is a bit more spontaneous, their voices louder and their touch a little rougher. With them the baby learns a new type of love, hearty and carefree. The familiar roughhouse of the typical household finds the baby the gleeful center. Now he's beginning to feel one of the gang. It took mother to nurse him through early infancy. It took father to teach him that men are good and very much a part of his life. Brothers and sisters round out his early emotional education by helping him feel that he belongs, that he is one of them—a part of the family.

Early in the child's life come other adults to strengthen and to modify the feelings built up toward parents. Relatives, neighbors, and teachers become substitute parents as the youngster tries out his parent-learned responses on them. These adults play important roles in the lives of children, giving them the comforting security so needed by youngsters growing away from early parent-child relationships. Baruch

---

[24] Smiley Blanton, *Love or Perish.* New York: Simon and Schuster, 1955, from a digest in *Woman's Home Companion,* January, 1956, p. 76.

gives a particularly clear illustration from a nursery school in the following episode:

. . . a two year old is having trouble making his adjustment in the new situation. He has been raised by his grandmother, and now his grandmother has gone to work. He sulks at the teachers and shrugs away. But, after a while, he navigates into the kitchen, settles himself there on a chair, and does not wish to budge. The head-teacher, observing, suddenly realizes, "It's the cook." As she said later, "The rest of the staff was so much younger than the only mother he had ever known. But not the cook. She's an elderly, comfortable, grandmotherly soul. So, we suggested that she take over and that she give him some loving between paring carrots and potatoes. He spent two days sitting in the kitchen, dragging the toys in under her feet, until he got the feeling of anchorage and belongingness, and could wander further apace.[25]

Most of us remember the warm, friendly adults who made us feel important back in those days when we went exploring for new relationships. Unfortunately, not all adults were equally friendly, and some of us also remember the shame and ignominy of early experiences with sarcastic, blaming persons, some of whom were teachers who shamed and ridiculed us and rebuffed our struggling efforts to please. All too few educators realize the importance of selecting leaders and teachers who can take the place of parents in the molding and directing of love responses in growing children. Teachers especially should be persons who are themselves emotionally mature enough to guide the affectional as well as the intellectual development of their charges. The typical experience of the youngster falling in love with his scout leader or teacher should be a happy one, guided and understood by the adults involved. It is a further step in the direction of the mature, heterosexual love which unites people in marriage.

Some young people become fearful of social intercourse and avoid the very gatherings that they most crave. Others mask their insecurity by a pretense at sophistication and play the bravado role of the "wolf." They may go in heavily for petting rather than explore the fuller personal meanings of boy-girl relationships. The trauma and the disappointment of many of these blind-alley experiences then affect the ability to love and seem to be related to later marital unhappiness.

Teen-agers who have had a hearty experience in loving and being loved in a happy family circle make these adjustments relatively successfully. There are two reasons for their success: (1) they have parents who are adequate examples of people in love, and (2) they have

[25] Dorothy W. Baruch, "Are Teaching Techniques Meant for Children?" *Journal of Consulting Psychology*, Vol. 8, No. 2, March-April, 1944, p. 111.

had years of practice in learning to respond with affection and consideration to loved ones.

Love beyond oneself

The Greeks had two words for love—*eros* and *agape*. *Eros* tends to center in sexual love. It is that love for another that comes spontaneously and longs to be reciprocated.[26] It is possessive and demanding. Erotic love wants something in return and if frustrated may turn to hate. This is the "hell has no fury like a woman scorned" brand of love —primarily self-love. *Agape*, in contrast, cannot be frustrated because it is not demanding. It is outgoing, overflowing joy in fellowship. Its pleasure is in being and in giving. It releases the freedom of cooperation that people find in thinking, yearning, developing, and achieving together.

There are satisfactions of personal needs in every marriage, often rich and intense. But if there is nothing more to it than satisfying selfish needs, the marriage will not long endure. Love that lasts involves a real and genuine concern for others as persons, for their values as they feel them, for their development and growth. As time goes by, those we love become increasingly dear to us. We watch their progress with joy. We are saddened by their sufferings and disappointed with them in their mistakes. Because we love them, we are able to lose some of our petty selfishness in thoughts and actions directed beyond ourselves. This outgoing type of love has capacities for infinite variety and for satisfying deep hungers within us. This is the love that builds a strong, enduring marriage.

Expression of affection is learned

Families differ widely in the ways in which their members express affection for one another. In some homes loving words and gestures are rare; in others, the children grow up from babyhood surrounded by warm assurances of love. Some married couples hide their love for each other behind a wall of reserve, while others continue to show their affection by all the small, meaningful signals that develop through years of close association. Children growing up in a home where father kisses mother good-by in the morning and returns affectionately to her side in the evening learn that "papa loves mama." Children who have been taught how to express their feelings for others as they grow up, reach marriage with the fundamental skills required for living intimately with another person.

Young adults purposively continue their various learnings to become more adept. You polish your table manners as you get out into society, starting from where your family patterns left off and going on from there. You develop your own tastes and refinements as you gain ex-

---

[26] Esther Adams, "Eros and Agape," *Marriage Guidance*, August, 1950, pp. 6–7.

perience in the varieties of settings that are open to you. So too, you build on your family patterns of expressing affection, your own individual forms and methods and values that express you more fully in smooth, loving ways. Even your ability to gauge the extent and depth of your own feelings is learned through actual experience and developing understanding of yourself and the forces that are involved.

What Are the Differences between Love and Infatuation?

Love feelings may be in the nature of a transient appeal that disappears after a few heavy dates or they may foster a relationship that becomes stronger with the years. It would be folly to decide whether to marry or not solely on the basis of the love sentiment at any given moment. In some instances the very intensity of the feeling may be a danger signal. How can you know then whether any particular love is of the sort upon which a happy marriage can be based? What are the differences between infatuation and love that can serve as a sound basis of decision for future plans?

First of all, recognize that it is not just a question of—"Is it love or infatuation?" There is no clean, clear-cut line between the two emotional experiences. Indeed, in many cases infatuation appears to be an early stage in the development of love. What starts out as infatuation may in time develop into something permanent and deep. What the young teen-ager first experiences may not last in itself, but it quite possibly paves the way for his or her further development of the capacity for lasting love. With this distinction in mind, let us review what is known about the predominant characteristics of infatuation as compared with love.

1. *Infatuation is associated with immaturity, love with relative maturity.*

Many statistical studies and a great deal of clinical evidence indicate that infatuation is far more frequent among children and young adolescents than among more mature individuals. Early in one's heterosexual development there are the feelings of "being in love with love" that may become attached to almost any convenient person. It is as though the first stirrings of maturation within a young adolescent boy or girl found their outward expression in yearnings for close attachments to members of the other sex unlike anything hitherto known to the individual. This is the "puppy love" that has been the subject of so much amusement through the years. After numerous "dress rehearsals" in playing at loving through earlier experiences, the person reaches a level of capacity to love another deeply and fully. It is not only that now he (or she) knows what he wants, but that now he is mature enough emotionally to give and to receive affection, in lasting grown-up ways.

2. *Infatuation is characterized by unsuitability, love by relative appropiateness.*

The indications are that infatuations are common between "impossible" partners. These may be the appeal of the exotic and the different. More often they appear to be deliberate, unconscious efforts to escape from some unsolved problem or some difficult situation. The most common illustration is that of the young teen-ager who is "crazy about" someone whom the parents are sure to vigorously oppose. The parents' disapproval is indeed an important part of the motivation in the attachment. It is as though the youngster were rebelling from parental control and authority by becoming attached to someone they surely would object to as a sweetheart or a mate for him.

There are many cases too, where a young man or girl purposefully, although unconsciously, "falls head over heels in love with" a quite unavailable person, *because* of his or her unattainableness. The young girl falls for her minister, the young fellow is infatuated with an older married woman, members of both sexes moon over quite remote movie and TV stars, just because these persons are inaccessible. It is their very impossibility that makes them safe objects for the young person who dares not get involved with anyone who would expect him or her to do something about it. Later on, when the young person feels more adequate, he develops the courage to make attachments with more attainable persons. Until then, he protects himself by mooning over unsuitable love objects who demand nothing of him.

In contrast, love attachments are usually between persons who are appropriate. Two people who are in love, enough to plan a marriage for instance, want their parents' blessing. They tend to seek suitable, compatible persons both as sweethearts and as mates. They are not using love as an escape but in a wholesome direction of becoming a unity based upon common interests, values, and ways of life.

3. *Infatuation is often mainly sex attraction, while love tends to involve the whole personality.*

"The call of the wild" is dramatic, exciting, and exhilarating. It is a universal experience, instinctual, fundamental, powerful in its impact. Yet by itself alone it does not necessarily unite two human beings over a long period of time. There is some indication that strong sex desires

TABLE 10. *How 500 College Girls Felt When They Were in Love* [27]

Behavior Response	Percentage of Girls Answering Each Response			
	Very Much	Moderately	A Little	Not at All
I had more energy and ambition as a result of being in love	52%	24%	10%	14%
I felt real friendship for him	71	18	8	3
I was more interested in life than I usually am	33	40	16	11
I was sure of myself more than usual and more confident	48	29	15	8

are related to early intense feelings of attraction in girls [28] as well as in boys. However, there is little if any evidence that erotic elements alone make for permanence of a love relationship Love tends to be a many-faceted relationship involving the whole personalities of the two lovers. Such a broad base provides an adequate foundation for permanence as well as richness and fullness of the unity through the years. Love may begin with strong sex appeal, but to develop into a strong relationship sturdy enough to stand it must develop many other facets in a rich repertoire of interaction of the two-in-one.

4. *Infatuation, more often than love, is marked by frustration, guilt, and insecurity.*

Confused and anxious feelings about one's love and one's lover are not infrequent in infatuation because of the predominance of poorly understood sex drives. If the strong sex feelings are repressed, feelings of frustration are evident. If there is direct expression of sex without the components of tenderness, affection, and mutual concern, feelings of guilt and insecurity are almost inevitable.

Love affirms, motivates, and vitalizes. The person who is really in love is vitally alive, and is more creative than before in all areas of his life. This is evident in the college girls' responses in Table 10.

5. *Infatuation, more often than love, is reluctant to face reality, to change, and to grow.*

Infatuated partners tend to idealize each other to the point where it becomes difficult to distinguish between the "dream mate" and the real person. This is the "love is blind" phenomenon. The lover becomes

[27] Albert Ellis, "A Study of the Love Emotions of American College Girls," *The International Journal of Sexology*, August, 1949, p. 2.

[28] Albert Ellis, "Some Significant Correlates of Love and Family Attitudes and Behavior," *The Journal of Social Psychology*, Vol. 30, 1949, pp. 3–16.

so enmeshed in fantasies, dreams, and idealizations that he does not appear as a real person. The infatuation remains "stuck" on a level which offers little change or development to either of the pair or to the relationship itself.

In contrast, partners in love recognize the realities of each other's personality and each encourages the other to become more and more what he is striving to be, so that the identity of each partner is re-affirmed. Realistic love can grow and change to take in the shifting moods in a relationship, and thus new dimensions in the love relationship are possible.

The flux of love—the oscillation between attraction and repulsion—*is a normal part of every marriage.* True love between two people does not mean that one must become completely absorbed in the other. The partial maintenance of one's own identity is a basic requirement of normal existence and it would be a fallacy to interpret it as a sign that love has died.[29]

6. Infatuation can be instantaneous, love takes time to develop.

This is probably the most helpful criterion of all in telling the difference between infatuation and love. One can become infatuated upon very short acquaintance. However, no one can tell whether that first feeling of attraction will develop and grow, or subside and die, least of all the person involved. But if over a period of time, two people become more and more fond of each other, in more and more ways; if the better acquainted they become the more they love each other, then the chances are that their love will last, precisely because it has.

How Can You Know Your Love Will Last?

There is no magic test by which you can measure the depth or the permanence of your love feelings. Yet, if you are going to try to base your marriage upon love you must have some criteria by which to judge whether yours is the kind of love that may be expected to continue to grow in marriage. Here are seven ways to distinguish lasting love from its short-lived substitutes.

LASTING LOVE . . .

has many facets: tender, passionate, comradely, protecting, highly specific in its focus, widely general in its diffusion.

is outgoing: radiating out in its values, concerns, and interests to others' happiness and well-being.

is motivating: releases energy for work, is creative, brings an eagerness to grow, to improve, to work for worthy purposes and ideals.

---

[29] Blanton, *op. cit.*, p. 75.

is sharing: what one has and what one is striving to be; thoughts, feelings, attitudes, ambitions, hopes, interests, all are sharable.

is a we-feeling: thinking and planning are in terms of "we"; what *we* want, how *we* feel, what *we* will do, rather than "I" centeredness.

is realistic: faults, weaknesses, and problems are faced together as part of reality; willingness to work on building the relationship.

changes and grows with time: time is the surest test—if the relationship has grown through many emotional climates, further association, developing interests, and deepening feelings, the chances are that it will continue to grow as long as the persons do.

As you get to know yourself, you learn what to expect of yourself in love as in other situations. As you gain insight into yourself you begin to catch glimpses of why you feel as you do about particular persons, in a variety of circumstances. As you explore your past and present involvements you learn in some measure how to appraise the depth and strength of any particular relationship. You discover something of the feelings you are capable of, you find out what emotional responses you seem to need, you work out ways of relating yourself to a loved one that are mutually fulfilling. When you can love another person deeply enough to lose yourself in the values that are common to both of you, you quite probably have the kind of love that is solid enough to marry on.

Until then, the very process of loving is a learning experience, and it can be a pleasure in itself, if you don't expect too much from it. Of all the many persons you will learn to love in your lifetime, you probably will marry but one. So, this may be a good time to realize that you do not have to make a production out of every love sentiment that hits you. You can learn to enjoy the sweetness of loving and being loved for itself alone. You can take the waxings and wanings of your own feelings, safe in the knowledge that over time you are true to the love that within you lies. You can stand up under the bombardment of romantic stereotypes around you, because deep within yourself you know what love is and how it operates.

READINGS

Blanton, Smiley, *Love or Perish*. New York: Simon and Schuster, 1955.

Blood, Robert O., Jr., *Anticipating Your Marriage*. Glencoe, Illinois: Free Press, 1955, Chapter 4, "Growing in Love."

Bowman, Henry A., "The Diagnosis of Love," Chapter 9, Morris Fishbein and Ruby Jo Reeves Kennedy (eds.), *Modern Marriage and Family Living*. New York: Oxford University Press, 1957.

Burgess, Ernest W., Paul Wallin, and Gladys Denny Shultz, *Courtship, Engagement and Marriage*. Philadelphia: Lippincott, 1954, Chapters 2, 3, 4, 5.

Duvall, Evelyn Millis, *Facts of Life and Love*. New York: Association Press, 1956, Part 3, "Loving and Being Loved."

Duvall, Sylvanus M., *Before You Marry*. New York: Association Press, 1959 revision, Chapter 2, "*How Do You Know It's Love.*"

Folsom, Joseph K., "Steps in Love and Courtship," Chapter 7, Howard Becker and Reuben Hill (eds.), *Family, Marriage and Parenthood*. Boston: Heath, 1948.

Fromm, Erich, *The Art of Loving*. New York: Harper, 1956.

Kirkpatrick, Clifford, *The Family*. New York: Ronald Press, 1955, Chapter 12, "Dating and Love."

Magoun, F. Alexander, *Love and Marriage*. New York: Harper, 1956, Chapter 1.

Montagu, Ashley (ed.), *The Meaning of Love*. New York: Julian Press, 1953.

Waller, Willard, and Reuben Hill, *The Family*. New York: Dryden Press, 1951, Chapter 7, "The Sentiment of Love."

Winch, Robert F., *The Modern Family*. New York: Holt, 1952, Chapter 14, "Romantic Love in American Life."

4 Choosing Your Mate

Who cares whether or not you make a good choice?

Do opposites attract?

What about mixed marriages?

How much choice is there?

How can you find the right person for you?

What factors are involved in whom you marry?

CHOOSING your marriage partner puts to the test everything you have learned about choosing friends and dates over many years. Choosing and being chosen are not new but familiar experiences. The difference in choosing a mate is in the finality of the commitment and the tremendously large number of people who care whether or not you make a good choice.

Many of the same principles of attraction summarized in the opening chapter about friend and date selection hold for mate selection. Almost no American ever found himself engaged to a girl he had not first met and courted. Indeed, in mate selection, as in friend and date selection, you tend (1) to seek those who have values similar to yours, (2) to search for individuals whose needs dovetail with yours, (3) to continue relationships with those "who seem to speak your language," and (4) to perpetuate relations with individuals who rate high in your friends' esteem. These similarities between the two processes make full participation in friendship making and dating useful for later mate selection.

How then do the two differ? Dating tends to be random, play- and recreation-oriented, leading only to further dates. Mate selection is marriage-oriented, and further contacts lead toward increasing involvement, with marriage as the most likely outcome. Friendship making

71

differs from mating in its undifferentiated ignoring of gender and age lines, whereas mate selection is clearly heterosexual and limited to similar age groups. Finally, friend and date selection operate in an ever-widening circle of acquaintances, whereas mating is a narrowing process in which others are progressively excluded.

Who Cares Whether or Not You Make a Good Choice?

Your family, your friends, and a few neighbors will be interested in whom you choose to marry. It may be surprising to learn how many others bring pressures to bear if you propose marrying outside the limits of what is considered suitable. If you mention that you have wondered what it would be like to be married to someone of a different race, nationality, or faith you will see how quickly your associates form a front opposing such a marriage. The idea of inter-class, inter-race, and inter-national marriages is repugnant to many people. These pressures are brought primarily to bear, however, on eliminating ineligibles, deflecting you from unlikely candidates, rather than pinpointing the exact person you should marry.

Ministers, teachers, youth leaders, and others are influential in providing the precepts and the rules of eligibility about who should marry whom, and tend to organize the social affairs where young people meet. People meeting at public dance halls, at bars, or at bowling alleys may undertake their initial contacts relatively anonymously, but a high proportion of young people meet under the more sheltered and supervised auspices of church, school, and social set. It is no accident, therefore, that most marriages occur between two people of the same family background, religion, and class. Those who arrange parties, make introductions, and provide opportunities for social intercourse have been busily at work sorting and eliminating, with the end in view of minimizing hybridization and crossings. Collaborating with these hostesses and unofficial matchmakers are friends of the couples who pull apart and alienate ineligibles while cheering those who seem suitable.[1]

Your family are the most interested in whether you make a good choice. However, time and the ideal of freedom of mate selection have pruned the power of final selection, which was once the prerogative of parents. Except for underage candidates, they have by now even lost the power of veto. To suggest that parents no longer participate ac-

---

[1] That friends withhold their negative opinions of a match, permitting unlikely relationships to form, is also true, see John E. Mayer, "The Self-Restraint of Friends," *Social Forces*, Vol. 35, March, 1957, pp. 230–238.

tively in the process of mate selection would be inaccurate, however. They are as interested as ever, and as you read in Chapter 1, exercise subtle controls on their children during the friend and date selection stages. In mate selection they exercise influence in a variety of ways. Students report that they can always tell how their family feel about the persons they date, even when no outward evaluation is given. The welcome mat would seem to be out for all acceptable comers, but the girls particularly notice that some boys are more warmly greeted and made more a part of the family than others.

If you were to conform to your parents' and friends' wishes you would limit your affairs of the heart entirely to members of your own group. In Chapter 1, which dealt with friend and date selection, in-group choice was labelled "homophily." In mate selection we term it "homogamy" (the tendency to marry a person like oneself). How conforming are American young people in this respect? In Hollingshead's study of New Haven, Connecticut, homogamy is higher in some groupings than in others:

Mismatching versus mismating

> None of these marriages were inter-racial
> 10 per cent were inter-faith
> 42 per cent were inter-class
> 44 per cent were inter-ethnic [2]

New Haven couples rarely crossed group boundaries with respect to race and religious affiliation, although nationality background and class were heeded less often in mate selection. Homogamy results in part from geographical proximity. People who live, work, and worship in the same place are more likely to meet, share the same values, and marry.

Social homogamy is a matter of primary concern to your immediate public, and most young people follow its rules. In an analysis of 88 marriages of college students, the half who first met in their home communities came from more similar backgrounds than the half who met after coming to college. The influence of parents in insuring suitable homogamous matches in the home community is said to explain the differences between the two groups.[3]

At one time, wide discrepancies in age between the bride and groom

---

[2] August B. Hollingshead, "Cultural Factors in Selection of Marriage Mates," *American Sociological Review*, Vol. 15, 1950, pp. 619–627. Hollingshead's estimates of inter-faith marriages are substantially lower than Thomas's country-wide estimates for Catholic-Protestant crossings, see our discussion of inter-faith marriages, page 78.

[3] Gerald R. Leslie and Arthur H. Richardson, "Family Versus Campus Influence in Relation to Mate Selection," *Social Problems*, Vol. III, 1955, pp. 117–121.

were not uncommon, with the groom often a number of years older than the bride. Today the age gap has narrowed to under three years, on the average. In the New Haven study, of the men twenty to twenty-four years old, 70 per cent married girls from the same age bracket, and nearly 100 per cent married girls within five years of their age bracket.[4] In the United States as a whole, from 1947 to 1950, in 65 per cent of all first marriages men married women differing from them in age by no more than four years.[5]

Do Opposites Attract?

According to romantic folklore, the secret of mating is to select someone who will be radically different in make-up. Accordingly, if you are a spendthrift you need a wife who will pinch the pennies, or if you are hyperactive you need a wife who is slow and easygoing. The tales go even further when they say that opposites have a fatal attraction for one another, that brilliant men marry the beautiful but dumb, that brunets seem drawn to blondes. The generalizations from folklore are probably based more on the striking exceptions than on an accurate count of the total marrying public. There have been well over one hundred studies of personal attributes, all of which suggest the falsity of the "opposites attract" theory. Couples who marry tend to be similar in height, age, weight, intelligence, and interests. If opposites do attract each other, it is only a temporary attraction. The tendency is for similars to marry.

On seventeen physical traits there are greater resemblances between mates than dissimilarities.[6] Moreover, physical attractiveness seems to run in pairs.[7] Intellectual ability is shown in a large number of studies to be as similar between husband and wife as between children from the same family.[8] High similarity of attitudes about religion, feminism, and everyday interests are also noted.[9]

In a monumental study of one thousand engaged couples, Burgess and Wallin found also that the similarities between married couples

---

[4] Hollingshead, *op. cit.*, p. 622.

[5] Paul C. Glick, *American Families*, New York: Wiley, 1957, Table 82, p. 125.

[6] Harold E. Jones, "Homogamy in Intellectual Abilities," *American Journal of Sociology*, Vol. 35, 1929, pp. 372–373.

[7] Clifford Kirkpatrick and John Cotton, "Physical Attractiveness, Age, and Marital Adjustment," *American Sociological Review*, Vol. 16, 1951, p. 85.

[8] Helen M. Richardson, "Studies of Mental Resemblances Between Husbands and Wives and Between Friends," *Psychological Bulletin*, Vol. 36, 1939, pp. 105–107.

[9] Clifford Kirkpatrick, *The Family As Process and Institution*, New York: Ronald Press, 1955, p. 303.

TABLE 11. *Social Characteristics Showing Greatest Similarity Among Engaged Couples* [10]

Courtship Characteristics	Age at beginning of courtship
	Number of going-steady experiences
	Number of persons consulted about engagement
Conceptions of Marriage Held	Attitude toward married women working
	Attitude toward having children
	Number of children desired
	Attitude toward divorce
Family Attachments	Happiness of parents' marriage
	Attachment to father
	Attachment to siblings
Religious Behavior	Religious affiliation
	Church attendance
	Active membership
Social Habits and Participation	Drinking habits
	Smoking habits
	Leisure time preferences
	Extent of participation in organizations

had not developed subsequent to their marriages but were present at the time of engagement.[11] This team found much more homogamy in social characteristics, such as religious affiliation and behavior, social backgrounds, courtship behavior, conceptions of marriage, social participation, and family relationships than they did with regard to temperament and personality makeup. Table 11 lists the social characteristics found most frequently to be similar among the thousand couples.

Of forty-two personality traits appraised by Burgess and Wallin, fourteen showed greater and none showed smaller than chance similarities between couples. There is a tendency for persons with neurotic symptoms to become engaged to neurotics and for non-neurotics to prefer non-neurotics. Persons who characterize themselves as possessing "easily hurt feelings" or as "being touchy on various subjects" are more likely to become engaged to individuals possessing the same disabilities.[12]

Why do so many conform to the homogamous pattern? Social pressure from friends and parents helps to limit marriages to one's race, class, and faith, but hardly explains the tendencies for similar physical, intellectual, and interest types to pair off. Two explanations, neither entirely satisfactory, are offered. One is that much of the attraction we

---

[10] Drawn from E. W. Burgess and Paul Wallin, *Engagement and Marriage*, Chicago: Lippincott, 1953, Table 14, p. 206.

[11] Burgess and Wallin, *op. cit.*, pp. 204–211.

[12] Burgess and Wallin, *op. cit.*, p. 209.

have for others is really self-love, which tends to direct us toward persons who are similar in personality make-up to ourselves.

A more defensible explanation is that we attempt, through mating, to perpetuate the satisfactions of our parental family relationships, and to select a marriage partner who resembles a favorite parent, brother, or sister. For example, a girl who likes her brother and resembles him because of common heredity and association tends to marry a man who resembles her brother and likewise herself. Kirkpatrick points out that this explanation assumes that there is more satisfaction than dissatisfaction with family members. If the reverse were true, one would expect a tendency to heterogamy in mating.[13]

Winch makes a strong argument for keeping the issue of homogamy and heterogamy open for further investigation. He sees social homogamy operating to establish a field of eligible persons from whom marriage partners can be selected freely. But within the field of eligibles, he hypothesizes that individuals tend to choose those whose need patterns generally *complement* their own rather than those whose need patterns are similar to their own.[14]

In an intensive study of twenty-five recently married college-age, middle-class couples, Winch confirmed his theory that mates tend to select each other on the basis of complementary needs.[15] Bowerman and Day, attempting to duplicate Winch's findings, but using a different classification of needs, found scanty support for the Winch hypothesis, asserting ". . . the relationships might be complementary in some instances and homogamous in others, and would probably be in terms of patterns of personality characteristics rather than single variables." [16]

Winch has opened up the issues of personal preferences and motivation in mate selection. It is unfortunate that answers remain elusively difficult to these questions. In time it is hoped the necessary research will be completed to indicate the dynamics which are at work. The best we can do at the moment is to counsel self-study. What do you know about your own needs and how they may function in choosing a mate?

---

[13] Kirkpatrick, *op. cit.*, p. 304.

[14] Robert F. Winch, *Mate Selection: A Study of Complementary Needs*, New York: Harper, 1957, pp. 3–28.

[15] Robert F. Winch and Thomas and Virginia Ktsanes, "The Theory of Complementary Needs in Mate Selection: An Analytic and Descriptive Study," *American Sociological Review*, Vol. 19, June, 1954, pp. 241–249; see also Winch, *Mate Selection*.

[16] Charles Bowerman and Barbara Day, "Test of the Theory of Complementary Needs," *American Sociological Review*, Vol. 21, October, 1956, pp. 602–605.

What about Mixed Marriages?

Despite the prevailing pattern of homogamy in mate selection, dissimilars do meet and marry. Their unions are known as *mixed marriages* when the parties have crossed the boundaries of race, faith, nationality, or class. However, Blood points out that a number of these unions prove upon inspection to be *pseudo-mixed marriages* with more in common than many couples who marry within their own group. He identifies two types of pseudo-mixed marriages, (1) those where group membership is only nominal—the parents are practicing members but the child no longer accepts the doctrines, and (2) those where one of the two has not simply drifted from his parents' group but has actively joined another, such as in the case of the social climber or the religious convert.[17]

A genuine mixed marriage exists when each partner retains his identification with his separate group, when each holds different beliefs and values, and follows a different way of life. The following extract in which the daughter of a socially prominent family is attracted to a young lawyer of another religious faith illustrates how parents sometimes react to differences in religious and social background.

"Why?" he repeated, looking at her. "All right, I'll tell you why. I don't want my daughter to go through life neither flesh, fowl nor good red herring, living in a kind of no man's land where half the people you know will never accept him, and half the people he knows will never accept you. I don't want a son-in-law who'll be an embarrassment to my friends, a son-in-law who can't be up at my club and who can't go with us to places where we've gone all our lives. I don't want a son-in-law whom I'll have to apologize for and explain and have to hear insulted indirectly, unless I can remember to warn people off first."

"We want you to marry someone—someone like us. Someone who'll fit in and whom we can"—Margaret Drake caught her breath, then managed to say —"can all be proud of," and suddenly shoving back her chair, she got up and left the room.[18]

Most authorities in the field of marriage, including Catholic, Protestant, and Jewish leaders, are agreed that inter-faith marriage is risky, if not undesirable. But young people themselves increasingly disregard these warnings. A recent study by John L. Thomas, an outstanding

Inter-faith marriages

---

[17] Robert O. Blood, Jr., *Anticipating Your Marriage,* Glencoe, Illinois: Free Press, 1956, pp. 38–39.

[18] From Gwethalyn Graham Erickson Brown, *Earth and High Heaven,* Philadelphia: Lippincott, 1944, by permission.

Catholic sociologist, has discovered a marked increase, since 1910, of mixed Catholic marriages in 132 parishes through eastern sections of the United States. Roughly 30 per cent of all marriages sanctioned by the Roman Catholic Church in 1950 were inter-faith.[19] In another analysis of marriages in Iowa, it was found that 42 per cent of all marriages involving a Catholic in 1953 were mixed. Mixed marriages were twice as common in a second marriage as in a first marriage.[20] If these figures are generally applicable, nearly half of all Catholics who marry in this country take non-Catholic mates.

Thomas suggests that the inter-faith marriage rate of Catholics is related to the availability of marriage partners within the Catholic group. Intermarriages are high in the Southeast, where Catholics make up only 2 per cent of the population, and low in areas where Catholics are in the majority. Where the Catholic group is bound by distinctive ethnic ties, the intermarriage rate is low. This is also the case within the small Jewish minority (5 per cent) in this country.[21]

The intermarriage rate goes up also as one moves from the low income groups in the center of the large city to the high income urban suburbs. The chances of intermarriage therefore appear to increase with (1) exposure to eligible mates of other groups, (2) low ethnocentrism (identification with one's ethnic group), and (3) improved economic and educational conditions. These trends suggest more rather than less intermarriage in the future.

The objections that the three major religious faiths have had historically [22] toward inter-faith marriages are based upon the traditional positions of Catholic, Protestant, and Jewish groups.

Catholic. Catholics regard their religion as the only true faith, the only form of Christianity which is both complete and without error. If a Catholic marries a non-Catholic, he is not supposed to permit the

---

[19] John L. Thomas, "The Factor of Religion in the Selection of Marriage Mates," *American Sociological Review*, Vol. 16, No. 4, August, 1951, pp. 487–491. Bossard and Letts found a comparable increase in mixed marriages for Lutherans in a countrywide study. They increased from 46 per cent mixed marriages 1936–40 to 58 per cent mixed 1946–50. See James H. S. Bossard and Harold C. Letts, "Mixed Marriages Involving Lutherans—A Research Report," *Marriage and Family Living*, Vol. 18, November, 1956, pp. 308–310.

[20] Loren E. Chancellor and Thomas P. Monahan, "Religious Preference and Interreligious Mixtures in Marriages and Divorces in Iowa," *American Journal of Sociology*, Vol. LXI, No. 3, November, 1955, pp. 233–239.

[21] Milton L. Barron, *People Who Intermarry*, Syracuse: Syracuse University Press, 1946, and "Research on Intermarriage: A Survey of Accomplishments and Prospects," *American Journal of Sociology*, Vol. LVII, November, 1951, pp. 249–255.

[22] *Ibid.*, pp. 22–47.

ceremony to be performed by someone other than a Catholic priest. If he does, he is automatically dropped from the Church and lost to the "true faith." If the non-Catholic signs the following agreement to bring up the children in the Catholic faith, the priest will perform the ceremony. Even then, there is a fear that the non-Catholic may fail to live up to his agreement, or, by the very fact of not being himself a Catholic, he may weaken the faith of his children.

ANTE-NUPTIAL AGREEMENT

To Be Signed by Applicants for Dispensation from Impediment of Mixed Religion or Disparity of Cult.

Non-Catholic Party

I, the undersigned _____ of _____, not a member of the Catholic Church, desiring to contract marriage with _____ of _____, who is a member of the Catholic Church, propose to do so with the understanding that the marriage bond thus contracted can be broken only by death.

And thereupon in consideration of such marriage, I, the said _____ do hereby covenant, promise, and agree to and with the said _____ that he (she), the said _____ shall be permitted the free exercise of religion according to the Catholic faith without hindrance or adverse comment and that all the children of either sex born of such marriage, shall be baptized and educated only in the faith and according to the teachings of the Roman Catholic Church, even if the said _____ shall die first.

I hereby promise that no other marriage ceremony than that by the Catholic priest shall take place.

I furthermore realize the holiness of the use of marriage according to the teaching of the Catholic Church which condemns birth control and similar abuses of marriage. I shall have due respect for the religious principles and convictions of my Catholic partner.

Witness my hand this _____ day of _____ 19 _____ at _____ in the County of _____, and State of _____

Signed in the presence of

Rev. _____   _____

Signature of Non-Catholic

Catholic Party

I, the undersigned _____ a member of the Catholic Church of _____ Parish, _____, wish to contract marriage with _____, a non-Catholic, hereby solemnly promise to have all the children of either sex, born of this marriage, baptized and reared only in the Catholic faith.

Furthermore, I promise that no other marriage ceremony than that by the Catholic priest shall take place.

I also realize my obligation in conscience to practice my religion faithfully and prudently to endeavor by prayer, good example and the reception of the Sacraments, to induce my life partner to investigate seriously the teachings of the Catholic Church in the hope that such investigation may lead to conversion.

Witness my hand this _____ day of _____ 19 _____ at _____ in the County of _____, and State of _____

Signed in the presence of

Rev. _____   _____

Signature of Catholic

Protestant. Many Protestants think the Catholic religion is in serious theological error, and that those of "sound faith" ought not to run the risk of being led astray by it and should not expose their children to its "false teachings." Ideological objections are common. Many Protestants feel that Catholics are under the domination of an ecclesiastical dictatorship. Unless the Catholic is willing to give up his church, the non-Catholic must agree to bring up his children in a religion which he regards as a relentless foe of his democratic ideals. He feels that a parent has no right to sign away in such an arbitrary fashion the rights of his children to grow up as free men and women.

Jewish. Since orthodox Judaism regards the preservation of Jewish tradition and practices of utmost importance, intermarriage threatens the purity and strength of the Jewish faith. In the Bible, Nehemiah cursed, struck, and pulled the hair of Jews married to foreign women. Ezra led a movement to require all Jewish people to divorce foreigners to whom they were married. However, today many liberal Jews feel quite differently, viewing inter-faith marriages with greater tolerance, and generally do not disinherit their children who marry outside the fold.

All faiths fear, what is fairly well proved, that people of mixed marriages will be less loyal to any faith, as seen in their attendance at church services, than those in which both are members of the same faith.[23]

Most people who marry are not too concerned about the effects of their marriage upon their church. They want to know, "What will union with a member of another faith do to my marriage?" From the first contact the inter-faith combination is more vulnerable to breakup. Fewer inter-faith steadies survive to become engaged, and the breaking of inter-faith engagements is high. Burgess and Wallin found that 41 per cent of their inter-faith couples broke their engagements compared with 27 per cent of the couples belonging to the same church.[24] Inter-faith marriages are equally vulnerable. In a study of marriages in Iowa it was found that inter-faith couples are not only more likely to divorce, but they divorce three years earlier than couples of the same faith.[25] Clearly there is a selective process going on which weeds out all but the hardiest inter-faith marriages by the fifth year of marriage. If we define success in marriage as invulnerability to divorce, the inter-faith marriage is more hazardous than the homogamous marriage. However, if we define success in marriage as happiness or adjustment in marriage and wait to take our measures of success until after a few years have elapsed, inter-faith marriages stand up very well.

Religious difference and marriage failure

In the Iowa study, marriages in which both members of the couple were Catholic had half the divorces of the marriages in which one member was Catholic and one Protestant.[26] Landis' study of 4108 couples in Michigan provides even more striking findings (see Fig. 6), indicating that there is a difference within Catholic-Protestant combinations in their vulnerability to divorce. The Protestant father–Catholic mother has a low rate of 7 per cent divorced, one third the rate of 21 per cent of the Catholic father–Protestant mother. Since the children usually follow the faith of the mother, the first combination succeeds much more frequently than the second. It is also true that the Catholic mother can take the consequences of failing to use birth control methods with fewer frustrations, and she is less likely to regard divorce as a solution to her marital problems.

Since inter-faith marriages are more likely to end in divorce, it is natural to expect that they would also be handicapped in marital ad-

---

[23] See the results of a study conducted by Murray M. Leiffer, "Inter-faith Marriages in U.S.A.," *Lumen Vitae*, Vol. 4, July, 1949, pp. 442–454.

[24] Burgess and Wallin, *op. cit.*, p. 289.

[25] Thomas P. Monahan and Loren E. Chancellor, "Statistical Aspects of Marriage and Divorce by Religious Denomination in Iowa," *Eugenics Quarterly*, Vol. 26, September, 1955, p. 170.

[26] Chancellor and Monahan, "Religious Preference and Interreligious Mixtures," *op. cit.*, p. 238.

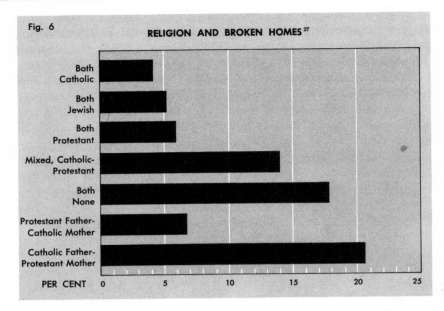

Fig. 6

RELIGION AND BROKEN HOMES[27]

justment. However, Dyer and Luckey, in a follow-up study of several hundred couples who attended the University of Minnesota, find that inter-faith combinations of Lutherans, Catholics, Protestants, and Jews are likely to be as happy as when man and wife are of the same faith.[28] Moreover, similarity of religious affiliation is not listed in any of the marital happiness studies as an important predictive factor in marital adjustment.[29]

Although still in the minority inter-faith marriages are on the increase. While they are initially more vulnerable to divorce those which survive are not as handicapped in achieving happy marriages as has been popularly supposed. Mixed marriages can succeed; the great majority do. If yours is a mixed marriage, you may have to work harder to make it succeed, but it is by no means doomed to failure. Church affili-

---

[27] Percentage of Marriages of Mixed and Nonmixed Religious Faiths Ending in Divorce or Separation, 4,108 Couples in Michigan, "Marriages of Mixed and Nonmixed Religious Faith" by Judson T. Landis, *American Sociological Review* (June, 1949), Table 1, p. 403.

[28] Dorothy T. Dyer and Eleanor Luckey, "Religious Affiliation and Selected Personality Scores as They Relate to Marital Happiness of a Minnesota College Sample," unpublished manuscript.

[29] Lewis M. Terman, *Psychological Factors in Marital Happiness*, New York, McGraw-Hill, 1938; E. W. Burgess and Leonard S. Cottrell, *Predicting Success or Failure in Marriage*, New York: Prentice-Hall, 1939; and Burgess and Wallin, *op. cit.*

ation is but one of a number of factors which can make for failure or success. Far more important are such qualities as character, mental health, and the attitude which the husband and wife take toward their differences, religious or otherwise.

The major problem of inter-faith marriage will probably emerge when children arrive; then the church may step in, not only in the person of the priest or minister but also in the form of devoted family members. Usually the children follow the religion of the mother,[30] regardless of signed agreements or other factors, unless the father is especially strong in his convictions.

If you are planning an inter-faith marriage here are some questions you should consider.

1. *How intense is the loyalty of each to his own religious group?* Mary was a Catholic and Jim was a Methodist, but neither of them cared anything about church nor had attended for some time. They were married by a justice of the peace, and after their marriage both continued to stay away from church, just as they had before. Their families made no attempt to interfere. In consequence, their differences caused almost no problem.

On the other hand, Bill and Sally, who belonged to two different and extremely narrow sects, each regarded the teachings of his or her church as the only true religious faith, and felt that the other lived in darkness and sin. They had agreed beforehand that each was to go his separate way, but after marriage neither could bear to see the loved one going to hell. Therefore, each made ardent efforts to convert the other, in which their families heartily joined. Bill and Sally never divorced or separated, but the constant tension which developed between them embittered the whole relationship and had an especially unfortunate effect upon their children.

2. *How many complicating factors are there, such as relatives or influential friends?* The church is not merely a religious body; specifically it is Mother, Father, and Uncle Bill. If they object to the faith of the married partner, it is natural that they should bring considerable pressure on behalf of their church, especially as the children are born. Many parents give up their children with considerable reluctance and sometimes welcome any chance to keep a hold on the life of the young adult. Zealous friends and members of the clergy are often eager to push the claims of their church. Sometimes these pressures bring serious discord into the marriage.

---

[30] Landis finds this to be true for 65 per cent of the boys and 75 per cent of the girls in his Michigan study of 4108 couples; see Landis, *op. cit.*, p. 405.

3. *What aspects of religion does each feel most strongly about?* Some Christians regard dancing or attending movies on the Sabbath as a sin, whereas others openly encourage such activities. Among Jewish groups the conflict between those who observe kosher and other orthodox regulations and those who disregard them may prove to be painful. If the person to whom you are married freely indulges in activities which you have been brought up to regard as immoral, it is inevitably a strain on the whole relationship. Differences in theology, indicated by such terms as "modernism" and "fundamentalism," may also cause difficulties.

Husband and wife sometimes disagree over how actively they want to support their church. Fred believed strongly in the church and was an ardent worker in its activities. Before his marriage he had been president of his church youth group, later he became superintendent of the Sunday school. His wife, Ellen, belonged to the same church but was decidedly lukewarm in her interests. Sunday mornings she wanted to sleep or take a trip into the country. If Fred insisted that she get up and go to church with him, she resented it. On the few occasions she persuaded him to skip church and visit relatives he felt guilty and disloyal. As time went on, both found other persons more sympathetic to their own interests, and questioned the desirability of their marriage.

4. *Is there danger that religious differences will be used as a means by which one can dominate the other?* Sally and Bill both honestly believed that their desires to convert each other were inspired solely by religious motives. A psychiatrist would have thought differently. He would have seen in their efforts subconscious attempts to dominate, with their religious ardor used as a smoke screen behind which to conceal their desire to control. So it often is, as we have suggested, with interfering family members.

5. *Are there other strong bonds to compensate for the religious difference?* Doris was a highly educated Catholic with a liberal viewpoint. Jacob was a reformed Jew. Both, however, regarded their own religious groups primarily as social institutions designed to perform social functions. Both were vitally interested in good housing, the improvement of government, and social welfare. The children, when they came, were given a social interpretation of the religious groups, and as they grew up were encouraged to choose their own affiliations. This breadth of attitude made possible not only a harmonious but an enriched relationship which brought them close together. Their marriage was successful because both believed in the same thing—the religion of humanity. When the fundamental values of each are similar, the religious label is of less importance.

Young people can hardly be expected to be more rational in religion than they are in other matters related to marriage. Those who are determined to cross faith lines, however, can increase the likelihood of success by frankly facing the situation and coming to some agreements before the marriage. These should involve specific and definite decisions on such questions as the following:

1. Who, if either, will change his church affiliation? If this is done at all it should be done before the wedding.
2. If each retains his separate faith, where will they attend church, if at all?
3. In what faith, if any, will the children be brought up?
4. Are parents and relatives to be consulted? This is one of the most crucial and difficult problems, since parental approval is significantly related to later success of the marriage. Will you keep your parents informed as you go along, or just keep quiet about the whole matter, marry, and let them howl about an accomplished fact? The latter policy has in some instances proved to be the less difficult. It also has its risks.

All marriages are mixed in some degree. You marry outside your parental family group. You marry a member of the opposite sex. The differences found not only in inter-faith, but also in international and inter-class crossings, are important to consider in marriage because they are indicators of different ways of life in our society which are burdensome to reconcile within a marriage.

For many years marriages between people of the same race and ethnic backgrounds in Hawaii have had higher divorce rates than mixed marriages between Americans, Japanese, and Europeans.[31] Moreover, a study of marriages in Hawaii, involving 324 war brides and husbands of European and Japanese ancestry, showed better marital adjustment among the international combinations (70 per cent good adjustment, wife European—husband Japanese; 75 per cent good adjustment, wife Japanese—husband non-Japanese; compared with 51 per cent good adjustment, both non-Japanese; and 39 per cent good adjustment, both Japanese). Similarly, the in-law relationship was poorer where the wives and husbands shared the same cultural background than where they were of mixed backgrounds (72 per cent good adjustment with in-laws for Japanese wives of non-Japanese husbands, 60 per cent for European wives of Japanese husbands, compared with only 48 per cent of Japanese brides married to Japanese husbands). Evidently sharing the cultural background tends to restrict personal relations to the prescribed forms and to hamper spontaneous interaction

International marriages

---

[31] Romanzo Adams, *Interracial Marriage in Hawaii*, New York: Macmillan, 1937, p. 224.

while, where cultural backgrounds differ, behavior is determined by the necessity to adjust one's self to another on the basis of the situation at hand.[32]

Strauss, in a study in Chicago, also found more harmony than strain in the international marriages which braved the disapproval of the anti-intermarriage policy of the military in Japan. He cautions, "This is not to go overboard and claim that homogamy between husband and wife is of no importance in marital selection or in the involvement of domestic fates. However, the easy assumptions that interracial marriages are doomed to destruction or that the couples must have something extra-special to make a go of the marriage are much over-simplified notions." [33] Strauss suggests there is need for re-evaluation of this variety of mixed marriage to take into account the special conditions of contact, selection, and living conditions which make mixed marriages more fragile and vulnerable to trouble. In the specific marriages he investigated the couples were more harmonious than conflicted.

Perhaps it is safe to say that where racial and national boundaries are crossed, couples need to be assured of sufficient flexibility and compatibility and enough interests in common so that they can overcome the differences between them and withstand the social disapproval of their marriage.

Successful intermarriages of any kind seem possible where the essentials for a happy interpersonal adjustment are present: (1) similar attitudes about work, play, children, and the meaning of life, (2) reasonably good personal and couple adaptability, and (3) temperamental compatibility. These essentials are by no means assured in non-mixed marriages and are probably more important in choosing a marriage partner than the group affiliations we have been discussing.

How Much Choice Is There?

Under our system of mate selection, the ultimate choice of whom to marry, when to marry, and how to marry is yours. Your "public" has tried to assure you a good match by setting limits on those suitable for one of your station, but this still leaves you with many more thousands of eligibles than you can consider seriously. It is humanly impossible to make very many firsthand contacts. Chance factors largely operate to narrow the list down to more manageable proportions.

---

[32] Yukiko Kimura, "War Brides in Hawaii and Their In-Laws," *The American Journal of Sociology,* Vol. 63, July, 1957, pp. 70–79.

[33] Anselm Strauss, "Strain and Harmony in American-Japanese War Bride Marriages," *Marriage and Family Living,* Vol. 16, May, 1954, pp. 99–106.

Blood states it well when he reminds us that "In actual practice, more couples are thrown together by sheer accident than by either the magic of romance or the strategy of intelligence. . . . The typical young adult drifts through life assuming that sooner or later he will get married. He dates—whoever attracts his fancy or is conveniently available. Chance factors determine pretty largely whom he dates. And, as expected, sooner or later he does get married to someone." [34] How much the individual can guide his own destiny by rational thought and improve on his marriage by deliberate choice is still a subject for research and evaluation.

Let us assume that you wish to make as deliberate and rational a choice as possible. Here are some basic conditions which are necessary:

1. You must have a sufficient number of acquaintances to insure a range of individuals from which a choice can be made.
2. You must achieve sufficient depth with your acquaintances to enable you to appraise their marriageability and mutual compatibility so far as personality and values go.
3. You must be able to involve others and be willing to make commitments yourself if you are to reach the stage of making a firm choice.

In actual practice few of these conditions are met by the majority of young people, hence they tend to marry without the data necessary to make a wise choice. Fortunately, chance factors work to bring compatible as well as incompatible combinations together, and parents, friends, and engagements enlighten still other unsuitable mates before they marry. Let us look more closely at the process of narrowing the field as it appears to University of North Carolina seniors.

These seniors were asked to compute their number of dates per week in high school and in college, to get a picture of the *volume of acquaintances* which they had made during those eight years. The number of dates totalled several hundred per student. However, when the students attempted to record the number of *different persons* represented by the hundreds of dates they had had, the range of acquaintance varied from a low of one person to a high of one hundred different persons, with the average student dating fewer than twenty different persons over an eight-year period. Is this a wide enough range to assure a good marriage choice?

A more crucial question to test the conditions for wise mate choice involves the depth of acquaintance achieved with one's dates. The North Carolina seniors were asked how many persons in high school

---

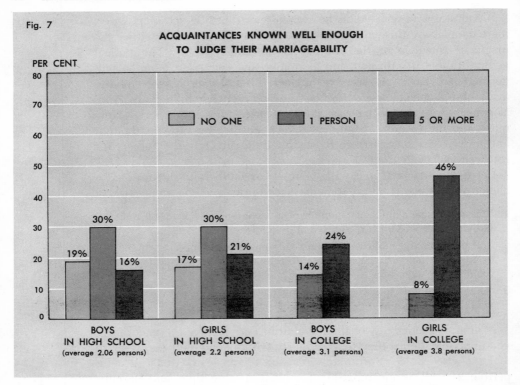

Fig. 7

ACQUAINTANCES KNOWN WELL ENOUGH
TO JUDGE THEIR MARRIAGEABILITY

and how many persons in college they became well enough acquainted with to judge their marriageability (see Fig. 7).

The volume of dating by these one hundred seniors was high enough to assure wide contact. And since it was with relatively few persons, roughly twenty per student, it should have permitted depth of acquaintance; yet the results are quite modest. Girls claim better acquaintance, leading boys both in high school and especially in college. Are they better listeners, or more interested in increasing the depth of acquaintance? See Fig. 8 for the number of persons these seniors had seriously considered marrying.

How much choosing is there here? The average graduating senior reports depth of acquaintance sufficient to judge marriageability with only two persons in high school and three in college. Since these five acquaintances were cultivated over an eight year period in a series rather than simultaneously, they were not available at any one time to choose from. Is the choosing occurring in dating before couples know one another well enough to judge their marriageability? Are highly marriageable boys eliminated because they dance poorly or appear more interested in studies than in dating? Are highly marriageable girls eliminated because they do not fit the stereotype of the popular girl who knows how to maintain a conversation harmlessly at the chitchat level for dating, or do not wear clothes to the best advantage? It would appear that the much-valued pattern of dating does not facilitate depth of acquaintance even though it does bring about increasing involvement and commitment.

The intelligent person needs to ask himself how he can increase the number of his acquaintances and how he can know them well enough to make an intelligent choice for marriage. He does not really choose among several girls but chooses rather whether to continue with one relationship or to break it and negotiate another. Girls are even more handicapped in the range of effective choices they can make, since the freedom to take the initiative in negotiation is conventionally not theirs to exercise.

The problem of mate choice is one of *judgment* about the potential success or failure of one's contemporary combinations against other possible combinations the future might bring. This is quite different

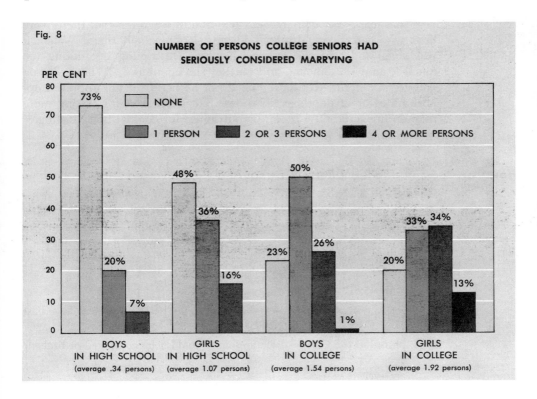

Fig. 8

NUMBER OF PERSONS COLLEGE SENIORS HAD
SERIOUSLY CONSIDERED MARRYING

from the classic problem of mate choice which is seen as choosing among several suitors the one who "suits" you best. Moreover, this new statement of the problem fits the realities better. The man in search of a wife is not like a purchaser looking for a car. Cars are everywhere in endless supply, each equally indifferent to being chosen. Marriageable women of the right age and background, by contrast, are in short supply and vary greatly in their interest in being chosen by just any man. They require courting and loving attention and react violently to any suggestion that they are the object of comparison with other dates. The task of choosing is further complicated by the need to so conduct yourself that there is reciprocity—the object of your choice must also want to choose you!

Critics of campus dating assert that the conventions about dating conversations restrict the subject matter and circumscribe the discussions on party dates so severely that couples learn relatively little about each other. At the conversation level, little is asked of the date and little is given in return. Conversation is kept strictly within the bounds of safe neutral topics not calculated to reveal intellectuality or spirituality. As one coed remarked, "Last night I had the first date in over a year that made me really think. I had almost forgotten that there were boys who cared enough about ideas to argue about them." When it was suggested that she might have been restricting her dating too much to movies, dancing, and parties, she countered, "Where else do you go on a date?" Yet dating need not be bereft of self-appraisal opportunities or of depth explorations. It can be used for testing more than dating suitability. It can be put to use for compatibility testing. [35]

How Can You Find the Right Person for You?

How will you ever make a good marriage choice? You have been for some time choosing dates and evaluating them as possible marriage partners, perhaps not systematically or calculatedly. In order to use good judgment in making a marriage choice three questions may be considered:

1. Self-Appraisal: For what range of persons would I be good?

2. Other-Appraisal: What types of persons in my past and present have best met my needs?

3. Appraisal of the Current Relationship: Should it be continued or broken?

---

[35] See Chapter 1.

One aspect of self-appraisal asks what kinds of persons you can best get along with. As you look back over your relationships with others, what kinds of persons have you been able to serve best? Are you equally good for confident and for fearful persons? Did you ever ask yourself how different the list of possible mates for you would be if you phrased the question: "What range of persons would I be good for?" rather than the familiar query: "Who would be best for me?"

A second phase of self-appraisal asks what kind of a person you are yourself and what your needs are. For example, what are my basic and peculiar needs in courtship and marriage with which someone is going to have to cope? What are my pet hates and irritations that will have to be taken into account? What services will I be asking for from a partner? Someone to make decisions for me? give me self-confidence? offer me challenge? new experience? give me direction and purpose? baby me when sick? love me and listen to my stories? What do I miss when I am alone that I would expect my life partner to be able to give me? What do I now receive from my parents and siblings which my mate will need to give to keep me happy? Looking at the persons to whom I have been attracted in the past, what do they have in common that might suggest needs for which I am seeking gratification?

In mate selection the eye is often on the other person. How adequate is he in meeting my requirements? Does he leave me feeling elated? satisfied? contented? Judgment is needed in other-appraisal, however, on questions beyond the stimulus of pleasant feelings. What persons tend to round me out into a finer, more effective person, stimulate me to greater achievements, give purpose and meaning to my life? Foote has suggested the close parallel of the relationship of well-mated lovers to that of the artist and his critic who sees what the artist is capable of and urges him to realize it.[36] In appraising these others in your life, how capable are they of acting as great critics? What do you know about their potentials and your competence in activating these potentials?

The choice of a marital partner is registered in the decision to con- tinue one love relationship and discontinue all others. Soul-searching self-appraisal is important, objective other-appraisal is necessary, but the test of compatibility is found in the interpersonal relationship itself. Is it a good relationship for both parties and does it promise to be mutually rewarding in the future? The marriage decision reflects the compatibility achieved in the premarital period. Here are some questions which if answered affirmatively would argue that the relationship itself is basically sound:

[36] Nelson, Foote, "Love," *Psychiatry*, Vol. 16, August, 1953, pp. 245–251.

1. Is the relationship stimulating and growth-promoting?
2. Is it tolerant of differences, utilizing them effectively in increasing the range of mutual understanding?
3. Is the relationship building a repertory of problem-solving techniques and procedures for using them?
4. Is the relationship comforting, satisfying, and communicating?
5. Is it deepening and extending in the scope it covers?
6. Is the relationship secure and predictable for each rather than a source of mixed feelings and doubts?

If you are interested in making the best possible marriage choice, you will utilize the counsel and wisdom of parents, ministers, other professional counselors, and, of course, your friends. Parents' blessing and friends' approval has been shown to be predictive of later success in marriage, suggesting that they can possibly see evidences of incompatibility as well as unsuitability somewhat more objectively than do the participants themselves. It is actually a bad sign if both parents and friends oppose the relationship. They may be more likely to be right than the couple in the long run.

A certain amount of help in self-appraisal can be obtained from personality tests interpreted by a competent counselor. Marriage counselors, physicians, and ministers often provide premarital conferences that are a good help in deciding whether this is a relationship which will thrive or wither in marriage (see Chapter 6 for further details).

One of the greatest helps others can provide is a sounding board for your own doubts, misgivings, and enthusiasms, enabling you to ask questions which might otherwise not be voiced in the decision of whom to marry, and when.

What Factors Are Involved in Whom You Marry?

The process of mate seeking and choice is not done alone but in concert with many participants—parents, brothers and sisters, friends, neighbors, teachers, and ministers. While these participants are especially concerned about suitability and eligibility of couples they do not pinpoint who should marry whom within the list of eligibles.

Most young people are socially homogamous, observing the rules of eligibility and concentrating their dating and mating contacts within their own race, church, nationality, and class affiliations. Moreover, most young people also practice personal homogamy, choosing for mates persons with physical, personal, and social characteristics similar to theirs. The only exception to this phenomenon of "like choosing like" is with respect to temperamental characteristics, where the theory of complementary needs is advanced to explain the "opposites attract" theory.

It is clear that Americans have great freedom of mate choice despite active participation by elders in setting the limits within which choosing occurs. Through the dating system, wide acquaintance is theoretically possible. Actual practice shows the range of acquaintance is quite modest. The depth of acquaintance is so shallow that the effective range of suitors known well is exceedingly small—between two and three persons in four years of college dating. Young people enter upon commitments to marry, therefore, with too few persons from among whom to make a rational deliberate choice. Contemporary dating and courtship practices fail to provide range, depth, and self-appraisal opportunities required to make the best marriage choice. More accent is placed on suitability than on compatibility testing.

Increasing the range of choice and depth of acquaintance involves attending functions and participating in activities which cut across class, religious, and ethnic lines. It involves a more imaginative use of dating beyond the "party type" date to include a wider range of situations where new aspects of the self can be expressed naturally: church discussions, forums, student politics, ski trips, crusades, and so on. It involves getting to know the parents, brothers and sisters, and friends of the dating partner. It includes becoming interested in dates as persons, becoming an interested inquirer, and reciprocating by making one's own life open to discussion.

Finally, the procedures for choice making, assuming adequate range and depth of acquaintance, require (1) candid self-appraisal to ascertain one's needs and gratification possibilities, (2) generous other-appraisal to discover the marriageability and potentials of one's suitors, and (3) appraisal of the contemporary relationship to determine whether it should be continued or broken. The competence required to fulfill these procedures is clearly a combination of self-understanding, other-centeredness, and judgment which can be improved by consultation with professionals concerned with the improvement of compatibility in marriage.

READINGS

Barron, Milton L., *People Who Intermarry*. Syracuse: Syracuse University Press, 1946.

Becker, Howard, and Reuben Hill, *Family, Marriage and Parenthood*. Boston: Heath, 1955, Chapter VIII, "How Mates are Sorted."

Blood, Robert O., Jr., *Anticipating Your Marriage*. Glencoe, Illinois: Free Press, 1955, Chapters 2–3, "Narrowing the Field " and " Finding the Right Person."

Bossard, James H. S., and Eleanor S. Boll, *One Marriage, Two Faiths*. New York: Ronald Press, 1957.

Bowman, Henry A., *Marriage for Moderns*. New York: McGraw-Hill, 1954, Chapter VIII, "Choosing a Marriage Partner—Mixed Marriages."

Cavan, Ruth Shonle, *The American Family*. New York: Crowell, 1953, Chapter X, "Cross-Cultural Marriages."

Duvall, Sylvanus M., *Before You Marry*. New York: Association Press, 1959 revision, chapters 6, 7, 8, 9, and 10.

Kirkpatrick, Clifford, *The Family As Process and Institution*. New York: Ronald Press, 1955, Chapter 13, "Selection of the Marriage Partner."

Landis, Judson T. and Mary G., *Building A Successful Marriage*. Englewood Cliffs: Prentice-Hall, 1958, Chapter 12, "Mixed Marriages."

Rutledge, Aaron L., *Responsible Marriage and Family Living: A Text with Adapted Readings*. New York: Harcourt, Brace, 1960, Chapter 2, "Choosing a Mate."

Thomas, John L., *The American Catholic Family*. Englewood Cliffs: Prentice-Hall, 1956.

Winch, Robert, *Mate Selection: A Study of Complementary Needs*. New York: Harper, 1957.

5 Are You Ready for Marriage?

What will marriage require of you?

What aptitudes are needed in marriage?

What makes for competence in interpersonal relations?

Can interpersonal competence be improved?

When is the best time to marry?

What about a military marriage?

What backgrounds favor stable marriages?

IT is more important to know *when* to marry than it is to know *whom* to marry, say the psychiatrists. The timing of marriage is crucial to its success. There is probably an optimum time for every individual to marry, and an optimum point where a couple should leave off testing their compatibilities and make a firm decision to marry. In these statements three issues are involved: (1) the *aptitude* and *competency* of the person entering marriage, (2) the *readiness* for accepting marital responsibilities, and (3) the *timing of* the decision to marry. Because marriage involves two persons who must develop into a functioning unit, it is helpful to view the problem of marriageability both as an individual problem, "Am I ready for marriage?" and as a problem for the engaged couple, "Are we ready for marriage?" In this chapter we will take up the problem of the marriageability of the individual, leaving for Chapter 6 the problem of the readiness of the engaged couple for marriage. Let us begin by asking what are the peculiar properties of the marriage relationship for which aptitudes are needed. Viewing marriage as a career, what does it demand of those who would pursue it?

97

What Will Marriage Require of You?

Marriage may be seen as a joint career for two people which starts with the husband-wife relationship, shifts in emphasis for a period of childbearing to more complex group relationships of father-mother-child, father-child, and mother-child, and becomes even more complex as additional children join the family. Eventually the children depart for marriage and careers of their own, and the husband-wife relationship becomes again the most prominent feature of the marriage. What are the properties of the husband-wife pair for which aptitude and training are indicated?

First of all, the marriage pair is "a divided house," by virtue of its two sexes. The more the young woman has been trained to be feminine and to abstain from activities regarded as masculine, and the more the groom has been reared to be masculine and protected from the values of the world of women, the greater the cleavage between the two in marriage. Heterosexuality is at once a major source of the attraction which draws the sexes together and the basis for the different appraisal of the world which so irritates and alienates the sexes when they are yoked together in marriage. A candidate for marriage might ask himself, "How well do I understand the opposite sex?"

A second feature of the marriage relation is its *extreme intimacy*. The protective barriers which preserve privacy between the sexes are withdrawn in marriage. Demonstrative affection is expected to be given and received. The marriage relation, moreover, is supposed to be one in which no secrets are kept from one another. The disposition to share is nowhere so elaborated as in marriage. Even the barriers which in most social contacts protect the ego from exposure to criticism are expected to fall within the confines of marriage. A second question, therefore, might be, "How capable am I of sharing, of expressing affection, and of accepting criticism?"

Closely related to the intimacies and sharing of the relation is the phenomenon of companionship. Interdependence on one another for the satisfaction of the basic needs of security, response, and recognition is most characteristic of American marriage. Individuals expect in marriage the warmth of belonging, even more than competence in household management.

The marriage pair must become a decision-making unit, a planning and executing group, if it is going to carry out its functions. The couple must be able to communicate well enough to perceive a problem, break it down into its components through consultation and discussion, and agree upon a plan for action. Once a workable plan is achieved, the activities become routinized, bringing about a real saving of time and energy. Married couples have to concern themselves with efficiency, routines, and shortcuts.

Finally, the marriage pair is one of the few groups in our society which plans for permanence. It is expected that the newly married will build a relationship which can survive personality changes, illness, disabilities, and financial reverses. The marriage relation requires domesticity, constancy, and loyalty over an adult lifetime. Individuals who abhor routine, domestic tasks, or the confinement of monogamy find marriage more frustrating than satisfying. The husband-wife relation is expected to transcend the competitive pulls of professional ties, the demands and needs of children, and other entrancing love objects which cross the stage in various forms during the marriage life span.

Marriage is usually thought of as an option which women face as an alternative to an occupational career. Yet in a real sense husband and wife are both involved in building a *joint career* which has to compete seriously with other concomitant careers.

What Aptitudes Are Needed in Marriage?

Given this view of the marriage relation, admittedly a most American picture, marriageability involves great emotional maturity and self-mastery, and high competence in interpersonal relations. Ideally, the individual should have (1) an understanding of the opposite sex, (2) the capacity to give and receive love, (3) the ability to foster and sustain an intimate interpersonal relation, and (4) skills in communication, consultation, and problem-solving. He should, moreover, be willing to subordinate himself to a joint career for which he should bring high expectation of success. Do such paragons of marriageability develop by the marrying ages of twenty to twenty-five? Research findings may be helpful in confirming or clarifying the aptitudes important for success in marriage.

Marital aptitude, as defined in research studies, consists of a complex of attitudes, likes, dislikes, opinions, values, and preferences that seem to predispose a person to successful adjustment to the demands of marriage. These value orientations seem to motivate people to make the necessary sacrifices of other conflicting values that successful marriage demands. As Bernard puts it, lack of marital aptitude doesn't necessarily imply neuroticism, it merely means these people's values and interests do not lie in the area of domesticity, but in other directions. They are just not the "marrying kind." [1]

---

[1] Jessie L. Bernard, *Remarriage,* New York: Dryden Press, 1956, pp. 101–102.

Johnson and Terman have identified personality features which distinguish the happily married, the unhappily married, and the divorced. The unhappily married woman lacks the warm sympathy and emotional balance of the happily married woman, and the rugged individualism, ambition, and efficiency of the divorced. "She is inclined to be egocentric, irritable, and intolerant. . . . She is neurotic, indecisive, and unmethodical. . . ." [2] The unhappily married man "differs from the happily married man in being less amiable, tolerant, and sympathetic, less interested in social welfare activities, and more irritable, moody, and seclusive. He differs from the typical divorced man in showing less initiative, self-confidence, and personal ambition, and in his greater tendency to conservatism." [3]

Terman and associates [4] provide a profile of the happily married women:

Happily Married Women as a Group

1. Are characterized by kindly attitudes toward others and by the expectations of kindly attitudes in return.
2. Do not take offense and are not unduly concerned about the impressions they make upon others.
3. Do not look upon social relationships as rivalry situations.
4. Are cooperative.
5. Do not object to subordinate roles.
6. Are not annoyed by advice from others.
7. Enjoy activities that bring education or pleasurable opportunities to others and like to do things for the dependent or underprivileged.
8. Are methodical and painstaking in their work, attentive to detail, and careful in regard to money.
9. In religion, morals, and politics they tend to be conservative and conventional.
10. Their expressed attitudes imply a quiet self-assurance and a decidedly optimistic outlook upon life.

The temperament of the happily married woman fits the demands of the marriage career rather closely, and her activities and interests are

---

[2] Winifred B. Johnson and Lewis M. Terman, "Personality Characteristics of Happily Married, Unhappily Married, and Divorced Persons," *Character and Personality*, Vol. 3, June, 1935, p. 297.

[3] *Ibid.*, p. 297.

[4] Lewis M. Terman and associates, *Psychological Factors in Marital Happiness*, New York: McGraw-Hill, 1938, pp. 145–146.

not competitive with it. She shows evidence of self-mastery, is other-oriented in her kindliness and interest in helping others. She addresses herself to the maintenance of the marital relations in her willingness to accept subordinate roles, her lack of rivalrous tendencies, and her ability to take counsel. She fits the demands of domesticity in her attention to detail, her methodical patterns, and her careful stewardship of money. Her quiet optimism carries her through the crisis situations met by the family.

Terman's happily married men differ from happily married women in some respects: [5]

Happily Married Men as a Group

1. Show evidence of an even and stable emotional tone.
2. Their most characteristic reaction to others is that of cooperation.
3. This is reflected:
   a. In their attitudes toward business superiors, with whom they work well.
   b. In their attitudes toward women, which reflect equalitarian ideals.
   c. In their benevolent attitudes toward inferiors and underprivileged.
4. Tend to be unself-conscious and somewhat extraverted in a gathering of people.
5. Compared with unhappy husbands they show:
   a. Superior initiative.
   b. Greater tendency to take responsibility.
   c. Greater willingness to give close attention to detail in their daily work.
6. They like methodical procedures and methodical people.
7. In money matters they are saving and cautious.
8. They are conservative politically and socially.
9. They have a favorable attitude toward religion and strongly uphold the sex mores and other social conventions.

In some respects the description of the happily married man would fit the requirements for success in business and the professions as well as marriage. Terman finds him more self-confident, less likely to get rattled under stress, and less dependent upon others for recognition and approval (showing more autonomy) than the unhappily married man. He takes the family maintenance function seriously, being more likely than the unhappy man to concern himself with the longtime economic future of the family. Terman writes, "In the happy marriage it is the husband who does the worrying." If, in this joint career of marriage, a division of aptitudes is required, it would appear that happily mar-

---

[5] *Ibid.*, p. 155.

ried men bring to marriage the competencies which assure economic success and social stability while evidencing the optimism and cooperation needed to make a cooperating family possible.

Locke,[6] contrasting the personality attributes of happily married and of divorced in Indiana, reported that the happily married more frequently rated themselves and their mates as directorial, adaptable, demonstratively affectionate, and sociable than did the divorced. His findings support Terman's at a number of points but add still other characteristics of marital aptitudes. The divorced, compared with the happily married, rate themselves and their partners lower on the culturally approved virtues of responsibility and decisiveness and ascribe to themselves more frequently the culturally disapproved vices of stubbornness, domination, and quick anger. Happily married couples are more generous in their ratings and view themselves more frequently as having the aptitudes considered important for marital success.

Emotional maturity and self-development

Another way of viewing marriageability is to ask the question: "Are you mature enough for marriage?" A thoughtful listing of evidences of maturity is provided by Bowman (see Table 12).

This list places heavy emphasis on "self-mastery and self-integration," which adolescents often lack and which college students still find troublesome. The process of achieving mastery over one's urges continues

---

TABLE 12.   A Mature Person [7]

1. Profits by his own experiences and the experiences of others
2. Has some knowledge of social life, how it is organized, what the requirements are for living in a society
3. Has a reasonable respect for authority and tradition
4. Lives in a world of reality
5. Faces an unalterable situation with poise and a minimum of conflict
6. Uses the present rather than the past as a point of departure
7. Accepts his chronological age for what it is
8. Is independent of his parents in his ability to make decisions
9. Does not easily take offense at slights
10. Accepts the responsibility for his own acts
11. Controls his behavior, acknowledging possible undesirable appetites in self but controls them
12. Operates on the basis of principles rather than pleasure or pain
13. Has an attitude toward sex, love, and marriage compatible with adulthood

---

[6] Harvey J. Locke, *Predicting Adjustment in Marriage*, New York: Holt, 1951, pp. 171–245.

[7] Modified and adapted from Henry Bowman, *Marriage for Moderns*, New York: McGraw-Hill, 1953, pp. 94–151.

into adulthood. This means that many young people marry while still unfinished in this respect—marriage becomes for them a "finishing school." From Bowman's table one can identify at least five expressions of self-mastery and integration:

✓ Self-accepting: accepting one's body, one's sex, name, and color
✓ Self-directing: establishing one's own goals, making one's own decisions
✓ Self-understanding: knowing self, who am I, who would I be good for, why do I do as I do, what are my limitations
✓ Self-confidence: feeling adequate to handle life situations, jobs, school, and marriage
Self-control: able to manage one's tensions, to postpone satisfaction, to sustain pain and disappointment

Self-integration in this multiple sense is the product of a process of growth and development which begins in infancy and continues through the progressive differentiation of personality into childhood, adolescence, and adulthood. It begins with the first *recognition of self* as different from *things not self,* an achievement of high order. It continues with the discovery of areas of life over which he, the child, has power and autonomy and areas where he is dependent upon others. His first power assertions are seen as he takes control of his own physiology in refusing to defecate, to eat, and/or to sleep, differentiating between the things *I do* for myself and things that must be done for me.

Recognition and acceptance of sex differences occur early in the building of one's sense of identity: I am a girl like mother, not a boy like father; or I am a boy like father, not a girl like mother. Now the self has grown from an undifferentiated something into a gender of a recognized form. To get approval, the child discovers he/she must act right—that there are different ways for boys and girls to act; and *self-control* tied to one's gender becomes valued. Boys further differentiate themselves from girls in the activities they engage in, placing heavy emphasis on physical prowess, skills in *doing things,* playing with *things,* toys, trains, trucks, or playing at occupations like soldiers, cowboys, all clearly masculine in orientation. Girls elaborate by contrast the nurturing roles, playing with dolls and housekeeping equipment, imitating the mother-child relation. This may account in part for the fact that college men tend to judge their marriageability by their economic and occupational competence (Am I competent to earn an adequate living?), whereas girls gauge their readiness for marriage more by their ability to make a man happy and to facilitate the interpersonal relationships socially and within the family.

For both sexes there comes with maturity a sense of self that makes it possible to associate intimately with others without being personally threatened. As you find satisfying answers to your own deepest questions—"Who am I?" "What is life, and where do I fit in?" "What kind of person am I and what can I do?"—you gain a sense of your own identity as a person. This inner assurance of selfhood is necessary, says Erikson, before young people can cope with the problems of intimacy.[8] As you achieve your own identity by going beyond the simple self-placement you learned as a child—to accept your name, your ancestry, your gender, your body, your status among others—and come to feel secure deep down within yourself about who you are and what you can do, you become ready to merge with another intimately.

When once you know who you are, you are not afraid to fuse with others and become fully intimate, that is in sexuality and in love. . . . Otherwise early marriages are often used by the partners to fight for their identity. Many young marriages break up over this point.[9]

Maturity sufficient for marriage, then, involves enough ego strength so that you do not have to fight for your selfhood in constant intimate relationships with your mate. Your ego is strong enough to stand alone without defenses to safeguard it and without having to constantly run in with reinforcements to prop it up. You know who you are securely enough so you can gracefully encourage your partner to reveal himself. You are free to enjoy each other for your differences as well as your similarities, because each of you is first of all a socialized human being and accepted as such, each by the other. Self-development continues throughout the marriage, stimulated by creative interaction, in solving the problems of marriage and parenthood.

What Makes for Competence in Interpersonal Relations?

The skills and abilities taught in the socialization of children from babyhood to adulthood have been termed *interpersonal competencies* by Foote and Cottrell.[10] Four of the components of interpersonal competence are especially relevant to marriageability: empathy, autonomy, judgment, and creativity.

1. *Empathy.* Empathy refers to the ability to put yourself in anoth-

---

[8] Erik H. Erikson, *Childhood and Society,* New York: Norton, 1950, pp. 227–231.
[9] Erik H. Erikson, *Healthy Personality Development in Children,* New York: The Josiah Macy Foundation, 1952, p. 93.
[10] Nelson Foote and Leonard S. Cottrell, *Identity and Interpersonal Competence,* Chicago: University of Chicago Press, 1955.

er's shoes, so that you can think as he thinks, feel as he feels, and perceive as he perceives. It involves correctly predicting a person's feelings and thoughts from his overt behavior. It has been referred to by some writers as "taking the role of the other." Empathy requires the capacity to listen, to be so effectively other-centered that you arrive accurately at the other's answer. Correct other-perception in marriage should be accompanied by sympathy for the spouse, since high empathy alone would make many types of manipulation and exploitation possible (the confidence man empathizes very effectively with his victims).

Empathy moreover can be used as a test of adequacy of interspousal communication. Unpredictable behavior on the part of the spouse is good proof that communication has been inadequate. A husband commonly errs in misperceiving his wife's ideas by supposing that she thinks as he does. The husband imputes his views to his wife, when actually she has ideas of her own. A common error made by wives is to suppose that their husbands feel as "all men" are supposed to feel, only to discover that husbands are individuals with idiosyncratic reactions of their own.

It is obvious that empathy is needed to become efficient in solving marital problems. Recent research by Hobart and Klausner in California demonstrates that accurately perceiving one's spouse is related significantly to good marital adjustment. Empathic skills in wives correlated more frequently with good marital adjustment than it did in husbands, suggesting that wives may use their skills in empathy to achieve resolution of differences more frequently than do husbands.[11]

2. *Autonomy.* A person who acts autonomously acts *with security*, as he *chooses to act*. The person acts confidently, with poise, with the conviction that he is adequate to the situation. When you say you are acting autonomously, you are saying, "I can comfortably handle this situation in any of several ways, according to my choice." [12]

In a recent experiment by Oscar and Eleanor Eggers, a number of people attempted to improve on their capacity for autonomy by participation in spontaneous and extemporaneous skits, called "role playing," followed by reflective discussion. Some of the statements made by the participants at the conclusion of the experiment were:

I have freer emotional expression
I am more realistic about myself

---

[11] Charles W. Hobart and William J. Klausner, "Some Social Interactional Correlates of Marital Role Disagreement, and Marital Adjustment," *Marriage and Family Living,* August 1959, pp. 256–263.
[12] From an unpublished manuscript by Thomas L. Gillette, *Interpersonal Competency,* Chapel Hill, North Carolina, pp. 1–4.

. . . . more confident, can act as I want to
. . . . more objective in evaluating my own reactions
. . . . better able to share myself with others
. . . . better able to let others know what I am like and how I feel
. . . . more honest in dealing with people
. . . . more able to act hostile sometimes
. . . . less inclined to act in a dominating way, as I feel more secure
. . . . not so afraid of people's reactions to me
. . . . more comfortable generally
I have more confidence in functioning in a group
I see things about myself that were covered up
I can say "no" more often
I can discuss personal feelings with less difficulty
I find it easier to give a speech

Through all these statements run the themes of increased self-confidence, greater clarity about self, freer ability to act in the way one wishes to act, greater freedom from compulsive conformity to others, and greater freedom from compulsive self-demands. Gillette, reporting on the Eggers' experiment, indicates there are a number of types of autonomy deficiency:

One type is *submissive.* It is seen in the person who is passive, easily influenced, hesitant or uncertain. It may take a variety of forms: . . . excessive sweetness, a reluctance to criticize or disapprove, or disagree.

Another type is seen in *rebellious action* . . . the guy who is quite easily irritated, who has a chip on his shoulder, and is seen in the refusal to listen to the other's point of view, unwillingness to admit an error, or a tendency to argue at the drop of a metaphor.

A third type is designated as *rigid behavior.* This is seen in the avoidance of emotional expression, objectivity or aloofness in giving or receiving affection, and a high degree of intellectualization in interpersonal relations.[13]

Autonomy as a component of interpersonal competence develops rapidly as the personality arrives at an acceptance of his "identity." Indeed, this appears to be a prerequisite for the full acceptance of others. Unexplored yet is the concept of "pair autonomy" which an engaged pair begin building as they try on the "Mr. and Mrs." designation for size, begin making plans, and undertaking decisions about their "joint career" of marriage.

3. *Judgment.* Of importance for the longtime success of marriage is the component judgment, the capacity to estimate and evaluate the possible outcomes of various ways of acting in interpersonal situations. It involves the ability to choose among values as well as the capacity to

---

[13] *Ibid.,* p. 3.

make correct decisions about intimates. Bad judgment is revealed by one's mistakes, as time proves one's evaluations faulty. People with good judgment possess (1) the ability to select the important issues in a complex situation, (2) the skill of marshalling evidence quickly in choosing a course of action, and (3) the vision to take into account the future consequences as well as the immediate consequences of any given social interaction. Current research by Brim and his associates suggests that the ability to take into account both short-run and long-run consequences of an action is all too rare among the parents they studied.[14]

4. *Creativity*. The concept of creativity, used more frequently in connection with the arts, also has a place in interpersonal relations. It is best seen in the redefining of old situations with new perspectives, endowing old goals with new meanings, and devising new means for attaining one's objectives. Creative people are said to be original, flexible, venturesome, and innovative.

Creativity is needed as a couple meets new and undefined situations for which their past experiences are inadequate. Someone has said, "Every marriage is an undefined situation, impossible to predict, and therefore full of surprises." The uncreative person is often in a dilemma seeking to make "the old bottles do for the new wine," when what is needed is something of the venturesomeness and the risk-taking capacity of the explorer.

The abilities of empathy, autonomy, judgment, and creativity make for an interpersonally competent person capable of handling himself in a changing world where the guides for behavior are in flux. Such a person has insight into himself, is sensitive to the needs of others, and anticipates those needs accurately. He is able to maintain his goals and his poise despite social pressures and is able to come quickly to good decisions in new and complex situations. Moreover, he is able to innovate new roles in collaboration with his spouse when traditional roles fail.

Can Interpersonal Competence Be Improved?

The research on the processes of improving one's competence in interpersonal relations is as yet modest and exploratory. Empathy has received the most attention, autonomy has been studied, but judgment

---

[14] Orville G. Brim, Jr., David C. Glass, and David E. Lavin, *Correlations Between Husbands and Wives in Characteristics of Child Rearing Decisions*, New York: Russell Sage Foundation, September, 1958, Working Paper No. 6, pp. 1–5.

and creativity are just beginning to be explored. Dymond demonstrated the close relationship between empathic skill (understanding and sensitivity to others) and insight (accurate understanding of self), suggesting that the ability to take the role of the other accurately (empathy) is made of the same stuff as the ability to stand off and look at ourselves from another's point of view (insight).[15] Kirkpatrick and Hobart sought to discover whether couples' empathic skill depended on the stage of their involvement. They found, as you would expect, first of all, that individuals who were dating or engaged were much more accurate about one another's values than randomly paired individuals not in daily association with each other. Second, they found significant improvement in empathy between couples at the "favorite date" stage and "going steady" and between the "engaged" and "married" stages of involvement, but very little difference between "going steady" and "engaged." They found no association between duration in any stage of involvement and empathy scores, and suggested that perhaps the improvement that occurs from one stage of involvement to another is due more to mutual rejection by non-empathic couples, and survival of more empathic couples long enough to get married.[16]

Vernon and Stewart find their data demonstrate improvement in empathy with continued association. As couples become better acquainted with each other, those with high empathic ability become more accurate in their perceptions of one another's ideas and interests, they suggest. They found errors of empathy less frequently among the engaged than among the going steady or the just dating couples. They also found the empathic scores higher among couples who had dated one another more than ten times than among those who had fewer than ten dates together. Their findings suggest that empathy between couples may well improve over time as they mutually expose their inner preferences and ideas, making it possible to replace intuitive guessing with knowledge and understanding of others.[17]

Thus far attempts to improve empathy and autonomy experimentally have been conducted under the direction of Mark and Dorothy Flapan

---

[15] Rosalind F. Dymond, "A Scale for the Measurement of Empathic Ability," *Journal of Consulting Psychology*, Vol. 13, 1949, pp. 127–133.

[16] Clifford Kirkpatrick and Charles Hobart, "Disagreement, Disagreement Estimate, and Non-Empathetic Imputations for Intimacy Groups Varying from Favorite Date to Married," *American Sociological Review*, Vol. 19, February, 1954, pp. 10–19. Hobart has duplicated this Indiana study on California data with almost identical results, see "Disagreement and Non-Empathy During Courtship, A Restudy," *Marriage and Family Living*, Vol. 18, November, 1956, pp. 317–322.

[17] Glenn M. Vernon and Robert L. Stewart, "Empathy as a Process in the Dating Situation," *American Sociological Review*, Vol. 22, February, 1957, pp. 48–52.

(empathy) and Oscar and Eleanor Eggers (autonomy) at the Family Study Center of the University of Chicago. Using discussion, role playing, and self-evaluation primarily, the Flapans carried a number of groups through twelve sessions each. Their unpublished findings show substantial improvement in empathy for individual couples in each group, moderate improvement for others, and little improvement for the balance.[18]

The Eggers, working at autonomy with similar methods, showed substantial improvement in half the participants in six experimental groups they served. They estimated that the sessions failed for a fourth of the couples served. Easiest of the autonomy components to master was the recognition of identity problems and the direction of change one wished to take. Most difficult was the undertaking of change in ascribed role sets, and the communicating of one's new identity unequivocally with the group.[19]

When Is the Best Time to Marry?

Differences in socialization, in rate of maturation, and in self-development may make one person ready for marriage at twenty while another may not be ready until much later. There is a tendency for the socializing experiences which prepare one for the responsibilities and tasks of marriage to continue into the late teens and early twenties. There is real advantage in waiting to marry until these experiences have been assimilated.

For those who wish to postpone marriage until the middle twenties the statistics on divorce and separation should prove comforting. The U.S. Bureau of the Census reports that marriages in the 15–19 age bracket are three and a half times more likely to be broken by divorce or separation than marriages in the 25–29 age bracket.[20] The Landises, in a study of more than 1,000 marriages, reveal that the divorce rate falls as the age at marriage increases (see Fig. 9).

Age and marital success

A number of studies of marital success agree that very youthful marriages tend to be unstable. Good marital adjustment is positively associated with the husband being twenty-four or over in four studies

---

[18] Mark H. Flapan, "A Conceptual Analysis of the Empathic Act." Paper presented at the annual meeting of the American Sociological Society, Urbana, Illinois, September 8, 1954.

[19] Oscar Eggers, "Order of Movement in Developing Interpersonal Autonomy." Paper presented at the annual meeting of the American Sociological Society, Urbana, Illinois, September 8, 1954.

[20] 1950 Census of Population, Vol. IV, Special Reports, Part 2, Chapter E, "Duration of Current Marital Status."

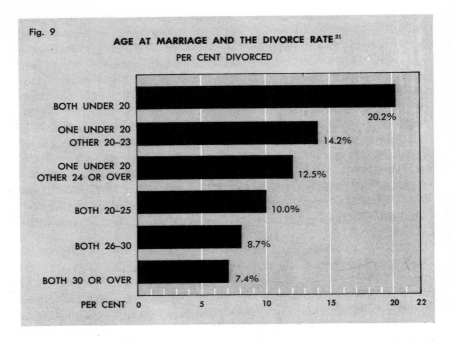

Fig. 9

AGE AT MARRIAGE AND THE DIVORCE RATE [21]

PER CENT DIVORCED

BOTH UNDER 20 — 20.2%
ONE UNDER 20 OTHER 20–23 — 14.2%
ONE UNDER 20 OTHER 24 OR OVER — 12.5%
BOTH 20–25 — 10.0%
BOTH 26–30 — 8.7%
BOTH 30 OR OVER — 7.4%

PER CENT   0   5   10   15   20   22

(Hart, Davis, Terman and Oden, and Locke), two studies found good adjustment beginning at age twenty-two (Burgess-Cottrell, and King with Negro couples). Good marital adjustment begins with wives at earlier ages in all studies, with 19–21 being the minimum ages for good adjustment.

The average age at first marriage for men in the United States has dropped from 26.1 in 1890 to 22.7 in 1955, and for women has dropped from 22.0 in 1890 to 20.2 in 1955. The most common marrying ages today are 21 and 22 years for men and 18 and 19 years for women, and almost a third of all marriages occur at these particular ages. However, less than 10 per cent of men marry before they are nineteen, and less than 10 per cent of women marry before seventeen. At the older extreme, fewer than 15 per cent of men and 10 per cent of women waited until they had passed thirty years of age before marrying.[22]

As you time your marriage decision, keep in mind that marriages before twenty appear hazardous, marriages in the early twenties are general, and although marriage for men is likely to be associated with in-

---

[21] Judson T. Landis and Mary G. Landis, *Building a Successful Marriage,* Englewood Cliffs: Prentice-Hall, 1958, p. 156.
[22] Paul C. Glick, *American Families,* New York: Wiley, 1957, pp. 54–57.

stability until the mid-twenties, to wait longer brings the individual into a diminishing supply of eligibles. The likelihood of ever marrying decreases rapidly after thirty, although 62 per cent of men and 55 per cent of women thirty and over eventually do marry.

Education is perhaps more relevant to readiness for marriage than age because it reflects adequacy of preparation for marriage and parenthood. The question of when to marry may be put in terms of readiness to leave school for marriage and homemaking, or for marriage and gainful employment. Census figures for white couples in the United States as a whole demonstrate that divorce and separation are twice as great for young people who fail to finish high school as for college graduates.[23] Studies of marital success also find good marriage adjustment begins with couples with education beyond high school (King, Schroeder, Hamilton, Terman, Burgess-Cottrell, and Locke), suggesting the importance of some college education.[24]

Education and marital success

Certainly age at marriage is correlated with education at marriage.[25] This is most marked for women, where college graduates marry, on the average, 4.7 years later (23.8) than girls who have had some high school but didn't graduate (19.1). The comparable difference between men is 3.2 years, college graduates (26.0), and high school nongraduates (22.8). Likewise, amount of income expected and type of occupation are affected by amount of education received by the husband. Since marriage induces men to leave school to enter gainful employment, and brings about the discontinuation of schooling for motherhood and possible gainful employment for girls, it is important to take the issue of completing one's schooling into account in timing the decision to marry.

A much greater proportion of young people in the United States today remain in school long enough to become high school students than was once the case, thus increasing the likelihood of marriages being recorded as "high school marriages" which yesterday would have been "marriages of out-of-school young people." Nevertheless, it will be some time before it is fashionable to undertake marriage while in high school. In studies in California and Nebraska, the number of girls marrying was not substantial until the senior year (see Fig. 10). Many fewer boys (about one-tenth the figure for girls) marry while in high school, but if they do marry, they tend to marry a girl who is still in

High school marriages

---

[23] *Ibid.*, p. 154.

[24] Ernest W. Burgess and Harvey J. Locke, *The Family*, New York: American Book, 1953, p. 413.

[25] See Paul C. Glick and Hugh Carter, "Marriage Patterns and Educational Level," *American Sociological Review*, Vol. 23, June, 1958, pp. 294–300.

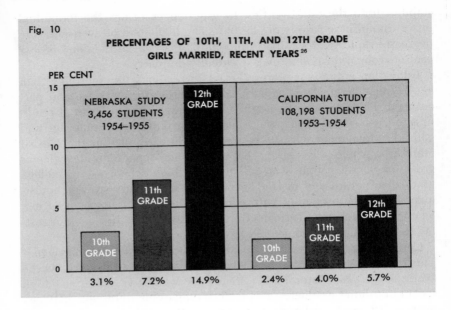

Fig. 10

PERCENTAGES OF 10TH, 11TH, AND 12TH GRADE
GIRLS MARRIED, RECENT YEARS[26]

PER CENT

NEBRASKA STUDY
3,456 STUDENTS
1954–1955

CALIFORNIA STUDY
108,198 STUDENTS
1953–1954

10th GRADE   11th GRADE   12th GRADE   10th GRADE   11th GRADE   12th GRADE

3.1%   7.2%   14.9%   2.4%   4.0%   5.7%

school. The majority of girls who marry while in high school marry out-of-school young men; only 7 per cent of the California girls married boys in the same school.

Another report [27] on the Nebraska study found that the girls who married were slightly older than their classmates. The boys they married, who were, on the average, five years older than they, were engaged in trades that required no further education. The married girls proved less well-adjusted than their non-marrying classmates on items of morale, family relations, and emotionality, but otherwise as students have been as free of problems as the students who did not get married.[28]

While it is said that high school marriages tend to occur in lower-class households, in Nebraska this does not prove to be the case. The educational backgrounds of parents of the girls who married in high

[26] Kenneth L. Cannon, "Report of Study of High School Girls Who Marry Under 19 Years of Age," mimeographed report, University of Nebraska, Lincoln, Nebraska; and Judson T. Landis and Kenneth C. Kidd, "Attitudes and Policies Concerning Marriages Among High School Students," *Marriage and Family Living*, Vol. 18, May, 1956, p. 129.

[27] J. Joel Moss and Ruby Gingles, "A Preliminary Report of a Longitudinal Study of Early Marriages in Nebraska." Paper presented at research section, National Council on Family Relations, Eugene, Oregon, August, 1958.

[28] *Ibid.*, Table 1.

school were almost identical with their non-marrying classmates, fathers averaging 9.86 years of schooling in both groups, and mothers averaging 10.31 years of schooling in both groups. The background of high school brides was found to be similar in a study in Iowa. The majority of these girls married home-town boys; three-fourths were wed in the county of residence, and 92 per cent were married by a clergyman.[29]

The most marked difference between the girls who married in high school and those who did not was in the extent of involvement. Nearly a third of the non-marrying group were "not dating" at the time of the survey, compared with only 3 per cent of the group who later married. Almost 40 per cent of the non-marrying group were engaged in random dating, compared with 13 per cent of the marrying group. Only 2 per cent of the non-marrying group were engaged compared with 40 per cent of girls who later married. The proportions going steady were almost the same in the two groups. These figures suggest that random and steady dating do not precipitate marriages, that the significant step is engagement.

Of these married high school students three-fourths advised graduating first or arranging to finish high school after marriage. They saw a high school education as insurance for getting a job or as help in raising a family:

I would tell them to wait until they have graduated because even if they think they are ready for marriage, I don't think they are.

Both graduation and marriage are important in your life and I would want to be sure of doing both jobs as well as possible; therefore, I think they can be done best separately.

Wait and go with more than one fellow, because I went with only this one. Make sure you are good and ready.

Do not go steady with one certain fellow until the last of your senior year. Make sure you want to spend the rest of your life with this person.

Don't ever let anyone talk you out of graduating from high school. Even if you don't graduate with high honors and maybe you'll never need a job outside of being a housewife but you'll always be proud of yourself for graduating, you'll never regret it.[30]

Among the obvious disadvantages to high school marriages are: cutting short one's formal education, freezing one's economic potentials, and shortening the period of preparation for marriage and parenthood.

---

[29] Lee G. Burchinal and Loren Chancellor, "What About School Age Marriages," *Iowa Farm Science*, Vol. 12, June, 1958, pp. 12–14.

[30] This section has been drawn from the two reports by Cannon, *op. cit.*, and Moss and Gingles, *op. cit.*

People are much more likely to think they are ready to marry in college than in high school. One author writes, "The feeling that marriage is an attractive proposition does not develop out of thin air but follows when people have drunk deeply of the 'heady wine' of freedom, have found it good, but are ready now for something more nourishing." [31] For many people this readiness to settle down comes during the college years despite lack of money, parental disapproval, and the fact they are still students. The attitude toward college marriages has changed markedly since World War II. The G.I. college marriage provided a model for other students to follow, and today from 10 to 20 per cent of college students across the country are married. Students in professional schools of medicine, law, and in the graduate schools are even more likely to be married, and few colleges can now avoid the pressure to provide apartments for married students along with the dormitory accommodations for single students.

It costs married college students more to live, especially if they have a baby. They are pressed for time because of a tendency to combine work and study. Social life is cut, not only because of time and financial pressures, but because campus activities are organized primarily around single students. Marriage requires shifting from the on-campus activities of single students to the activities of friends and neighbors in the apartment units. In spite of these disadvantages, most college marriages are satisfying to their participants. In studies at Michigan State University [32] and at Purdue University [33] roughly three-fourths of the married students said if they were starting college over they would again marry. Only 15 per cent of the Purdue group felt they had definitely made a mistake to marry when they did. The marriage adjustment scores of these latter marriages suggest that the students were responding not so much to the question of the "timing of the marriage" as the wisdom of marrying the person they had married. If they had waited to marry and had first become better acquainted, they might not have married each other at all.

From the studies of college marriages it is apparent that they are no longer considered precarious, but that they are qualitatively different in form must be recognized. To marry in college successfully requires high adaptability and an acceptance of a drastically cut level of living,

---

[31] Robert O. Blood, Jr., *Anticipating Your Marriage*, Glencoe, Illinois: Free Press, 1955, p. 157.

[32] Judson T. Landis, "On the Campus," *Survey Midmonthly*, Vol. 84, January, 1948, pp. 17–19.

[33] Harold T. Christensen and Robert E. Philbrick, "Family Size as a Factor in the Marital Adjustment of College Students," *American Sociological Review*, Vol. 17, June, 1952, pp. 306–312.

compared with single student life. Couples economize in order to marry, and scrimp even more severely when children arrive. They must be willing to accept graciously occasional help from parents and to sharply curtail their social life.

When both members of a married couple are attending classes and working part time, or when one is in school and the other working, the household tasks must be divided up flexibly.

A man who expects to be waited upon at home, who considers it beneath him to do dishes, scrub floors, and diaper babies, is likely to be a problem husband in a college marriage. And a girl who wants to be a queen, above hard work and struggle, and who cannot be happy if she has to miss any of the whirl of college social life, should not marry while she is still in college.[34]

The couple must be prepared for the possibilities of parenthood, since the best laid plans can be upset in this respect. Of 212 couples at Michigan State University who had had their first baby, the researchers found that only slightly over one third had definitely planned the first pregnancy, suggesting ineffective practice of birth control.[35]

Marriage in college can be a success if (1) the partners view with equanimity the challenge of much work and low pay, (2) they practice birth control, (3) the husband is willing to cooperate in the housework and care of the children, and (4) the wife does not place too much value on completing her own education.[36] These conditions may be too harsh for some to meet, but they will be a challenge to others.

What about a Military Marriage?

Since military life is organized essentially for single men and a serviceman's first duty and responsibility is supposed to be to his military unit, couples are faced with questions such as these: Shall they marry at once or postpone marriage until the intensive early part of military service is past? If they marry immediately, shall she follow him so that she may have as much time as possible with him? Would it be better to dissolve the engagement entirely and return to circulation, with the understanding that they will keep in touch during his service and re-

---

[34] Landis and Landis, *op. cit.*, pp. 187–188.

[35] Shirley Poffenberger, Thomas Poffenberger, and Judson T. Landis, "Intent Toward Conception and the Pregnancy Experience," *American Sociological Review*, Vol. 17, October, 1952, pp. 616–620.

[36] Blood, *op. cit.*, p. 163.

new their engagement when and if they are both free and interested at the completion of his military duty?

The prudent who marry after college and after military service have a higher likelihood of success in marriage, because they face a simpler marriage situation at a more mature age, than those who marry earlier. The military service marriage in which the husband may be sent overseas and separated from his wife for a long period is difficult for newlyweds who need to spend as much time as possible together during the first weeks and months of their marriage to grow closer together in their habits and ways. In spite of this many couples marry before military service is completed because they fear that separation would break up their relationship. The girl doesn't entirely trust her man, nor does she trust herself. The young man has similar doubts. In wartime such marriages would have been called *war marriages,* because they are characterized by haste, impulsiveness, and a sense of urgency. It is quite true that had these couples waited, their relationship would not have survived the separation. Each would have become lonely and started dating others, and would have eventually drifted into other involvements.

Other couples marry during military service because their relationship has matured to the point where marriage is clearly indicated. They have completed their schooling and have been engaged long enough to prove the staying quality of the relationship. They are prepared to face marriage in military service as a special challenge. While they don't welcome the separations which military service requires they don't fear them because they have ways of keeping the relationship actively growing while separated. In a study of adjustments to war separation, Hill found the number of letters written, the number of topics covered, and the adequacy of communication related to good adjustment of the wife.[37] The more adequate the communication, the better the wife's morale and the less likely she was to build up false pictures of the husband. Even so, there is a temptation to build a letter-to-letter relationship to replace the face-to-face relationships of everyday family living, which complicates the adjustments to reunion when the service husband returns.

Courtship in military service also presents greater hazards than courtship in college. The coeducational college is in some respects the ideal marriage market, bringing together as it does young people of common interests and similar family backgrounds for prolonged periods of acquaintance during which they can ascertain their suitability

---

[37] Reuben Hill, *Families Under Stress*, New York: Harper, 1949, pp. 141–142.

and compatibility. In the military environment the atmosphere is not conducive to prolonged courtships and the exercise of good judgment in mate selection. Courtships are undertaken for the momentary satisfactions of companionship and affection rather than from the perspective of civilian community and family responsibilities.

Timing of the marriage decision should probably not be a function of the urgency of war, the possibilities of separation, or the advantages of a secure officer's pay, but should weigh more heavily the readiness of the two persons as individuals to assume the responsibilities of marriage.

What Backgrounds Favor Stable Marriages?

Some highly marriageable individuals find the cards stacked against them in marriage because of unfavorable backgrounds and upbringing. Other less marriageable individuals face a relatively secure future in marriage because of favorable contingencies due to birth, education, and position. In a series of more than twenty studies of the factors making for happiness in marriage, a number of generalizations have been constructed which may be used to point out favorable and unfavorable climates for the development and testing of one's marriageability.

Similarity of cultural backgrounds (1) simplifies the forging of workable marriage routines, (2) facilitates the arrival at mutually acceptable solutions to problems, and (3) increases the likelihood of quick and open communication when one's needs are not met.

Similar backgrounds

Extensive and strong evidence supports the claim that happiness of parents' marriage is favorable to marital adjustment of offspring. This in turn appears associated with a history of happiness in one's childhood and with mild but firm discipline with only moderate punishment. However, young people whose home experiences have been unhappy are not infrequently highly motivated to avoid similar mistakes in their own marriages and make great strides under proper guidance.

Emotional atmosphere of family

Fairly strong evidence supports the favorable relationships between attachment to parents and good marital adjustment. Lack of conflict with parents is favorable. Other expressions of emotional attachment such as equal intimacy with both parents, regarding the parent of opposite sex as attractive, and lack of attachment to one's siblings are only slightly correlated with good marital adjustment.

There is extensive evidence that adequate sex information, especially from encouraging parents, is favorable to marital adjustment. Parental frankness in answering the questions of children about sex and in giving them adequate information tends to develop healthy attitudes to-

Climate of attitudes concerning sex

ward the sexual experiences of marriage. These in turn are undoubtedly related to achieving similarity of sex desires, developing orgasm capacity in the wife, and other tasks of sex adjustment in marriage.

Contingency factors

To a limited extent, the couple appraising their future career together can foresee and control contingencies which might be unfavorable to their marriage. The choices of a minister instead of the justice of the peace and of marrying in a church are usually under the control of the couple. Occupational choice may be less easily controlled, yet type of occupation (the professions) and stability of employment are associated with good marital adjustment. There is rather striking evidence that husbands playing an equalitarian rather than a patriarchal role in the marriage is favorable. Sociability, common friends, and participation in community organization argue well for the happiness of the relationship.

Predicting success in marriage

Kirkpatrick [38] has arranged the factors most highly associated with marital success by order of the extent of confirmation in several studies:

Premarital Factors

Happiness of parents' marriage

Adequate length of acquaintance, courtship and engagement

Adequate sex information in childhood

Personal happiness in childhood

Approval of the marriage by parents and others

Engagement adjustment and normal motivation toward marriage

Ethnic and religious similarity

Higher social and educational status

Mature and similar chronological age

Harmonious affection with parents during childhood

Post-Marital Factors

Early and adequate orgasm capacity

Confidence in the marriage and satisfaction with affection shown

An equalitarian rather than a patriarchal relationship, emphasis on husband's role

Mental and physical health

Harmonious companionship based on common interests and accompanied by a favorable attitude toward the marriage and spouse

Perhaps this discussion and listing is enough to indicate the contexts of marriageability which tend both to set limits on one's achievements and to spur one on to overcome obstacles to marriage success. Each individual brings to marriage his backgrounds, registered as part of his past, his personal competencies, which enable him to function more

---

[38] Clifford Kirkpatrick, *The Family as Process and Institution*, New York: Ronald Press, 1955, pp. 350 and 354.

or less effectively in the present, and his potentialities for growth, which are reflected in his needs, hopes, and goals.

Fortunately, the most single important item in predicting good adjustment in marriage is good adjustment in engagement. It is the best test of compatibility and marriageability as yet devised. For the individual who feels personally ready for marriage, there is still the question of pair readiness, "Are *we* ready for marriage?" The engagement period can be a rigorous test of both individual and pair marriageability. It occupies the bottleneck position through which most marriages-to-be pass, and one of its assignments is to discourage mismatings and eliminate the as yet unmarriageables from marriage.

READINGS

Becker, Howard, and Reuben Hill (eds.), *Family, Marriage and Parenthood.* Boston: Heath, 1955, Chapter VI, "Producing Marriageable Personalities."

Blood, Robert O., Jr., *Anticipating Your Marriage.* Glencoe, Illinois: Free Press, 1955, Chapter VI, "Deciding When to Get Married."

Bowman, Henry A., *Marriage for Moderns.* New York: McGraw-Hill, 1953, Chapter V, "Age for Marriage."

Cavan, Ruth S., *American Marriage, A Way of Life.* New York: Crowell, 1959, Chapter 3, "Personal Readiness for Marriage."

Christensen, Harold, *Marriage Analysis.* New York: Ronald Press, 1958, Chapter VI, "Social and Emotional Maturity."

Foote, Nelson, and Leonard S. Cottrell, Jr., *Identity and Interpersonal Competence.* Chicago: University of Chicago Press, 1955, Chapter 2, "Interpersonal Competence."

Himes, Norman, and Donald L. Taylor, *Your Marriage* (Rev. Ed.). New York: Rinehart, 1955, Chapter 6, "Choosing a Mate Wisely."

Landis, Judson T. and Mary G., *Building A Successful Marriage.* Englewood Cliffs: Prentice-Hall, 1958, Chapters VII and VIII, "Marriageability" and "Maturity for Marriage."

LeMasters, Ersel E., *Modern Courtship and Marriage.* New York: Macmillan, 1957, Chapters X and XII, "Military Service and Courtship" and "Personality Factors in Marital Adjustment."

Levy, John, and Ruth Munroe, *The Happy Family.* New York: Knopf, 1938.

Terman, Lewis M., "Marital Adjustment and Its Prediction" in Morris Fishbein and Ernest W. Burgess (eds.), *Successful Marriage* (Rev. Ed.). Garden City: Doubleday, 1955, pp. 111–126.

6 Getting Engaged

What are the advantages of an engagement?

Are short engagements better than long ones?

Should engagement mean "no stepping out"?

How much intimacy during engagement?

Does every engaged couple have doubts?

What engagements should be broken?

How do you build your engagement into marriage?

THE meaning of engagement, the interpretation of its obligations and duties, varies tremendously from couple to couple. For many it is regarded as an end in itself, like a degree or a diploma, rather than a period of preparation for greater responsibilities in marriage and family life. For many it is dominated by the thrills of novelty and new experience rather than by the solving of problems and testing of personalities.

Engagement is more than a hurdle before marriage. The betrothal has values of its own. Time invested in a conscientious engagement returns dividends in more successful marriage later on. It is a necessary bridge between the irresponsibility of youth with its "single blessedness" and the married responsibility of adults.

What Are the Advantages of an Engagement?

Many couples, especially in the working classes, marry without getting engaged at all. In wartime it is not uncommon to bypass the engagement in the haste to marry. What are the hazards of this procedure, and the advantages of a full and adequate engagement?

121

Engagement is commonly thought to mainly concern women. On the face of it the formal aspects of the engagement, the showers and parties and notices in the society pages, emphasize the girl's good fortune and neglect the young man. Actually there are substantial advantages to both people in a modern version of the betrothal:

1. The engagement may save a man from being dazzled by the supposed glamor of his fiancée, since it gives him opportunities to see her in everyday clothes over a period of time.

2. The engagement enables both to become much better acquainted with the other's family and to become accepted by them. In-laws are valuable assets, and their approval is a factor in predicting marital success. If parents disapprove, they may act as a wedge to separate the pair when the first crisis develops.

3. The engagement provides the opportunity to create an amorous monopoly in which "old flames" and rivals are eliminated as love objects.

4. The engagement provides insight into the relative responsiveness of the other. Even though there be a minimum of sex experimentation in the engagement, such deficiencies as frigidity, lack of capacity for demonstrating affection, and childhood fears about sex will show up in the normal love play of the engagement.

5. The engagement gives full opportunity to discuss children, child discipline, wife working, handling of money, extramarital friendships, and other vital issues which often don't seem appropriate in the dating and courtship stages.

6. The engagement provides time to arrange financial affairs and to gradually get ready for the economic burden of marriage, sharing business and professional interests, and discovering similarities and differences in this realm of marriage.

7. The engagement also gives both participants a chance occasionally to slip into the roles of husband and wife and to learn some of the ropes while still in the engagement period. Nothing succeeds like success, and the engagement enables the novices to succeed by starting them out with premarriage problems and inducting them slowly into the complications of married life.

These seven advantages presuppose substantially greater activity together as a pair than characterized formal engagements of the past. Today engagement is increasingly viewed as a "testing period" rather than a "promise to marry"; indeed, the Harts have characterized it as the period during which the idea of marriage with this particular mate is being explored as a working hypothesis.[1]

---

[1] Hornell Hart and Ella B. Hart, *Personality and the Family, Revised,* Boston: Heath, 1941, p. 178.

The testing and exploring which the engagement makes possible are necessary because parents have largely lost their control over the mate selection procedure. It is up to the young woman to investigate the background and future prospects of the man to whom she is engaged. Similarly, the man continues to test the suitability of his choice before it is too late. Within the privacy and intimacy of the new relationship, these detailed checks on their reactions to each other are invaluable since they reveal whether a couple will be compatible in temperament and values.

A final advantage of the engagement is as a stabilizer of the relationship. The newly engaged want to be assured that the professing of love isn't part of the line, that this is really love. The girl wants to feel the tenderness of her fiancé without the threat of rivals to disturb them. The members of an engaged pair inevitably bring from courtship certain resentments, memories of injustices, and painful jealousy, as a result of the insecurity of the relation in competitive courtship days. Now is the time to bring out the unresolved differences and conflicts that have covertly plagued the relationship. Each can now speak his piece with more security. There are no longer rivals who might take immediate advantage of any temporary alienation. It is no longer necessary to jockey for position. The line, used originally to cover up the insecurity of the participants, can now be put aside. People leave the pair alone a lot more now, so they can be quite frank about themselves.

Are Short Engagements Better than Long Ones?

How long should the engagement be? To answer this question requires an intimate acquaintance with the history of each engagement pair. Each engaged couple is unique in experience and background, and each interprets engagement somewhat differently. Much depends, for example, on the length of acquaintance before engagement and the degree to which the couple may have undertaken the personality-testing and problem-solving functions in the pre-engagement period. Many students who have read books or attended classes on marriage problems discuss during courtship questions that other couples less well oriented postpone for the engagement.

In both the Burgess-Cottrell and the Terman studies of marriage success, there appears to be a positive relationship between length of engagement and marital happiness.[2] The longer couples are engaged,

---

[2] Lewis M. Terman and associates, *Psychological Factors in Marital Happiness,* New York: McGraw-Hill, 1938, p. 198, and Burgess and Cottrell, *Predicting Success or Failure in Marriage,* New York: Prentice-Hall, 1939, p. 167.

these studies show, the more satisfactory is their later marital adjustment. Actually, these statistics may not show a completely true picture because there probably was a selection of the hardier couples of superior character who could survive a long engagement. Unfortunately, since these studies were limited to engaged couples who got married, we have no assessment of adjustment for those couples whose engagements were broken because they attempted to prolong the engagement beyond a sensible point.

The highest happiness scores in the Burgess study went to those married couples who had been engaged for two years or longer before marriage. Only 11 per cent of this group showed poor marital adjustment, while of those who had been engaged less than three months, 50 per cent showed poor adjustment. The mean happiness scores of Terman's couples went up steadily in relation to length of engagement, reaching a peak among those who had been engaged five years or longer. One of these authors concludes from his findings that companionship rather than romantic love forms the best sustaining force for a mutually satisfying love relation. He questions the lasting quality of a relation based primarily on romantic love, suggesting that there should be an opportunity for the relationship to mature over a considerable period of time before marriage.[3]

There are obvious values in engagements which are long enough to prepare couples for marriage. Engagements need to be long enough to act as a screening device to alienate incompatible couples who would otherwise marry, only to separate more painfully after some years of marriage. The answer to the question of length of engagement is given best not as a definite number of months or years but in terms of the indefinite "long enough." The engagement, then, should be *long enough* to perform the many functions of testing, discussing, learning, fighting, and loving which underlie successful marriage. If the student requires a more specific figure, it is probably safe to say that the engagement should rarely be shorter than six months and rarely longer than two years, depending on the length of previous acquaintance and the extent to which the engagement functions have already been started in the courtship period.

How long an engagement is too long? Henry Bowman has established rough criteria which may be helpful:

An engagement is too long if an excessive amount of nervous tension is generated; if the couple experience a sense of frustration; if they become more than usually tired of waiting; if they grow discouraged; if they become in-

---

[3] Burgess and Cottrell, *op. cit.*, p. 168.

different to each other; if they begin to accept the *status quo* as a substitute for marriage and lose interest in the latter; if the engagement constitutes more than a relatively small fraction of the total period from meeting to wedding. . . . We wish to counteract the opinion so commonly expressed among students to the effect that on the basis of a few months' courtship a couple may without risk enter upon an engagement of several years' duration.[4]

In computing the length of the engagement period it is important to consider the distance which separates the engaged couple. The engagement of individuals parted for long periods of time because of war, employment, prolonged professional training, or other enforced absences is hardly to be compared with the engagement of young people who see each other day in and day out.

Engagements in the face of separation

In the ideal engagement the announcement should normally be followed by more or less constant association. The pair needs time to win the approval of the families, relatives, and friends of both parties. This necessitates being seen in public together long enough for people to say, "I think they make a fine pair; they ought to hit it off nicely." The support of the public is not to be disregarded, even in these times, and it is hard to obtain public support of the marriage-to-be by correspondence. There are, however, young couples who are working out their engagement duties quite conscientiously by correspondence. How are they doing it?

First, every effort is made to keep letters full of information about day-to-day experiences which tell about the changes in personality. The correspondents go in for frequent exchange of candid photographs and snapshots. These keep the couple up to date on physical appearance (new clothes, changes in weight, etc.) and give a visual picture of the places and people each is meeting. These tokens later act as a source of common experience to tie the couple together.

Second, the couples find that some questions may be discussed more deeply and somewhat more objectively by correspondence than in face-to-face chats; for example, attitudes about children, money, religion, a wife's working, the use of leisure time, and the place of sex in marriage. Letters most certainly should not preclude many face-to-face talks on these subjects at some later date, but during the separation they can serve to clear up many questions.

A third approach used by successful correspondents is to refer to particularly enjoyable books and newspaper and magazine articles as a means of getting the reaction of the other on questions of mutual in-

---

[4] Henry Bowman, *Marriage for Moderns*, New York: McGraw-Hill, 1948, p. 249.

terest. "I read an interesting article you may enjoy. Remember your discussion about women working? Tell me what you think of it."

Certain engagement functions have to wait until the pair is reunited to be worked out satisfactorily. The aspect of marriage preparation having to do with living together in intimate association is an art that takes practice; the skills of getting along together must be learned. Engagement by correspondence prepares only for a marriage in which most contacts are by correspondence and might be good preparation for marriage with a traveling salesman. For normal, settled married living, however, there is no substitute for daily association over a period of time to learn the art of resolving conflicts, of cooperative planning, of joint functioning, all of which are learned only by doing.

Should Engagement Mean "No Stepping Out"?

While it should be understood that an engagement is a monopoly, when the couple is to be separated indefinitely does that preclude dating others? Some couples will find it to their advantage to continue dating while separated, regarding it as recreation and as a valuable social experience, while other couples who have doubts may well decide to forego dating until their own engagement is firmly established.

In a survey at the University of Wisconsin, 65 per cent of 608 students disapproved of stepping out, 14 per cent approved, and the balance were undecided.[5] This study was made in peacetime rather than wartime when many engaged couples are separated for long periods of time. Bowman[6] favors a policy that permits dating for engaged students who attend colleges in widely separated towns, feeling that otherwise an engaged student's social life is too curtailed for his own best development. Such dating, moreover, may help to relieve the strain of separation. Bowman adds, "It is also a good test of the couple's devotion, for if their love and trust cannot withstand a simple test like this, they are not ready to marry and their engagement is insubstantial."[7]

There are several suggestions for dating with others while engaged: (1) The dating should be for recreation or convenience without amorous interest in the other person. (2) The dating should not be limited to one person exclusively. (3) The dating should be with the full understanding and approval of the affianced. (4) The dating should not

---

[5] Unpublished study by Reuben Hill.
[6] Bowman, *op. cit.*, p. 253.
[7] Bowman, *op. cit.*, p. 254.

be expected to come up to the standards of enjoyment of dating with the affianced, and unfavorable comparisons should not be made.

A question which frequently troubles young people entering upon an engagement is how much of the past should be revealed to the other. In the Wisconsin survey, 29 per cent of the women disapproved of revealing the past and 33 per cent were undecided, 24 per cent of the men disapproved and 33 per cent were undecided.[8] There should be frank discussion during the engagement period; indeed, that is one of engagement's major functions. However, there is no obligation to rattle all the family skeletons in a recital of past misdeeds and foolish indiscretions. These might be better taken up with a counselor, minister, family physician, or trained specialist who will hear them out without becoming emotionally involved. *Revealing the past*

Items having a bearing on the couple's future that should come out in the frank discussions of the engagement period are: (1) a previous marriage and any financial obligations which that might entail; (2) hereditary or other defects which might involve reasons for not having children; (3) a history of tuberculosis, heart disease, venereal disease, mental breakdown, etc.; (4) an imprisonment record; (5) debts or similar obligations which might handicap the marriage.

How Much Intimacy during Engagement? [9]

One of the most difficult of the questions of the engagement period is the extent of physical intimacy. Some caressing and expressing of warm affection is normally expected and is helpful in the processes of preparation for the intimacies of marriage. But while some love-making is desirable, full expression of the sex urge in premarital sex intercourse often brings hazards of guilt and shame which are extremely difficult for conventionally reared couples to overcome. Not all couples are so troubled, however. Burgess and Wallin in their study of one thousand engaged couples divided them into three groups on the basis of their experience with the problem of premarital intercourse: [10]

1. The first set constitutes couples firmly opposed to premarital relations whose firmness of conviction leads them to limit their physical intimacies. Their ideals and restricted stimulation combine to make them relatively free of strain in refraining from intercourse.

---

[8] See Chapter 5.
[9] For other discussions of the issues of intimacy before marriage, see Chapter 8.
[10] Ernest W. Burgess and Paul Wallin, *Engagement and Marriage*, Chicago: Lippincott, 1953, pp. 387–390.

2. The second group are couples who engage in sex relations without violating their own particular religious, moral, ethical, or rational standards. Both man and fiancée agree in regarding intercourse as desirable and proper for them, seeing it as a private affair. Premarital intercourse for these couples appears to be satisfying and constitutes no problem.

3. The third group, probably the majority, are those for whom intimacies in engagement present a real dilemma. They suffer conflict between the intensity of desire for intercourse and the inhibiting effects of their moral standards. They fear pregnancy, being found out, losing respect for one another, and often report little satisfaction from sexual union when they do cross the line.

By far the strongest deterrent to sex relations of the engaged persons before marriage is their belief that it is not right. This reason leads all others including fear of pregnancy, of hurting parents' feelings, or of social disapproval.

Intercourse is not used to test compatibility, Burgess and Wallin report, but as a culmination of couples' frequent and intensive erotic stimulation. It occurs more frequently among couples having no religious affiliation, or of mixed religious backgrounds, and is associated with previous sexual experiences with other persons. It occurs more often in less well-adjusted engagements and in broken engagements, and also tends to occur more frequently in couples engaged longer than sixteen months.[11]

The incidence of sexual intercourse among engaged couples is about 50 per cent, according to the studies by Terman, Locke, and Burgess and Wallin. For those engaged couples who need help in setting limits on intimacies it is wise to have some kind of understanding on the matter of "how far shall we go?" so that each can notify the other when they approach the boundaries set. Such understandings may naturally emerge out of the day-to-day contacts themselves. Some days Jim may be able to take less of Mary's tantalizing proximity than other days. If he whisks her from his lap with a gentle indication that she is too much for him at the moment, she may accept both her attractiveness and his response to her. When recognized in time, such experiences need not be as frustrating as they are later on in intense love play. Here are some of the signs of "time to stop and do something else":

1. When either is flushed and uncomfortable, driven on by an urgency to continue the petting.

2. When either finds himself restless and sleepless for extended periods after being with the other.

---

[11] *Ibid.*, pp. 353–390.

3. When the love play becomes for one or both an unpleasant memory with aspects of shame or guilt.
4. When being with the loved one is fun only when there are physical contacts.

The student will be able to add his own guideposts to these general ones in setting up his own boundaries for engagement conduct.

Does Every Engaged Couple Have Doubts?

Engagement uncovers almost as many problems as it solves. Fortunate indeed is the couple that does not end the probation period with many doubts and mixed feelings. The disillusionment spoken of so frequently as occurring during the first year of marriage may come before the wedding as a result of the questions raised in the engagement period. Still, it is probably better to face these realities all along the way than to meet them unexpectedly in early marriage.

An engaged couple will do well to recognize at the outset that they will have occasional misunderstandings accompanied by mixed feelings and inner doubts. These differences need not be a source of shock, however, if the couple expects them to occur and develops methods for ironing them out instead of dwelling on the seriousness of the conflicts.

Engagement is entered into by most people in America during the transition between adolescence and adulthood, a period of doubts and uncertainties. Those who are engaged may make the mistake of ascribing these feelings of uneasiness to the engagement and the new relationship. Realizing the fact that everyone in this stage of life faces many problems may help relieve the situation for some; part of the difficulty is just that of growing up. Another source of doubt may be in the discrepancy between the flesh-and-blood person and the dream the affianced has built up. The fact that no couple faces marriage with absolute knowledge and conviction of its ability to survive the crises ahead remains a source of insecurity throughout engagement; the jittery couple applying for a marriage license is an American stereotype.

How widespread is this phenomenon of doubts and mixed feelings about the engagement? Burgess and Wallin report that nearly half of their engaged couples had hesitated at some point: 25 per cent broke up one or more times during the engagement, 22 per cent wished they had not become engaged, and 15 per cent broke the engagement before the study was completed. Clearly an engagement is a tenuous relationship.[12]

---

[12] Burgess and Wallin, *op. cit.*, pp. 180–183.

Elopement as
an escape

Some couples, faced with doubts about engagement, feel they may escape part of the responsibility by eloping. An elopement is often as much an impulsive escape from the realities of engagement and marriage as the hysterical breaking of an engagement on the eve of the wedding. Although conflict with parents is frequently the alleged cause, the desire to escape reality is prominent. The elopement is usually carried off in haste, is inappropriate to the situation, and bodes poorly for marital happiness. Popenoe studied 738 elopements and grouped those who eloped to avoid publicity, those who eloped to escape elaborate, expensive weddings, and those who eloped because of pregnancy. The marital adjustments of the eloped couples were poorer than those of other married couples; apparently their escape from doubts and inner conflict was poorly conceived—they "jumped from the frying pan into the fire." [13]

Apart from the escape element there are objections to elopement. The eloping couple are bypassing the testing and exploring functions of the engagement period during which the gradual preparation for marriage occurs. Furthermore, they are alienating their in-laws and friends whose support they will need frequently in the days ahead.

What Engagements Should Be Broken?

One of the most important functions of the engagement is to eliminate from marriage those matchings which cannot stand the experience of intimate association. Many engagements should be broken; a high rate of broken engagements is preferable to a high rate of divorce and desertion. Burgess and Wallin, in a study of engaged couples, report almost a third of the girls and a sixth of the men had had two or more engagements.[14] If the possibility that an engagement may be broken is recognized in the beginning, the break will be less severe for both persons. While the habits of association are difficult to cast off, in the long run a broken engagement is less painful than a separation after marriage.

What are reasons for breaking an engagement? In general, any crisis which changes the basis on which the engagement was launched justifies a re-evaluation, with sufficient discussion to arrive at an agreement as to the proper course to follow. This is good procedure in any pair relationship, whether it be engaged partners, marriage partners, business partners, or research collaborators. All find it necessary to review

---

[13] Paul Popenoe, *Modern Marriage*, New York: Macmillan, 1943, pp. 222–225.
[14] *Ibid.*, p. 136.

their relationship whenever crises occur, in order to keep the partnership intact. There is strong consensus that the following reasons justify re-evaluation of the engagement, with the possible agreement to sever the relationship: (1) recognition of fundamental feelings of alienation arising out of the more intimate relations of engagement, not just doubts and misgivings but strong feelings of incompatibility; (2) recognition that the engagement was made originally under pressure from relatives or circumstances, and that the main reason for refraining from breaking the engagement is the fear of publicity; (3) recognition that either member of the pair is emotionally dependent on parents and too immature to stand the rigors of marriage; (4) changes in the economic future due to serious accident or health breakdown or similar disaster affecting ability to earn a living and carry on the functions of parenthood.

While these reasons for breaking the engagement are rejected in individual cases, they should not be rejected because of fear of publicity, fear of admitting that one has made a mistake, fear of homicide or suicide threats, or fear that the break will ruin the other's future. "In the great majority of instances, suicide threats never get any further than the self-pity stage, and relatively few are ever carried out." [15] Threats of vengeance or of suicide exhibit a type of neuroticism that would be highly undesirable in a marriage partner and are ample reasons in themselves for breaking the engagement.

There are two reasons for allowing the girl to announce the breaking of an engagement. First, she loses status in terms of marriageability unless she is permitted to issue the announcement of the break. Second, no breach-of-promise suit can be carried out successfully against any man if the woman has announced the dissolution of the engagement. Established historically as an indemnity for the woman whose opportunities for marriage were impaired by the broken vows, breach-of-promise suits still occur occasionally. The promise to marry is a legal contract, the breaking of which gives grounds for suit for damages. One of the happy results of the improved status of women in our society is the growing feeling of disfavor toward breach-of-promise suits.

How Do You Build Your Engagement into Marriage?

The engaged couple expects to make a success of their marriage. All their plans are laid with that expectation in mind, and the public supports them in their resolutions. Some day there may be special orienta-

---

[15] Bowman, *op. cit.*, p. 260.

tion classes in every community to introduce engaged couples to marriage as a civilian is processed into army life. Industrial plants consider it important to give their new employees weeks of orientation into their policies and objectives, as well as into the ways of behavior in the organization, before entrusting them with free access to the plant. Marriage is worthy of even more careful attention. Some communities are now offering classes for engaged couples and there are marriage courses in over 1200 colleges and universities. In time, young people everywhere will be able to receive such instructions. There are now many helpful books and pamphlets available, as well as several tests and prediction scales.

Few people attempt to build a house without consulting an architect. Marriage, also, is given design and symmetry only after careful planning and study. Intelligent couples say, "Nothing's too good for our marriage," and the careful planning which their premarriage interviews stimulate gives them a head start on less careful students.

Premarriage counseling

Premarital counseling often starts early in the courtship period and continues throughout the engagement. In addition to marriage prediction scales that test the similarity and compatibility of home and family backgrounds as well as certain social factors, the premarital counselor has available other personality tests that help determine the emotional readiness of individuals for marriage.

These tests in the hands of a skilled counselor can be extremely revealing. Suppose they indicate emotional dependence and nervousness, with tendencies toward blues and depressions. The counselor may advise remedial attention just as the physician would advise a couple to postpone having a baby until a kidney infection cleared up. The couple will not want to take a chance on marrying immediately, but will recognize that the period in which these questions are best cleared up is during engagement, not after marriage.

Some counseling centers describe their premarital guidance as a "premarital consultation." Actually the guidance program may take weeks and sometimes longer if problems are uncovered which deserve detailed attention. The premarital consultation is a personal course of instruction adapted to prepare young people for marriage by giving special attention to the individual background and specific needs of the couples concerned. In general, it includes: (1) a review of the personal and family backgrounds in an effort to locate the important factors that may influence marriage and avert avoidable mismating; (2) a study of the characteristics of the person, the temperament, disposition, and other emotional inclinations and attitudes, by means of interviews and tests; (3) specific sex instruction geared to clear up misconceptions, questions, and fears; (4) guidance in the healthiest approach to marriage, its problems and responsibilities as well as its possibilities for growth and development; (5) conferences and consultations with both members of the couple, and separately at the discretion of the counselor. Group conferences and classes in marriage and family courses also provide helps to the engaged couple anticipating marriage; (6) a thorough physical examination by a qualified physician.[16]

The engagement is the best preview of the marriage pattern for any given couple. The optimum length of engagement is best stated as "long enough"—to perform the many functions of testing, discussing, learning, fighting, and loving which underlie successful marriage. All the processes welding a couple together in courtship continue with greater force in engagement, but they operate with less uncertainty, because there is less danger that the relationship will be disrupted. The engagement provides opportunity for maximum planning, and learning how to make jointly choices which both parties can accept and support individually. The engagement operates as a preventive of divorce, since in breaking up those matchings which cannot stand the experience of intimate association, in effect it brings about a divorce before marriage itself.

Summary

READINGS

Becker, Howard, and Reuben Hill (eds.), *Family, Marriage and Parenthood*. Boston: Heath, 1955, Chapter IX, "The Engagement."

Burgess, Ernest W., and Paul Wallin, *Engagement and Marriage*. Chicago: Lippincott, 1953, especially Chapters V through VIII.

Cavan, Ruth S., *American Marriage, A Way of Life*. New York: Crowell, 1959, Chapter 9, "Engagement, the Anticipation of Marriage."

Duvall, Evelyn M., "Courtship and Engagement" in Morris Fishbein and Ernest W. Burgess (eds.), *Successful Marriage* (Rev. Ed.). Garden City: Doubleday, 1955, pp. 28–41.

Duvall, Sylvanus M., *Before You Marry*. New York: Association Press, 1959.

Himes, Norman E., and Donald L. Taylor, *Your Marriage*. New York: Rinehart, 1955, Chapters 7–8, "Engagement Problems" and "Engagement Planning Opportunities."

Mace, David R., *Marriage*. New York: Doubleday, 1952, Chapter 2, "Are Engagements Necessary?"

Magoun, F. Alexander, *Love and Marriage*. New York: Harper, 1956, Chapter 8, "The Period of Engagement."

Waller, Willard, and Reuben Hill, *The Family: A Dynamic Interpretation*. New York: Dryden Press, 1951, Chapter 12, "The Engagement: A Bridge to Marriage."

---

[16] See the details covered by the physician in his examination, in Chapter 7.

7 Sex Structure and Function

What are the basic facts of life?

Is doing what comes naturally enough?

How does a baby get started?

How many children can you have?

What is the danger of venereal infection?

Why get a premarital examination?

Most couples look forward to marriage as establishing their right to live together as man and wife. They usually have many questions about the nature of man and of woman and what happens in marriage. The evidence is that, although sex is widely discussed today, there are few men and women who clearly understand even the most elemental facts of life.[1]

What Are the Basic Facts of Life?

This chapter reviews the knowledges pertinent for young adults at the threshold of marriage. The names of the sex organs, functions, and conditions are italicized as an aid to adequate vocabulary, so important in communication in the sex side of marriage.

The male sex glands are two firm oval bodies about one and one half inches long which hang from the lower part of the front of the body between the thighs in a sac called the *scrotum*. These are called *testes* and have two important roles to play. They produce a *hormone* (chemical substance) called *testosterone* which is largely responsible for the

Male sex organs

---

[1] Kenneth S. Clarke, *Sex Knowledge Inventory of College Students in Selected Classes,* Master's Thesis, University of Illinois, Urbana, 1957.

135

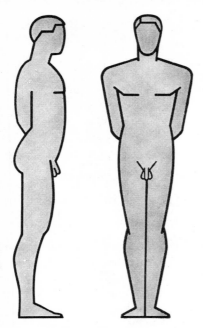

ADULT MALE BODY

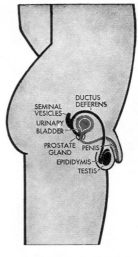

SEMINAL
VESICLES

DUCTUS
DEFERENS

URINARY
BLADDER

PROSTATE
GLAND

PENIS

EPIDIDYMIS

TESTIS

MALE UROGENITAL SYSTEM

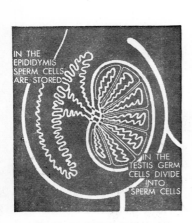

IN THE
EPIDIDYMIS
SPERM CELLS
ARE STORED

IN THE
TESTIS GERM
CELLS DIVIDE
INTO
SPERM CELLS

DETAILS OF TESTIS (Schematic)

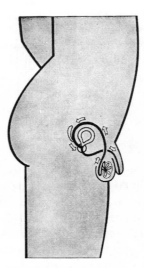

PATH OF SPERM CELLS

From *Life and Growth* by Alice V. Keliher (Appleton-Century)

Fig. 11 MALE SEX ORGANS

development of masculine characteristics, and they produce the male germ cells known as *sperm cells, spermatozoa,* or *male gametes,* by means of which a man is able to produce children.

Testosterone is absorbed directly into the blood stream and is carried to all parts of the body. Its presence produces the male type of body build, hair distribution, vocal range, and all other characteristics that go to make up the maleness of an individual.

Sperm cells are formed within tiny tubules in each *testis.* These empty into the *epididymis,* which leads into a slender tube, the *ductus deferens,* or *vas deferens.* A vas rises on either side and through it the spermatozoa travel slowly upward. Each vas runs upward from the scrotum into the lower part of the body, ending behind the bladder. Close by on either side, the *seminal vesicles* furnish the bulk of the fluid in which sperms are suspended. Surrounding the *urethra* in the region where the two *vasa deferentia* (plural of vas deferens) open into it, is a firm globular gland known as the *prostate.* This produces a secretion which nourishes and activates the sperm cells. Together the spermatozoa, the fluid from the seminal vesicles, and the prostate make up the *semen.*

The urethra runs through the *penis,* which in its relaxed position hangs just in front of the scrotum. At times of sexual excitement, the penis becomes engorged with blood and stands erect from the body. When *ejaculation* occurs sperms spurt out of the reservoirs through the ejaculatory ducts, through the prostate, and with the seminal and prostatic fluid are carried out of the body through the urethral opening in the penis. Hundreds of millions of sperm cells are present in the half-teaspoonful of semen that is released in the average ejaculate.

Semen is released during sexual intercourse, masturbation, or unconsciously during sleep. The latter process is known as *nocturnal emission,* or "wet dream," and is nature's way of eliminating stored secretions when there has been no other more active form of expulsion. Such release occurs first at *puberty* (period of establishment of sexual maturity) and continues to take place with some degree of regularity during intervals of sexual *continence* (abstinence from intentional ejaculation of semen). It has definitely been established that a man may remain continent for long periods of time, or indeed for a lifetime, without injuring his health or destroying his masculinity.

The sex glands in the female are about the same size as those in the male, but they lie within the abdominal cavity, low on the right and left sides. They are called *ovaries,* and like the testes, have two important functions. They produce the hormones which control the femininity of the individual, the two most important of which are known as

Female sex organs

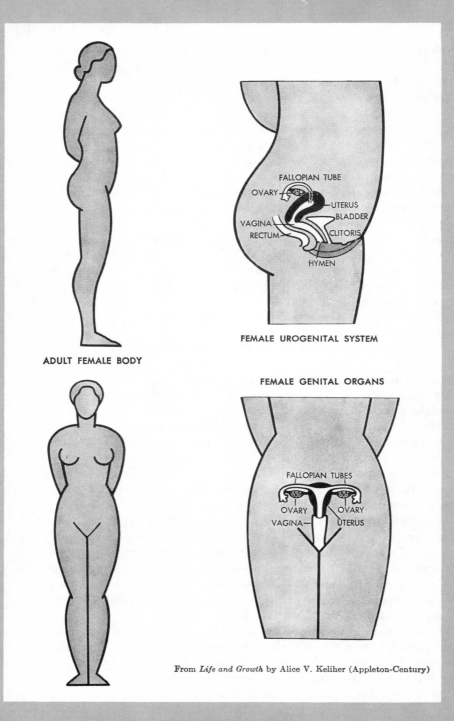

ADULT FEMALE BODY

FEMALE UROGENITAL SYSTEM

FALLOPIAN TUBE

OVARY

UTERUS

VAGINA

BLADDER

RECTUM

CLITORIS

HYMEN

FEMALE GENITAL ORGANS

FALLOPIAN TUBES

OVARY

OVARY

VAGINA

UTERUS

From *Life and Growth* by Alice V. Keliher (Appleton-Century)

Fig. 12 FEMALE SEX ORGANS

estrin (*estrogen*) and *progestin,* and they also produce the female germ cells which are known as *female gametes, ova,* or *eggs.*

Millions of sperm cells are formed daily during the active life of the male, but the female is born with all of the ova she ever possesses. From the time of puberty until the *menopause* (that period which marks the termination of the ability to bear children, commonly known as "the change of life") one ovum each month ripens and is expelled from the ovary. The production of hormones is related in large measure to the ripening of the ova. As an ovum begins to mature, estrin is produced and is carried by the blood stream from the ovary to the *uterus.* This stimulates the growth of the inner lining of the uterus and produces an initial preparation for pregnancy. When the ovum is mature it is expelled from the ovary (*ovulation*), and progestin is produced in the ovary. This hormone is also carried by the blood to the uterus and acts upon it to bring about the final preparation for pregnancy. After the ovum is expelled from the ovary it enters the Fallopian tube where, if sperm are present, *fertilization* (entrance of the sperm into the egg) occurs, and subsequently the fertilized egg journeys into the uterus, where it becomes implanted into the already prepared wall. The secretion of progestin continues throughout pregnancy.

If the ovum is not fertilized it dies within a few hours after its expulsion from the ovary. Despite this the uterus, under the influence of progestin, continues its preparation for pregnancy for ten or twelve days. By the end of this time the production of progestin ceases. The sudden cessation in the production of progestin affects the uterus and causes the vessels in the lining to bleed. This bleeding is the result of the fact that the body has prepared for pregnancy, but no pregnancy has taken place. This flow is called *menstruation* and consists of blood, mucus, and shreds of uterine lining. It lasts for three to five days. Before the menstrual flow stops, another ovum begins to mature; estrin is again formed and another period of preparation for pregnancy is on its way. This is what is called the menstrual cycle.

The female internal organs of reproduction other than the ovaries are the *Fallopian tubes, uterus* (*womb*), and *vagina.* The vagina forms the lowermost portion and is the canal into which semen is ejaculated from the penis during sexual intercourse. The uterus hangs above the vagina; it is a muscular, pear-shaped organ consisting of a lower small, cone-shaped or cylindrical portion known as the *cervix,* which extends into the vagina, and a large upper portion, in which the baby develops during pregnancy.

Extending up and out from each side of the upper portion of the uterus are the Fallopian tubes. The outer funnel-shaped ends of the tubes lie close to the ovaries so that when an ovum is liberated it is drawn into the open end of one of the tubes. Spermatozoa which may have been deposited in the vagina move upward through the opening of the cervix, into the main cavity of the uterus, and on into the Fallopian tubes. Fertilization normally takes place in one or the other of the tubes.

The lower end of the vagina has a puckered, crescent-shaped, pliable thin cuff of membrane called the *hymen*. In some virgins this is but a narrow rim of tissue; in others it forms a partial membrane which is easily stretched during cleansing procedures or at the time of first intercourse; and in others its thickness necessitates dilation or surgical nicking before sexual intercourse can take place.

The *external genitalia* (outer sex organs) include two hair-covered folds called the *labia majora* and two small inner folds known as *labia minora*. Between these lie the openings of the vagina and the urethra, and situated above the latter is a small structure called the *clitoris*, which is not unlike a rudimentary penis. This organ, located at the front meeting of the labia minora, is usually the seat of woman's early localized erotic (sex) response, and its manipulation usually leads to her sexual excitation.

The sex act   The couple approaching marriage should understand what happens in *coitus*, how the sex responses of man and woman differ, and how to acquire the skill necessary for mutual satisfaction. Though women respond more slowly than men, a sexually awakened woman may be aroused to a high and sustained pitch that is exquisitely desirable. Woman's response is not localized to the same degree as man's and usually takes more time to arouse in the love *foreplay*, that precedes the actual introduction of the penis into the vagina. Caressing, fondling, and assurance of endearing love are as much a part of the sex act as the more highly dramatic climax that is to follow, and they must be given enough time to bring both of the partners to a readiness for the next step.

Orgasm in the man is noticeably marked by the ejaculation of semen. The woman's climax is marked by rapid breathing and a series of spasmodic sensations which release her tension. Orgasm in both man and woman is followed soon by supreme feelings of satisfaction and tenderness. Occasionally a woman is capable of and desires a multiple orgasm. When the man is not able to accomplish another erection immediately, his manual manipulation of her clitoris and vulva may be satisfactory. Any activity or position in coitus is normal and acceptable if it brings satisfaction to the couple. The duration of the sex act varies from a few minutes in its basic biological component to an hour or more where the foreplay and afterplay are extended. The frequency of intercourse differs widely. During the first few weeks of marriage it might take place nightly. Later in the marriage it may take place one, two, or three times a week. Crests in the woman's desire may make for more frequency at certain times of the month. A great deal of variation is normal so long as the partners themselves find the arrangement satisfactory.

Is Doing What Comes Naturally Enough?

It is commonly assumed that as soon as a man and his wife are alone together, they will find ecstatic bliss in doing whatever their instincts command. This is a reason for a great deal of unhappiness and disillusionment in early marriage. Actually, few couples make a mutually satisfactory adjustment to each other in their most intimate associations from the very first.

The establishment of a good sex adjustment is often not accomplished immediately after marriage. It may take the couple many weeks or months to achieve.[2] This is especially true if the bride is not fully ready for the consummation of the marriage. Such factors as a tough and resistant hymen, or a slight spasm of the muscles at the opening of the vagina, may be painful and so add to the fear and resistance of the bride. The husband's impatient urgency in possessing his bride can be frightening to the girl who is less sexually aroused and ready. Conditions conducive to a satisfactory sex experience such as personal hygiene, and quiet, private surroundings often are not as incidental as they may seem.

Sex manuals have so stressed the importance of both husband and wife reaching the climax simultaneously, that many young couples feel inadequate in their first efforts. Actually, the young husband's response is usually more rapid than that of his bride. Only as the man gains experience with his wife is he able to quicken her readiness and to slow down his crescendo of passion to more nearly approximate hers. The young bride, meanwhile, must throw aside her inhibitions and learn to relax in the delights of her marital bed. There comes a time in many marriages when husband and wife do often reach the climax at approximately the same time. But such perfect timing is not essential for mutually shared satisfaction.

---

[2] Judson T. Landis, "Adjustments after Marriage," *Marriage and Family Living*, IX, May, 1947, pp. 32–34.

Impotence, frigidity, and sexual incompatibility

It sometimes happens that the husband or wife or both find that they cannot respond effectively as sex partners. The inability to have or maintain an erection on the part of the man is called *impotence*, and is likely to be humiliating and difficult for both the man and his wife. This inability to perform the sex act in a desirable manner results usually from deep-seated psychological fears and feelings of guilt that yield best to psychiatric attention rather than to any localized or purely physical treatment. Quacks have exploited men for years with promises of quick return of full sex functioning.

Lack of sex response in the woman is even more frequent and is the cause of much distress in married living. *Frigidity* in the woman may be expressed in absence of sensation, with an inability to experience orgasm or to get release in intercourse, or in an active dislike of the whole experience, with accompanying pain, nervousness, and feelings of revulsion. This condition frequently results from one of the following causes: (1) faulty early sex education, (2) a feeling that sex is shameful, (3) resentment at being a woman, (4) hostility toward the husband, or (5) fear of being hurt or becoming pregnant. Any of these is sufficient to make the woman unable to enter eagerly into the relationship. Temporary withholding of sex relationships because of anger is not infrequent even among fairly well-adjusted women, and is a mild manifestation of chronic frigidity.

Few women enter marriage sexually awakened and ready for complete response in the sex act. Many American girls are brought up to be "nice," to repulse the advances of men, and to refrain from any genital stimulation. Marriage demands a completely different pattern of behavior, and it is extremely difficult to remake oneself overnight. To overcome the conditioning of a lifetime and replace it by the attitude of mature marital cooperation takes time. An understanding husband and/or professional help before an unsatisfactory pattern becomes too well established prove helpful in correcting this condition in many women.

So-called *sexual incompatibility* is rarely a physical problem, but rather one that emerges through the lack of the knowledges, skills, attitudes, and appreciations necessary to build mutual compatibility. Any two relatively normal man and woman can become sex partners in a purely mechanical sense. But achieving the potentials of the sex relation as love-in-action is quite another matter.

The language of sexual communication

Sex is a highly complex type of interpersonal communication. As such it must be learned—much as any other language has to be mastered before it is spoken fluently or understood fully. The beginner is clumsy and awkward, literal and unfamiliar with the many phrases, forms, and idioms that could express his feeling. With time and devoted practice couples develop many idiosyncratic love gestures which they use to advantage in communicating their love for one another.

Marital communication begins with the initial step of expressing pleasure and displeasure. When the wife lets her husband know which of his love-making efforts are enjoyable and which are painful, she gives him the cues he needs for learning the particular forms of caressing that awaken her most fully. If the man can indicate to his wife more specifically just what he enjoys he encourages her to take her part in the sexual responsibility they both share.

In those instances where couples mutually defy each other by withholding response they communicate hostility rather than love. They practice the devices of hatred that make of marriage a nightmare and a mockery. These are not solely problems of sex adjustment as such, but rather indications of personality maladjustment being expressed through the sex act. Marriage counseling and psychiatric help are indicated before such difficulties become either critical or chronic.

For the majority of married couples, there is a great deal of devotion and affection expressed in the personal language of love This is achieved by patiently practicing many varied communicative arts in their most intimate moments together. Realizing that such complete intercommunication does not come all at once in married love any more than it does in any other language, helps each encourage the other to effectively and fully express what otherwise might be inarticulate between them.

How Does a Baby Get Started?

During intercourse semen is discharged from the penis into the upper end of the vagina. Many sperm pass through the opening in the cervix into the body of the uterus and out into the Fallopian tubes. Here fertilization takes place if an ovum is present.

The steps in fertilization are:

1. The ovum ripens in the ovary
2. The mature ovum escapes from the ovary into the tube
3. The ovum goes through the tube toward the uterus
4. Sperm cells deposited in the vagina travel up into the tubes
5. One sperm cell unites with the ovum in the tube
6. The fertilized ovum is implanted in the uterus

Immediately after the egg is fertilized it begins to divide rapidly into many cells, and by the time it has passed down through the tube and has reached its final point of attachment in the uterine lining, considerable development has taken place. Continued division and specialization of cells soon produce the *fetus* (baby within the uterine cavity), *surrounding membranes* enclosing fluid within which the fetus lies, and the *placenta,* a structure to which the fetus is attached by the *umbilical cord* and through which the fetus receives all of the oxygen and food material necessary for its development. There is no direct connection between the circulation of the mother and that of the fetus. Blood of both enters the placenta but always remains separated by vessel walls, and all exchange of food takes place across these membranes. Growth is very rapid, and at the end of nine months the fetus has increased in weight 800,000,000 times!

The baby is born through the birth canal (vagina) in a three-stage process known as *labor.* The first stage may last for fourteen hours or more for the first baby, and consists of muscular contractions which dilate the cervix sufficiently to allow the baby to pass through. The second stage of labor (one or more hours) is marked by intense bearing-down pains which expel the baby. Usually the head comes first. The final stage is the separation and expulsion of the *afterbirth.* See the series of photographs and the fuller treatment of this subject in Chapter 18.

How Many Children Can You Have?

The normally fertile couple may expect one pregnancy to follow the previous one by intervals of a year or two more or less. Some women are physically able to take such frequent pregnancies without injuring their health or increasing the hazards for the newcomer. Many families, however, prefer to space the arrival of their children to provide adequately for the care of the children already in the home, the optimum well-being of the mother, and the readiness of the family for an additional member. For these reasons the normal healthy couple consider seriously the means by which they may limit the number and plan for the arrival of their babies. This usually means the use of some type of contraceptive device or technique. Abstaining from intercourse except for procreation is so extremely difficult for the normal couple living together that *continence* is rarely advocated. *Abortions* are so dangerous (see fuller discussion in Chapter 18—"Where Babies Come From") that they are generally deplored as the most unfortunate means of limiting family size.

In wider use in the voluntary prevention of pregnancy are the efforts to prevent the sperm and the egg from meeting. This is called *birth control,* or more accurately, *contraception.* There are many procedures, devices, and materials, some of which the man may use, and others which are the woman's responsibility. Of the methods now in use, no one is 100 per cent certain and all leave something to be desired in simplicity, effectiveness, and personal acceptability.

One of the oldest attempts at contraception is *coitus interruptus,* in which the man withdraws the erect penis from the vagina before the ejaculation. This abrupt interruption of the full sex act robs the couple of complete fulfillment, and is rarely acceptable to a well-mated pair. Furthermore, since droplets of semen containing live sperm appear before the ejaculation, this method is not reliable in preventing conception.

The *rhythm method* is dependent upon an accurate plotting of supposedly reliable regular periods of fertility and sterility in the monthly cycle of the woman. The fertile period occurs roughly midway between menstrual periods, leaving the days just preceding and immediately following the menstrual flow as "safe" periods. Fluctuations in length of the cycle and variations in the time of ovulation make an accurate plotting of the occurrence of ovulation difficult.

Doctors and birth control clinics prescribe mechanical devices and chemical preparations to prevent conception. These are fitted to the needs of the particular couple and have become widely accepted. Moreover, the religious, social, and medical needs of the couples are respected and taken into full consideration by expert marriage counselors in the premarital conference discussed later in this chapter.

In case of chronic illness (such as severe heart disease, active tuberculosis, etc.) of the wife, and for other serious reasons where having children would be dangerous, permanent prevention of pregnancy may be accomplished by *sterilization.* This procedure in no way interferes with menstruation, or with the normal sex life of either the man or the woman. Tying the tubes of the woman to permanently prevent the meeting of sperm and egg is a major operation. Cutting and tying of the vasa deferentia of the man is a simple procedure and in no way affects the masculinity of the husband or interferes with normal sex desires and intercourse.

What Is the Danger of Venereal Infection?

Two persons who have limited their sex intercourse to each other face no problem of venereal disease. When either of them has consorted with someone else, before or after marriage, the possibility of venereal disease is introduced. Syphilis and gonorrhea, the two most serious venereal infections, are contracted by sexual contact.

Gonorrhea in the woman has its start in an infection of the urethra and cervix. If not treated skillfully it may move up from the vagina, through the cervix, and the uterus, into the tubes, and even on into the abdominal cavity, where it may cause peritonitis. The tubes frequently close as a result of the infection, causing sterility thereafter, since the sperm can no longer get through to meet the egg.

The progress of gonorrhea in the man is somewhat similar. Starting at the point of contact, it may progress up through the entire genital tract, leaving blockages in its wake. It is the most frequent cause of male sterility, since it produces closure of the tubes of the epididymis.

The early symptoms of gonorrhea are frequent burning, and painful urination, and a lemon-yellow discharge from the site of infection. Prompt, effective medical treatment is imperative. The use of sulfa or penicillin has greatly increased speedy and complete recovery, especially if treatment is started at the outset of infection.

It is of utmost importance to understand that the germ of gonorrhea can easily be carried (by means of towels, hands, etc.) from infected and discharging parts to the eyes of the person having the disease. This may result in a severe infection of the eye which, unless promptly and properly treated, may result in blindness. Blindness in the newborn has been almost entirely eliminated by the use of a suitable drug in the eyes of the baby at birth. This kills the gonococci (germs of gonorrhea) that may have been present in the mother and could infect the baby's eyes in its passage through the vagina.

Syphilis is caused by a minute corkscrewlike organism called a *spirochete* ("ch" as "k"). This germ is caught from the infected person at the point of contact—usually the genitalia and rarely the lips or mouth. A few days after the infection a hard sore called a *chancre,* teeming with spirochetes, appears at the point of infection. The second stage of skin rash and patches on the mucous membranes follows. The disease may then become latent for months or years, after which severe damage to the central nervous system (brain and spinal cord), to the heart and blood vessels, or to other vital organs may cause insanity, paralysis, and death. Because of its many different manifestations, syphilis is frequently called "the great masquerader." It is one disease which cannot be self-treated. A reliable physician or clinic should be sought as soon as possible after infection may have taken place, and the treatment must be continued until the patient is completely cured and officially released.

Treatment of the syphilitic mother greatly reduces the likelihood of *congenital syphilis* in infancy, especially when treatment is begun before the fifth month of the pregnancy. For that reason routine tests for syphilis (Wassermann or Kahn) are given expectant mothers so that if the disease is present treatment may be started while there is still time to protect the baby.

The man may protect himself from infection by the use of a protective sheath or other prophylactic materials, with immediate resort to physician or prophylactic station following contact. No similar prophylactic measures are available to the female because of the more generalized nature of her sexual contact.

So-called "innocent infections" through nonsexual contact have been reduced through the wide use of paper drinking cups, paper towels, and the general acceptance of hygiene. Venereal infection of the adult through nonsexual contact is rare.

Laws have been passed in most states requiring the examination of both men and women before marriage for presence of venereal infection. Syphilis is diagnosed by Wassermann or Kahn blood tests, and gonorrhea by the microscopic examination of a smear from the cervix and urethra. Infected persons are allowed to marry only when treatment has reduced the disease to a noninfectious stage.

Why Get a Premarital Examination?

The premarital examination has been a boon to many couples in detecting and clearing up a variety of treatable problems and in offering an opportunity to raise the questions pertinent to the establishment of a successful marriage. What may be expected in the premarital examination depends upon both the physician and the couple. Here are some of the things a well-trained doctor and an alert couple keep in mind to be included.

1. Medical history including the previous sex history of both the man and the woman, possible heredity problems in either line, and the menstrual history of the woman.
2. Clarification of any questions one or both members of the couple bring in, along with any that arise during the consultation. Selected books may be recommended as helpful.
3. Brief review of the anatomy and physiology of both male and female genital systems in the human (with charts or films if desired).
4. General physical examination including blood and urine studies, heart, lung, and pelvic conditions, and search for any possible pathologies in both the man and the woman.

5. Pelvic examination of the woman with especial attention to the condition of the vaginal orifice and the adequacy of the vagina for sexual intercourse.

6. Possible instruction in a program of hymen dilation, where indicated and compatible with the attitudes of the couple.

7. Examination of the clitoris, and plan for freeing the clitoris as indicated.

8. Laboratory study of cultures from vagina and cervix with especial concern for the presence of gonorrheal infection, with immediate program of treatment if tests prove positive.

9. Examination of the male genitalia with laboratory tests and a program of treatment for possible infection. (Sperm count and motility may be included if desired.)

10. Blood tests for the detection of syphilis in both individuals. Positive findings are followed at once by adequate treatment. No evidence of the disease is the clean bill of health required in most states before the license is issued.

11. Discussion of plans for contraception, as requested, with particular reference to the initial period of the marriage, and the religious factors that may be pertinent: (a) plan for plotting the "safe period" if rhythm method is to be used, or (b) fitting a diaphragm if religious and personal factors allow it.

12. Specific advice on vaginal lubricants and coital procedures as requested and indicated.

Obviously such a program of premarital consultation cannot be carried out effectively in one brief office call. It is usually wise for the couple to go for their first premarital consultation as soon as the definite date has been set for the wedding (see Chapter 9, "Your Wedding Plans").

At that time, the general exploration of common factors included in items one through three above may be covered, and appointments made for more detailed physical examinations of both man and woman at separate times, and possibly by different physicians. It is important that the pelvic examination of the female be done some time before the marriage when possible so that a program of dilation of the hymen and correction of any remediable conditions may be effected well before the actual marriage date. It is not uncommon for the girl to take her mother or some close woman friend with her for this first pelvic examination, although it is not essential to do so.

Premarital counseling includes not only the physical examination discussed here, but also the exploration of the personality, social, cultural, family, economic, and religious factors that are important for the building of a marriage.

Happiness in marriage is dependent not alone on perfecting the physical sex act to the point of mutual fulfillment. As studies and clinical evidence have richly indicated, it lies more within the personality adjustment of each member of the couple and in their larger relationships as two whole persons than in any physical tricks or techniques. True married living revolves around such interchange as is found in planning for the children, spending the family money, making plans for vacations and holidays, rejoicing over personal advances, and comforting one another in times of illness or disappointment. It is these day-by-day experiences in common that set the stage for the fullness of sexual response which, for most couples, symbolizes their unity and is far more satisfying than the purely physical release involved.

READINGS

Blood, Robert O., Jr., *Anticipating Your Marriage*. Glencoe, Illinois: Free Press, 1955, Chapter 12, "Achieving Sexual Satisfaction in Marriage."

Brown, Fred, and Rudolf Kempton, *Sex Questions and Answers*. New York: McGraw-Hill, 1950.

Butterfield, Oliver, *Marriage and Sexual Harmony*. New York: Emerson Books, 1957.

Chesser, Eustace, *Love without Fear*. New York: Signet Books, 1949.

Clark, LeMon, *Sex and You*. New York: Bobbs-Merrill, 1949.

Duvall, Evelyn Millis, *Facts of Life and Love for Teen-Agers*. New York: Association Press, 1956.

Ellis, Albert, *Folklore of Sex*. New York: Boni, 1951.

English, O. Spurgeon, "Sex Adjustment in Marriage," Chapter 16 in Morris Fishbein and Ruby Jo Reeves Kennedy (eds.), *Modern Marriage and Family Living*. New York: Oxford University Press, 1957.

Kinsey, Alfred, Wardell Pomeroy, Clyde Martin, and Paul Gebhard, *Sexual Behavior in the Human Female*. Philadelphia: Saunders, 1953.

———, *Sexual Behavior in the Human Male*. Philadelphia: Saunders, 1948.

Landis, Judson, and Mary Landis, *Building a Successful Marriage*. New York: Prentice-Hall, 1958, Chapter 16, "Sex Adjustment in Marriage."

Levine, Lena, *The Modern Book of Marriage*. New York: Bartholomew House, 1957, Chapters 6, 20, and 21.

Rainer, Jerome, and Julia Rainer, *Sexual Pleasure in Marriage*. New York: Messner, 1959.

Rock, John, and David Loth, *Voluntary Parenthood*. New York: Random House, 1949.

Stone, Hannah, and Abraham Stone, *A Marriage Manual*. New York: Simon and Schuster, 1952.

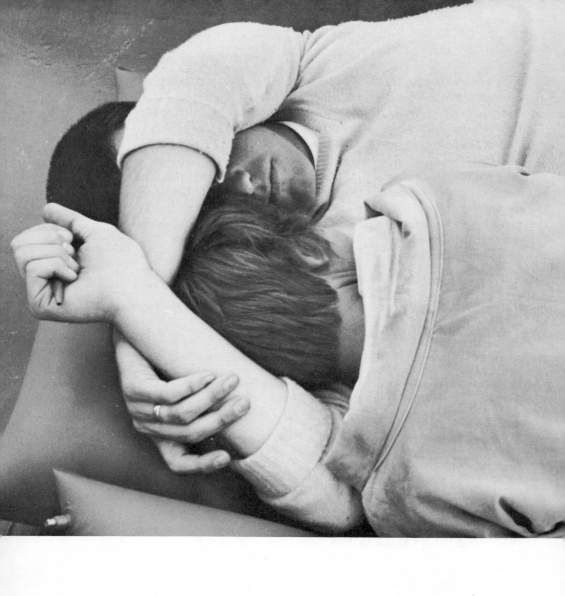

8 Sex Manners and Morals

Why are moral decisions so difficult today?

What sex outlets are there for single young people?

Is your sex conduct anyone's business but your own?

What's the harm of stepping outside the code?

How is responsive integrity developed?

What kind of person are you?

IT is hard to be sure of what is right and wrong in sex conduct today. This is largely because our society as a whole has not yet made up its mind. A half century ago the American public was narrow-minded about sex, but at least young people knew what was and what was not acceptable behavior. There was then, as there always is, extensive violation of the moral code, but there was no basic disagreement as to what it was.

Why Are Moral Decisions So Difficult Today?

Great social change has dramatically affected sex manners and morals in America in the past fifty years. Rapid industrialization with the accompanying growth of city living, two great world wars, the assimilation of people from around the world, and the intermingling of different cultural groups, have combined to raise doubt as to the validity of former sex codes for today's society. The greater freedom of women, the weakening of rigid family and community controls, and an expanding economy of abundance have resulted in high valuations of pleasure and a minimizing of the former virtues of saving for the future, hard work, and discipline.

The first sharp break with the past came at the time of the first world war when sex morals underwent a dramatic change. As Frederick Lewis Allen vividly records the spirit of the 1920's:

A whole generation had been infected by the eat-drink-and-be-merry-for-tomorrow-we-die spirit which accompanied the departure of the soldiers to the training camps and the fighting front. There had been an epidemic not only of abrupt war marriages, but of less conventional liaisons. In France, two million men had found themselves very close to filth and annihilation and very far from the American code and its defenders; prostitution had followed the flag and willing mademoiselles from Armentières had been plentiful; American girls sent over as nurses and war workers had come under the influence of continental manners and standards without being subject to the rigid protections thrown about their continental sisters of the respectable classes; and there had been a very widespread and very natural breakdown of traditional restraints and reticences and taboos. It was impossible for this generation to return unchanged when the ordeal was over.[1]

The basic change in attitude has been from one that regarded sex as essentially dirty to one that affirms sex as essentially wholesome and good. In the pendulum swing from sex rejection to sex acceptance has come widespread flaunting of sex in all areas of life. Speech and clothing, song and story, personal and social behavior all extol the charms of the human body and its potentialities for sexual pleasure. Cigarettes, cosmetics, cars, and business machines are sold with the help of scantily clad young women of promising proportions. Films and novels often owe their popularity to scenes of seduction repeated in never-ending variety. Everywhere the delectable pleasures of sex are proclaimed. Today, all but the most conservative groups acclaim sex as basically desirable and profoundly good.

Different groups have reacted in different ways to these drastic shifts in manners and morals. Opinions about sex today vary all the way from the most conservative religious position that labels any deviation from the traditional sex codes as mortal sin, to a completely non-moralistic stance in which sex is seen as a natural appetite to be appeased freely without restriction. Sexual practices within any given community differ tremendously. Some persons are openly exploitative to the point of sadism. Others seek deep spiritual and emotional meanings in their sexual communion. Some are proudly promiscuous while others find their satisfactions with complete monogamy. Where does all this leave the individual trying to decide which of the moral paths to follow?

Analysis of thousands of young people's questions finds today's youth greatly confused and eagerly seeking sound answers to their ever-present sex questions.[2] Just what is expected of a girl on a date? Should

---

[1] Frederick Lewis Allen, *Only Yesterday,* New York: Harper, 1931, p. 94.

[2] Evelyn Millis Duvall, *Facts of Life and Love for Teen-Agers.* New York: Association Press, 1956. Based upon an analysis of 25,000 questions from high school, college, and out-of-school young people of both sexes.

she kiss her escort good night the first time she goes out with him? How does she refuse and still remain his dating partner? Does a girl have to pet to be popular? If she doesn't will she lose her boy friend to some girl who will? If she does will he think less of her? How can a girl avoid sex-toned situations with a boy she does not care for? How does a girl go about keeping a particular relationship within the bounds that are appropriate to it? Just what is appropriate in various situations, relationships, and stages of involvement?

Boys' questions are quite as searching. Is a boy expected to "sow his wild oats" before he settles down in marriage? Does he have to prove his masculinity by getting sex experience during his teens? If he does should he be proud of his premarital adventures or ashamed of them? These questions reflect a cultural contradiction on what is expected of a man in his relationship with women. The official sex code calls for premarital chastity. The man's world of locker room, barracks, and dormitory magnifies the importance of sex experience and withholds its praise of the male virgin. Kirkendall's exploratory study [3] finds that the boy who has followed the moral code in premarital chastity is apt to be apologetic and embarrassed about his lack of experience. When the other boys are bragging about their conquests, the inexperienced boy keeps quiet or feigns more sophistication than he has.

Quite as confusing to a boy is the question of how to approach a girl. If he is fond of her, he is expected to treat her gently and to be tender and considerate in expressing his affection. On the other hand, he sees the Great Lover of screen and story aggressively thrusting himself upon his struggling conquest until she melts in his embrace. Research in male sex aggression finds that the majority of sexual advances offensive to college girls are abrupt and unprovoked—58 per cent in a study of the reports of 657 university freshmen women.[4] It is possible that a goodly number of these boys were honestly confused about just what was expected of them in their relationships with their girl friends.

The older moral directives have lost their influence and as yet few others have come to take their place. Granted that we are well rid of the narrow, rigid social controls of previous generations, modern men and women still need some guide lines on which to base their personal behavior. With the disappearance of Mrs. Grundy, the community chaperone, sound sex guidance in building of personal controls is emphatically indicated.

---

[3] Lester A. Kirkendall, "What Kinsey Overlooked about Kids," *The National Parent-Teacher*, November, 1958, pp. 12–14.

[4] Eugene J. Kanin, "Male Aggression in Dating-Courtship Relations," *The American Journal of Sociology*, Vol. LXIII, No. 2, September, 1957, p. 201.

Wholesome sex guidance is woefully inadequate in present-day America, as is seen in the discussion of sex education in Chapter 20. Many a home, school, church, and youth agency still pass the buck in dodging the responsibility of guiding youth in what it means to grow up and meet modern challenges with inner strength.

What sex guidance there is tends to be physiological "organ recitals" about the structure and function of the complex reproductive systems of male and female. The psychological, emotional, spiritual, and moral aspects of sex conduct are rarely discussed in ways that make sense in today's world and give helpful direction within the complex of present day confusions. Many a mother admonishes her daughter departing for a date, "Be careful, dear," with little to indicate what she should be careful about or how to go about taking care. Many a pastor preaches on "The Home" with scant reference to the powerful forces that sweep youth into marriage. Many a teacher gingerly skirts the issue even when students bring it into the classroom. Many a youth leader stays clear of the subject that might get him in trouble with his constituency. So youth, according to survey after survey, continue to educate themselves as best they can in the mysteries of the way of a man with a maid.

What Sex Outlets Are There for Single Young People?

There are ten years, more or less, between puberty and marriage for most young people. These are the years when the male sex drive is at its peak,[5] and when members of both sexes combine high stimulation with limited socially accepted release of sexual tension. Just how young adults manage their sex impulses before they marry varies with the individual. Such factors as social class, level of education, religious affiliation, family background, and personality predispositions all affect the amount and type of sexual activity a single man or woman experiences.

What the general population of unmarried college students do has been studied by the Indiana University Staff of the Institute for Sex Research, as summarized in Table 13.

The majority of sex expressions in single college students involve no other person. Eight out of ten of the sex outlets of single men are solitary—nocturnal emissions and masturbation; seven out of ten of the sex outlets of unmarried college women are in sleep or masturbation.

---

[5] Alfred C. Kinsey, et al., *Sexual Behavior in the Human Male*. Philadelphia: Saunders, 1948, p. 240.

TABLE 13. *Frequency of Five Sex Outlets for 16 to 20-Year-Old Single College Men and Women* [6]

Sex Behavior	Percentage of Total Sex Outlet	
	Men (N-2,861)	Women (N-3,299)
Masturbation	66%	65%
Orgasm in Sleep	16	4
Premarital Intercourse	10	10
Petting to Climax	5	18
Homosexual	3	3
Total Sex Outlet	100%	100%

In the eyes of some religious groups, masturbation is morally wrong. The official position is that the sex organs were created for the propagation of the species rather than primarily for the pleasure of the individual.[7]

Until relatively recently, secular writers also regarded masturbation as an evil. Masturbation was reported to lead to insanity, to feeble-mindedness, to a shifty look in the eye, to acne, and to "long black hairs on the back of the hands." Girls as well as boys were cautioned against the evils of the "secret sin" and the "solitary vice." These superstitions are without foundation in fact, yet they persist in essence in the minds of many people.

Attitudes toward masturbation

Contrary to the fear-inducing taboos of the past, many liberals today hold that masturbation in any form or frequency is simply an indication of normal wholesome sexuality. Says Magoun,

Absence of masturbation in a healthy youth is a matter of concern, not a matter of reassurance, to many intelligent parents. It probably indicates some frightening, early experience such as having seen an older boy masturbate behind the garage, and having repressed what was a shocking experience for fear of parental disapproval.[8]

Some authorities claim that a history of masturbation in the woman before marriage facilitates her early sexual response to her husband.

---

[6] Alfred C. Kinsey, Wardell B. Pomeroy, Clyde E. Martin, *Sexual Behavior in the Human Male*. Philadelphia: Saunders, 1948, p. 378; and Alfred C. Kinsey, Wardell B. Pomeroy, Clyde E. Martin, and Paul H. Gebhard, *Sexual Behavior in the Human Female*. Philadelphia: Saunders, 1953, p. 563.

[7] John L. Thomas, *The American Catholic Family*. New York: Prentice-Hall, 1956, p. 54.

[8] F. Alexander Magoun, *Love and Marriage, Revised*. New York: Harper, 1956, p. 144.

The best documented of these studies reports, "Among the females who had never masturbated before marriage, or whose masturbation had never led to orgasm, about a third (31 to 37 per cent) had failed to reach orgasm in the first year, and nearly as many failed in the first five years of their marital coitus. Among those who had previously masturbated to the point of orgasm, only 13 to 16 per cent were totally unresponsive in the first year of marriage." [9]

There are clinicians who question both of these extreme attitudes toward masturbation. They agree with the most liberal in the harm caused by the unfortunate and unnecessary fear induced by the older repressive approaches. Yet they cannot accept the completely permissive attitude as well founded. They report such problems as fixations, regressions, introversion, and failure to progress beyond masturbation to make a good marriage adjustment with a sex partner as repercussions of obsessive masturbation in their patients. It is possible that, since such warnings come from those who treat personality disturbances, they do not entirely apply to the relatively healthy person.

Authorities agree that the most serious effects of masturbation are the feelings of guilt aroused in persons whose conditioning has been to repress such activity. Biologically there is no harm in non-obsessive autoeroticism. Legally and socially there are no barriers to discreet private periodic release of sex tensions. Emotionally, if a person considers masturbatory experience as immoral, dirty, or shameful, and yet practices it, the result almost certainly is feelings of guilt and self-accusation. Persons who have no compunctions against occasional self-induced release of mounting sex tensions take these experiences in stride as part of the price of premarital chastity. Even in married pairs, there are periods of separation, illness, and continence in the latter part of pregnancy when masturbation plays a role in maintaining equilibrium until marital relations are re-established on a continuing basis.

These matters are not often discussed, largely because actual practice differs so widely from the official moral code of articulate groups, and repressive measures of the past have repercussions in present-day taboos. Likewise, other normal aspects of sex are but rarely acknowledged in any but the most confidential settings.

Release in sleep

The normally virile male who limits his sex experience finds periodic involuntary sexual release in nocturnal emissions in which seminal fluid is emitted during sleep. These episodes are popularly known as "wet dreams" because they usually are accompanied by erotic dreams and sexual fantasies. Quacks and charlatans for years exploited impression-

---

[9] Alfred C. Kinsey, et al., *Sexual Behavior in the Human Female*, p. 390.

able boys with their remedies for this so-called "loss of manhood." Such misrepresentation of normal functioning fortunately is being gradually discouraged by adequate sex education early enough to help boys know what to expect and how to accept their normal sexuality.

While sexual release during sleep is practically universal in men, according to the Kinsey reports [10] less than 5 per cent of unmarried college women report having experienced orgasm during sleep. Girls have many sex-toned dreams that express sexual energy whether the individual acknowledges them or not.

Some 3 per cent of both college men and women report having had some type of homosexual contact between the ages of 16 and 20 (see Table 13). Before that age, crushes on members of the same sex are much more frequent. As both girls and boys enter puberty there is a period when intense attachments to members of the same sex serve to help the growing person to identify himself as a member of his own sex group. The boy often is devoted to a boy of his own age, to his coach, or to some other attractive male who serves as a model of masculinity. The girl fastens her attention on one special girl friend, on a much beloved teacher, movie or television starlet, or other attractive woman as her ideal of womanhood for a time. **Contacts with the same sex**

With healthy maturity boys leave their all-male world to find girls attractive. Even earlier the girls of their age and grade have begun to seek them out in their first heterosexual explorations. Usually by the time an individual reaches college he or she has balanced his love diet so that, while he still enjoys members of his own sex, those of the other sex are particularly attractive as well. By the late teens most persons of either sex have made real progress in heterosexual attachments.

Homosexual contacts are so severely punished that the homosexual offender keeps them as secret as possible. The individual's problems then lie in fear of discovery, guilt feelings, and in the limitation of contacts with the other sex in the normal process that leads to marriage.

The person whose development has been arrested at the homosexual stage may be helped in psychotherapy to work through his or her blockages. For the vast majority of college people the recognition that the problem is not simple can be helpful. It is not a question of there being men, women, and "homos" but rather that sex tendencies are on a scale from the very masculine men to the extremely feminine women with many intermediate types including a very few true homosexuals.

Some necking and petting are expected as part of the dating and courtship experience. The question is not so much whether there shall **Necking and petting**

---

[10] Kinsey, et al., *Sexual Behavior in the Human Female*, p. 218.

be any expression of affection between men and women before marriage, but rather with whom, when, and how much.

Young people of high school and college age make a distinction between necking and petting. Necking refers to the lighter forms of love-making literally "above the neck"—kissing, snuggling, caressing the hair, face, neck, and ears of the partner. Petting generally is recognized to involve the more intimate forms of erotic stimulation of those parts of the body usually covered by clothing. Thus defined, necking is generally approved and expected especially between couples who are fond of one another. Petting, on the other hand, is a matter of controversy viewed differently by the older and younger generations, the members of both sexes, as well as by individuals from various social backgrounds, religious and moral climates, and emotional predispositions.

In general, young people tend to accept necking and petting more freely than do members of the older generations. Boys generally are more inclined to expect necking and petting on their dates than are their feminine partners, as studies of what girls find offensive about their dates so fully document.[11] Sex play that stops short of actual intercourse is more frequent and more elaborate among young people at the college level than it is among working-class youth for whom premarital coitus is more generally accepted.[12] Sex stimulation outside of procreation in marriage is immoral in the eyes of certain religious groups, while it is accepted or condoned by the more secularly inclined. There are wide individual expectations ranging all the way from the boy who feels he has to fondle even the most casual date to the girl who "can't bear to be touched," however lightly.

On many college campuses, necking and petting have become substitutes for premarital intercourse. The problem is that since these activities are by nature sexually stimulating, how can they be kept within bounds so that the couple does not go too far? These are the questions that rain in upon a leader of student discussions of courtship practices.[13] Although there is much that can be said on the whys and hows of conducting oneself in amorous situations within the bounds set by one's own moral principles, the standards of one's group, and the larger societal codes, discussions with reliable guides are all too infrequent.

Dubbé finds that the question of petting is the most difficult area of

---

11 Eugene J. Kanin, "Male Aggression in Dating-Courtship Relations," *The American Journal of Sociology*, September, 1957, pp. 197–204.

12 Alfred C. Kinsey, et al., *Sexual Behavior in the Human Male*, Chapter 10.

13 For detailed treatment of typical student questions see Evelyn Millis Duvall, *Facts of Life and Love for Teen-Agers*, New York: Association Press, 1956; and *The Art of Dating*, New York: Association Press, 1958.

life for both college men and women to discuss with their parents.[14] Kanin finds that only one in six of the freshmen college women he studied appeal to parents or other adults when they experience offensive male aggression on the part of their dates.[15] One of the main reasons for the reticence of adults in considering petting as a premarital activity is their recognition that it serves as a prelude to intercourse in marriage, and setting powerful sexual drives in motion among the unmarried opens the way to premarital intercourse.

Depending on the study, from 20 to 80 per cent of unmarried males by the age of twenty-five have had premarital intercourse. The estimates of Kinsey and his associates, the highest reported to date, indicate that premarital intercourse accounts for 10 per cent of the total sex outlets of college men and women (Table 13). *Premarital intercourse*

Deviation from the code of premarital continence and marital fidelity is the only instance in our society where one instance of nonconformity places a person in the category of being a deviant permanently. Stealing, lying, and cruelty are not uncommon among young people, and even among older people, yet if the person is honest, truthful, and kindly 90 per cent of the time, his behavior is generally regarded as conforming. With regard to sex, however, there is a tendency to divide young people into two camps, those who are virginal, that is, have never experienced sex union, and those who are nonvirginal, which groups together all who have experienced intercourse one or more times.

There are great differences among those who have had sexual relations before marriage. There is the boy or girl who once stepped over the line and ever since has refrained. There is the girl who has known many men intimately, and the one who gives herself fully only to the man she is about to marry. There are those who are demanding, exploitative, and sexually aggressive, while others are tender, considerate, and mutual in their love-making. There are those whose mating is chiefly biological and others who express in sexual union deep spiritual and emotional communication.

Clinical and statistical studies indicate at least five kinds of persons who go all the way before marriage, as distinguished from those who do not:

1. The unconventional person with few or no spiritual roots. Religious young people tend to be faithful to the code—and to each other in marriage.

---

[14] Marvin C. Dubbé, "What Young People Can't Talk Over with Their Parents," *The National Parent-Teacher*, October, 1957, pp. 18–20.

[15] Kanin, *op. cit.*, p. 203.

2. The lower-class young person. In general, the middle-class boy or girl values chastity more highly, has higher aspirations for the future, and more often refrains from going all the way before marriage.

3. The person who has a compulsive need for love—at all costs. Some emotionally hungry persons will do anything to get attention and re-assurance.

4. The rebellious youngster who indulges sexually just to prove that he or she can. This sort of individual breaks rules as a matter of policy; he gets pleasure from nonconformity rather than from the act itself. He (or she) often runs headlong into trouble in impulsive efforts to "express" himself sexually or otherwise.

5. The couple who are deeply in love but cannot marry. These peo-ple may be completely faithful to each other and committed to a policy of fidelity both before and after marriage.

Premarital coitus between members of an engaged pair is discussed in Chapter 6, "Getting Engaged." There remains the even more contro-versial question of more casual premarital liaisons. Relationships with prostitutes and pick-ups are generally considered risky not only in terms of venereal infection and unscrupulous exploitation but also im-moral because they perpetuate unwholesome social practices and insti-tutions that are often tied in with a community's criminal elements. Taking advantage of an immature child is severely punished, as it should be. Exploiting a casual dating partner for sexual gratification is considered fair sport in some circles, and yet generally is recognized as short-lived and unethical.

Kirkendall finds little or no conversational, intellectual, or emotional communication in coital situations marked by exploitation, in contrast to highly developed interaction between persons who deeply care for and respect one another before, during, and after the sex act.[16]

Some people define sexual morality in terms of the function of inter-course. A man is moral who uses the sex act as a way of expressing the deepest feelings and the highest values man and woman have for each other. A man is moral to the extent that he sincerely cherishes his mate and seeks her welfare in his conduct with her. A woman is moral as she values her man as an end in himself rather than as a means for the fur-therance of her own personal goals alone. They both behave morally as they find with each other selfless devotion as well as self-gratifica-tion, lasting loyalty as well as momentary pleasure, and commitment to their larger responsibilities as well as their satisfactions with each other.

---

[16] Informal communication, April, 1958.

Others sympathetic to these spiritual values put their major emphasis on the social responsibilities involved in sex behavior. They recognize that in all areas of life, everything from the most infantile behavior to the most shameless exploitation masquerades as high idealism. They regard with suspicion the noble "love" of those who seek intense physical satisfactions without providing for its full legal and social security within marriage. They question the belief that a sexual relationship can be a private act that involves no one else.

Is Your Sex Conduct Anyone's Business But Your Own?

Before you have been dating very long, you have to make important decisions about sex conduct amidst a wide variety of points of view. You hear some others insist that sex is only a normal, natural appetite, like thirst, that ought to be satisfied as the urge arises. If you and your dating partner satisfy your sex desires directly, whose business is it but yours? The answer is that you can take a drink of water without involving anyone else. This is not true and at present cannot be true of sexual intercourse. Sex cannot be a "private affair."

Societies and cultures vary widely in what they expect and demand of people, but in no case has sex conduct ever been regarded as a strictly private affair. In every society studied, sex conduct is regulated as part of the total social system and absolute promiscuity has never been encouraged or supported by the moral codes. In America we live in a culture that approves of the companionship of the sexes, socially and intellectually, but restricts sexual intimacies to married couples. Jealousy and strife are minimized by insisting upon continence before marriage and marital fidelity to one partner after marriage. This enables us to maintain tenderness as an integral part of our love life and makes possible exclusiveness among lovers. Over the years a moral code meeting these specifications has been formulated and has proved relatively workable. That code is monogamous marriage—one man for one woman—at a time.

Social controls are universal

What you do about your sex life matters to your family, your friends, your sex partner, and to you personally. Sex is the most powerful force in human society. As such it is often explosive and frequently unpredictable. Of one thing you can be sure—that it matters.

Who cares what you do?

Your family cares what you do. Get into trouble and your family bears the burden of your behavior. They may not take the "never darken this door again" attitude. But if your mother has to "explain" things to the neighbors, or your father has to assume responsibility for unanticipated expenses, or if you have to sneak away for a quick, quiet ceremony instead of the public announcement that your family rightly expects, your conduct matters to them—tremendously.

Your friends and associates care what you do. When you yield to the pressures of one group, you may find yourself an outcast among others whose friendship over time might mean a great deal to you. Your future dates and marriage opportunities depend upon the reputation you build, the groups you relate yourself to, and the standards of conduct you maintain.

Will you lose your friends if you don't go along with the demands of the let's-live-it-up boys? Repeated polls of both high school and college students indicate clearly that the "fast worker" is rarely well liked. The majority of girls avoid the boy with a reputation of being a wolf. The girl who is known as too "easy" or promiscuous usually is not popular among either the boys or the girls. If a girl loses her boy friend by refusing to allow him intimacies she can assume that he was pursuing not her friendship but her sexual favors. If she oversteps the bounds of what is expected of a "nice girl" her partner may be the first to think less of her and to drop her when he starts to think seriously of marriage. One of the most frequent difficulties a girl faces with her sweetheart is that of granting him sexual privileges because she loves him, only to find that having had intimate access to her his ardor cools and he loses interest in her.

There is a good chance that *you* care what you do. You may start out with a casual "love 'em and leave 'em" attitude. But you may release a Pandora's box of complications that soon get out of hand. In many cases one of the partners becomes so deeply involved that any threat of breaking off becomes intolerable. The sordid stories played up in the tabloids often started with a simple sharing of a mutually enjoyable experience. In time one of the lovers came to care so much that when the other threatened to break it off, somebody got hurt. For every case in the public eye there are hundreds of less known private dramas in which bitterness, recrimination and heartbreak are the fruits of foolhardy "freedom."

There is considerable clinical evidence that women especially become intensely attached to their sex partners. What they may have thought would be a brief and casual episode turns into a deep and compulsive need that only the security of marriage can satisfy. Your sex partner may appear to be able to take the consequences of his or her behavior. But time may tell a different story. Your sex behavior affects you, your partner, and your feelings about and for each other in ways that you may not foresee.

What's the Harm of Stepping Outside the Code?

The sex code in twentieth-century America says something like this to young people of both sexes—"Go out and have a good time. Date whom you will as often as you want to. Go where you will and meet all sorts of interesting people. Fall in and out of love along the way, several times. Then when you find the one person you want to spend the rest of your life with, enjoy a deeply meaningful courtship and get married when you are ready to settle down in a home of your own. Only one thing is required—that you reserve your full sexual intimacy for marriage with your marriage partner." Fundamentally, our moral code today, as yesterday, calls for premarital chastity and marital fidelity.

The couple who "feel married" in their mutual affection for each other are in a quandary about their sex conduct before marriage. The Hollywood stereotype of filmed romance says in effect, "Anything is all right if you are really in love." Yet this is at variance with the sex code that denies the couple the right to sex experience before they are married. What is a couple to do? Suppose they go all the way before marriage, what is the harm?

The dangers of sex intercourse before marriage can be spelled out fairly clearly. First in the minds of many people is the possibility of pregnancy. Even with modern contraceptive devices and techniques there are many unplanned pregnancies among married couples. Studies of married college students find that although most of them try to postpone their first baby until after graduation, nearly two-thirds of their first pregnancies are unplanned.[17] For the unmarried the probabilities of having an unplanned baby are too high to be treated lightly.

In spite of great medical progress in detecting and treating such infections, venereal disease is still widely prevalent among young people.[18] There is no way in which a man or a woman·can tell whether a sex partner is diseased; the only completely reliable safeguard is restricting sexual activity to each other as previously continent partners.

For many couples the fear of discovery is rarely anticipated to be as haunting as it is. Our society makes little provision for liaisons among

---

[17] Harold T. Christensen and Robert E. Philbrick, "Family Size as a Factor in the Marital Adjustments of College Students," *American Sociological Review*, June, 1952, pp. 306–312; and Shirley Poffenberger, Thomas Poffenberger, and Judson T. Landis, "Intent toward Conception and the Pregnancy Experience," *American Sociological Review*, October, 1952, pp. 616–620.

[18] Periodic bulletins from the American Social Hygiene Association, 1790 Broadway, New York City 19, N. Y.

unmarried people, so surreptitious secrecy must surround premarital sex experience. Moments together snatched from under the interested eyes and ears of family, friends, neighbors, and curious strangers are in the shadow of the ever-present possibility of being found out.

With exposure of an affair comes the possibility of loss of reputation for the girl, and in some circles for the boy as well, the chance of losing one's job, and at least some of one's friends. The girl who has to pack up and leave college in disgrace is an object of pity or superior amusement in the eyes of her fellow students. Her welcome home can hardly be jubilant, and her relationship with family members, friends, and neighbors is apt to show the strain of their disapproval.

This used to be considered a woman's problem. Increasingly today men are recognizing that they too have a price to pay for premarital indiscretions. One of the most difficult questions asked by high school and college boys is, "My girl is pregnant, do I have to marry her?" If he doesn't he feels that he is a cad to leave her carrying his child. If he is forced into marriage, it may mean the end of his education, a sharp curtailment of his vocational, family, and social plans, and marriage with a girl whom he may not love or respect . . . a heavy price for a few moments or months of sex enjoyment.

The wisdom of sex regulation[19] The average girl is unable to attain physical gratification without abundant affection and attention. Sexual gratification for her is not a simple affair. She needs a basic personal security to achieve it. She needs understanding, tenderness, and constancy. There is clinical evidence that she needs a series of experiences, rather than single isolated experiences, and it is important that they be with the same person. Time and experience in becoming accustomed to each other are necessary to achieve complete satisfaction. Short-run, surreptitious affairs lack both of these requisites. Because sex is personal in addition to being biological, it is unlikely that promiscuity can produce the desired satisfactions.

Unfortunately, the history of couples who establish full sex relations outside of marriage is not encouraging to read. The experimenting couple may expect their love to be strengthened by their increased physical intimacy. But there are many indications that their idealized images of one another may be shattered thereby, as the sense of mystery vanishes. Interest in the other wanes at the end of the chase, sex tensions lose their titillating power as they are released, and the couple realize that they have "gone the limit." These ingredients of the roman-

---

[19] This section is based upon Sylvanus M. Duvall, *Men, Women and Morals,* New York: Association Press, 1952.

tic complex are lost simultaneously with the recurrence of guilt feelings. Because they expect romantic love as a necessary prerequisite of marriage, its lessening is interpreted as meaning that they were really not meant for each other, that the relationship should be broken off so that each may hunt for someone else.

Much the same transformation of emotional relationships takes place within marriage and partly for the same reasons. When romance wanes after marriage, however, it is not so hazardous. By then the ties have been formally sanctioned through the wedding ceremony, and the couple has established a common household with its many satisfactions and interlocking functions.

If the experimenting couple is not engaged and has no plans for marriage, the emotional involvement may be fully as complicated. Once a couple attains a state of satisfactory sexual union, either the boy or (more usually) the girl begins to wish for something more permanent. If the relationship is satisfying, one or the other tends to become involved emotionally and begins to press for marriage.

Sex can be safe and satisfying, only under circumstances which make possible the full and rich development of its emotional involvements. If the physical aspects were all, those who know how to guard against physical dangers of disease and pregnancy might safely have as free a sex life as an alley cat. But they are not. Because of the psychological aspect, the temporary affair is almost all risk and little promise. Sex requires for its satisfaction a complete response of the whole personality. As a general policy, this means marriage. People can go the limit, psychologically, only within the security of a sound and permanent marriage relationship.[20]

Until recently young people in our society needed only conscience to tell them what was correct behavior, at least in the area of sex relations. Today many young people are entering adulthood with the necessity of answering for themselves whether they will remain continent until marriage or include sexual experimentation in their premarital experience. No longer can one's conscience be one's only guide. Added to it must go insight into the consequences of premarital experimentation, into its effects upon personality and on the future of the relationship. The responsibility for these decisions is too great to place on young people until they are thoroughly informed. Young people acquire insight by learning the consequences of deviant behavior, the results of promiscuous relations, and the need for permanency to achieve a satisfying relation.

One of the helpful outcomes of the relaxation of the older sex code

---

[20] S. M. Duvall, unpublished manuscript.

has been the lifting of the ban on discussion of sex and sex problems. Frank discussion of moral problems and enrollment in marriage education courses can provide young people with a picture of the consequences of behavior which, on the rational level, can supplement the conscience, which is on the emotional level, as an important guide to conduct.

A famous physician, wise in the ways of sexually disturbed people, recently pointed out the principles of sex morality in a question-answer session with several hundred students in a marriage class. He had been asked the question, "Is it all right to pet if you think you are in love?" His answer appeared to be directed toward the boys of the class: "I would say you should be able to answer the following questions: Is it genuine, this affection? Is it fair to the girl in the long run? Are you hurting yourselves emotionally by building up appetites you can satisfy only in marriage? I find that patients who come to me for help are disproportionately drawn from individuals who were promiscuous before marriage. An act is right if it makes for the development of personality and human welfare. An act is wrong if it leads to the destruction of human personality. Sex is powerful, but neutral, neither bad nor good; how it is used makes it right or wrong. With this start I feel you should be able to construct the type of situations in which petting would be all right and the situations in which it would be all wrong."

How Is Responsive Integrity Developed?

Once an individual recognizes within himself the capacity to *enjoy others as persons* rather than as potential sex partners, he frees himself for much wider and more varied relationships with members of the opposite sex. In exploring personality, in sharing points of view, and in collaborating in creative work he sees possibilities which are closed to the person hampered by the feeling that every friend must be fondled and caressed to be enjoyed.

The "wolf" (male or female) whose aims are sex-directed is often not so much sex-starved as in need of ego-bolstering. The girl who leads a man on to prove to herself that she can, is often so insecure as a woman that she must constantly prove to herself, as well as to others, that she is desirable. The heart-hunter usually collects conquests because he or she needs evidence of personal power.

More fortunate are those persons who are free to know and enjoy and to love a wide variety of fine people of both sexes in a variety of situations, for theirs is the love that frees them for further growth of personality. As such emotional growth takes place, mate love is enhanced rather than challenged, since the sex channelling of affection remains exclusive while the emotional responses grow richly inclusive.

Responsive integrity is the ability to respond to another person honestly and as a whole person without having to block off or deny basic aspects of the self. If we are honest we must admit that we find all sorts of people attractive and lovable. The desire to attract and be attracted to others does not cease with marriage. Conscience tells us that we belong exclusively to one mate; so the tendency to feel guilt, shame, and a denial of our real feelings dams up the out-going responses. As long as this repression is successful we cannot allow ourselves to respond honestly to others. If, on the other hand, the emotional currents become so strong that they overflow the limits set by the conscience, they may set up a whole sequence of unacceptable behavior. Neither alternative is wholesome, since both prevent us from responding as a whole; either we must deny our feelings of affection, or we must break with our own ideals of right and wrong. Responsive integrity enters in when we accept our feelings for others, when we learn how to channel them in ways that are acceptable, and to enjoy wholesomely and freely the emotional satisfactions of our relations with others. Refusing to admit our dislike or our love for another does not lessen the potency of the feeling. Repression only masks the emotion, which somehow, someway, must burst forth eventually with accumulated force and vigor.

Responsive integrity does not mean going around with emotions unbuttoned, letting feelings spill over as they will without control. Necessarily involved is a great deal of self-imposed restraint and control to keep expressions of feelings within the bounds of the particular relationship. The gushy girl who fusses around her brother does not share as much of him as does the sister who expresses her affection in more acceptable sisterly ways. The touchy person who flies off the handle shares fewer confidences than the poised, unshockable one with whom people feel safe. Self-control for the sake of the recognized values of the relationship allows more freedom of access to others than is granted the less disciplined, who find themselves in emotional hot water much of the time.

Take Sue and Emma, for instance. They both admire and work closely with an attractive married man in their office. Emma flashes her lashes and maneuvers for compliments and opportunities to be close to him. She goes to great lengths to let him know that he touches off her affectional responses. Yet she cannot win. If he responds to her advances, he will either be turned away from her by his own feelings of guilt, or he will take advantage of her availability without the loyalty and permanence most girls need to make sex satisfying. Or by completely succumbing to her seduction, he faces the possibility of breaking up his home, which would inevitably be fraught with guilt, some ostracism, and pangs of conscience. More likely he will find her advances uncomfortable and take steps to remove himself as far as possible from her silly, one-sided flirtation.

Sue, on the other hand, just as honestly admits her interest in her colleague. But she lets her affection stimulate her productivity in the job they are doing together. She throws herself wholeheartedly into doing the kind of work that he will admire and that will do credit to them both. She expresses her admiration for his achievements and so spurs him on to greater creativity. Theirs can be a growing relationship with a depth and breadth of permanence, because neither threatens the other with demands that are not intrinsically a part of their own working relationship.

Responsive integrity, then, means wholehearted response to others through the avenues provided by the particular relationship. Responsive integrity is established when a person, accepting both his impulses and his conscience, exerts the self-controls that allow him freely to channel the full power of his feelings within the moral code. It is one important aspect of emancipation, of freedom to grow, because it opens up opportunities for friendships and working relationships with men and women which might otherwise have to cease with marriage's traditional exclusiveness. Persons with responsive integrity can frankly recognize that real affection is a source of motivation in working with other people and that the enjoyment of work and play with others need not be followed by sexual contact.

What Kind of Person Are You?

Ultimately, the kind of person you are determines your sex manners and morals. In a world where old forms are being challenged and new patterns have not yet become fixed, you as a person are responsible for your conduct.

You are a person with a past. The way you were brought up, the values your family and friends have held through the years, and the convictions you have had about yourself have made their imprint on you as a growing person. If you accept your past without question, you probably will follow its influence through your present and into your future. If you are in the process of questioning certain elements in your past, this is the time when you challenge what you have been in terms of what you want to become. If you have tended to think of yourself as a creature of impulse with little worth waiting for, you may have been sorely tempted at every pleasant prospect. As you sense the promise of the future and know who you are and what you are becoming, you tend to choose the pathways that lead toward your life goals. Your past and your future meet and fuse in what you do day by day in the present.

You are a person in society. You are governed by its rules and enjoy the freedom to grow that it allows you as an individual. With your freedom goes the responsibility for disciplined behavior that preserves rather than threatens the basic tenets upon which your particular society is based. If you are to enjoy the satisfactions of happy marriage and sound family life, you are bound to the principles that assure their stability.

You are a person among other persons. Your sex life is only part of your wholeness as an individual, and only a fraction of your relationship with others. As you see others as personalities to be enjoyed as whole persons, rather than as sex objects to be exploited, you take a giant step toward learning the art of mutual fulfillment. Your sex manners and morals are shaped by your fundamental attitudes toward others, toward yourself, and toward life itself.

READINGS

Binkley, Robert C. and Frances W., *What Is Right with Marriage?* New York: Appleton, 1929, Chapter 16, "Marriage and Sex Monopoly."

Blood, Robert O., Jr., *Anticipating Your Marriage.* Glencoe, Illinois: Free Press, 1955, Chapter 5, "Giving Physical Expression to Love."

Burgess, Ernest W., and Paul Wallin, *Engagement and Marriage.* Philadelphia: Lippincott, 1953, Chapter 12, "Assessing Premarital Intercourse."

Christensen, Harold T., *Marriage Analysis* (Rev. Ed.). New York: Ronald Press, 1958, Chapter 8, "Sexual Perspective."

Duvall, Evelyn Millis, *The Art of Dating.* New York: Association Press, 1958, Chapter 14, "Sexual Relations before Marriage."

Duvall, Sylvanus M., *Men, Women and Morals.* New York: Association Press, 1952.

Ehrmann, Winston, *Premarital Dating Behavior.* New York: Holt, 1959.

Hiltner, Seward, *Sex Ethics and the Kinsey Reports.* New York: Association Press, 1953.

Kinsey, Alfred C., et al., *Sexual Behavior in the Human Female.* Philadelphia: Saunders, 1953.

———, *Sexual Behavior in the Human Male.* Philadelphia, Saunders, 1948.

Magoun, F. Alexander, *Love and Marriage.* New York: Harper, 1956, Chapter 5, "The Premarital Sex Problem."

Seward, Georgene H., *Sex and the Social Order.* New York: McGraw-Hill, 1949.

Sorokin, Pitirim A., *The American Sex Revolution.* Boston: Porter Sargent, 1956.

9 Your Wedding Plans

Do you have to have a wedding?

How informal can a wedding be?

Who should be invited to your wedding?

What has to be done to prepare for the wedding?

Why a special wedding ceremony?

What if yours is a special case?

Weddings have become so commercialized and so elaborate that some couples frankly prefer omitting them in favor of a simple inexpensive marriage ceremony. The bride-to-be and her fiancé become so enmeshed in family tangles over a multitude of wedding details that they may become estranged long before the actual ceremony itself. Other members of the family find the overly elaborate wedding quite as uncomfortable. One father of the bride, with head swimming over the mounting costs and complications of his daughter's wedding, offered her five hundred dollars if she would elope and stop the whole dizzy wedding procedure. Fortunately, a wedding does not have to be uncomfortably pretentious. In fact, there does not have to be a wedding at all.

Do You Have to Have a Wedding?

In the United States there are two main types of marriage ceremonies. The first is the religious ceremony in which the wedding is solemnized by an officiating clergyman, priest, or rabbi. The religious ceremony may be an elaborate wedding in church or cathedral, or it can be a simple affair in parsonage, home, or garden. The second type of marriage is the civil ceremony presided over by a Justice of the Peace or other magistrate. This is usually in his office or chambers in the presence of the required witnesses and often members of both families and friends of the couple. The civil ceremony is recognized by all states except Delaware, Maryland, and West Virginia where the religious ceremony is required.

Religious ceremonies are far more numerous than civil marriage ceremonies. DePorte examined the records for 1949 in New York State (outside of New York City) and found only one in ten (9.5 per cent) of all marriages had been civil ceremonies.[1] More recently, an even higher percentage of all Iowa marriages were civil ceremonies (see Table 14).

TABLE 14. *Marriages in Iowa by Type of Ceremony, 1951–1955* [2]

Year	Total Marriages	Religious Ceremonies	Civil Ceremonies	Not Stated
1955	24,493	19,741	4,743	0
1954	23,228	18,665	4,543	20
1953	23,180	18,705	4,464	11
1952	22,600	18,102	4,349	149
1951	24,301	19,918	4,195	188

In general, religious ceremonies are more numerous in the following categories: (1) rural brides, (2) first marriages, (3) younger brides and grooms, (4) couples belonging to the same faith, and (5) if the husband is a farmer or professional worker (see Table 15). Conversely, those who marry by civil ceremony tend to be urban, divorced, or widowed, older brides and grooms, belonging to different religious faiths, with the husband in unskilled or semi-skilled or service occupations.

Marriage by declaration   Less frequent than the civil marriage ceremony is the marriage by declaration. In Montana 4.4 per cent of all marriages in 1953–1956 were marriages by declaration. This recognized marriage is one in which the two persons simply appear before a notary public giving him the facts required by law (names, ages, residences of the parties, the fact of the marriage, the time of the marriage, and that the marriage has not been solemnized) and signing the declaration which he notarizes, subscribed by the parties and attested by at least three witnesses.[3]

[1] J. V. DePorte, "Civil Marriage in New York State apart from New York City," *American Sociological Review*, Vol. 17, No. 2, p. 233.
[2] Personal communication, November 6, 1957, from L. E. Chancellor, Director, Division of Vital Statistics, Iowa State Department of Health, Des Moines, Iowa.
[3] John C. Wilson, State Registrar, State Board of Health, State of Montana, Helena, Montana, personal communication, November 8, 1957.

TABLE 15.   *Marriages According to Husband's Occupational Group and Couple's Prior Marital History, State of Iowa, 1953* [4]

Occupational Group *	All Marriages	Per Cent Married by Religious Ceremony		
		First Marriages	Either or Both Divorced	Either Party Widowed Only
Farming	93.7	96.6%	75.0%	89.0%
Professional	88.9	94.6	70.9	96.6
Owner-Official	78.5	90.9	63.6	85.1
Clerical-Sales	82.5	90.5	66.5	83.3
Skilled	75.1	85.8	58.8	80.2
Semi-skilled	70.7	81.8	51.9	80.2
Service	61.6	78.4	50.2	78.1
Labor	71.7	79.1	55.4	73.5
Total	80.7	88.3%	59.5%	83.1%

* Excluding students, persons in military service, and the "retired." Coded in accordance with U.S. Census classification. Number of cases–23,180.

More general is the common-law marriage which is considered to exist when a couple live together openly as man and wife but have not been married in a religious or civil ceremony. The State of Montana recognizes the common-law marriage in these words: "The so-called common-law marriage is recognized as valid in this state, but, to be effective, there must be a mutual consent of parties able to consent and competent to enter into a ceremonial marriage, and an assumption of such relationship by consent and agreement as of a time certain, followed by cohabitation and repute." [5] Other states define, describe, and recognize the common-law marriage along somewhat similar lines. Since this type of marriage involves no records, it is impossible to know its extent or incidence.

Common-law marriage

How Informal Can a Wedding Be?

The type of wedding you have depends upon many factors: (1) your own hopes and dreams through the years; (2) the amount of money you want to spend; (3) the families you both come from, their wishes

[4] Thomas P. Monahan and Loren E. Chancellor, "Statistical Aspects of Marriage and Divorce by Religious Denominations in Iowa," *Eugenics Quarterly,* September, 1955, Vol. 2, No. 3, p. 166.
[5] *Ibid.,* p. 2.

and interests and social standing; (4) your location with particular reference to the kinds of places suitable for a wedding; (5) the number of friends and relatives you want to invite; and (6) the amount of time you have to plan ahead for the wedding.

Weddings range all the way from simple, informal affairs to large, formal pageants.

1. *Small home wedding* with members of the immediate families present, and whatever decorations, music, and refreshments seem suitable. Such a wedding is the least expensive in time and money, and can follow the individual wishes of the couple more freely than other types.

2. *Informal chapel wedding* to which immediate relatives and close friends are invited, with the couple receiving their guests in the foyer following the ceremony. Although there may be no reception as such, the immediate wedding party may go somewhere for a wedding breakfast afterwards if they wish. This type of wedding can be easily arranged, kept as simple as the couple desires, is inexpensive, and can be quite lovely. One modification of this is for the wedding to take place following a regular service in the bride's church, to which the guests come as soon as the previous service is over. This is convenient for organist, minister, and many guests. The altar is already decorated, and extra arrangements are kept to a minimum.

3. *Small wedding in church, home, or club* to which members of both families and friends are invited, followed by a reception, that may include a longer guest list, if desired. The reception may take place in the church parlors, in the home, the club, or in some other suitable place nearby. The longer guest list may be for the ceremony itself with only a few chosen friends and family members invited to the reception that follows in another place. When the reception is held at the place of the ceremony, all those attending the ceremony are invited to the reception as well.

4. *The home, garden, or club wedding and reception* for everyone in the same place. In this type of wedding there is a flow from the ceremony to the receiving line to the refreshment tables with all guests participating. This may be an elaborate affair of *The Father of the Bride* variety, or it may be a simple ceremony under the trees in the yard or at an altar improvised inside. A sit-down wedding breakfast, a buffet supper, or simple refreshments of the stand-up sort, around whatever menu is appropriate, is chosen depending upon the number of guests, the accommodations, personnel to serve, and of course the budget.

5. *Formal or semiformal church wedding,* followed by a small home or club reception to which a few friends and the two families are

asked. Here the pomp and splendor are in the ceremony, with the secondary interest in the reception. This can be as elaborate or as simple as the bride and her family may desire. The formal ceremony itself demands both time and money to be in accordance with traditional form. A wedding consultant to advise on the costuming of the wedding party, decorations, wedding processional, the recessional, and all such details, can be a great help in the formal wedding, which to be proper must conform to convention.

6. *Large, formal church, cathedral, or synagogue wedding,* followed by home, hotel, or country club reception to which all wedding guests are invited. Here, money is no object, and the bills may total many thousands of dollars. This may represent not only the family's investment in the couple, but as is often the case, is one way of attaining or maintaining social position and/or cementing business interests. Such a wedding lies outside the scope of this writing. Professional wedding services are in the business of arranging large formal weddings down to the last detail, under contract for a suitable fee.

Who Should Be Invited to Your Wedding?

It is usual for the family of the bride to invite the guests to the wedding. As soon as the decision has been made as to the type of wedding it will be, the bride and her family, in consultation with the groom and his parents, make out the list of persons to be invited. If the wedding is to be a small home affair, with only members of the immediate families present, the matter is a simple one except in problems of close relatives by blood or marriage who have been cut off from the family by distance, divorce, or estrangement. It is wise to invite all such family members as is at all possible. To exclude them from such an important occasion is often to widen the breach and to make for feelings of guilt and uneasiness among those present. Whether or not they are included, the decision should be the joint responsibility of all the family members planning the wedding.

Members of the immediate family and close friends may be invited to the small home, or informal chapel wedding, personally by the bride or her mother, by word of mouth, telephone, telegraph, or informal note, whichever is most convenient. In this case, announcements of the wedding are sent to all other relatives and friends as soon as the ceremony has been performed.

Guests to formal or semi-formal weddings are always invited by engraved wedding invitations according to prescribed forms available at the engraver's. These are mailed from three to four weeks in advance of the ceremony. The order should be placed with the engraver about six weeks before the mailing date. Outside envelopes in the quantity decided upon may be secured from the engraver at the time the order is placed, so that addressing may be done in pen and ink at home while the engraving is being completed. If the list is very long, it is well to alphabetize it and check for duplicates and omissions before addressing the envelopes.

The engraved invitation may be used also in informal weddings to which a considerable number of guests are being invited. If engraving is too costly an item in the wedding budget, there is a form of raised printing that is frequently used instead of engraving that is much less expensive. The same general forms, dates for mailing, and other customs are followed.

On the outside envelopes go the full names and addresses of the guests. Both husband and wife are invited as a Mr. and Mrs. unit, except in a case like the following. When the entire office force goes as a group to a wedding of one of its members at or close to office hours, it is not expected that the husbands and wives of members of the office staff will be invited.

If there is some question about the correct address of the guest, the return address of the sender may be included on the outside envelope; otherwise it is not necessary.

Names of members of the family not specifically indicated on the outside envelope may be written on the inside envelope of the wedding invitation, so that it may be clear just who it is that is being invited. In the case of a couple with two children, for instance, the names of each one of the four would be listed one under the other on the inside envelope. It is not necessary to invite the children to the wedding, but if one is invited, the other(s) should be included except for some important reason. Names of other relatives (brothers, sisters, mothers, etc.) living in the same residence may similarly be included in the listing of names on the inside envelope, or, somewhat more properly, they may receive separate invitations. It is usual for family members at different addresses and for members of an engaged couple to receive separate invitations.

Unless you put R.S.V.P. on the invitations to your wedding and reception, your guests are under no obligation to reply. So, if you need to know the number of guests to be expected, be sure to indicate on the invitation that a reply is expected, including the address to which the reply is to be sent, if there is apt to be some question about it. Replies to formal invitations are usually written in the third person and mailed first class. Informal invitations may be acknowledged by a simple note, or verbally by telephone, or by person to person.

If you have a considerable number of acceptances and regrets to keep track of, you will need some kind of system that will give you an accurate count. One bride-to-be simply set two boxes, one marked "YES" and the other "NO," on a convenient table. As replies came in the mail, or were given members of her family, they were dropped into the "YES" box if they were acceptances, and the "NO" box if regrets. Her tallies of each gave her a basis for an estimate for the caterer, and a final figure of total response. *Tip:* Always plan for a few extras; you never can tell!

Engraved (or raised printing for economy's sake) announcements of the marriage are sent to all relatives and friends who did not receive an invitation to the wedding. Announcements follow a slightly different form than invitations, examples of which are available to serve as models at any stationer's or engraver's office. Lists of persons to receive announcements are collected from both bride and groom and their families, compiled and checked for duplicates as is done for invitations. Envelopes are personally addressed in pen and ink at home while awaiting delivery of the announcements and the inside envelopes. These may be prepared ahead. But, they are not mailed until after the ceremony, usually by some member of the bride's family. An "at home" card giving the address of the newly married couple and the date by which they will be settled may be enclosed with the announcement, or included in it, for the convenience of those who may wish to call or send wedding gifts to the couple. **Announcements**

As with the invitations, the bride's parents' names are the first named on the announcement. In cases of death or divorce, the remaining parent's name alone is correct. When the bride is a mature woman long out of her parental home, she may announce her own marriage quite properly according to forms already developed and available as models.

If, for some reason, the formal announcement is not desired, either the bride or some senior member of her family may write to relatives and friends not present at her marriage, telling them about it, and thus announcing it informally. Likewise, the groom or one of his parents writes members of his family and friends about the wedding as soon as convenient.

As soon as invitations are out, wedding gifts begin to arrive. Each one should be personally acknowledged by the bride just as soon as possible. With all the other things she has to do as the wedding date approaches, some sort of system will help. It is wise to plan ahead on **Wedding gifts** where gifts will be kept and how they will be displayed. As each gift arrives, it is labeled with a number corresponding to that which the bride writes for it in her gift record. Such gift records appear in the back of wedding books given brides by some stores, or she may make her own in any way that seems most convenient for her to keep her gift record straight.

When a gift arrives, the bride may wait until her fiancé drops by before opening it, if they enjoy opening gifts together. Or, she may open it and enter it into her record at once, carefully preserving the card, and perhaps the packing slip from the store from which it was sent. (WARNING! Many gifts are multiple, so wrappings should be searched carefully before they are discarded.) If she keeps close by the spot where she unwraps her gifts such items as pen, note paper, stamps, and her address book, she will find that it does not take too long to immediately acknowledge each gift as it arrives. It is gracious of her to specifically mention the gift and express her warm appreciation for it and tell how she plans to use and enjoy it.

It sometimes happens that a couple will have no use for a gift that has been sent them. One couple received seventeen sugars and creamers, only a few of which could be expected to be used. In such a case, and in all other cases where the gift does not fit into the plans of the couple, it may be returned to the store from which it was sent and exchanged for something more suitable. It is therefore wise for the bride to save the packing slips and the inner box in which the gift comes, for use in case it is to be exchanged. In a situation like this, the bride may acknowledge the gift as usual, being careful not to say anything to offend or hurt the sender at the same time that she avoids telling a falsehood. She can always express her gratitude for being remembered without mention of the possible inappropriateness of a gift.

In the event that the engagement is broken, after wedding gifts have been received, the gifts are returned to the senders with a little note indicating that the wedding plans have been cancelled. Postponement of the wedding in case of illness, death, or for any other reason does not necessitate the return of the gifts.

What should you do if a gift is delivered in a damaged condition? If the gift has been sent by a store, it is quite proper to call or write the store saying that the item sent to you on such a date as a gift by Mrs. So-and-So has arrived in such and such condition, and asking them to pick it up and replace it. If the package was wrapped and sent from home, it is best to say nothing about its condition when acknowledging the gift. If the giver asks you specifically about the gift, of course you will have to tell her.

The undelivered gift is another cause of frequent embarrassment. Aunt Mary told Jane that she was sending her an electric toaster for a wedding gift. The wedding is long since over, and still no toaster, nor further word from Aunt Mary. Jane needs a toaster, but hesitates to buy one when Aunt Mary still might send it as she volunteered. What should Jane do? One real possibility is that Aunt Mary ordered the toaster to be sent as a gift, and the store failed to fill the order. Jane might operate on this assumption and, writing a pleasant note to Aunt Mary, mention her anticipation of receiving the toaster that Aunt Mary said she was sending. If Aunt Mary wonders why no acknowledgment of her gift has come, she can either have the store check its records, or she may tactfully ask Jane if the item has been delivered. Such a follow-up on either the giver's or the receiver's part is a kindness when carefully managed.

Many stores offer prospective brides a service, in which the bride goes over the stock and selects those things that she would like to have. The store then lists these, including her choice of silver pattern, household china and glassware, color schemes, etc., so that those who wish to send some suitable gift may choose from the list of possibilities registered with the store. This assures the sender of giving something that will be appropriate, and the bride and groom of receiving things that they want and can use.

Friends and family members often ask either the bride or her mother what would be acceptable as a wedding gift. It is quite all right to reply specifically if it is done in such a way that the sender is given some latitude for the cost of the item. For instance, if the giver indicates that she would like to send silver, the name of the pattern selected may be given her so that she may add a piece or as many pieces as fit her budget. Or, a list of several items of varying costs may be suggested. In answer to the direct question about the acceptability of some specific item: "Would you like an electric iron?" the reply may be frank appreciation or rejection of the suggestion; e.g., "Oh, we'd love one, thank you," or "Thank you, it's a grand idea, but Ted's mother has already sent us one."

In answer to the question, "Is money an acceptable wedding gift?" Emily Post says "No," listing as her reason the fact that the money is spent and the couple has nothing definite to remember the sender by. However, many couples who marry today find money a highly acceptable gift in many instances. Some couples are not able to establish a household of their own for some time. For them the problem of storing wedding gifts may be a difficult one. Other couples go to housekeeping in limited quarters where there will be no place to put many of the things that they get for their wedding. Most young couples start out with limited finances that must be stretched as far as dollars can go and, knowing just what they need and what they can do without for a while, can possibly more wisely spend the gift allotment than could all but their closest associates.

One possible compromise between Emily Post and modern expediency is the giving of a United States Government Bond, which may be turned in for cash at once if needed, or "salted away" as a gift of security from the sender until it matures, or until it can be used to purchase some much needed item for the new household.

What Has to Be Done to Prepare for a Wedding?

Your first thought in preparing for your wedding will probably be of what you will need. Your wedding clothes and those of your guests will be in keeping with the type of wedding yours is to be. Procedure for the formal wedding rigidly prescribes the clothing worn by bride, groom, and all members of the wedding party. More simple weddings allow considerable latitude within certain general conventions. Wedding clothes do not need to be expensive to be appropriate and effective. They may be as elaborate as the bride and her family may choose.

Wedding clothes

The bride chooses her wedding outfit as the keynote theme of her wedding. If the wedding is formal, her dress will be in traditional white or near-white in some suitable fabric, with a train from three to seven yards in length over which falls the wedding veil from the bridal headpiece of fabric, flowers, or jewels in keeping with the period and style of the gown. Depending upon its elaborateness the formal wedding gown may cost anywhere from several hundred to several thousand dollars.

Any bride-for-the-first-time may wear a traditional white wedding gown no matter what the type of her wedding. For the informal wedding, the bride's outfit may be a simple floor length model and either no train or one of a yard or so in length, with a veil that is finger tip length caught in a simple fabric headpiece, or a garland of flowers. She may wear the wedding dress that she has inherited from her mother or grandmother, fitted to her figure. She may buy her gown and veil, or have it made for her, or as some gifted girls do, she may make it herself.

The bride may choose to wear a ballet length gown in white or pastel color. Or she may wear a street length gown in some soft becoming color and fabric. Or, she may select a well-cut suit and blouse with which she would wear hat and gloves. Shoes and other accessories are chosen in keeping with the rest of her outfit.

There are just two rules for what bridesmaids should wear: 1. bridesmaids' costumes are in the same period as the bride's, and fit into the wedding theme that she has set. 2. bridesmaids' costumes are alike, except possibly in color. Fabric, styling, and accessories harmonize with the costumes worn by the bride and her attendant.

The matron of honor, or the maid of honor (if unmarried), is the personal attendant of the bride and chooses her costume to complement that of the bride. She may or may not wear a hat or headpiece depending upon the nature of the costume. When gloves are worn they are long with a short-sleeved dress or short with a long-sleeved dress. Her flowers may be in any harmonious color and style. Her outfit is usually slightly different from that of the bridesmaids but harmonizes in color and styling.

The flower girl, usually a child of the family or close friends, wears a dress like that of the bridesmaids or one that is of the same general type, with suitable accessories.

Whatever the type of wedding, the men of the party dress alike. At the formal evening wedding, the groom, his best man, and the ushers all wear full dress suits: "White tie and tails." For the formal daytime wedding, cutaway coats and dark gray striped trousers, gray tie and gloves are prescribed. A simple wedding calls for dark blue suits, white shirts, plain ties, and no gloves for the men of the wedding party. In summertime, informal white jackets and dark blue trousers are sometimes worn at informal weddings.

Only the men's boutonnières are different. The groom's lapel blossom is usually white, while those of the groom's attendants may be in color. The groom's boutonnière may be somewhat more elaborate than the best man's and the ushers'; some little distinction marks the groom as "the man of the day" apart from his attendants.

In some circles suits of the same material for bride and groom have been popular. The color usually is some shade of blue, although there is no reason why some other color becoming to both could not be chosen. Black is rarely worn at weddings because of its association with mourning. Brown and gray suits for men are not usual at weddings, but there is no absolute rule that forbids them. In general, although there are conventions about what is proper to wear, the choice is up to the bride and groom whose wedding it is.

Calendar

OF THINGS TO DO

THE WEDDING PLANNED WELL IN ADVANCE

Three to Four Months Before the Wedding
Set the wedding date (in consultation with members of both families in so far as is possible).

Consider possible types of weddings suitable to your situation and choose the kind of wedding you both and your families can agree would be best.

Select the place for the wedding and reserve it for your date.

Consult your minister, priest, or rabbi about your marriage and wedding plans.

Make arrangements for the reception, reserving the date, determining in general the kind of food, who will prepare and serve it, and the number of guests in round numbers.

Choose your wedding attendants and invite them, specifying the definite date and the type of wedding.

Select the color scheme and general motif of the entire wedding, keeping in mind the season of the year, the type of wedding chosen, the budget, and your own preferences.

Plan bride's wedding gown and accessories, and those for bridal attendants in keeping with your type of wedding, your over-all scheme, your budget, and whether the gowns will be handmade or purchased.

Start a master list of persons to be invited to the wedding, including those suggested by you both and your families. Make a plan for thinning if the list becomes too long to be accommodated. Develop a system for checking duplicates.

Two to Three Months Before the Wedding
Order invitations from your stationer or engraver according to the model and the script desired. Order in round numbers in lots of fifty or one hundred, allowing more than the total of lists compiled to date. Calculate the percentage of acceptances you can reasonably expect, and so estimate the number of invitations it will be feasible to send.

Arrange for announcements (to those not being invited to the wedding) according to the same plan of estimating numbers as for invitations.

Order informals for acknowledging your wedding gifts at this time if you prefer these to other simple suitable note paper. The number should approximate that of the size of the invitation list.

Explore possibilities for where you will live, making whatever tentative arrangements are possible. If you are fortunate in having a definite place into which you will move, it is not too soon to plan for its furnishing and to start getting it in order.

One to Two Months Before the Wedding
Bride goes to a good gynecologist for her premarital examination according to the suggestions outlined in Chapter 7. She follows through on his (or her) recommendations before the wedding, including a return for routine blood tests a week or two preceding the wedding date.

Groom gets his complete premarital examination, making appointment for blood tests.

Address the invitations in preparation for mailing three to four weeks before the wedding. The outside envelopes may be picked up before the engraving is finished if you wish. The envelopes are addressed in pen and ink in a legible hand by the bride with whatever help is offered by members of her family, the groom and perhaps members of his family. One bride made a party of it with both families gathered around the dining room table, address books at hand, following a pleasant informal meal in joint-family style.

Decide on your honeymoon plans considering the special interests of you both and the function of the honeymoon (see Chapter 10). Make advance reservations for accommodations and travel.

Select "going away" outfits and trousseau, including appropriate accessories.

Check your luggage needs.

Express interest in what both mothers will wear to the wedding, giving what suggestions and help seem to be indicated.

Three to Four Weeks Before the Wedding
Mail the wedding invitations (*not* the announcements, yet). First class postage is expected. Air mail is indicated only for relatives and friends in far distant places.

Order the wedding cake and make final arrangements for the wedding breakfast and/or the reception. Estimate the number to be served with final figure promised as replies come in, just before the wedding (two or three days to a week is usual).

Select the photographer and discuss with him what kinds of pictures you will want, and make definite appointments with him.

Check on the legal requirements for marriage in your state.

Arrange for out-of-town guests.

Bride gets a permanent if she needs one, and makes appointments ahead for the day before the wedding, or at a time that seems best.

Select and order your flowers for the wedding.

Arrange for decorations needed for the wedding, the wedding breakfast, and the reception.

Register your preferences at the wedding bureau of the store where your friends and family will most likely shop for your gifts.

Plan for the way in which you will acknowledge your gifts as they arrive, and how they will be displayed.

The Week or Two Before the Wedding
Final check with your doctors, routine blood tests preliminary to getting the license.

Go together for your marriage license.

Arrange transportation for the wedding party.

Make final preparations for the rehearsal and for presenting gifts to the wedding party. The rehearsal is usually the day before the wedding. A simple party in connection with the rehearsal is an acceptable time for bestowing gifts upon members of the wedding party. Caution: Do not attempt too elaborate an affair the night before the wedding. You'll want to be rested and fresh then.

Groom gets hair cut; bride gets hair done and whatever else that will make her feel lovely.

Allow plenty of time for dressing and last-minute details on your wedding day.

THE WEDDING PLANNED ON SHORT NOTICE

Set the date and decide the type of wedding, clearing the time with the minister and both families.

See your doctor(s) for a complete premarital examination and the blood tests required in your state.

Make arrangements for what you both and the other members of the wedding party will wear.

Write invitation notes and order announcements.

Arrange for wedding cake, refreshments, flowers, and photographer.

Get your marriage license.

Keep calm, share the responsibilities, enjoy every minute of it . . . it's your wedding!

Wedding rings

Wedding rings are of many types, but with a single purpose—to symbolize the marriage. It is customary in this country for the groom to place the wedding ring upon the third finger left hand of his bride at the time of their marriage. The ring is usually white or yellow gold, or platinum either plain or set with small precious stones. It matches the engagement ring, and the wife may wear it throughout the marriage either together with her engagement ring, or alone by itself.

The double ring ceremony has gained favor in recent years. In this the bride receives her ring from the groom and places the groom's ring on his third finger left hand during the ceremony. The design of both rings is usually similar and they are engraved alike with the couple's initials and the date of their marriage inside the rings. The jeweler does this when the rings are purchased.

The best man carries the bride's wedding ring during the ceremony until he passes it to the groom to place it on the bride's finger. The maid of honor holds the groom's ring until she hands it to the bride to put on the groom's finger. Thereafter both bride and groom wear their wedding rings as symbols of their marriage.

Wedding costs

According to convention wedding costs are assumed by both the bride and her family and the groom and his in the manner outlined below. Although this listing represents the general custom in the United States, it need not be interpreted rigidly. As in other aspects of wedding procedure it is well to know the traditional conventions so that you may know from what you depart when you plan your own wedding.

The Bride or Her Family Pays for . . .
Wedding gown and veil
Bride's personal trousseau
Wedding reception, breakfast, or dinner
Transportation to church and reception
Wedding decorations and music
Invitations and announcements
Gifts for the groom and the bride's attendants

The Groom or His Family Pays for . . .
Bride's bouquet and mothers' flowers
Bride's "going away" corsage
Wedding trip
Wedding ring
Minister's fee
Marriage license
Gifts for the bride, best man, and ushers

The Wedding Party

IN ORDER OF APPEARANCE AT 3 PHASES OF THE WEDDING

**PROCES-
SIONAL**
Just before usher escorts groom's parents to front pew right of center aisle

Bride's mother is seated by usher at left of center aisle (signal for the wedding march to begin)

THE PROCESSION

Ushers two by two

Bridesmaids two by two

Maid or matron of honor

Ring bearer—*if any* [6]

Flower girl—*if any* [6]

Bride on her father's right arm

(Groom, best man, and minister stand at the altar, facing the processional)

RECESSIONAL
Bride on groom's right arm

Flower girl alone or with the ring bearer

Maid or matron of honor alone or with the best man [7]

Bridesmaids two by two or paired with ushers

Ushers two by two or with the bridesmaids

As soon as the wedding party has gone out, two ushers return at once for mothers of the bride and groom

The guests then depart

**RECEIVING
LINE
(Left to right)**
Bride's mother

Groom's father [8]

Groom's mother

Bride's father

Bride

Groom

Maid or matron of honor

Bridesmaids (if preferred they may mingle with the guests, as the ushers and the best man do)

---

[6] If children are in the wedding party, they should be rehearsed carefully once or twice before the ceremony, at the place of the wedding.

[7] The best man may go directly to the vestry for the groom's hat and coat, and his own, joining the wedding party at the door, if this seems more convenient in what comes next.

[8] The bride's father may stand beside his wife, then the groom's mother and father, then the bride and groom. This more modern form keeps the principal couples together and is sometimes more pleasant and graceful for the receiving line.

Why a Special Wedding Ceremony?

Virtually all groups, primitive and civilized alike, have a special ceremony marking the transition from the courtship to married life. In our own history we had for hundreds of years two ceremonies: the betrothal, which was a business arrangement between the families to take care of property arrangements, and the wedding ceremony, which came somewhat later and carried the mark of finality.

The wedding ceremony was originally performed by the father among the Hebrews, the Greeks, and the Romans; but as the early Christian church became powerful, the priest's blessing was added to the ceremony. As the church concerned itself more and more with marriage, witnesses were added, and all marriages were performed by the clergy. With the Reformation the Protestants came to regard marriage as a civil contract, and the state undertook the responsibility of supervising the ceremony in Protestant countries. In Europe today it is not uncommon to be married by a civil court and then to repeat the ceremony at a church wedding. In America we have delegated to the clergy the civil authority to perform marriages, giving them thereby both civil and religious sanction over marriage.

The functions of the marriage ceremony today are:

1. To impress on the couple and all relatives and friends the changed status of the pair, both legally and psychologically.
2. To announce the new status; to give public support and stability to the relation emphasized by the titles *Mr.* and *Mrs.* and by the assumption of the husband's family name by the wife.
3. To give legal protection to the wife and to the children born of the union: to place the responsibility for their care and support with the pair and not with the state.
4. To glorify and sanctify the relation (religious marriage), giving it divine blessing and approval—God approves.

Weddings in the many churches of the various faiths differ widely. Not only the procedures prescribed by the particular church but the training and beliefs of the individual minister and the preferences of the couple play a part in determining the nature of the wedding ceremony. An occasional couple write a part of their own ceremony, incorporating their own convictions and commitment with the traditional vows. Some ministers have developed their own introductory statements that precede the usual vows in the wedding ceremony. The following is used by permission as illustrative.

WEDDING CEREMONY

Address to the Congregation

There is an ancient story which contains a profound insight: It is not good for man to be alone. We rightly approach a wedding ceremony with reverence and with awe. For marriage has welled up out of the depths of personal and social need. In it the fundamental impulses of the individual and the race, biological, personal and social, come to an overt focus. The ceremony itself is the public avowal of a new relationship, the most basic which can exist among men. It signifies that two people stand at one point along the unending stream of human development, a point at which count-less others have stood before and countless more will stand in ages which are to come. Yet it is for the human race, as for them, unique in the totality of timeless aeons. The centuries of the past have looked forward to this occa-sion. Those of the future should have good cause to regard it with respect and gratitude.

It is meet and proper that so awe-inspiring an occasion, when Eternity emerges as a visible point in the present, should be celebrated with dignity and solemnity. All races, tribes and cultures, from the most primitive to the most advanced, have made of this step an occasion for rejoicing and an expression through ceremony and rite of profound social concern. So today, society expresses its legitimate and inescapable interest. For a wedding is more than the joining of two persons to each other. It is the closing of a link in the endless chain of human relationships, a link which binds the pres-ent to the past and out of which the future can most advantageously emerge.

The wedding is properly a religious ceremony. For in marriage, basic forces which determine human destiny find their richest and most creative expression. The noblest sentiments and highest ideals of the human soul stand by in expectant concern for their future. The God who sustains all which is, ultimately presides.

Address to the Couple

For you, this ceremony will mean entrance into new relationships which will affect many aspects of your lives. Your legal status will be altered in important respects. The merger of names will symbolize an extensive change in your social status and relationships. Changed personal relationships, some of which may prove onerous, will remind you that things are no longer as they were.

It will mean for you a new security in your personal lives. For marriage is an oasis of refreshment and renewal in an often arid world, a point of sta-bility amid the bewildering and often alarming changes of a rapidly shifting social scene. Your marriage will mean that each of you will have one whom you know and can respond to as a whole personality. In all the welter of mass humanity and whirling shifts of friendships, you can find stability. Marriage will mean for you that intimacy which is necessary for the best satisfaction of the deepest needs of your souls. You will find a new security in acceptance, a security which is freely yours without the need for pretense and dissimulation. For you there will always be one situation in which you can be as you really are, without risk of rejection. Marriage means, in part, the weaving of a rope of relationships upon which each of you can put the full strain of your own worst, without fear that it will break.

You will find a new security and richness of love. Among the greatest needs of all is a two-way flow of affection. Marriage will increase and enrich this for you, unimpeded by conventions and unspoiled by fear of its loss. Such married love is above and beyond all other forms of human love. In it alone are intermingled the depth, intimacy, and permanence essential for your greatest satisfaction and growth.

Your wedding means a recognition and acceptance of new social obligations. To marry is to enter into partnership in a building enterprise. It means the construction of a social relationship which inevitably involves others. To marry is not only to establish a center of emotional security for yourselves. It is to create a basic unit of society. And in so doing you find your own greatest fulfillment.

The vows which you are about to take pledge you to fidelity, one to the other. This does not merely mean fidelity to taboos, or even to a person. The man and woman who live together secure in each other's love are being faithful to far more than each other. They are being faithful to a social situation which can produce people who can live without fear, who are sufficiently mature emotionally as neither to seek nor to need dictatorship and aggression. They are being faithful to the basic foundations of the social structure in which all are formed and nourished. They are being faithful to the provisions which society makes for the protection and the development of the deepest needs of persons. When you marry you do far more than to take unto yourself a spouse. You take a piece of the social future into your hands.

Then follow the usual vows and prayers.

What If Yours Is a Special Case?

There are many special situations in which the usual forms and rules do not seem to apply. Yours may be a special case along one of the following lines.

When members of two faiths marry, their wedding has to be worked out to meet the requirements of their respective churches as well as their personal preferences. If a Catholic is to have his or her marriage recognized by the Roman Catholic Church, it must be performed by a Catholic priest according to the rules of the church. Some faithful Jews feel married only when it has been done by the rabbi.

One Baptist bride called her pastor on the evening of her wedding day and begged him to "marry us again, for I just don't feel right being married only by his rabbi." This minister replied that it was hardly necessary to be married again, since they were already married, but that he would be willing to *reaffirm* their marriage and give it his blessing as a Christian clergyman. This pleased the bride, was satisfactory to the groom, and violated nothing in either's religion.

Some couples marrying across religious faiths plan for such a dual-wedding service in which all members of both families as well as the dictates of both churches will be satisfied.

Two couples (usually sisters or brothers) may marry without other attendants, each serving as the others' witnesses. Or the double wedding may have all the pomp and splendor of the huge church wedding. In the latter case, the older bride and her attendants enter first, then the younger bride and her attendants, with the recessional in the same formation with each couple leading its own bridal party. If the brides are sisters, one invitation may be issued for their double wedding, in which case the older sister's name appears first.

If the bride's parents are divorced, the invitations may be issued by her mother, with her present husband as host, if she has remarried. In this case, the bride's father may give her away if she wishes, after which he steps back to the pew behind her mother. Whether or not he remains for the reception is best decided by discussion well ahead of time. Except in most unusual cases, the absent parent is invited to the wedding.

The mature bride whose parents are divorced may issue her own invitations and announcements and walk down the aisle either alone, or on the arm of a favorite uncle or other older male relative.

Similarly, if the bride is herself a divorcée, she may issue her own invitations, and the couple may announce their own marriage. If the bride is a very young divorcée, her parents may announce her marriage as usual. The remarriage of a divorced woman is usually not formal, or in a white gown and veil. It may be held in a chapel, home, or garden, with one attendant (not a child by a former marriage).

The bride who is an orphan may have a formal wedding if she wishes, by asking some older woman to be her sponsor, and walking down the aisle on the arm of some favorite older male relative or close family friend.

The remarriage of a widow is usually simple and informal, and not in white wedding gown and veil, which is the symbol of first marriage. Her own children may attend her if she wishes. She may write personal notes as invitations and announcements, using her full name.

Sickness and death in wedding plans

An invalid mother, grandmother, or sister may attend even a formal church wedding in a wheel chair, or the wedding may be planned at home where she is. Bride, groom, or any of the bridal attendants may participate in any wedding in a wheel chair or on crutches if need be. In the case of a close member of the family being suddenly stricken ill just before the wedding, the ceremony may be postponed by notifying the guests by wire, phone, or note.

When one of the parents of bride or groom dies suddenly, the wedding usually is postponed with some such wording as this: "Owing to the sudden death of Mrs. John James Jones, the marriage of her daughter Janice to Gerald Raymond Brown has been indefinitely postponed." This notice may be sent to the local papers, and to all guests already invited to the wedding. The marriage may proceed on the date planned but then it is a simple quiet wedding with only members of the immediate family present.

Calling off the wedding

It is not only in Hollywood that something breaks up a couple before the wedding date; it happens in real life too. In such a case, there are two things to do at once: 1. cancel the wedding; and 2. return to the senders all wedding gifts. Guests already invited to the wedding must be notified that the wedding plans have been cancelled, whether or not they have sent gifts to the bride. Couples feeling embarrassed about cancelling their wedding should remember that it is far better to call off an unpromising marriage before it gets started than it is to carry each other into the anguish of an unhappy union. One of the functions of the engagement period is to sort out incompatible pairs.[9] It may take the wise guidance of a competent counselor to help the couple discover whether the break originates from something simple and superficial, or whether it stands for something basically wrong in the match.

Moving up the date

In these days when so many things may happen to change things, it is sometimes necessary to advance the date of the wedding. A military leave is granted earlier than expected, a vacation date is advanced, an opportunity opens up, all sorts of things may call for an earlier date than the one originally planned. The procedure for meeting this type of case is simply to contact the guests and tell them where and when the rearranged wedding is to be. A simple wedding can be arranged at the last minute in the chapel at the military post, in the bride's home, in a club or garden, or even after one of the regular services of the church, if the couple are flexible in their planning. Indeed, this might serve as a motto for wedding plans generally: "Be Prepared for the Unexpected."

---

[9] See Chapter 6, "Getting Engaged."

To be useful wedding plans should be based upon the values of those being married. If you realize that tradition has been upset many times, and that conventions serve but as guides, you can plan your wedding in ways that will be most meaningful to you and to those whom you love and want close to you on this your day of days.

Commercial establishments make weddings their business. They count on making money on the weddings they service, as of course they must if they are to stay in business. But that does not mean that you have to go along with all the expensive suggestions or elaborate plans that are offered you. The bride who realizes that simple weddings can be quite as lovely as commercially staged ones has the courage to see to it that her wedding expresses what means most in terms not of dollars spent but of personal values. It makes little sense to go bankrupt on an expensive wedding that will be over in a matter of minutes when a little careful planning would save the money for a home for the years.

In the long run, it is not what you wear or eat at your wedding, but what you are that counts. As you put your emphasis on *being* rather than on *buying*, you are establishing a sound policy for the foundation of your home.

Expressing your values in your wedding

READINGS

Bentley, Marguerite, *Wedding Etiquette Complete*. Philadelphia: Winston.

Blood, Robert O., Jr., *Anticipating Your Marriage*. Glencoe, Illinois: Free Press, 1955, Chapter 8, "Getting Married: the Wedding and Honeymoon."

Bossard, James H. S., and Boll, Eleanor S., *Ritual in Family Living*. Philadelphia: University of Pennsylvania Press, 1950.

Bride's Magazine, *The Bride's Book of Etiquette*.

Cavan, Ruth, *American Marriage: A Way of Life*. New York: Crowell, 1959, Chapter 11.

Fenwick, Millicent, *Vogue's Book of Etiquette*. New York: Simon and Schuster, 1948.

Hollingshead, August B., "Marital Status and Wedding Behavior," *Marriage and Family Living*, November, 1952, pp. 308–311.

Johannis, Theodore B., Jr., and Karen Many, "Financing Student Weddings," *Journal of Home Economics*, May, 1959, pp. 362–364.

Marshall Field and Company, *The Bride's Book*. Chicago: Marshall Field, 1950.

Modern Bride, magazine published by Ziff-Davis Company, 185 North Wabash Ave., Chicago 1, Ill.

Post, Emily, *Emily Post's Etiquette*. New York: Funk and Wagnalls.

Timmons, B. F., "The Cost of Weddings," *American Sociological Review*, April, 1939, pp. 224–233.

Vogue, "Invitation to the Wedding," Vol. LXXIX, No. 9, p. 84.

Woods, Marjorie Binford, *Your Wedding: How to Plan and Enjoy It*. New York: Bobbs-Merrill, 1949.

Wright, Jeanne, *The Wedding Book*. New York: Rinehart, 1947.

PART TWO

BEING MARRIED

10 Being Newlyweds

How does it feel to be newlyweds?

What type of honeymoon is best?

Are all honeymoon intimacies easy to take?

Is there an etiquette of intimacy?

Is disillusionment to be expected?

Will you like setting up housekeeping?

What are the major accomplishments of the first year of marriage?

T HE wedding is over. The unity which has been built up during courtship and engagement has now been publicly recognized and ceremonialized. Now at last the roles of husband and wife which have been played in fantasy many times may be tried out. Once married, the man and the woman start on a journey from which it is difficult to turn back. In the chapters that follow, the discussion turns to the situations couples face in marriage, the skills and abilities they need, and the normality of trouble and frustration as a new family is launched into operation. Key ideas that merit attention include the following:

1. Marriage is a more complex way of living than single life and therefore is likely to aggravate rather than cure symptoms of immaturity such as restiveness, uncertainty, and unhappiness.
2. A key need of early marriage is to settle down and work out the routines of daily living.
3. As romantic love is replaced by conjugal love, the marriage becomes stabilized.
4. Conflict in marriage is normal and may be used constructively to hold the partnership together.

5. Happily married couples, in adult terms, are not necessarily couples who never quarrel, but are those who have learned the techniques of resolving conflicts which arise.

6. Keeping channels of communication clear is important for marriage solidarity.

How Does It Feel to Be Newlyweds?

In the early weeks of marriage people are perhaps more impressionable than at any other time in their lives. Hope and expectation are keyed to a high pitch. Idealism is at its height. The newly married individuals continue the pattern of the engagement in ever increasing tempo, widening the range of their mutual exploration of one another's personalities. These processes parallel, or overlay, anxieties about the undefined future and the realization that this relationship which is so precious has the capacity to hurt. All these conditions can bring about a delicately balanced state of the emotions in which small embarrassments are capable of having a devastating effect.

Mace expresses the situation well:

> From one point of view, getting married could be represented as a rather terrifying experience. For something like a third of their life span two people have lived independent of each other, probably without even knowing of each other's existence. They have formed their own personal habits and learned to live their own private lives. Now, after a comparatively short acquaintance, they come together in the closest human intimacy, living together, sleeping together, yielding themselves up to each other. At the time, they don't think of this as an invasion of their privacy. Their strong desire for each other draws them together and they make their surrender eagerly. But for all that, the mutual unveiling of their bodies and minds can sometimes have profoundly disturbing and quite unexpected consequences. . . . To make these early adjustments as easy as possible, we have wisely provided the institution of the honeymoon.[1]

Full of excitement, thrills, and anticipation of delightful intimacies, the honeymoon may be the fulfillment of the bliss hoped for during the engagement period. Two sources of emotion flow over in most marriages during the first weeks: the growing pleasures of the sex experiences and the fears of the unknown and undefined future of the marriage. These are major components of romantic love. Indeed, the honeymoon marks the crest of the feelings identified as romantic love feelings. Thereafter the fear element, which has its source in the ap-

---

[1] David R. Mace, *Marriage: The Art of Lasting Love*, New York: Doubleday, 1952, pp. 46–47.

prehension of the unknown and unpredictable problems of marriage, subsides unless activated by extramarital thrill seeking or a new love affair. Romantic love feeds on the new and the unknown. As marriage settles down to a walking gait, romantic love is normally exchanged for a less exciting but more permanent combination of love feelings based on companionship and mutual interdependence, identified elsewhere as conjugal love.[2]

Conjugal love first appears in the companionable phase of the engagement relation and develops rapidly during the early months of marriage. During the honeymoon the couple may pick up souvenirs or buy furniture which are quickly given a sentimental value. The snapshots of the honeymoon trip and the views seen together are often reviewed. Thus the memories of the honeymoon make up some of the first tangible evidences of the conjugal love on which enduring marriages are based.

What Type of Honeymoon Is Best?

The wedding journey is designed to meet specific needs and should not be postponed for several weeks or months until, for example, the bridegroom gets his vacation. The value of the honeymoon lies in the opportunities it gives the newlyweds to meet the first experiences of marriage away from people who know them, thus providing them a little time to get over the self-consciousness that comes with playing new and untried roles. Point number one in planning, then, is to set the wedding date at a time when a honeymoon is possible.

Although the plans for the honeymoon are for the most part jointly laid, the exact dates for the wedding and wedding journey are rightly set by the bride. The timing of the menstrual period and the irregularities often accompanying emotional stress are factors which need to receive attention in launching the marriage.

The newlywed couple can add enjoyment to their first days of marriage if they depart from the trite honeymoon tours to Niagara Falls or Washington in favor of a trip that characterizes the individuality of their relationship. One couple who had met in Europe on a hosteling tour planned a similar tour by bicycle through New England. Another made their common passion for bird life the center of their plans for a week's outing at a bird sanctuary neither had visited before. A third couple spent most of their time in New York attending plays and operas when they weren't catching up on their sleep at a bohemian apart-

[2] See Chapter 17, "Strengthening Marriage Ties."

ment off Washington Square. The couple should plan to do something that both enjoy and can do reasonably well. A trout stream in the Rockies is no place for a couple of tenderfeet and life on a dude ranch can be very irritating if the couple doesn't know its cattle ponies. There will be other occasions for the new and unusual when both parties are surer of themselves and are under less emotional tension.

Two hazards to be avoided by honeymooners are excessive costs and overfatigue. If the engagement has been one of planning and discussion, the honeymoon costs will have been worked out along with the budget of the first year's expenses. Some estimate of the number of miles to be traveled and the number of things to be seen and done needs to be made. Trying to do too much in too little time results in overfatigue and sets the stage for quarrels when the couple is least able to cope with them. Here are a few points to remember in planning for a honeymoon:

1. Select a place where you can be completely alone and away from people who know you, and where privacy is assured.
2. Plan your trip to obviate overfatigue as much as possible.
3. Arrange for hotel or room reservations in advance.
4. Plan for time to loaf and sleep—newly married couples go to bed early and get up late.
5. Carry on with the planning and exploration talks of the engagement, discussing points on which you aren't able to find a basis for agreement as well as those on which you are.

Are All Honeymoon Intimacies Easy to Take?

The honeymoon customarily lasts a week or two and for obvious economic reasons rarely extends beyond a month. The wedding journey is an excellent introduction into marriage, providing as it does for a release of the tension that has piled up in the days before the wedding and for the maximum expression of idealism. The honeymoon also provides a point at which realities are allowed to intrude, as the pair prepares to return to familiar surroundings and mundane responsibilities. Fortunately, the period of ecstasy does not continue long, for moving from one thrill and discovery to another is exhausting.

The adjustment in the first years is sometimes most difficult for those couples who have restricted their love activities too prudishly in the courtship and engagement period. They find themselves suddenly in marriage with all the barriers down but with all too little preparation for the expression of the excitement and attraction which arise in the intimacies. It is not uncommon for one or both of the pair to experience feelings of guilt or revulsion, to the mutual distress of both.

Couples who have anticipated great thrills in the first sex relations sometimes feel disappointment—reality doesn't live up to the expectations. Said one such couple, "We were surprised that that was all there was to it; somehow we had expected more." The girl felt cheated, and the boy was hurt and worried that his wife wasn't thrilled. Both needed to realize that enjoyable sex response is a matter of learning and that it grows with the years. They failed to grasp the fact that early sex relations are necessarily awkward, both because of their newness and because of the anxiety both feel toward the unknown. Where fear is present, sex response is inhibited, and only after the couple have become thoroughly secure in their new role of husband and wife can they expect to attain the heights which the uninformed honeymooners feel is their right the first night.[3]

The honeymoon intimacies are taken almost as a matter of course by the couples who are able to recognize the sexual urges and expressions for what they are. They have studied what to expect, and after a certain amount of normal love play in the engagement period, the honeymoon presents to them an extended period of easily assimilated new experiences. They are able to recognize and understand their own urges and quickly learn how to satisfy them in marriage.

There is one group of people who "make the most" of the honeymoon experience because they feel that the intoxication of early marriage is the most desirable part of marriage, that marriage should be one continual courtship in which love is kept aglow with constant thrills. This is the school that reflects most closely the Hollywood pattern of perpetual romance and which judges a marriage by the continuation of the burning thrills of love. If the love-light dies, divorce ensues; and the light burns again only as new love appears, followed by another honeymoon, another trip to Reno, another honeymoon, and so on. These people take their fiction and movies too seriously and apparently know little or nothing about the studies of happily married men and women. Although the great majority settle down in time to more or less routine married living, there is usually an intervening period of disillusionment before they hit a normal stride. For these

---

[3] See Chapter 17, "Strengthening Marriage Ties." In Stanley Brav's intriguing study of honeymoons, nearly half of his respondents reported that they failed to achieve complete sexual harmony during their honeymoon, yet the majority considered their honeymoon a complete success. Sexual harmony was not considered essential to honeymoon success. See Stanley Brav, "Note on Honeymoons," *Marriage and Family Living*, Vol. 9, Summer, 1947, p. 60.

people the psychiatrists would list "coming to terms with reality" as the most important accomplishment of the first year of marriage.

Is There an Etiquette of Intimacy?

Interpersonal adjustment on a honeymoon involves the intimacies of personal hygiene. The early days of marriage could be greatly eased if young couples received more help about these matters. They would be spared a good deal of distress if, as well as preparing themselves for sexual union, they recognized also the fact that in close intimacy of marriage, men and women must learn a warm, tender consideration for the little details of bodily hygiene which are part of the business of living. Mace has pointed out that in the course of married life there are many lowly services which husband and wife must perform for each other. One of the important adjustments to be made in the early weeks together is to get over any false modesty which the couple may feel about their own or each other's bodies.[4]

Why should couples, in this day and age of frankness and freedom of inhibitions about sex, find the intimacies of sensory details connected with other bodily functions fraught with embarrassment and disgust reactions? The answer may not be obvious.

In America, the land of locked bathrooms and fully clothed people, of private bedrooms and dressing quarters, the child is often reared to adulthood carefully protected from the sensory details of the bodily functions of others. He is taught to disguise his intention of going to the toilet by asking if he may "wash his hands." Girls particularly are protected from vulgarity, as Americans define it. Added to and accentuating the problem is the universal tendency in the courtship and engagement period to idealize the other person, to endow one's lover with superhuman qualities, and to shrink from the thought that the other person carries on the same bodily functions as common folk.

Holding these ideas, the carefully protected boy and girl marry and face for the first time the details of married living, with the doors of privacy torn off. Body odors, menstrual products, and untidy bathroom practices are peculiarly noticeable in the early weeks of marriage, calling for the closest attention by newlyweds to personal hygiene and physical cleanliness. Sensory details can overwhelm a sensitive, sheltered girl and all too often produce reactions of disgust and revulsion.

Too much intimacy, too little privacy, in too short a period! Because

---

[4] Mace, *op. cit.*, p. 50.

of the way you may have been reared, you may have to preserve some of the illusions for a time, at least. A minimum of privacy will need to be maintained indefinitely, just because Americans react to bodily functions of urination and excretion the way they do. This is difficult in overcrowded apartments with no private dressing quarters and with shared bathrooms, but every effort should be made to ease the transition gracefully from the more spacious parental home with its privacy to the more restricted accompaniments of married life.[5]

Is Disillusionment to Be Expected?

Disillusionment sounds like an ugly word, but it means, simply, "facing realities." G. V. Hamilton's study of two hundred married persons, *A Research in Marriage*, showed the illusions of the engagement and honeymoon period to have lasted well into the second year of marriage for most of his cases. Twenty-nine per cent stated that they had settled down to facing realities after one year, and 20 per cent after two years. The balance didn't know how long it took them to complete the process of disillusionment.

Disillusionment today is more likely to occur to husbands than to wives, according to Hobart, who has studied the reactions of couples as they shift from engagement to marriage. He defined disillusionment somewhat ingeniously as the relative increase in disagreement imputed to the spouse on crucial issues of the marriage compared with the change in disagreements from engagement to marriage which had actually occurred. Using this information he found husbands to be more disillusioned in marriage than their wives, especially with respect to romantic issues and the amount of personal freedom in marriage.[6]

Many couples claim to have no difficulty in settling down after returning from the honeymoon. They say, "The process developed naturally," "We didn't expect marriage to be so very different and it wasn't," "It was a relief to find marriage so livable after all the ghastly accounts of divorce and separation," "We just kept on being good pals instead of going dramatic during the honeymoon, and we couldn't see anything to be disillusioned about." These couples started their period of disillusionment by facing realities in the courtship and engagement

---

[5] A searching analysis of the reactions of Americans to lack of privacy is given in Markoosha Fisher's *My Lives in Russia*, New York: Harper, 1944, pp. 59–76.

[6] Charles W. Hobart, "Disillusionment in Marriage and Romanticism," *Marriage and Family Living*, Vol. XX, No. 2, May, 1958, pp. 156–163.

period, as their statements reveal, and made the transition into marriage with a minimum of anxiety.

Walking is the best gait for most people, but most honeymooners hit a tempo more akin to a gallop in the series of thrills sought and experienced. The change of pace which must come is called "settling down," and is a phase of disillusionment. Disillusionment includes not only the removal of blinders which have kept the lover from seeing that wart on the chin of the loved one, but also the mutual discovery that marriage doesn't change personalities. "We are still our old familiar, boring selves, and we thought we would be different when married. It looked as if we could change when we were engaged and on the honeymoon, but now. . . ."

Disillusionment is partly due to the discrepancy between what you have imagined marriage to be like, or have been told it was like, or read it was like, and what you find it to be. Notice the discrepancy between the following stereotyped picture of the couple who lived happily ever after and the facts. It is the case of Mary Jane and Jim, who were married and settled down in a cute little house with checked curtains at the windows. They are supposed to have had three years of happy married life, writes our ad writer for marriage:

Mary Jane, in a crisp house dress kept spotless and unfaded by Lux, has laid out breakfast—everything Beechnut but the eggs. Jim Junior is busily eating up his cereal for the fun of finding the Mickey Mouse at the bottom of the dish, thoughtfully supplied by the makers of Cream of Wheat. Jim Senior, spruce in an Arrow collar and fortified by a perfect night's rest under the auspices of the Simmons Bedding Company, is about to make his way to the office to earn the thirty-five dollars a week which somehow are to pay for the hundred-dollar radio, the Monel metal kitchen, the dapper little car, and the self-satisfied look that comes to those who have provided nicely for retirement at fifty-five. This intimate view of American home life is familiar to us all through the kindness of advertising mediums of every variety and haunting ubiquity. We are fortunate because without their aid we should never see such a pretty picture.

Let us peek in again without the rosy spectacles supplied by the nationally advertised brands. Mary Jane's frock for mornings at home looks a little frayed and faded. Her apron has definitely seen neither Lux nor a harsh washing soap for several days. She scrapes dispiritedly at the breakfast plates, slightly repulsive with congealed egg yolk and slimy cold bacon grease. For the fourteenth time she exhorts Junior to stop dawdling and eat his cereal. She is not, at the moment, enjoying her marriage very much. Why should she? Washing dishes day in and day out is not the same thing as canoeing in the moonlight with your heart's beloved. . . . Mary Jane is remembering five o'clock with Jim waiting at the corner, of dinner with dancing, of going to the movies, or a concert, or the theatre, or just a long ferry-boat ride. Of the difficult good-night kiss and the ecstatic knowledge that soon she would have Jim all the time for always. She is thinking rather wryly of how entrancing, how full of promise, this battered dishpan looked when it first emerged from pink tissue paper at the shower the girls gave her. She may even think, a little cynically, as she surveys the grey grease pocked surface of her dishwater, of the foaming pans of eternally virgin suds she expected from her perusal of the advertisements. Well, she's married now. She has her own house, her own dishpan, her husband, and her baby. All the time and for always. She doesn't even go to the movies any more because there is no one to stay with Junior. She speaks so crossly to the child now that his tears fall into the objectionable cereal. Why on earth won't Jim let her get Mrs. Oldacre in to stay evenings? He'll be earning more soon; Mr. Bayswater practically told him he would be put in charge of the branch office as soon as old Fuzzy retired. Five dollars a week savings—much good that does anyway. Mary Jane's thoughts about her husband become quite uncharitable. "If he only had the least understanding of the kind of life I have, but all he notices is Junior's shoes are scuffed out, and he would not even try that Bavarian cream I fixed yesterday. It's all very well for him to think Jimmy Junior's cute when he sneaks out of bed—he doesn't have him all day and all night and nothing but Jimmy Junior."

Thus Mary Jane at nine o'clock of a Monday morning. At three P.M. the sight of Junior tugging a large packing box about the yard suddenly makes her heart turn over with delight and pride. What a duck he is. . . . She smiles to herself with pleasure at the sunlight falling through the peach curtains on the blues and browns of her livingroom furniture. That recipe for apple pan dowdy—she'll try that for supper. Jim will be home in two hours and a half, home for a whole lovely evening. And Monday is Philadelphia orchestra night on the radio. For no reason at all life is abruptly good, very good.

Jim, meantime, is having his own problems, big and little. Mary Jane is a frequent pain in the neck to him. He likes his eggs with the whites firm and the yolks runny. Mary Jane gets them wrong every time—sometimes leathery, sometimes slimy. Why does she have to be so cranky with Junior, and why can't she keep him quiet mornings? She should know a man needs all the rest he can get. He has to give his best to the job—marriage is too expensive to loaf or to be tired. Mary doesn't understand that at all. He gave up his big chance in the Texas branch just for her, didn't he? But does she appreciate it? And yet Jim, too, has his hours of excitement and delight, of deep satisfaction in his wife and his son and his home and himself in the role of father in the family.[7]

How do you react to this latter view of marriage? It is more accurate than the version thrust upon us by the advertisers, but it is still only

[7] Reprinted from *The Happy Family* by John Levy and Ruth Munroe, by permission of and special arrangement with Alfred A. Knopf, Inc.

the top layer, the part we see, the common-sense interpretation of satisfactions and discords in the lives of Mary Jane and Jim. The roots of conflict lie much deeper in the personalities of the two partners.

If the discrepancy between what you imagined marriage would be like and what it is in reality is as great as that presented above, don't feel marriage has cheated you. The first step toward permanent and satisfying marriage is disillusionment, the willingness to accept one's self and one's partner on the level of everyday living, to take the worse along with the better.

It should be pointed out that well-adjusted couples will recognize moments of rapture and the moments of disappointment, as well as the strong undercurrent of partnership in the run-of-the-mine emotions of daily life. The role of moods is important; some days we're up, some days down, some days romantic and some days realistic. Disillusionment, although primarily concerned with facing realities, includes finding a place for the delightful moments of the happier mood.

Will You Like Setting Up Housekeeping?

In the play called 3 *Is a Family*, the young mother breaks down and weeps after her exasperated husband has criticized her inefficiency and mistakes in keeping the house straightened up, and her failures with the baby. "You must have patience with me; I know I'm inefficient, but you see, I've never been a mother before." The job was too big for her to handle all at once. She knew she was in a mess but was powerless to climb out of it. New jobs are like that, and marriage with its new household tasks takes some experience and planning.

Both parties in a new marriage face adjustments to a level of living less well ordered and substantial than existed in the parental family. After all, it took their parents twenty to thirty years to provide their home with all its facilities and to organize their routines so faultlessly. The new husband may obtain an understanding of his wife's problems if he pitches in to help with the meal, setting the table and washing up the dishes afterward—as well he should. The new wife needs to realize she can't follow the same budget for her personal expenditures that she could under her father's high salary, and she should thank her lucky stars she has a wardrobe built up which will hold her over the first few years. These are only a few of the adjustments which occur in the shift from parental family living to the life of newlyweds.

Out of the clinical studies by psychiatrists of hundreds of housewives come these findings of value for new husbands: Personalities that require order—that a house be neat and spotless, that every chair have a special place and all clothes be put away, in other words, personalities which make wonderful housekeepers, rarely make adaptable, understanding, patient wives. Rarely can a wife be both a perfect housekeeper and an understanding, flexible companion. The husband may get a not-so-good housekeeper who won't worry and fuss about him and the children. But the compulsion to keep order that makes for perfection in household management is incompatible with normal rough and tumble married living.

What Are the Major Accomplishments of the First Year of Marriage?

Courtship, engagement, and marriage can merge imperceptibly without jarring adjustments. A student's letter to one of the authors shows how normally and easily he and his wife achieved this merger:

I didn't learn much about family in my first month of marriage, but I did learn a great deal about marriage. We moved into our own house, budgeted our time and expenditures; we consulted a physician about birth control methods and got a very good start on our adjustment to the new roles we had assumed. Nobody told us a great deal about how to manage our affairs and it seemed to come natural to us. . . .

If all marriages developed as naturally and normally as this, there would be much less justification for formal education in marriage and family life. These young people changed the company they were frequenting and took on the roles and responsibilities of the new relation, just as they might shift tempo and dance steps on the dance floor. Ordinarily a person has to learn the steps in a new dance, but if he has watched carefully and is supple enough, he can imitate the new step satisfactorily. In more stable communities young people have known each other since school days, and at maturity may slip quickly into the more intensified relationships of courtship and engagement with a pretty clear idea of the reactions they may expect from each other. They assume the responsibilities of marriage relatively easily because the examples of successfully married people are constantly before them. Married people, moreover, are available to check with as the marriage progresses.

This chapter tells of certain minimum expectations for couples in the first year of marriage. These couples have carried over into the honeymoon and first months of marriage the fascinating pattern of exploration and experimentation started in the engagement. They have learned how to live intimately together and may have achieved a satisfying sexual relationship. They have come to accept the realities of marriage with its routines and schedules and unromantic regularity. Romantic thrills are giving way to more companionable sentiments.

These newlyweds have come to think of themselves as belonging to the married set and now feel comfortable in the roles of husband and wife, both at home and elsewhere. They are winning a status in the community as married folk and will soon be inducted into the circles of gardeners, marketing specialists, and do-it-yourself artists. Some people may already have begun talking about the advantages of "having your babies while you are young."

Although there have been many quarrels and conflicts during the first year, the differences are being ironed out, and the friction has worn smooth the edges which seemed so easily irritated the first few months. The pair still has its differences but has come to know that quarreling is no longer any threat to its relationship, which in itself is a major accomplishment. The new husband and wife have come to accept married life with its ups and downs and are prepared now to take the worse along with the better. The first year of marriage has been stimulating and satisfying. For the couple who worried about the pitfalls of marriage, it is reassuring to know that marriage is sometimes full of fun.

READINGS

Blood, Robert O., Jr., *Anticipating Your Marriage*. Glencoe, Illinois: Free Press, 1955, Chapters 8–10.

Cavan, Ruth S., *American Marriage, A Way of Life*. New York: Crowell, 1959, Chapter 11, "Time and Place for Wedding and Honeymoon."

Duvall, Evelyn M., *Family Development*. Chicago: Lippincott, 1957, Chapter VI, "Beginning Families: Establishment Phase."

Himes, Norman E., and Donald L. Taylor, *Your Marriage* (Rev. Ed.). New York: Rinehart, 1955, Chapter 10, "Wedding and Honeymoon."

Kirkpatrick, Clifford, *The Family*. New York: Ronald Press, 1955, Chapter 18, "Marriage Adjustments."

Landis, Judson T., and Mary G. Landis, *Building a Successful Marriage*. Englewood Cliffs: Prentice-Hall, 1958, Chapter 15, "Achieving Adjustment in Marriage."

Levy, John, and Ruth Munroe, *The Happy Family*. New York: Knopf, 1938, Chapter 2, "Settling Down to Marriage."

Mace, David, "For Those Who Wear the Altar-Halter," *Woman's Home Companion*, 1949, essay on the early weeks of marriage.

Magoun, F. Alexander, *Love and Marriage*. New York: Harper, 1956, Chapter 2, "The Nature of Marriage."

Waller, Willard, and Reuben Hill, *The Family: A Dynamic Interpretation*. New York: Dryden Press, 1951, Chapter 13, "Married-Pair Living."

11 Relating to In-Laws

Do you expect in-law trouble?

How serious are in-law problems?

Who is the most difficult in-law?

Are you mature enough to be a good in-law?

Should you live with your in-laws?

What makes for good in-law relationships?

ADJUSTING to in-laws is more than just getting along with your mother-in-law and the others that become your relatives by marriage. It involves a complete realignment of family loyalties:

Every married couple belongs to three families. They belong first of all to themselves. They are the WE of the new family they are founding together. But, at the same time they belong also to *his* family, and to *hers.* If they are to establish a strong family unit of their own, they must inevitably realign their loyalties to the place where *our* family comes before either *yours* or *mine.*

This is the elemental triangle of married living. Unless the cohesive force in the new family unit is stronger than that which ties either of the couple to the parental home, the founding family is threatened, as we see in the figures.

In Figure a, (see p. 210) YOU have in-law trouble because MY family is too close. It may be because I am still immature and not ready to emancipate myself from my parental home. It may be that one or more members of my family is possessive and find it difficult to let me go. It may be that circumstances within my family require from me more loyalty and attention than I can comfortably give at the time that I am involved in building my own home and marriage. Whatever the reason, if the forces pulling me/us toward loyalties to MY home are too strong, the development of OUR common sense of identity is delayed and weakened.

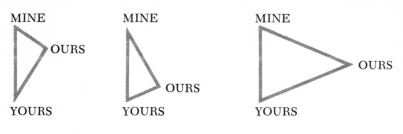

MY family is too close   YOUR family is too close   OUR family comes first

Figure a
YOU have in-law trouble

Figure b
I have in-law trouble

Figure c
No in-law trouble

In Figure b, YOUR family is too close, and so I have in-law trouble. Because YOU are bound so tightly to YOUR family, I am pulled away from mine, and WE make little progress in establishing OURS.

In Figure c, OUR family unit comes first in our joint loyalties. We are threatened neither by the ties that bind us to YOUR family, nor by the bonds that unite us to MINE. We are able to make progress as a new family because the force of our common identification pulls us out and away together into a home of our own. Now we can share in the common heritage of both your family and mine because we are not threatened by the pull from either. Only thus are WE free to enjoy being members of the entire extended family, without the stress of in-law strains.

The basic task in the early years of marriage is to cement the marriage bonds to the place where the two feel, behave, and fundamentally *want to be* ONE. This is the explicit commitment of the marriage ceremony in which the man and wife promise, "Forsaking all others, keep Ye only to him/her as long as Ye both shall live."

Any intrusion or threat from either his family or hers may be considered an in-law problem. The autonomy of the married pair is so imperative for the solidarity of the union that there is a peculiar sensitivity to any conflicting force emanating from either parental home. For this reason, anything that a member of his family or hers does that imperils the independence of the pair may be construed as an in-law difficulty.[1]

Do You Expect In-Law Trouble?

The chances are that you expect some difficulty with your in-laws, for at least one of the following reasons:

---

[1] Evelyn Millis Duvall, *In-Laws: Pro and Con,* New York: Association Press, 1954, pp. 278–280.

1. You have been influenced by negative cultural stereotypes about in-laws.
2. You have already experienced interference from your prospective in-laws.
3. Your sweetheart is having trouble getting free of his/her parental family.
4. You find it hard to emancipate yourself from your family.

You may already know and like your prospective parents-in-law, as many couples do. But even so, you may have been so bombarded by mother-in-law jokes that you may dread your future relationships with your relatives by marriage, and quite irrationally expect difficulty with them just because they *are* your in-laws.

Joking about the mother-in-law runs through our entire culture. An analysis of hundreds of mother-in-law jokes reveals several often repeated themes, such as: [2]

Stereotyped hostility

> Mother-in-law talks too much.
> She knows all the answers—the wrong ones.
> She is a meddlesome troublemaker.
> She is ego-deflating.
> She is mean.
> She comes too often and stays too long.

Americans are not unique in avoiding their mothers-in-law. In a cross-cultural survey of 250 societies around the world, Murdock found that 81 per cent of the societies had some form of mother-in-law trouble.[3] Briffault has said that one of the most constant rules in savage society is that a man may not speak to or look at his wife's mother.[4] Many different interpretations of the mother-in-law problem have been attempted by anthropologists, psychiatrists, and other social scientists,[5] but they all agree that there is a long history of taboos against the mother-in-law. Negative conditioning against mothers-in-law begins in childhood. One woman says:

---

[2] *Ibid.*, pp. 22–32.
[3] George Murdock, *Social Structure*. New York: Macmillan, 1949.
[4] Robert Briffault, *The Mothers—A Study of the Origins of Sentiments and Institutions.* Vol. L, London: Allen and Unwin, 1927.
[5] A summary of these is found in Duvall, *op. cit.*, pp. 33–35, drawn from original sources such as Sigmund Freud, *The Basic Writings of Sigmund Freud,* translated and edited by A. A. Brill, Book V, "Totem and Taboo," New York: Random House, 1938, pp. 815–819; Margaret Mead, *Kinship in the Admiralty Islands,* Anthropological Papers of the American Museum of Natural History, Vol. V, New York, 1934; C. S. Brant, "On Joking Relationships," *American Anthropologist*, 1948, p. 161; and Mildred Perlis, "The Social Functions of Marriage Wit," *Marriage and Family Living*, February, 1954, pp. 49–50.

> I remember hearing my first mother-in-law joke at the age of 8. At that time I couldn't understand too much the meaning of mother-in-law. At 15 I laughed with the others when jokes were made about her. At 17 those jokes were taken for granted like ice cream and pop. When I married at 20 I knew my mother-in-law would be everything I had heard about her . . . Imagine my surprise when she turned out to be as nice as *my* mother . . .[6]

This early conditioning brings many brides and grooms to the new family circle ready to bristle with hostility and to defend themselves at all costs against the mother-in-law.

It is encouraging to find that many young married couples actively reject the negative stereotype as unsound, unfair, and unfortunate. In an analysis of 3,683 letters, 264 of the husbands and wives wrote vigorous statements describing their personal campaigns to repudiate the mother-in-law stereotype. The following is typical:

> I do everything I can to keep my sons and daughters from swallowing all the nonsense they hear about how bad mothers-in-law are. We don't laugh at mother-in-law jokes at our house. And I go out of my way to praise my own mother-in-law in the children's presence, so that they will realize how I feel about her.

> Despite all the humor attending the mother-in-law myth, it is vicious and destructive of the good qualities in human beings. It is especially harmful to the children of a family who so early become aware of the negative attitude one is expected to have toward one's in-laws.

> That it is a *myth*, I am willing, anxious, and able to testify . . . my own mother-in-law has been a mother to me: warm, affectionate, helpful, critical when there was need for criticism, but loving at all times. During the sixteen years of my married life our friendship has become ever firmer until now it is unshakeable.[7]

Now, when good group relationships generally are dependent upon eliminating prejudice and exploding out-moded myths, there are indications that some young people are avoiding the cultural stereotype against mothers-in-law that might otherwise make for hardships in their early in-law adjustments. If you are wise enough to judge each of your prospective relatives by marriage for what he or she is (rather than discriminate against them as a family) you may avoid the negative attitudes that might otherwise hinder your early in-law relationships.

Unhappy previous experiences

You may dread your relationships with your in-laws because you have already had unpleasant experiences with one or more of them. In

---

[6] Duvall, *op. cit.*, p. 40.
[7] Duvall, *op. cit.*, p. 40.

one study of 136 young married couples, most of the men and women reported some parental attempts to influence their courtships. More interference from mothers than fathers was felt by both sons and daughters, and more girls than men remembered both parents' efforts to influence their courtship. It is quite possible that many of these efforts were resented, no matter how well-meaning from the parents' viewpoint.

Young persons who find it difficult to emancipate themselves from their parental families are apt to bring in-law problems into their marriages. The classic example is the "mama's boy" who finds it hard to untie the apron strings. Since his wife will resent the strong maternal

Difficulties in emancipation

TABLE 16. Attempts to Influence the Courtships of Sons and Daughters by Fathers and Mothers [8]

	Fathers Interfered	Mothers Interfered
Daughters' Courtship	68.7%	97.1%
Sons' Courtship	49.1	79.4

ties that endanger her full status as the Number One woman she may quite rightly anticipate mother-in-law trouble. A man, also, may foresee in-law problems if the mother of his bride-to-be is dominating, and quite understandably he will do what he can to protect himself and his home from the mother's efforts to run her daughter's life.

A further extension of the in-law problem is seen in the active rebellion against one's own parents projected upon the parents-in-law. Adolescents who have not yet established personal autonomy actively reject parent figures of all kinds, including anyone in a position of possible authority. The efforts that a girl makes to free herself from her too close dependence upon her parents often are continued as a repudiation of her parents-in-law. The young man who insists upon being completely independent will allow no help from either side of the family. More mature young people come to comfortable terms with their own parents and so can take their new relationships with their parents-in-law with more poise and grace.

How Serious Are In-Law Problems?

How much trouble do in-laws cause, and in what marriages are they most critical? Thomas reports an analysis he made of a sample of 2,000

[8] Alan Bates, "Parental Roles in Courtship," *Social Forces*, Vol. 20, No. 4, 1942, pp. 483–486.

disorganized Catholic families whose marriages had been dissolved. He found the following causes for marital breakdown in the "typical maladjusted Catholic marriage":

Factor	Per Cent	Factor	Per Cent
Drink	29.8	Sex	5.4
Adultery	24.8	Mental	3.0
Irresponsibility	12.4	Religion	2.9
Temperaments	12.1	Money	.8
In-laws	7.2	Unclassified	1.7

TABLE 17. *Factors Involved in the Breakdown of 2,000 Catholic Marriages* [9]

The in-law factor ranks fifth in this distribution of problem areas which suggests that in-laws sometimes do cause marital breakdown, at least among Catholic families.

In one study, the Landises found that in-law troubles were mentioned in second place by women and in third place by men as their most serious problem in achieving happiness in marriage. In another study of 544 university couples in the early years of marriage, in-law trouble was ranked as the most serious problem.[10] Such findings suggest that in-law problems are general early in a marriage, and then become chronic or are successfully worked out as the marriage progresses. Thomas found in-law problems much more frequent as a source for disorganization in the early than in the later years of marriage (see Fig. 13). He says, "When there is an in-law problem, some acceptable adjustment is worked out early in marriage, or the partnership fails."

Who Is the Most Difficult In-Law?

Mother-in-law leads the list of difficult in-laws by a wide margin, with sister-in-law named as the second greatest problem (see Table 18).

The Landises also find that husbands and wives name their mothers-in-law as the in-law with whom there was the most friction. Of a sample of 116 husbands and 160 wives reporting in-law friction, 46.7 per cent name the mother-in-law as responsible. They find too that many

[9] John L. Thomas, *The American Catholic Family*, Englewood Cliffs, N. J.: Prentice-Hall, 1956, p. 220.

[10] Judson T. Landis and Mary G. Landis, *Building a Successful Marriage*. Englewood Cliffs, N.J., Prentice-Hall, 1953, pp. 302–303.

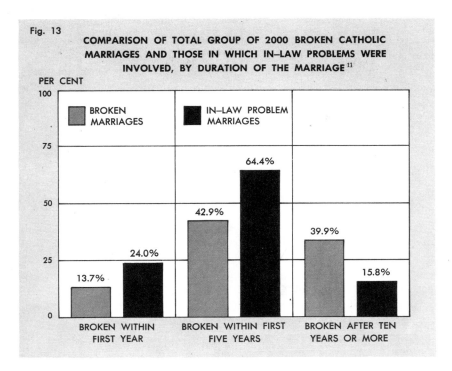

Fig. 13

COMPARISON OF TOTAL GROUP OF 2000 BROKEN CATHOLIC MARRIAGES AND THOSE IN WHICH IN-LAW PROBLEMS WERE INVOLVED, BY DURATION OF THE MARRIAGE[11]

PER CENT

■ BROKEN MARRIAGES

■ IN-LAW PROBLEM MARRIAGES

BROKEN WITHIN FIRST YEAR — 13.7% / 24.0%

BROKEN WITHIN FIRST FIVE YEARS — 42.9% / 64.4%

BROKEN AFTER TEN YEARS OR MORE — 39.9% / 15.8%

TABLE 18.   *The In-Law Named Most Difficult by 1,337 Men and Women* [12]

Most Difficult In-Law	Number	Per Cent
Mother-in-Law	491	36.8
Sister-in-Law	272	20.3
Brother-in-Law	72	5.4
Father-in-Law	67	5.0
Daughter-in-Law	37	2.8
Other Female in-Laws	22	1.6
"All in-Laws"	20	1.5
Son-in-Law	10	0.7
Other Male in-Laws	1	0.1
No Difficult in-Laws	345	25.8
Total	1,337	100.0

---

[11] Thomas, *op. cit.*, p. 234.
[12] Duvall, *op. cit.*, page 188.

more female than male relatives cause in-law friction in marriage.[13] Thomas too reports that mothers-in-law, sisters-in-law, and wives are involved more frequently in in-law friction than are the men of the family.[14]

The women of the family are more often named as troublemakers and they more frequently complain about having in-law problems. One reason for this is that the interrelationships within the family are generally felt to be the woman's responsibility. Any disharmony that arises is more a cause for the woman's concern than for her husband, who focusses his attention more on affairs outside the intimate interactions of relatives.

Another reason is that it is usually harder for a mother to release her children into marriage than it is for the father. When a woman's children marry she is left stranded with little to take the place of the mothering that has filled her twenty or more adult years. Not so with the father of the house. His major responsibility still is, as it always has been, in his work. When a man's children marry his life goes on much as it has before, whereas the woman faces a major readjustment in filling the vacuum left in her life by her children's departure.

Mothers-in-law are often called *meddlesome, possessive*, and *intruding*. Together these three faults account for more than half of all criticisms of mothers-in-law.[15] This kind of mother has difficulty letting her children go. She tries to mother them even after they are in homes of their own. In a sense, she is a problem because she continues to be a "Mom." [16]

The "Mom" kind of mother-in-law is a menace because she interferes with the maturing of her grown and growing children. Her continuing concern for them is such that they find it hard to fully develop as independent, emotionally mature men and women. She keeps her daughters too closely supervised, and becomes too closely attached to her sons to let them emerge freely as young adults. As a mother-in-law she forces her attention upon the young married pair, is over-protective of her own child, and intrudes generally upon the privacy and autonomy of the young couple. But, fortunately, not all mothers-in-law are of the "Mom" type.

---

[13] Landis and Landis, *op. cit.*, p. 304.

[14] Thomas, *op. cit.*, p. 235.

[15] Duvall, *op. cit.*, p. 191.

[16] Philip Wylie, *A Generation of Vipers*, New York: Rinehart, 1942; and Edward Strecker, *Their Mothers' Sons*, Philadelphia: Lippincott, 1946, characterize the American "Mom" as the clinging, over-protective mother who keeps her children emotionally dependent upon her.

TABLE 19.   Predominant Sentiments in 3,683 Letters on the Theme, "Why I Think Mothers-in-Law Are Wonderful People" [17]

Predominant Sentiment	Number	Per Cent
"I appreciate her as a person"	913	25
"I appreciate her gifts and services"	830	23
"I love her as my own mother"	540	15
"She reared my spouse to be a fine person"	483	13
"This is what 'they say' in mother-in-law jokes"	296	8
"The stereotype is unfair and untrue"	264	7
"I'm a mother-in-law and know what it's like"	193	5
"As a grandmother, my mother-in-law is wonderful"	48	1
Others (illegible, incoherent, irrelevant)	116	3
Total	3,683	100

An analysis of 3,683 letters, in a study of in-law relationships, reveals many men and women who love their mothers-in-law. They are grateful for all she does for them; they love her like a mother; they realize that she reared their marriage partners; they appreciate her as an individual, and feel that in their experience the stereotype against mothers-in-law is unfair and untrue (see Table 19).

Some mothers-in-law are appreciated

There are many situations in which a mother-in-law is especially appreciated. Orphans and persons from broken homes are apt to be especially fond of their mothers-in-law. Couples separated by military service often find that their mothers-in-law tided them over the strain of being apart. Couples in successful mixed marriages give credit to the mother-in-law who helped with the assimilation of the stranger.[18] The couple facing a critical or chronic illness, the birth of a child, accidents and other disabilities, or a death in the family, become devoted to the mother-in-law who sees them through the crises.

Parents can be classified into two main types according to whether their basic conception of parenthood is a developmental one or a traditional one.[19] Developmental parents emphasize the development of their children and of themselves as persons. They encourage their chil-

Developmental parents

[17] Duvall, *op. cit.*, p. 89.
[18] This is reported too in 72 per cent of the Japanese war brides of non-Japanese who enjoy congenial in-law relations, in the study of Yukiko Kimura, "War Brides in Hawaii and Their In-Laws," *American Journal of Sociology*, Vol. LXIII, No. 1, July, 1957, pp. 70–76.
[19] A distinction first developed in the study of mothers' conceptions of themselves as parents in Evelyn Millis Duvall, "Conceptions of Parenthood," *American Journal of Sociology*, Vol. 52, No. 3, November, 1946, pp. 193–203.

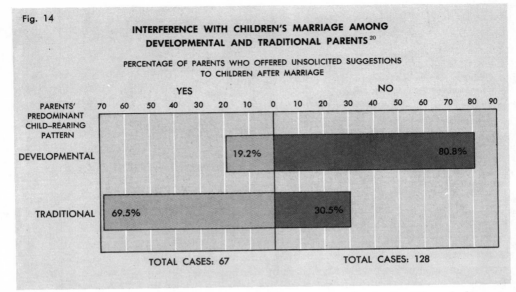

Fig. 14

INTERFERENCE WITH CHILDREN'S MARRIAGE AMONG
DEVELOPMENTAL AND TRADITIONAL PARENTS[20]

PERCENTAGE OF PARENTS WHO OFFERED UNSOLICITED SUGGESTIONS
TO CHILDREN AFTER MARRIAGE

dren to be free, growing, autonomous individuals. They believe a
mother should be "a calm, cheerful, growing person herself." Traditional parents, on the other hand, make a point of the importance of
keeping children neat and clean, and seeing to it that they obey adults
and respect property by "*making* the child good." It is not surprising to
find that traditional parents tend to interfere with their married children, while developmental parents adopt a "hands off" policy. Sussman's study finds considerably less parental interference of married
children on the part of developmental than traditional parents (see
Fig. 14).

In-law adjustments work two ways. Quite as important as the attitudes and behavior of the older members of the family is the readiness
of the young man and woman to stand on their own feet, to leave their
childhood roles and become young adults capable of building a successful marriage with a minimum of infantile tendencies.

Are You Mature Enough to Be a Good In-Law?

All studies to date indicate that in-law difficulties are in part related
to the young couple's immaturity. Typical in-law problems with roots
in immaturity of one or both of the young pair are: (1) the young hus-

---

[20] Adapted from Marvin B. Sussman, "Family Continuity: Selective Factors
Which Affect Relationships Between Families at Generational Levels," *Marriage
and Family Living*, Vol. 16, No. 2, May, 1954, p. 117.

band's inability to carry responsibility for his family which of necessity shifts back to the parents; (2) the young wife's tendency to "run home to mother" when marital problems become burdensome; (3) the couple's tendency to blame one set of parents or the other for their own failures; (4) the childish comparing of one set of in-laws with the other in competitive ways; (5) the couple's dependent leaning upon one or both sets of parents after marriage; (6) the pair's too rigorous insistence upon absolute independence from their parental families; and (7) the young couple's inability to handle effectively the interference of their parents.

One study of married students found that age at marriage was closely related to in-law adjustment. In general, the older the couple at the time of their marriage, the better their relationships with their in-laws (see Table 20).

Very young marriages are particularly vulnerable to in-law problems for several reasons. (1) The partners are not old enough to have achieved full emotional maturity before they marry. (2) The very young marriage may be a revolt, conscious or unconscious, against the parents from whom the adolescent is rebelling, with the unfinished struggle for emancipation continued in in-law as well as parental relationships. (3) The parents, not having full confidence in their child's readiness for marriage, interfere more than they would if they respected the child's judgment and maturity. (4) The young married couple have to be more dependent upon their families for support and help than if they had waited until they were better established financially before getting married.

To get along well with in-laws one must have attained a certain level of maturity. The young wife who has established herself as a person can accept and be accepted by her mother-in-law without severe ego threats. The young husband who has established his personal identity to the place where he can associate intimately with his wife can func-

TABLE 20. *Age of 544 Wives at Marriage and In-Law Adjustment* [21]

Age Married	Excellent	Good	Fair or Poor
17–19 Years	45%	34%	21%
20–21 Years	51	38	11
22–23 Years	60	28	12
24 or Older	63	30	7

[21] Landis and Landis, *op. cit.*, p. 311.

tion effectively as a son-in-law. Without the twin marks of maturity—identity and autonomy—the young couple is vulnerable in any in-law relationship which challenges their full status as adults.

Help from parents

A great many happily married people report having received all sorts of help from their parents-in-law. Letters from 1,853 men and women extolling parents-in-law for all the ways they helped out were analyzed as part of a survey of in-law relationships.[22] These letters show that married couples appreciate what their parents-in-law have done for them, such as helping them buy and establish their homes, seeing them through the birth of their children, nursing through illnesses and accidents, standing by with support through family crises, helping during the military service of sons and sons-in-law, and providing the young couple with a home for varying lengths of time. Sussman finds that parents help their married children in many tangible ways.

In 154 of the 195 cases in the sample, parents had established a pattern of giving moderate help and service to their married child's family. This included gifts, such as furniture, household, and kitchen equipment, to the young couple upon marriage; financial assistance in some of their larger expenditures, such as in the purchase or building of a house, loans or gifts of money to them; such services as gardening, landscaping, house construction, painting and repairing the house; and such personal assistance as care of grandchildren during their parents' vacation or provision of inexpensive vacations for them or the grandchildren. In return for this assistance parents expected from their children continued affectional response, inclusion in some of their activities, and personal service and attention.[23]

There appear to be limits beyond which most parents will not go in order to avoid being "used" or "taken for granted." Parents are often quite articulate about the importance of making their children responsible for what they are given, of being moderate in their assistance, and not making their children too dependent upon their help. As one parent puts it:

We have launched our children. We gave them cash, furniture, and helped them in buying their homes . . . and now they will have to carry on by themselves. We enjoy giving them gifts, especially something they can't afford . . . giving once in a while is all right, but not to give them money all the time. We don't think this would be right and besides I don't think our children would accept it.[24]

---

22 Duvall, *op. cit.*, pp. 89–121.
23 Marvin B. Sussman, "The Help Pattern in the Middle Class Family," *American Sociological Review*, Vol. 18, No. 1, February, 1953, p. 23.
24 *Ibid.*, p. 23.

Should You Live with Your In-Laws?

There is some evidence that the happiness of marriage is impaired when a young married couple lives with one set of parents or the other. In one study, fewer young couples living with parents rate their marriage as "very happy" than those whose marriages are assured of privacy in a room, trailer, or apartment.[25] Locke's comparison of a happily married with a divorced group suggests that "living with in-laws is unfavorable to marital adjustment, both in the case of the daughter-in-law and of the son-in-law."[26] Yet there are many husbands and wives who enjoy or "do not mind" living with their in-laws. Happily married, more than unhappy divorced, couples like living with their in-laws, as one would expect. Households can be shared with mutual advantage to both generations under many circumstances.

Doubling up with relatives becomes necessary under many conditions. In periods and places where severe housing shortages exist, living with relatives may be the only way a couple can manage and still keep their jobs or finish their schooling. When a man is in military service it is often necessary for his wife and children to move in with his family. Sickness, accidents, and other disabilities are further reasons for families to join forces under one roof for a while. Here are some recommendations for living with in-laws that have worked in actual situations and that are compatible with sound principles of personal interaction:

1. Develop together a clear understanding of financial, household, and other responsibilities so that each one may know just what is expected.
2. Be reasonable in your expectations of one another. No one is perfect. Everyone makes mistakes from time to time. Perfectionists are hard to live with in any family.
3. Make some provision for protecting the personal property of each member of the family. It may be little more than a closet or a bureau of his or her own, but everyone welcomes some place for his things that will be respected as his alone.
4. Respect each person's need for privacy. It is not only the great who need their "islands of solitude," as Adlai Stevenson suggests. The elderly, the adolescent, and all the rest of us from time to time desire undisturbed privacy. We have the right to open our own mail, answer our own phone calls, and make our own friends with some sense of privacy.

---

[25] Landis and Landis, *op. cit.*, p. 316.
[26] Locke, *op. cit.*, p. 120.

5. Encourage each member of the household to develop his own talents and pursue his own interests in his own way.

6. Jointly plan for whole-family activities so that each may have a share in deciding what is to be done, and what part he or she will play.

7. As disagreements arise, and they will from time to time, take the time to hear the other(s) out. Listen well enough to get what the situation means to those who differ with you. Respond to their feelings as well as to the "sense" of the situation.

8. Unify the larger family sharing the household by celebrations and rituals that bring the family closer together in its own most meaningful ways.

9. Take a positive attitude toward your joint living arrangement by being appreciative of the benefits derived from sharing the household, rather than merely bemoaning the sacrifices involved.

10. Gain some perspective by realizing that through the ages, families have lived more often together than in the little separate family units more popular today.[27]

What Makes for Good In-Law Relationships?

Good in-law adjustment and happiness in marriage go together. In-law relationships that are satisfying may contribute to marital happiness, or if the two people are happily married they may be pleasantly prepared to enjoy each other's family as an extension of the loved one. It is also true that both good in-law adjustment and marital happiness are the products of mature, well-adjusted people who so live that their human relationships generally are satisfactory and satisfying. Comparing approximately 190 happily married couples with 210 divorced men

TABLE 21. Happily Married and Divorced Men and Women Reporting Agreement or Disagreement with In-Laws [28]

Ways of Dealing with In-Laws	Men		Women	
	Married	Divorced	Married	Divorced
Always Agree	53%	29%	49%	31%
Almost Always Agree	34	19	37	23
Occasionally Disagree	12	15	12	17
Frequently, Almost Always, and Always Disagree	1	37	2	29

[27] Duvall, op. cit., pp. 323–324.
[28] Harvey J. Locke, Predicting Adjustment in Marriage: A Comparison of a Divorced and a Happily Married Group, New York: Holt, 1951, pp. 68–69.

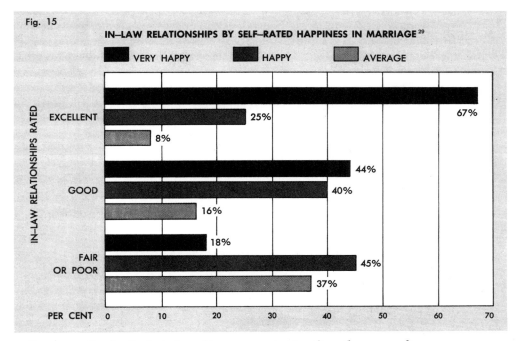

Fig. 15

IN–LAW RELATIONSHIPS BY SELF–RATED HAPPINESS IN MARRIAGE [29]

■ VERY HAPPY   ■ HAPPY   ▨ AVERAGE

IN-LAW RELATIONSHIPS RATED

EXCELLENT — 67%, 25%, 8%

GOOD — 44%, 40%, 16%

FAIR OR POOR — 18%, 45%, 37%

PER CENT   0   10   20   30   40   50   60   70

and women, Locke finds in-law disagreements significantly more often reported by divorced than married persons (see Table 21).

Combining the first two categories, 87 per cent of the happily married men and 86 per cent of the happily married women report that they always, or almost always, agree on ways of dealing with in-laws. In another study the Landises found more than two thirds of the couples whose in-law relationships were rated "excellent" considered themselves "very happy" in their marriages (see Fig. 15).

TABLE 22.   What Makes for Harmony among In-Laws [30]

Reason Mentioned	Number	Per Cent
Acceptance	306	40.9
Mutual Respect	257	34.3
No Opportunity for Discord	131	17.6
No Reason Given	54	7.2
Total Mentions	748	100.0

[29] Landis and Landis, op. cit., p. 304.
[30] Duvall, op. cit., pp. 330–331.

Many couples have no trouble getting along with their in-laws. One fourth of a group of 1,337 married men and women indicated that they had had no in-law problems. Three out of four mention some form of acceptance and mutual respect as responsible for their good relationships with their in-laws (see Table 22).

"They accept me" is the most frequently mentioned factor in relating successfully to in-laws. This is repeated in many forms and phrases of which the following are typical:

They have taken me in as one of them. They have shared with me. They have been kind to my people.

They are kind to me. They treat me as one of the family. They take my part if an argument arises.

We have pleasant family reunions at intervals with *acceptance of* me as a *real member* of the family.

From my wedding day I called my husband's parents "Mother" and "Father," and my in-laws accepted me from the beginning as a member of their family.

"We respect each other's personalities" is the second most frequently mentioned factor given as the reason for harmony between in-laws. These include such comments as:

They respect my relationships as wife. They respect our authority as mother and father of our children. They treat us as equals and dear friends.

My in-laws have never interfered in my immediate family problems, and they have never burdened us with their problems.

Complete trust, liking and confidence from all in-laws with whom there has been contact.

I have not had any trouble with my in-laws. Reason—I try to give everyone a right to their own opinions.

I have great respect for my mother-in-law. I never felt that my husband should ignore his mother the moment he slipped a wedding ring on my finger, nor ever after, either. She was the first woman in his life, I the second. That was good enough for me, for I fully understood that whatever good there was in him was a part of her. Good in-laws are an asset to any family.

The greatest handicaps members of the younger generation face in relating to in-laws are immaturity and prejudice. The greatest problem for the older generation is that of letting married children grow as individuals and as a couple without too much interference or "smothering." These are two-way problems with mutually achieved solutions. Parents and children together attain true maturity. As young people encourage their parents, especially their mothers, to find interests beyond their children, both generations benefit as persons and as members of the family. As young people mature and carry their responsibilities competently, their parents and in-laws are freed to play their part in building new relations of interdependence and continuity between the generations.

READINGS

Blood, Robert O., Jr., *Anticipating Your Marriage*. Glencoe, Illinois: Free Press, 1955, Chapter 15, "Functioning as a Married Couple."

Burgess, Ernest W., and Paul Wallin, *Engagement and Marriage*. Chicago: Lippincott, 1953, Chapter 18, "Marital Adjustment."

Duvall, Evelyn Millis, *In-Laws: Pro and Con, and Original Study of Inter-Personal Relations*. New York: Association Press, 1954.

Duvall, Sylvanus M., *Before You Marry*. New York: Association Press, 1959 revision, Chapter 10, "The Family You Marry."

Grinstein, Alexander, and Editha Sterba, *Understanding Your Family*. New York: Random House, 1957, Chapter 16, "Other Adults."

Landis, Judson T., and Mary G., *Building a Successful Marriage*. Englewood Cliffs: Prentice-Hall, 1958, Chapter 17, "In-Laws and Marriage Adjustment."

LeMasters, E. E., *Modern Courtship and Marriage*. New York: Macmillan, 1957, Chapter 15, "In-Laws: Friends or Enemies."

Levine, Lena, *The Modern Book of Marriage*. New York: Bartholomew House, 1957, Chapter 5, "Getting along with Parents and In-Laws."

Locke, Harvey J., *Predicting Adjustments in Marriage: A Comparison of a Divorced and a Happily Married Group*. New York: Holt, 1951, Chapter 4, "Marital Disagreements and Conflicts," and Chapter 6, "Parental Influences on Marital Adjustment."

Sussman, Marvin B., "Family Continuity: Selective Factors Which Affect Relationships between Families at Generational Levels," *Marriage and Family Living*, Vol. 16, No. 2, May, 1954, pp. 112–120.

———, "The Help Pattern in the Middle Class Family," *American Sociological Review*, Vol. 18, No. 1, February, 1953, pp. 22–28.

Thomas, John L., *The American Catholic Family*. Englewood Cliffs: Prentice-Hall, 1956, Chapter 7, "The Disorganized Family," and Chapter 8, "The Disorganizing Factors."

Waller, Willard, and Reuben Hill, *The Family: A Dynamic Interpretation*. New York: Dryden Press, 1951, Chapter 14, "Bases of Marriage Conflict," and Chapter 20, "Parenthood: Launching Stage."

12 Living on Your Income

What will be your probable income?

What about working wives?

How can you make your money go farther?

What can a budget do for you?

How much does it take to live well?

Ⅰт costs money to get married. There are the costs of the wedding, the trousseau, and the honeymoon. Afterwards, staying financially solvent involves having enough money to support the family and living within your income. Two cannot live as cheaply as one, especially when they are married. For with marriage come new desires and expenses—furnishing a home, financing a car, and having a baby. Family incomes vary considerably. As you see in Fig. 16 more than half of America's families get along on less than $5,000 annual income.

What Will Be Your Probable Income?

In estimating your prospective income you may consider not only the husband's probable income, but also what you can make in home production, what return you may expect from allotments, gifts, and investments, and possible income from other members of the family, notably the wife and older children.

The husband's actual income includes both his regular earnings and other special increments. Between two and three million Americans hold down two jobs, one of which may be part-time. A considerable number of teachers supplement their salaries by working during vacations, evenings, Saturdays, and holidays at jobs other than their regular employment.

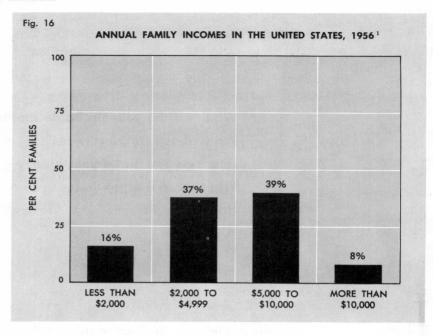

Fig. 16

ANNUAL FAMILY INCOMES IN THE UNITED STATES, 1956[1]

᷉ *Home production* is a hidden source of income in many a modern family.[2] When a couple buy an unfinished house for $3,000 less than they would have to pay for it complete, and finish it themselves with $500 worth of materials, they have added $2,500 to their income. If the husband can repair a leaky faucet that might have cost an $8 visit from the plumber, he has added this amount to their income. If the wife makes drapes for $50 that would have cost $200 to buy, she has increased the income of the family by the amount of the difference. One wife bought battered but basically sound furniture from secondhand stores and refinished and re-upholstered it at home. Before long her family had fine furnishings for a fraction of what they would have been new. Such home production has high economic value. The "do-it-yourself" movement is for some only a more or less expensive hobby. For others it is a way of adding considerably to their family incomes by home production. Everyday services such as shopping wisely, preparing meals, laundering, and sewing are difficult to estimate but are real income stretchers nevertheless.

---

[1] Special report, United States Bureau of the Census.
[2] For an excellent discussion of this see Howard Bigelow, *Family Finance*, Lippincott, 1953, Chapter 6.

▽*Allotments, gifts, and investments* as part of your prospective income include such items as veterans' benefits, gifts from friends, and aid from relatives, as well as all income from investments. If you own your own home, the rental value of the house minus costs is additional income to you. If you rent out a spare room, the net gain is also investment income. There is a chance that you will own some stocks or bonds. In 1955, 8 per cent of all American families owned some stock, including 4 per cent of those with annual incomes under $3,000.[3] Ownership of bonds is even higher. The longer you are married the higher your income from investments is likely to be.

○*Earnings of other family members* sharing your household may be part of the total family income. According to one study,[4] high school students in this country earn some four billion dollars a year. While most of this is not turned over to their families, much is used to provide spending money and to buy what otherwise the parents would furnish. Long before the children are old enough to work, the wife's earnings are a definite possibility.

What about Working Wives?

Rightly or wrongly, and for better or worse, nine out of ten women work outside their homes in the course of their lives. The proportion of working wives has steadily increased during the twentieth century (see Fig. 17).

What has happened, simply, is this. Modern industry has taken away from the family many of the production jobs that formerly belonged to the wife, such as making soap or clothing or much of the preparation of food. Modern equipment greatly simplifies the tasks of cleaning and laundry. If the modern wife is to make the kind of economic contribution to the family that her ancestors used to make, she can do it only by getting a job on the outside. In other words, the employed wife is only doing what wives have always done, only she is doing it in a different place and in a different way.

The general pattern seems to be somewhat as follows. Most unmarried women not in school are employed. When they marry, as half do before they are 20 and 93 per cent do before they are 35, 60 per cent continue on with their jobs. Most of them stop work when their babies come, although 18 per cent of young mothers with pre-school chil-

---

[3] *Statistical Abstract of the United States,* 1957, p. 470.
[4] "What It Costs to Be a Senior in High School," *The Family Economist,* April, 1957.

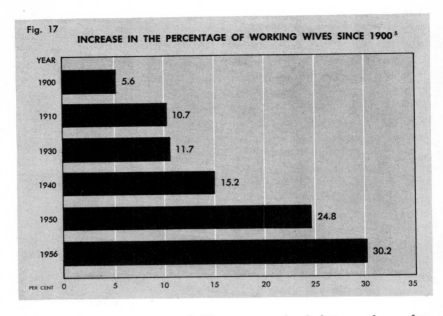

Fig. 17 INCREASE IN THE PERCENTAGE OF WORKING WIVES SINCE 1900 [5]

dren remain employed. As children enter school their mothers often return to work, 34 per cent of those from 35 to 44 years of age being employed. This percentage has doubled since 1940 and probably will continue to rise markedly. The United States seems definitely headed for the time when most urban married women will continue to work before their children come and after they have all entered school.

Why wives work

Until quite recently work by wives was often a matter of necessity. Many women worked because the husband was alcoholic, improvident, or otherwise incapacitated and there were few Aid to Dependent Children provisions. If such wives did not work they or their families would have suffered acutely. Financial need is still an important reason. A study made in 1951 revealed that when the husband's income was less than $5,000 a year, 55 per cent of the wives without young children were employed, but in the $5,000 to $7,000 bracket this dropped to 30 per cent, and in the $7,000 to $10,000 bracket to 8.6 per cent.

Aside from stark need, wives work because they and their families want to enjoy the higher standard of living that their additional income will provide. In 1954 about 22 per cent of individual families had incomes of from $6,000 to $10,000 a year, but when husband and wife

---

[5] From *The Statistical Abstract of the United States, 1957*, pp. 208, 209; the National Manpower Council's study, *Womanpower*, Columbia University Press, 1957, pp. 9–69; and various reports of the U.S. Bureau of the Census.

both worked, approximately 40 per cent enjoyed this income. The United States Bureau of the Census found in 1955 that farm families in which wives were employed had incomes 60 per cent higher than families in which she did not work. Yet money is not always the main consideration. After the husband's income reached $10,000, the percentage of employed wives jumped from 8.6 per cent to 21.1 per cent, a striking increase.[6]

The higher percentage of working wives at the upper income levels possibly reflects the continued employment of the married professional woman. The woman doctor, architect, lawyer, artist, writer, home economist, teacher, or nurse is quite likely to have demands on her professional skills after marriage as before. Her training represents a real investment for her personally and for society at large. Her husband may be proud of her talents and achievements and encourage her to remain at work and to maintain her status in her chosen field. Her earnings from highly saleable skills more than replace her at home in tasks that less talented domestics can perform as well. Her time is more her own than it is for the less educated working girl, so that she can plan her work around the needs of her home and family. Her satisfactions from her work are real and her associates stimulating in a way not so usual in manual labor. Thus it is not surprising to find significantly more talented wives of men in the higher income brackets working than among less privileged women.

Despite the fact that the employment of wives outside the home is widespread, growing, and generally accepted, many people still raise serious questions about it, including some of the employed wives themselves. One simple question is, "Does it really pay?" What the wife earns, even her take-home pay, is not clear gain. Her increased income may put the family in a higher income tax bracket, so that she and her husband must pay higher taxes. Her work may require additional expenses, such as transportation, more expensive clothing, and outside meals. If she must hire someone to replace her even partly at home, all the financial advantages may be soaked up. One woman, working from a sense of obligation to support an ailing mother, found that her job actually cost her family $650 more than she brought in.[8]

If the couple have no children, or if their children are old enough to

Problems of working wives [7]

---

[6] Daniel Bell, "The Great Back-to-Work Movement," *Fortune*, July, 1956.

[7] For a summary discussion of this question, see Stella B. Applebaum, *Working Wives and Mothers*, Public Affairs Pamphlet #188, Public Affairs Committee, New York, 1952.

[8] Cited in Frances L. Feldman, *The Family in a Money World*, New York: Family Service Association of America, 1957, p. 141.

assume some of the household responsibilities so that no replacement need be hired, there is probably some real economic advantage. But if a replacement must be employed, the family should scrutinize any supposed gains most carefully.

○A second concern is that employment puts too much of a burden on the wife. In our culture the main responsibility of cooking, cleaning, entertaining, and the care of the children falls upon the wife. If, in addition, she has as heavy a work schedule outside the home as her husband, this will probably leave her over-burdened. This can have serious consequences for her health, happiness, and her relationship with her family. Three things operate to keep the wife from becoming over-burdened. In the first place, the husband also has his home responsibilities. He usually is expected to be responsible for the yard, the repairs around the house, and many other domestic chores. These have increased since a growing number of families own their own homes. In the second place, husbands today commonly assume some of the responsibilities formerly assigned to women. Several studies show that modern husbands help with the cleaning, the shopping, meal preparation, and care of the children, so that their burdens are much more equitably distributed. Frequent wails that men are losing their "masculinity" and have abdicated their rightful place as "head" of the household emanate from general observations that husbands are now willing to accept their fair share of responsibility for the household in a cooperative and democratic relationship.

More serious is the charge that if the wife and mother works the husband and children are neglected. Maladjustments and delinquencies often are blamed upon the working mother. It seems probable that children of employed mothers do get less attention from them than they otherwise would. That this is necessarily damaging to their development and growth is questionable. One of the needs of every child is some "good, wholesome neglect"; some families are apt to give too much "smothering." The employed mother often feels better about herself, and is a better and more understanding person than she would be if she had only her family to care for. When a mother works, the children are much less likely to be spoiled, parasitic "brats." Actually a number of studies have shown that children of both employed and non-employed mothers can be either wholesome and well adjusted, or neglected and delinquent, depending upon the total relationship in the family.

Last comes the question of the effects of outside employment on the husband-wife relationship. For husbands who have an emotional need to dominate, the independence that comes from significantly sharing in the economic responsibilities for the family unquestionably threatens the man's status. For those who wish wives who are worthy of respect and admiration in their own right, employment can bind them more closely together in an interdependent relationship. This presumption is substantiated by a number of studies. For example, Locke and Mackesprang, in a study of 525 divorced persons and 404 happily married ones, found no differences between the marital adjustments of wives who had full-time jobs and those who were full-time homemakers.[9]

We should clearly recognize that husbands and wives differ widely, both as individuals and in the situations in which they are involved. Their decisions about employment should be based upon an intelligent understanding of who they are, what they want, and the problems with which they are confronted. Here are eight factors that both should and will affect decisions.

1. Some women are temperamentally so built that if they do not have a job of their own they either "blow up" or constantly meddle in the affairs of their husbands, and possibly those of other husbands as well. With them a real job outside the family meets a vital psychological need.

2. A few women have special talents and skills which ought not to be wasted. In this class belong some of our more talented teachers, authors, artists, and executives. Such women may take time out for children, but will and should remain employed for most of their productive years.

3. Wives of certain professional men, such as ministers, governmental officials, or big business executives, may find their full-time employment as helpers and hostesses for their husbands.

4. Wives of farmers usually have full-time jobs where they are.

5. Many women really are employed extensively outside their homes, but are not so classified because they are not paid. They are prominent in church work, P.T.A.'s, and various civic and community organizations and enterprises. A woman is not unemployed because she is not paid for her work.

6. Most wives have neither the strength nor the ability to carry on a very big job outside the home while their children still need careful supervision. Most wives in cities could carry on a real job, at least part time, before their children come and after they are grown.

7. Some women are so lacking in health and talents or interests that housekeeping, even without children, taxes their energies and capacities to the utmost.

8. Some women do not want to be employed, their husbands do not want them to be, and their families do not need the money.

---

[9] Harvey Locke and Muriel Mackesprang, "Marital Adjustment and the Employed Wife," *American Journal of Sociology*, May, 1949.

There is one further problem for a newly married couple to consider —what to do with the earnings of the wife. During the first few years of marriage, the income of the husband probably will be relatively low, while the expenses are relatively high. There is furniture and equipment to be bought and paid for, and the couple will want to save up enough money to make the down payment on the first baby. If the husband and wife "live up" all that they both earn, they are highly vulnerable. As soon as the baby comes, their expenses go up while their income may be cut almost in half. Couples can protect themselves from this by living on what the husband earns, and saving all the net income of the wife. Some of what the wife earns may go for home furnishings, which is a type of saving. The rest is banked. When the baby comes, their income for ordinary expenses remains the same, while they have a nest egg to take care of the extra expenses.

How Can You Make Your Money Go Farther?

There are, in general, two major ways of living better on your present income. One is to get more for your money. The other is to put your money where it counts most. Let us look at each of these in turn.

Getting more for your money

The simplest way to live better on your income is to avoid throwing money away. If yours is a typical American family you lose considerable sums, either by worthless schemes and products or by buying what is not worth its cost to you. Here are some of the more common forms of wasteful expenditures:

Participating in confidence games or frauds. You may never have bought fake oil stocks, but what about the panhandler on the corner whose "take" averages $30 a day? What about the numerous fake charities that abound? Did you pay a registration fee to that so-called employment agency? Or fall for the "free lot won with a lucky ticket" gag? Poor families which can ill afford the loss are annually mulcted of sums which run into millions. Approximately $200 per family is lost annually in such deals. Two hundred dollars would really help your budget.

Gambling. There is little bona fide gambling in the United States. Most of what is called gambling is really the donation of suckers to swindlers. Slot machines pay off from five to thirty cents on the dollar. Pools and bookie bets often give odds no better.

Buying worthless products, especially drugs. Do you pay good money for stuff in bottles guaranteed to take your unpleasant breath away, massacre bacteria, prevent colds, and warm up cold love affairs? Know, then, that most of these mouth washes, antiseptics, and patent medicines in general are essentially frauds. If your weight reducer potion is only a fraud, you are lucky. If it were effective, it might be highly dangerous. One way of helping your budget is looking in your medicine cabinet.

 Buying things you don't want. We all see things in stores which attract us. But when we get them home we wonder why we ever bought them. Anyone who goes through the stuff he has bought but never used or cared about will get the idea. These white elephants cost money. Cut them out and you can increase your income considerably.

A second possibility is to get more for less. Consider, for example, the following instance. Two wives, Mrs. Squander and Mrs. Canny, went to the same shopping district on the same day and bought the following items at the indicated prices.

	Mrs. Squander paid	Mrs. Canny paid
6 percale sheets and pillowcase sets	$ 24.54	$ 18.00
3 men's broadcloth shirts, 2 x 2 ply	14.00	8.00
3 nylon jersey slips	15.90	11.90
1 pair ladies' shoes	11.40	8.10
1 bottle, 100 5 gr. aspirin tablets, USP	.50	.19
1 large bottle, make-up base	1.80	1.20
	$ 68.14	$ 47.39

With the remainder of her money, Mrs. Canny was able to get in addition:

1 chenille bedspread, good quality	$ 7.95
1 slip cover for chair	9.00
1 roll aluminum foil (large, heavy duty)	1.69
1 sponge mop	1.37
2 magazines at 35¢ each	.70
Grand Total	$ 68.10

Do you see why Mrs. Canny's family was able to live so much better than Mrs. Squander's and on the same money income? Here are some suggestions for how your family, too, could live better.

 Buy the best, rather than the most expensive. Some people assume that by paying more Mrs. Squander got better quality. Actually, she did not. The quality was identical, in all but the sheets where Mrs. Canny got the better quality. Her sheets had a tensile strength of 71 and 72, while Mrs. Squander's had 62 and 67. Thousands of tests have shown that the most expensive is not always the best. Here are some ways to determine quality.

Judge quality, not on the basis of price or advertising claims, but standardized tests. Obviously you cannot maintain a private testing laboratory. But you can get the reports from such services as *Consumers' Research,* and *Consumers Union.* They are not always complete but their findings and recommendations are far better than guessing. In many instances they enable you safely to buy nonadvertised brands at considerable savings and to distinguish between advertised brands on the basis of quality.

A second way to get a good quality at low price is to buy the brand name products of the big chains. The large grocery chains commonly offer products under their own brand names that are quite as good as, and usually sell for less than, more widely advertised goods. From mail-order houses you can often get such items as electric refrigerators, washers, dryers, tires, and even garages at very considerable savings, with a big and reputable firm fully backing their products.

Different members of your family can specialize by studying up on various products. This can be done by special reading, talking with agents and repair men, and following up other sources of information. If you do this there will be another possibility for savings in secondhand or discontinued models.

Consider discontinued models and secondhand items. The new model car may be a completely redesigned and decidedly superior product. Or it may be just a "face-lifting" job with no essential changes from the previous year. In a car, the depreciation is so great that it may not pay you to get a new discontinued model, even at a tremendous discount, unless you plan to keep it four years or more. But in items that last for years, like refrigerators, TV sets, air conditioners, or washers, the discontinued model may be quite as good and very much cheaper. Another possibility for substantial savings is the floor sample. One family saved $150 by buying a dishwasher with a scratch on one side which did not affect the mechanical operation or guarantee, and did not show at all when it was installed between two cabinets. There are stores that specialize in such products in most large cities.

Secondhand goods present more risk, especially if they have motors or mechanical parts that wear out. With furnishings in good condition, however, you often can get considerable savings. The best plan is to have a friend who is an expert, or to employ an expert to go with you, even if you must pay him a consultant's fee. This precaution is especially important if you buy a house, whether new or old.

Buy it for less. The simplest way to do this is to take advantage of sales. Some supposed sales are frauds. But reputable stores periodically have sales in which such goods as furniture, clothing, and white goods are offered at considerable discounts. Grocery chains have specials on featured products and occasional special days when they offer attractive savings.

Another rule is to shop around. This is especially worth while when you have decided what you want. One lady set out to buy a certain make and model of vacuum cleaner. Various stores offered her from five to twenty dollars off the list price. In such items, the manufacturer's list price may be purposely set so high that any store can offer a substantial "discount."

Save money by paying cash. By paying cash you can save in two ways, by getting discounts and by avoiding carrying charges. About some goods it is said that "only saps pay retail prices." But such discounts may require cash. The other place where you save considerably is on carrying charges. Credit necessarily is costly. Bookkeeping, collections, and bad debts are expensive. A merchant who extends you credit must borrow the money and pay interest on it. These costs he must add to his prices, either directly or indirectly. Paying cash enables you to avoid such charges.

Many families willingly pay these additional costs in order to get their goods sooner. You may ask, "Why should we wait years and years for our needed furnishings, refrigerator, or car, just to save a little money?" The answer is that you may not have to. In many cases you can borrow the money you need from a bank or a credit union for a fraction of the store's carrying charge and pay cash. What you cannot borrow for you may not be able to afford anyway.

Keep what you have in good repair. A stitch in time may save the entire garment. Judicious use of moth crystals may save a complete wardrobe. A little glue, a screw properly placed, may save an entire piece of furniture. The ability to see needed repairs before they become too serious, and the willingness and skill to keep things in good working order can add greatly to your income.

Getting more for your money is one way to live better on what you have. The other possibility is to shift your expenditures so that your money goes for what means most to you.

If you are an economic infant who lacks restraints, there is little that this or any discussion can do to help. But if you are reasonably mature you may be able to live much better on your present income simply by shifting some of your expenditures. Here are some of the more promising possibilities for saving.

Putting your money where it counts most

Families naturally want to do some entertaining. If this includes expensive foods and liquor, the costs run up. One couple moved in a "set" in which almost everyone was running behind. They frankly announced, when their turn came to entertain, that from now on, they would serve only simple sandwiches and soft drinks. This one change saved them $20 a month, enough to balance the budget. Their friends? The spongers dropped away. The others, greatly relieved, stayed and followed suit.

Another couple was baffled because, in spite of both their earnings they did not seem to be able to scrape enough together to make the down payment on a house. They were in the habit of dining out every Sunday and once during the week at a fairly expensive place at a cost of about ten dollars a time, or twenty dollars a week. When they saw this, not merely in terms of money but in terms of the house they wanted, they decided that once a month would do. In the course of a year they had saved over $800 on this one item alone which, combined with other savings, was enough to enable them to make the down payment on a house.

One of the surest ways to keep "poor" is to buy or rent a place that costs more than you can comfortably afford. In most cities you can get comfortable homes and apartments for considerably less than those with a swanky address. One couple who moved from their expensive place to another quite as commodious if less "modern," saved enough in one year to buy a good TV set, a fur scarf, two nice pieces of furniture and a serviceable secondhand typewriter. They had learned how to live better on what they had.

In 1955, 82 per cent of all childless couples in this country owned a car. Whether you regard it as essential or not, you should at least know what it costs. A "low priced" American car, purchased new and turned in every two years can easily cost $100 a month. One couple who began to compute the costs of licenses, gas and oil, depreciation, finance charges, and interest on their investment, found that their car cost ten dollars a month more than did their house payments, and about 37 per cent of the husband's take-home pay. By getting a small car, or a secondhand car, you can trim these costs, especially if you can do some of your own repairs. But for the very least that a car will cost, you could live in a nicer place and afford many other things. If you want really to live better on your income, however, you should go over all your expenditures carefully and plan them so that your money will go for what you want most. This is the essence of budgeting.

What Can a Budget Do for You?

Good budgets perform several important services. They help you spot the big items that might keep you poor. They also can help you guard against the dribbles that, small in themselves, in the aggregate mount up and keep you from getting what you could otherwise afford. They can help you not only to save, but to avoid oversaving, or saving in the wrong places. They can help greatly in the timing of expenditures.[10]

Like most families you occasionally must make large payments. Unless properly planned for and budgeted, they can throw you off badly for a long time. You may have to scrimp and deprive yourselves of wanted or needed things that you could easily have had. Large payments may force you into expensive and unnecessary debt. Good budgeting may enable you to take them in your stride.

A good budget should be tailored to your interests and your needs. No printed budget, or even the items of such a budget, can be applied to your situation without change. There are several reasons why. In the first place, budget needs vary within the family life cycle. The newly established family, for example, properly may spend for permanent equipment and furniture a proportion that would be ridiculous for an established family. The family with several growing children should spend for food a proportion that might be way out of line for a couple without children. When children have grown, the couple should provide for their coming retirement by a savings program that might have proved impossible before.

A good budget reflects individual tastes. Some families would rather enjoy better housing and keep the car until it falls apart. Others prefer to spend larger proportions of their money for music, books, and magazines. Others enjoy the theater and would rather spend their money for entertainment. A budget is designed to help you get what you want and need, not what some supposed authority thinks you should want.

Although budget studies and recommendations are not to be slavishly followed, they can be helpful. They can help you by suggesting a range within which your own expenditures should fall. For example, if you are a family of four with an income of $2,500 a year, you should spent at least a third and not as much as half of your income for food. If you receive $12,500 annually anything above a fourth for food would be excessive. The following table is offered as suggestive.

---

[10] For good general discussions on budgets, see Helen Fowle and E. C. Harwood, *How to Make Your Budget Balance*, Great Barrington, Massachusetts: American Institute for Economic Research, 1950; Lillian Gilbreth, et. al., *Management in the Home*, New York: Dodd, Mead, 1954; and Oreana Merriam, "How Young Families Spend Their Money," *Journal of Home Economics*, May, 1955; as well as appropriate chapters in more general books on family finance.

SUGGESTED BUDGET FOR A FAMILY OF FOUR [11]				
Income (annual)	$2,500	$4,500	$6,500	$12,500
Food, including outside meals	35–45%	25–35%	20–30%	15–25%
Housing, including rent, house payments, fire insurance, and real estate taxes	20–30%	18–30%	15–25%	15–25%
Household, including help such as sitters and cleaning woman	1–5%	3–8%	5–15%	8–20%
Capital purchases, including all installment payments	5–15%	5–15%	10–20%	10–20%
Clothing	8–12%	9–13%	9–15%	9–15%
Transportation, including car	5–8%	6–9%	7–12%	7–12%
Health and personal	3–6%	3–6%	4–8%	4–8%
Donations, including personal gifts, church, and charity	2–5%	3–8%	4–9%	5–12%
Income taxes, state and Federal	3–5%	6–8%	12–15%	20–30%
Savings and insurance	2–5%	4–6%	4–8%	6–15%

Because of the fluctuating nature of some expenses, such as heating, clothing, taxes, and insurance, your budget should be built on an annual basis. But because of such items as rent, payments on the house, and utilities, and department store bills sent in monthly, most families find it most convenient to organize their budgets on a monthly basis.

How to work out a budget
There are at least two possible ways to organize your budget. The more usual one is to base it on what the money goes for, such as food, rent, donations, etc. Some families, however, prefer to organize on the basis of predictability. Some items, such as rent, telephone, income tax deductions, and installment payments you can know in advance. Others, like food, are regular, but fluctuate somewhat. Some others, like clothing, may fluctuate extensively. You may pay more for clothing in the one month of September, when you are outfitting yourself and your family for the coming season, than you pay in all the eleven other months put together. Other costs are occasional, such as the down payment on the car, or a new sofa bed or curtains. Choose whichever plan seems best to you, and do not hesitate to shift from one to the other until you know which one suits you best.

Some couples begin to work out an intelligent budget as soon as they return from the honeymoon. Others have been married for some years before they have learned to take budgeting seriously. Regardless of when you begin, one essential of good budgeting is to keep a fairly accurate record of your actual expenditures over a period of time. Do not be a fanatic and try to account for every cent. But get a fairly good

---

[11] Adapted from suggested budget in Feldman, *op. cit.*, p. 164.

idea of how much you have actually been spending for this or that. A good budget is like a good girdle, it should be firm enough to give real support, but not so tight as to be uncomfortable.

When you first begin to plan, your records may tell you that your actual expenditures have been quite different from what you had intended. You have spent more for music and less for movies, more for the household and less for food than you budgeted. This could just mean an "off" month. Or, it could mean that your budget does not reflect what you really want. Keep reviewing your budget so as to bring it more in line, not only with what you have to spend, but with what you want most.

The following list of items is suggested to help you both to record your expenditures of the past and to budget those of the future.

A. INCOME TAXES (Federal, State, and Local).

These are usually deducted in advance, so that you look upon your income only as your take-home pay. Yet you should certainly know what your income taxes amount to, at least for the record.

B. FOOD.

You may want to divide this into two items, groceries and meals out, or you may not. Your groceries are likely to include some items that actually are not foods, such as cigarettes, soaps, detergents, and brooms, as well as sales taxes. But most families find it more convenient just to lump these items all together. You may want to know, however, how large your tobacco bill actually is.

C. HOUSING.

This includes a number of items, some of which you may want to keep separate, such as:

1. Rent or payments on the mortgage.
2. Real estate taxes.
3. Insurance on the house and furnishings, including not only fire, but liability and other types.
4. Upkeep and repairs, including the plumbing bills, etc.
5. Utilities. These usually include gas, electricity, water, and telephone. If you buy coal or oil, include these. If you rent, the real estate taxes, insurance on the building, repairs and usually the heating are included in your rent.

D. HOUSEHOLD.

1. Certain items of purchase, such as linens, dishes, refrigerators, washers, and the installment payments on same. It ought also to include soaps and cleaning costs, but these are probably in your grocery bills.
2. Certain services, such as baby sitters, and repairs on the equipment, such as the vacuum cleaner or the TV set.
3. Miscellaneous items.

E. CLOTHING.

1. Purchases, including shoes and hats.
2. Laundry, cleaning, and repairs.

F. TRANSPORTATION.

1. The car. The payments on your car will, of course, be known exactly in advance. Gas and oil in "normal" months when there are no special trips, can be reliably estimated. Licenses and insurance can be known exactly but likely will be heavily bunched in certain months. Repairs are the item most difficult to estimate in advance.
2. Other transportation. This will be big only if you must commute regularly some distance to your work by public transportation. In any case you should be able to tell in advance about how much it will total each month.

G. HEALTH AND MEDICAL EXPENSES.

1. With hospitalization insurance you can take much of the uncertainty out of your budget. Sickness and accident insurance and company health plans may come as a fringe benefit to further reduce your risks and costs.
2. Doctors' bills are more likely to be unpredictable, except in obstetrics cases where almost the exact cost can be known and planned for in advance.
3. Dental bills are often a large unknown, especially when your family has increased in size. Even an unusual extraction can rock your budget, and orthodontia can blow a big hole in it. In this case, however, the costs can be definitely known in advance.

H. LIFE INSURANCE.

This can, of course, be exactly known and planned for in advance. Any uncertainties are likely to be on the favorable side in the form of dividends that help your budget.

I. PERSONAL EXPENSES.

1. Allowances for each member of the family old enough to spend his own money.
2. Grooming. With haircuts and permanents, this can amount to considerable money.
3. Dues. Include not only membership in volunteer organizations, but also any union dues, even if deducted in advance.

J. RECREATION AND EDUCATION.

1. Ordinary recreation: movies, shows, entertainments, and the like, unless they come out of personal allowances.
2. Vacations. This can come to a sizeable sum, and usually all at one time. Either you must save up for it in advance or go into debt for it.
3. Books, magazines, daily papers, tuition for courses, etc.

K. DONATIONS.

1. Gifts to individuals, especially around Christmas, but also for such events as weddings.

2. Gifts to agencies and causes, such as church, community chest, the Red Cross, and YMCA. Barring special emergencies and appeals you should be able to predict this with considerable accuracy.

L. SAVINGS.

Money deposited in a checking account to be used for expenses is, of course, not saved. Savings will ordinarily be of two kinds.

1. Temporary savings for specific purposes, such as having a baby, vacations, making the down payment on a house or a car, which you expect to use up.
2. Investment, which is money saved for the purpose of producing income on a relatively permanent and continuous basis.

M. OTHER.

This is, of course, a catch-all for items not included elsewhere.

Some of the above items will not be applicable to your budget. Therefore you should make your own list and use it as a basis of both recording and planning your own expenditures.

How Much Does It Take to Live Well?

No income, however high, is "enough" for some families. In survey after survey, families have been asked, "How much would you have to have to live comfortably and well?" The answer usually is "Just a little more than we now have," regardless of the size of the income. An occasional family reports that they are doing well on what they have. Most families, even those who make ends meet, feel pinched. Usually they are quite sure that if they had a sizeable increase, they would be on "easy street." They are sometimes amazed to find that after each increase they are further behind than they were before.

One survey found that of those with incomes under $3,000 a year, 56 per cent were running behind an average of $666 a year; and of those with incomes twice as great, almost as many (52 per cent) were running behind an average of $1,235, or almost twice as much.[12]

The story of a small family struggling unsuccessfully to live on $25,000 a year [13] illustrates the dilemma of the "well-to-do." Far from having saved anything, the family is nearly $20,000 in debt, not counting the mortgage, and is falling behind at the rate of $200 a month.

---

[12] These figures are taken from a table compiled from government and private sources by *Changing Times,* the Kiplinger magazine, and reprinted in the *Ladies' Home Journal,* February, 1958.
[13] "We Can't Live on $25,000 a Year," *Ladies' Home Journal,* February, 1958.

The husband feels that their only hope is an increase in his income. This is almost certainly an illusion; he talks sadly of his inability to afford servants, a yacht, and membership in a country club, so that any increase is more than absorbed by his present wants. It is doubtful that this family could make ends meet on twice the husband's salary.

A rise in income may leave families financially worse off than they were for two reasons: (1) They celebrate expensively. One man, after a $10 a month raise, threw a party that cost $150—more than the entire increase for the year. (2) They splurge. Many families have lists of things they want as soon as they have the money. One family, given a $500 yearly raise, went out and bought $2,500 of goods. The man with the $25,000 income celebrated a raise by buying a house that costs $7,000 a year to maintain.

Many families get along well on surprisingly little. In the survey mentioned above, 27 per cent of the families receiving less than $3,000 a year, and more than half of those with incomes less than $5,000 a year, were able to save money—an average of $260 and $472 respectively. The conclusion is clear. Your ability to live on your income depends far less on the size of your income than upon you and the person you marry.

Problems of marrying "up" or "down"

Marriages between the "rich" and the "poor" are usually complicated by differences in social, cultural, and educational backgrounds. Not every Cinderella would be at home with her Prince and his family. Had she married the boy-next-door she might have agreed on far more aspects of daily living than she can living in the castle on the hill. A married couple coming from essentially the same economic background, finding their income about what they expected, can expect to agree on money policies and to handle their financial conflicts with relative ease.

If they both come from low economic backgrounds, there will be trouble if one or both have "millionaire" demands. He may have grown up with "Horatio Alger" ideas that anyone willing to work hard enough can get rich. He throws himself into his job with great energy, only to discover that his work merits only ordinary income. He becomes frustrated, then embittered, and finally gives up, perhaps developing some "illness" to conceal his failure from himself. Or he may strive to "get rich quick" by some "invention" or other.

In any case, the prognosis is not good. His wife, deceived by his glowing promises or deceived by her own wishes, may have married expecting some financial miracle. When he fails to meet her expectations, she may turn on him with nagging and recrimination, condemning him as a failure. His reaction is resentment which, coupled with feelings of shame and guilt, brings a serious breach in the relationship. The outcome is either complete resignation or hostile retaliations ranging all the way from withdrawal to desertion or violent physical assault.

If both are from relatively wealthy backgrounds and must for a while after their marriage live at a much lower economic level, their adjustments may have to be considerable. Their lower income may increase their personal conflicts, or it may bind them closer together. One thing is sure, it will do something significant to their relationship.

A poor couple that suddenly comes into money may adjust to their sudden affluence in any of a number of ways. They may go on a buying binge. They may cut themselves off from former friends, fail to find acceptance among their new neighbors, and find themselves socially isolated. They may irresponsibly lunge in separate directions, shattering family unity and resulting in associations that bring them into bitter conflict with each other. They may, of course, continue as before, only on a somewhat more comfortable level, making an optimum adjustment.

If the wife has been used to far more than the husband has, they both face problems. If she uses money of her own, or if her father continues to subsidize her heavily, the husband may resent this. If she consents to try to live on his salary, she may find it difficult to live on what they can afford. What happens to the marriage will depend primarily upon the kinds of persons that they both are. If they both have good mental health, a sound sense of values, and a determination to work things out, they probably will make a go of their marriage. If one or both lack any of these essentials, the relationship may be threatened.

It might seem that the ideal situation would be for him to be rich and her to be poor. Then she will demand little and appreciate much. Yet even this situation can cause trouble. He may feel it important that his wife dress expensively and operate the household on a luxury basis. Because of her background she may find this difficult, or even regard such "extravagance" as a sin. The above illustrations are not exhaustive, but illustrate the kinds of difficulties that may arise. In marriages that are "mixed" because of economic differences, as in marriages "mixed" on other bases, the couple should foresee and face the problems they will confront with great care. Then they enter the marriage with some knowledge of the kinds of difficulties that they will have to work out.

The question "How much does it take?" must be answered mainly in terms of your demands. Inability to make ends meet may result from one of the following: (1) compulsive spending, (2) impulsive spending, or (3) competitive spending.

Compulsive spending [14]   You are familiar with the nature of compulsive drinking, or alcoholism. You know that the alcoholic drinks, not because he wants to or enjoys it, but because he cannot help himself. Some people are the same way about spending. One man with a fairly adequate but modest salary had managed to save up over $5,000 at the time of his marriage. Then he "bought" (by making the down payments) in rapid succession, a $25,000 house, $10,000 worth of furniture, and a private airplane. He thereby pledged himself to payments of more than twice his take-home pay. One wife has for several years been spending as much on clothing for herself as her husband earns. Some people buy because of some neurotic need in themselves. For such individuals, appeals for economy, budgets, and promises, even the threat of hunger and deprivation, are usually ineffective. Living on their incomes may require extensive psychotherapy.

Impulsive spending   At times you—like everyone—spend impulsively. You go to the store with a list and while there you buy items that you had not planned on getting. Within limits this may not be serious as long as you remember that what you spend this way cannot go for something else that you may want even more. The great problem is that impulsive buying can get out of hand. Many families whose incomes could be ample go without actual necessities because "money just slips through my fingers," for what they have no idea.

Competitive spending   Some people are what David Riesman calls "other directed." They not only do what others expect, but they feel they have to do as they do, including buying whatever they buy. They cannot make ends meet because "the neighbors are always buying things we cannot afford." The financial difficulties of many families are due largely not to the high cost of living, but to the costs of impressing others.

Living on your income is more than knowing how much income you can count on and then planning its expenditure wisely. Like many of the basic problems of living, money difficulties are often brought on by personality hungers within the individuals themselves. As you strive for maturity, mental health, and good personal adjustment, you greatly increase your chances of living happily within whatever income is yours.

---

[14] For a discussion on some of the psychological factors in spending, see Allan Fromme, *The Psychologist Looks at Sex and Marriage*, New York: Prentice-Hall, 1950, Chapter 8; George Katona, *Psychological Aspects of Economic Behavior*, New York: McGraw-Hill, 1951; and Albert Lauterback, *Men, Motives and Money*, Ithaca, N.Y.: Cornell University Press, 1954.

READINGS

Bergler, Edmund, *Money and Emotional Conflicts.* Paterson, N.J.: Pageant Books, 1959.

Bigelow, Howard F., *Family Finance.* Chicago: Lippincott, 1953.

Consumer Bulletin published monthly by Consumers' Research, Inc., Washington, N.J.

Consumer Reports published monthly by Consumers Union of U.S., Inc., 256 Washington Street, Mount Vernon, N.Y.

Duvall, Evelyn M., *Family Development.* Chicago: Lippincott, 1957.

Duvall, Sylvanus M., *Before You Marry.* New York: Association Press, 1959 revision, Chapter 5, "Financing Your Marriage."

Feldman, Frances Loman, *The Family in a Money World.* New York: Family Service Association of America, 1957.

Fowle, Helen, and E. C. Harwood, *How to Make Your Budget Balance.* Great Barrington, Mass.: American Institute for Economic Research, 1950.

Gilbreth, Lillian M., et al., *Management in the Home.* New York: Dodd, Mead, 1954.

Gordon, Leland J., *Economics for Consumers.* New York: American Book, 1953.

Household Finance Corporation, *Money Management Booklets.* Chicago: Consumer Education Department, Household Finance Corporation.

Katona, George, *Psychological Aspects of Economic Behavior.* New York: McGraw-Hill, 1951.

Ladies' Home Journal, February, 1958—a series of articles on the budget problems of various income levels entitled: "We Can't Live on $25,000 a Year"; "We're Doing Fine on $8,400 a Year"; "More Dreams than Money."

Lauterback, Albert, *Men, Motives and Money.* Ithaca, N.Y.: Cornell University Press, 1954.

National Manpower Council, *Womanpower.* New York: Columbia University Press, 1957.

National Manpower Council, *Work in the Lives of Married Women.* New York: Columbia University Press, 1958.

Rutledge, Aaron L., *Responsible Marriage and Family Living: A Text with Adapted Readings.* New York: Harcourt, Brace, 1960, Chapter 12, "Work, Money, and the Family."

13 Establishing Financial Policies

How should your family income be allocated?

Who makes the major money decisions?

How can you keep your credit good?

Is it cheaper to buy or to rent?

What insurance program is best?

What savings program should you adopt?

What are your long-range goals?

S TUDIES by Terman, Burgess, Cottrell, and Wallin found that money problems in marriage were usually symptomatic of more basic conflict, and in themselves not too important. More recent studies, and a re-evaluation of earlier investigations, place more importance upon financial difficulties in both established and broken marriages.[1] While money is certainly not the root of all evil in husband-wife relationships, you should carefully consider the kinds of financial adjustments that you must make and establish sound financial policies as the basis for making them.

How Should Your Family Income Be Allocated?

Mr. X was a hard-working and prosperous farmer with a considerable cash income. He owned his farm free and clear and everything on it was the best that he could buy. He had modern, fire-proof, and well-ventilated barns, the best and most recent tractors, milking machines,

---

[1] For discussions of this see William J. Goode, *After Divorce*, Glencoe, Illinois: Free Press, 1956; and E. E. LeMasters, *Modern Courtship and Marriage*, New York: Macmillan, 1957, pp. 401–405.

and other equipment. Everything on the place was in excellent condition except the house which had been built in 1910 and had not been essentially changed since. There was no inside toilet or running water. His wife cooked over a wood stove and pumped her water for washing dishes from a cistern. Drinking water came from an outside well. Whenever improvements inside the house were suggested, the husband insisted that they could not afford them. All their extra money went to buy either more land or new equipment for the farm.

This situation persisted partly because the family assumed that the husband had a complete right to determine all purchases. Small sums of money were doled out by the husband to the wife and children, often with considerable reluctance and ill will. Had the wife been a woman of more strength, or had she grown up with different ideas of husband-wife relationships, there would have been far more conflict, but ultimately probably more happiness.

This may seem to be an extreme case, yet every family must make some adjustment to the basic problem. Does either husband or wife have the right to buy an expensive hi-fi set and records to play on it without regard for the total budget? Does he bring home flowers to his beloved, instead of the steak that she would greatly prefer? Should the family go to the expense of buying a new car because one family member feels embarrassed about the old one? By whom and how should such questions be decided? In the "old days" when both husband and wife assumed that he would control the purse strings, the allocation of income often remained the basis of a running fight between them both during their entire marriage. He would dole out as little as possible. She, on her side, might resort to tears, public embarrassment, running up bills, or like Vinnie Day in *Life with Father* develop elaborate programs of manipulation to gain her ends. She might be aided and abetted in her stratagems by the children. It was inevitable that what started out as an effort to gain control of the purse strings easily became efforts to use the purse strings as a means of gaining control over other aspects of the relationship.

Money as a means of control

In the conflicts of married life, husband and wife, and later parents and children, may resort to any available weapon to win. Parents are known to try to control their children by threatening to withhold allowances or to deny special treats and favors. Husbands may seek to control their wives through the giving or the withholding of money. In this struggle the wives have an advantage because their husbands are legally responsible for their debts. Money can be and often is used as a means of control—a possibility that calls for significant adjustments in marriage and family life.

Different families have different systems for the allocation of their money. Five of the more common ways are the dole system, the family treasurer system, the division of expenses system, the joint account system, and the budget system.

The "dole" system. If mutually accepted, the dole can work fairly well. If it is not fully accepted, it can make for constant conflict, either open or concealed behind trickery. It is not likely to work in most modern American families.

The "family treasurer" system. This may outwardly appear like the dole system, but differs greatly in the spirit and nature of relationship. Usually each member of the family old enough to spend money gets an allowance. The rest is turned over to the "treasurer," who may be husband, wife, or even an older child. This treasurer pays all bills and often does most of the buying. He (or she) does not make unilateral decisions, however, regarding major expenses. This system works well provided (a) you have someone who likes, and can handle, the responsibilities, and (b) all other members of the family really accept it.

The "division of expenses" system. Certain expenses are assigned to the husband, such as the rent, the car, and his personal expenses; and others are the responsibility of the wife, such as food, utilities, and clothing for her and the children; with each assigned enough money to cover these costs. Special expenses or other expenditures not so allotted are decided by joint decision.

The "joint account" system. The earnings of both husband and wife are put in a common checking account upon which either may draw to pay both common and personal expenses. Children are cared for by personal allowances. Any unusually large expenses are decided by joint consultation. This works well when both members are responsible, in essential accord, and when the income consistently runs above expenses.

The "budget" system. For most families, this is the best system. Expenses are budgeted in advance by common agreement. This budget includes a personal allowance for each member of the family old enough to handle money, which he may spend as he chooses without consultation. Any excess goes into a common fund which is saved, or spent only by common agreement.

Any of these systems involves adjustment and can cause conflicts. Even with the best plans there can be considerable conflict over the budget itself. If the wife especially enjoys eating and cooking, she may want to spend too much for food. The husband may enjoy music and want more to go for records. Clothing may mean much to one and little to the other. A second problem is in keeping to the agreed-upon budget. Obviously when Uncle Bill comes to visit that calls for some increase in the regular food budget. But does she have to serve him crab meat and steak? Or do they really have to take Cousin Sue and her boy friend to the best restaurant in town? And out of what part of the budget are such extra costs to be taken?

Major expenditures constitute a third area of contention. Should the couple buy a new car, or new furnishings for their home? Should they have a family vacation or should they stay at home this year and save the money toward buying a house? Should they save for a new roof or "live it up" as they go? Who decides, and how?

Who Makes the Major Money Decisions?

A series of studies of a cross section of families in all parts of the United States over a period of years (1954–1956) queried husbands and wives as to which one made their family financial decisions. In general, buying the family car is decided by the husband and almost never by wives alone. Decisions to purchase household goods are made jointly or by wives alone. In handling money and bills and saving, responsibility is often shared; where it is not, the wife is more likely than the husband to play the dominant role [2] (see Table 23).

These nation-wide surveys find husbands and wives in essential

TABLE 23. *Reported Decision Making within Families* [3]

	Who in your family decides . . . ?			
	When it's time to buy a car	About savings	About money and bills	When it's time to buy household goods and furniture
Wife Only	3%	27%	40%	25%
Wife Predominantly	1	4	2	11
Both Equally	28	48	28	54
Husband Predominantly	7	3	2	4
Husband Only	51	15	27	4
Don't Buy (Don't Save)	8	3	—	1
Not Ascertained	2	—	1	1
Number of cases	(651)	(644)	(959)	(661)

[2] Elizabeth H. Wolgast, "Do Husbands or Wives Make the Purchasing Decisions?" *Journal of Marketing*, October, 1958, Vol. 23, No. 2, pp. 151–158.

[3] From "Husbands and Wives as Decision Makers," *Family Economics and Review*, March, 1959, page 13, from Wolgast, *op. cit.*

agreement as to who makes the decisions in their families, indicating that family roles are well defined and well understood among the members of established homes. Among less experienced and younger married couples there are more efforts at joint decisions and there seems to be more uncertainty as to who has the greater influence in money matters.

"Will you or your spouse have the greater influence in making financial decisions in your marriage?" is the question that Kenkel put to undergraduate married students living on the Iowa State University campus. When he asked husband-wife pairs to assume that they had received a gift of $300 and to decide between themselves just how the money would be spent, less than half (42 per cent) thought that each of them would have about the same amount of influence. Of all the spouses, 48 per cent expected the husband to have the greater share of influence and 10 per cent anticipated the wives would have somewhat more influence. In actual decision-making sessions, taped and analyzed for study, the husbands did the greater amount of talking, came up with more ideas and suggestions, and had the greater influence in deciding what to do with the money. Eighty per cent of the wives performed most or more of the actions that kept the discussion running smoothly —raising the husband's status, showing affection, joking, laughing, and showing consideration and appreciation. The wives who contributed most of the social, emotional actions had the most influence in the husband-wife decisions.[4]

Although the roles of college husbands and wives were clearly defined in action, with the husbands having the greater influence in the decisions and the wives playing the emotionally supportive roles, neither the husbands nor the wives were able to predict and recognize with clarity the roles they each played.[5] This suggests that married college students may not clearly understand what to expect of themselves or of each other in the process of making family decisions about money.

Early in your marriage you have to decide what and when and how to buy such basic essentials for housekeeping as linens and enough dishes and kitchen equipment to enable you to sleep and serve meals at home. You will need furniture and furnishings, including curtains

---

[4] William F. Kenkel, "Influence Differentiation in Family Decision Making," *Sociology and Social Research*, September–October, 1957, Vol. 42, No. 1, pp. 18–25.

[5] William F. Kenkel and Dean K. Hoffman, "Real and Conceived Roles in Family Decision Making," *Marriage and Family Living*, November, 1956, Vol. 18, No. 4, pp. 311–316.

and drapes, necessary durable equipment such as a stove, refrigerator, washer, and vacuum cleaner, along with optional items such as a television set, a camera, a record player, golf clubs, and a sewing machine, as well as the most expensive item of all—an automobile.

Who makes the decisions in your family, and how, depends upon a number of factors: How you each define your roles as man and woman in marriage, which of you feels the more intensely about a given purchase, what community and family pressures operate in your situation, and how experienced you are in the process of decision making. You two are free to choose what you will, as you want to, at the time that makes sense for you.

Very few young married couples start housekeeping with everything they need already furnished. Your responsibility is to arrange in order of priority the major items that you will need and buy them when you decide you can afford them. Since many pieces of major equipment may be bought on the installment plan, or with some other form of credit, you inevitably face the question of what borrowing policies will work best for you.

How Can You Keep Your Credit Good?

In an earlier age it was often felt that, except for mortgages and extreme emergencies, families should avoid any form of debt. Today, credit in some form is a normal part of family economics. Yet it is important to avoid going from one extreme to the other. Therefore you should know something of the kinds of credit and debt and how to keep them within bounds. There are three major types of credit for families.

Major types of credit

Open-account credit or "charge accounts." One distinguishing feature of this is the monthly bill. It would be difficult to pay cash for your electricity or gas, and inconvenient for your telephone. Doctors and dentists also find it more convenient to send bills, at least to their regular patients. Larger department stores, too, commonly extend credit to approved customers. Like all credit this has its costs, although bad debts and collection costs are usually less than with other types of credit. These costs are included in the prices of the merchandise so that the store makes no extra charge to the customer. About a third of all retail trade is conducted on charge accounts.

For the customer open-account credit has both advantages and risks. You can shop without having first to go to the bank and carry around large sums of cash. You may get better treatment, especially in exchange privileges, and receive advance notice of specials and sales.

The danger is that the ease of getting things just by ordering them will lure you into getting more than you can afford. To pay for too many goods carelessly bought, you may have to scrimp on essentials or resort to costly borrowing.

Charge accounts with stores are commonly used only with relatively costly purchases not frequently made. In "dime stores" and grocery stores the cash outlay at any one time is usually so small that credit would not pay either you or the store. In other stores you will find the charge account an advantage, provided that you buy only what you want most and can well afford.

Installment credit.[6] Almost 80 per cent of borrowing by families is done by installment credit. The advantages are that you can have the use of what you want without waiting. Furthermore, installment payments may make you save money that you would otherwise fritter away with nothing to show for it. The disadvantages are the high financing costs that cut the amount of money you have to spend for other things and the danger that you will buy so much that you will have to live close to the margin in more important things in order to keep up the payments. Studies show that in over 40 per cent of young families installment payments lap up a fifth of their take-home pay. If you do buy on the installment plan never get so committed that circumstances, such as loss of pay from illness or a new baby, will push you over the edge. Some installment contracts allow the store not only to take back what you bought but to make you continue your payments for what you no longer have.

The revolving charge account. This works like installment credit except that it is payment on your total debt rather than on some particular item. In some one month you may want to buy far more than you could pay for within thirty or even ninety days. The revolving charge account enables you to spread your payments over six months or even a year. It works like this. On the basis of your annual income, say $4,500 a year, the stores that are in on the plan allow you a total combined credit up to $900. You do not have to use it all. But on whatever you do use, you pay one twelfth each month. It is revolving in that, as you reduce your debt you can get other things on credit up to the full amount of your maximum. On any unpaid balance you pay a finance charge of 1 per cent to 2 per cent a month.

The great danger, as found by one survey, is this. Some families

---

[6] A number of books on family finance have discussions of this subject. For a simple, popular discussion, see C. Hartley Grattan, "Buying on Time: Where Do You Stop?" in *Harper's Magazine,* April, 1956, or watch other magazines for current articles.

feel that as long as they have this credit they may as well use it up to the limit. This policy of buying, not because they want the goods but because they can get them, keeps them permanently in debt, cuts their income through the finance charges, and prevents them from building up savings and reserves.

Credit ratings

In almost any city of any size, merchants and others establish a composite list of those who use credit. Before long you will be on this list, as a good, slow pay, or poor credit risk. Keep your credit rating good, (1) by not buying more than you can easily afford to pay for; (2) by making all payments, and (3) paying all bills promptly. If for some reason you are unable to do so, get in touch with your creditor, tell him what you can do and make whatever arrangements you can. Unless you have been taken in by some "gyp" concern, you will find your creditors reasonable and willing to make any necessary concessions.

Borrowing

All credit is a form of borrowing in which you get goods, rather than money. By borrowing you are getting money, rather than goods, "on credit." Family borrowing should ordinarily be done only for one of two reasons: (1) to tide you over in case of emergency, or (2) to enable you to finance purchases at less expense. In the case of some illnesses, serious fire or other loss, or loss of job, borrowing may be necessary. You should, however, save up a "cushion" so that it will be less necessary. A legitimate reason for borrowing is to enable you to finance some major purchase, like a house, a car, or a freezer, stove, or furniture. It is a good idea to know in advance the main possibilities for loans for any purpose.

Friends and relatives. If you find yourself without carfare or money with which to pay the dinner check, borrowing from friends may be essential, but as a general practice avoid it. Despite some exceptions, one of the surest ways to lose your friends is to borrow or to lend them money.

Borrowing from relatives should depend mainly upon the nature of the relationship and how well the relative can afford to loan or even to lose the money, A simple rule is this. The borrower should regard it as he would any other loan, to be repaid in full if at all possible. The lender should be willing to regard it, if necessary, as a gift.

Borrowing on collateral. The most common form of this is a mortgage. You borrow the money to buy a house and, as security for this loan, pledge the house itself. A second common type is a loan on an insurance policy. This is a way of getting the cash surrender value of your policy without cancelling your protection. You pay a nominal interest rate because making the transaction involves some costs, and because the interest on this money has been paying part of your premium. If you own stocks, bonds, or other securities, you can use them as security for loans from a bank. On stocks you can get from 50 per cent to 70 per cent of their market value, and on bonds, somewhat more, depending upon their grade. For such loans you may pay from 5 per cent to 6 per cent a year, far less than you would pay in financing costs on the installment plan or revolving credit. Pawnbrokers loan relatively small sums on personal property, but the amounts are so small and the cost so high that they are unlikely to be used by most families.

Borrowing without collateral. (1) *Salary advances.* An advance on your salary may help out in a temporary crisis when you need extra money only for a week or two. (2) *Credit unions.* Many industries, labor unions, fraternal orders, and some other groups operate credit unions that loan money to members. The usual rate is 1 per cent a month or 12 per cent a year. This is usually less than most financing costs and far less than you can get unsecured loans from other sources. (3) *Legitimate loan companies.* In most cities there are companies that make small loans without security and without using dishonest practices. Partly because of high costs of collection, they charge from 2.5 per cent to 3 per cent interest a month, or 30 per cent to 36 per cent a year. While this rate is both legal and perhaps legitimate, it is higher than most borrowers need to pay. (4) *Loan sharks.* These are the "gyp" financiers that may charge you several hundred per cent. Never borrow from anyone who charges more than the legal rate of interest. Seek legal advice if you get into the clutches of a loan shark. If his interest rates are beyond the legal rate he cannot collect.

In summary, using credit or borrowing so that you can live beyond your means is to be avoided. It is often an evidence of neurosis, and can bring nothing but grief. Credit as a convenience has a proper place in family economy, provided you limit your buying to what is already in your budget. Installment buying and revolving credit may be useful, but will cut your income and should be scrutinized with great care. Emergency borrowing may be necessary but should be kept to a minimum. Borrowing money so that you can get cash discounts and save on financing charges can increase your income, provided you do not go beyond what you can well afford. Borrow where you can get the best rates.

Is it Cheaper to Buy or to Rent?

In order to avoid the work and headaches of home ownership and to be freer to move about you may prefer to rent, regardless of cost differences. Or the satisfactions of your own place may outweigh any additional costs. The answer to the question "Which is cheaper?" varies with the locality and the situation. If there are many houses for sale and few places for rent, buying may be much cheaper. If there are a number of vacant apartments and few houses, renting may be much less expensive. There are many factors to be considered.

The Henry Browns, married for several years, are now renting. They find a nice house that they can buy for $20,000 with a $3,000 down payment, an amount which they have. The monthly payments including interest, principal, and insurance to cover the equity of the mortgage will be almost exactly what they are now paying for rent, and at the end of twenty years the mortgage will be completely paid off. At first the economic advantages of home ownership seem obvious. If they rent, at the end of twenty years they will have nothing but a pile of rent receipts. But if they buy, for the same monthly payments, at the end of this same period they will own a $20,000 home.

Then they begin to do some estimating. If they do not buy, at the end of twenty years they will have in addition to their rent receipts, the $3,000 that they did not have to use for a down payment. At present this is in a Savings and Loan Association, earning 4 per cent. If they leave it there, at the end of twenty years it will be about $6,500. Then they remember that in addition to the monthly payments there will be other costs now included in the rent, such as taxes, heat, and repairs. Those will average in their city, about $50 a month, or $600 a year. If this were added each year to the $3,000 already on deposit, at the end of five years they would have rent receipts plus about $7,000. In sixteen years this amount would have grown to somewhat over $20,000 and at the end of twenty years they would have, not only rent receipts but more than $26,000. The Browns decide that anyway they would rather live in a house. But they know that over the twenty-year period it will cost them $6,000 more to buy than to rent. Yet if inflation continues their rent might have so greatly increased, along with the value of their house, that they would more than break even.

Whatever you decide, estimate the relative economic advantages and disadvantages realistically. In any case, if you decide to buy, have an expert go over any property you are considering. Otherwise you may find that major repair bills will add considerably to what you have paid for your house. A relatively small consultant's fee could save you thousands of dollars.

What Insurance Program Is Best?

Americans are the most insured people in the world. A recent study indicates that 80 per cent of all American families have some form of life insurance. This percentage has been growing rapidly. Between 1900 and 1950 the number of policies taken out increased seven times as fast as the population, and the value of these policies fifteen times as fast. Between 1950 and 1955, the increase in the number of policies written was approximately double the increase in the population. By 1955 the amount of life insurance in force was 50 per cent higher than the national debt of that year, and the assets of all insurance companies were almost a third of the national debt. Life insurance occupies an important place, both in our total economy and in the programs of most families. It is important to know something about it.[7]

The primary purpose of life insurance is to protect those who are financially dependent in some way upon the insured. We usually think of dependents as wife and children. The "dependent" may also be a creditor who has insured the life of a debtor so that in case of death he can get his money back. A company may find its manager so valuable that they insure his life for a huge sum to protect themselves against the loss of his direction. In any case, you do not take out life insurance because *you* need it, but because your dependents (of whatever type) need it.

Life insurance should be taken out when you have dependents who need it, and not before. You would not take out automobile liability insurance before you have a car, or fire insurance on your "Dream Home" not yet built. Likewise do not take out life insurance before you have dependents—except in the case of G.I. insurance which is so much cheaper than ordinary insurance that you should take it out while you can still get it. If you take out life insurance at a younger age the rate will be lower, but you will be paying for more years and the total cost will be greater. No insurance company can insure you for extra years, even the younger years, without additional cost.

The more dependents you have the more insurance protection they need. As a man's family increases, so does their need for insurance. As the children grow up and become independent, this need will decline. How can a family get high protection while the children are young without saddling itself with a huge burden which later will be unnecessary? The answer is the kind of insurance which gives you the greatest protection at the least cost and automatically terminates when you no longer need it. This is term insurance. With some companies you can get this renewed each year without further examination, at an increas-

When to take out life insurance

---

[7] The statistical data in this discussion have been taken mainly from various issues of the *Life Insurance Fact Book,* published annually by the Institute of Life Insurance, 488 Madison Avenue, New York City; and from the *Statistical Abstract of the United States,* 1957.

ing rate. Or you can get it for a specific period—five, ten, or twenty years—for the same rate each year the policy is in force.

A good family plan is for the husband and wife to each take out a policy to protect each other, the husband taking out the larger amount. They should expect these policies to continue until death. The children, however, do not need protection after they are old enough to take care of themselves. Therefore with each pregnancy the father would take out another twenty-year term policy on himself. For the same money he can give his children twice the protection he could with ordinary life insurance. Furthermore, when this protection is no longer needed, his cost will decline.

Should you insure the children themselves? If they have dependents, yes. If not, no. If you want to build up a fund to put them through college, invest in good bonds, or a Mutual Fund, or in Savings and Loan. They will have a better chance of going to college if you insure yourself, not them.

How much insurance?

Statistics show that many families take out more insurance than they can or will keep up. On the surface the lapse and surrender rate may not seem excessive. For ordinary life insurance it ranged from a low of 2.2 per cent in 1944 to a high of 11.9 per cent in 1932, while industrial insurance rates were 6.8 per cent in 1944 to 27.9 per cent in 1932. But these rates are for all policies in force, *and for one year only.* You get a truer picture if you compare the amount given up each year with the amount bought each year. During the low years, people gave up more than they bought, not including normal maturing. In the best year, 1944, they gave up a third as much as they bought of the ordinary life, and more than half as much as they bought of industrial policies. One study made in New York State covering ten years showed that over half of all ordinary life policies taken out were given up, and three fourths of all industrial insurance policies. So don't let an agent talk you into overloading. Better take a small amount and hang on to it. How much you should take will depend largely upon such considerations as:

1. The size of the family and the ages of your children.
2. The standard of living which the protected family expects.
3. What the wife could earn. A woman who is a permanent invalid needs more protection than one who is strong and healthy. The wife who has some training or skill, like nursing, stenography or a license to teach, needs less protection than one who would face widowhood without abilities or skills.
4. Other economic resources. In time, savings or the gradual accumulation of property may lessen the need for insurance protection. Included here

also should be any forms of social security, governmental or private, by which the family is protected.

Wealthy people may need large policies in order to get cash with which to pay heavy inheritance taxes. For the ordinary family, the investments in insurance are for two purposes: to "level off" payments and to invest savings. The first kind is seen in the whole life policy. As people become older their insurance costs rise. If the payments are to remain the same throughout life, the company must "overcharge" people while they are young, so that it can "undercharge" them when they become old. The excess paid in the early years is saved by the insurance company and appears as the loan or cash surrender value of the policy. The interest on this saving is used to help pay the total costs of the policy. On the average the savings will be enough to pay off the entire policy by the time of death. This investment is actually a type of convenience to the policyholder, making it possible for him to meet the costs of later years without payments being too high.

Insurance as an investment

Savings may be invested through the endowment policy. This is really a form of term insurance at about four times the cost. The excess is saved and invested by the company. If the person outlives the term of the policy its face value (say $1,000) is returned in a lump sum. But if he dies before the policy expires his beneficiaries get only the same amount they would have received from a term policy. The company keeps the excess. If he had bought a term policy and saved the difference in cost, in case of prior death the beneficiaries would have received the thousand plus all the additional savings. These could amount to over $900. Endowment insurance is a "tails I lose" "heads I break even" proposition; not the wisest choice, even if you live. It has one defense. Some people seem unable to save anything. If they have to make payments on an endowment policy they may end up with savings which otherwise they would have squandered.

Finally, remember that insurance agents are human beings. Most of them are not dishonest; neither are they saints. Expect of them what you would of any salesmen; that they will do their best to sell their products. When they sell protection they are often rendering a valuable service. When they try to sell their banking and investment services, their efforts are more questionable.

For those who can get it, G.I. insurance is the best insurance available. But most people have to buy their insurance through regular companies. Some of these are ingenious at developing all kinds of "special" policies. But if you understand a few basic principles you can easily reduce them to a few major types. For example, one policy pro-

The best type of policy

vides for low payments during the first five years (when your earnings are presumably low) and substantially increase after that. This is likely to be a term policy that automatically becomes converted to whole life after five years.

Industrial insurance is not really a different kind of insurance, but rather a way of paying for insurance. Instead of making monthly or annual payments, you pay a collector who stops in each week to collect. Because of the costs of such collection this is the most expensive type of insurance. The limited payment policy is not a different kind of insurance, but merely a way of paying for whole life insurance more rapidly, so that at the end of a specified period the interest on your reserve takes care of all future insurance costs and you need pay no more yourself.

Group insurance is cheap and valuable for those who, because of physical disabilities, cannot get any other kind. A group, such as the employees of a certain company, are insured as a whole. When you leave the employ of the company, your protection automatically ceases. In other words, it is term insurance, the term being the length of time you remain with the same firm.

In general, insurance should be used for protection only, and not for investment. There is one exception—the annuity policy. This is a type of social security operated by the insurance company instead of the government. If your retirement pension is not already adequately provided for, and you wish to be assured of an income for your old age, the annuity policies of insurance companies should be given serious consideration. You pay a certain amount each year into the fund. When you reach the retirement age stated in the policy, the company either pays you a flat sum or a stipulated income for the rest of your life. If you die before the policy becomes due, the amount already accumulated is paid to your estate.

Buying life insurance

The first rule in buying life insurance is to buy it rather than merely to allow someone to sell it to you. Many people never give enough intelligent thought to it. Just before they marry, or perhaps some years before, an agent calls. Before he leaves, without ever having made any study of the matter or any comparisons with other companies, they have signed up. If you buy a freezer or a car, you may sign up for payments for the next six months to two years. But in life insurance you sign up for payments that can be for fifty years or more. So do not let anyone rush you into it. Here are some things to consider.

1. Does your vocation make you eligible for policies covering preferred risks? If you are a minister, a teacher, or a YMCA secretary, for example,

there are insurance companies especially organized to cover members of your profession at a decidedly lower than average cost.

2. Are you a member of a religious denomination or a fraternal order that insures its members at especially favorable rates? G.I. insurance available to veterans is the most generally known of this type.

3. In some states, including New York, savings banks sell certain kinds of policies at a cost below the usual rate. See whether such policies are available in your state.

4. If you buy your insurance from a regular company through a regular agent, shop around before you decide. See several agents and compare their figures. It can make a considerable difference. A study was once made of the net cost of $1,000 of insurance taken out at the age of 18 in ten major companies. The cost of one company was 50 per cent higher than that in another company that was both larger and probably stronger. Why pay 50 per cent more for something perhaps not as good?

5. Make a personal study of the costs of policies with different companies. For a few dollars you can buy a compendium that gives rather complete information about the kinds of policies and their costs, issued by all major American insurance companies. *Flitcraft* and *Spectator's Life Insurance Year Book* are among the better known. Your public library or a local insurance office can give you their addresses and costs. Spend a few evenings studying the costs of those companies in which you may be interested to find out which offer the best buys. Evenings so spent can easily be worth a hundred dollars or more each in savings.

In addition to life insurance, a well-rounded program includes at least the following types: **Other types of insurance**

Hospitalization insurance may not take care of all hospital expenses, but it will pay enough to make the costs far less burdensome. You should have a policy that covers your entire family. It should include obstetrical care.

Sickness and accident insurance usually pays a cash indemnity for specific losses, such as eye or foot, plus cash payments for each week you are laid up after the first week. This is often more difficult for women to secure, but cover the entire family if you can. Be especially careful in investigating the company that insures you. Such insurance lends itself to irresponsible companies from whom it is difficult to collect. Read the policy carefully for "jokers," or have a competent person read it for you. Otherwise you may find that the accidents and sicknesses you are most likely to have are not covered.

Medical insurance to cover medical bills and similar expenses other than hospital costs is not available everywhere, but the possibility of getting it should be carefully considered. Cover the whole family if you can.

Automobile insurance should cover liability first of all. Juries today have become increasingly generous with other people's money. A high coverage is not much more expensive than a low coverage, and may be well worth its cost. A second type that every owner should have is fire and theft. This will not only protect you in case of loss, but the insurance company may also take over much of the worry and burden.

Collision insurance is much more questionable, especially because of the usual $50 deductible clause. Many people drive for many years without ever having a repair bill for an accident over $50. If you have not owned a car for as long as ten years or so, take the case of your parents' car and see how much they would have gained or lost in that time by carrying a $50 deductible collision insurance policy.

Shop around for your automobile insurance. If you live outside a large city, some agency like the Farm Bureau may be able to insure you at considerable saving. If you do not drink, the Preferred Risk Mutual may offer you real savings. At least one mail order house offers insurance at especially attractive rates. Here, again, some time spent in studying different possibilities can bring real savings.

Property insurance. The payments on a house you are buying usually include enough for fire insurance to cover the equity of the mortgage holder. The rule is that any property that could be lost or damaged should be insured. If you own furniture, insure it against loss by fire. If you own anything that could be easily sold if stolen, you may wish to take out theft insurance. If you own property on which someone might be hurt, you should take out liability insurance. You can do this conveniently by taking out a "package" policy that covers the house and all furnishings against fire, theft, liability, wind damage, falling trees, and similar losses. Again, shop around before buying. In so doing, consider mail order houses and cooperatives as well as regular companies.

A well-rounded and complete program of insurance costs money. But it can also keep you from suffering disastrous losses or even being wiped out.

What Savings Program Should You Adopt? [8]

Putting money in a bank may not be saving, but only a safe and convenient way to keep it until you use it. On the other hand, buying dur-

---

[8] Kiplinger Magazine's *Your Job and Your Money, 1958 Success Book* contains a number of excellent articles on various types and aspects of a sound savings program. See also J. K. Lasser and Sylvia Porter, *Managing Your Money,* New York: Holt, 1953.

able goods that you need, such as linens, furniture, and household equipment is a form of saving, provided you need and can use what you get. So are the installment payments on goods so bought.

There are several kinds of saving. One is saving for a particular item or expense, such as the down payment on a house or a car, a baby, a vacation, or some relatively expensive item like a dryer, a rug, or a boat. A second kind of saving is investment. A third kind that should be high on your list from the start is a cash reserve for emergencies. The amount of this will vary with your income and the size of your family. Every family should have enough to tide it over in case of illness or loss of job, or to take care of such unforeseen extras as moving expenses or sizeable repairs on the house.

Investment is a problem that has become steadily more difficult. A few years ago the ordinary family could follow a simple formula—"Buy government bonds"—and let it go at that. Now with any bonds you risk loss through inflation, and U.S. government bonds lack the tax exempt advantages that other high grade bonds possess. Here are some major possibilities for investment.

Property. Buying a house is, among other things, a financial invest- Investment
ment. It may well be, as we have seen, more expensive to buy than to possibilities
rent. But it does protect you against inflation. As prices rise, so ordinarily, does the value of your house. Also, you may be able to rent a room, at least before the children come, and thus add to your income.

If you are a bit more venturesome and willing to assume some of the responsibilities of a landlord, consider buying a two-flat building and renting the other apartment. A two-flat building is usually small enough so that you can take care of it yourself without the expense of a janitor. If you are handy you may be able to do much of the repair work yourself. Furthermore with only one extra flat it is relatively easy to keep it rented to desirable tenants. Some people have gotten enough from the rental of the extra flat to carry the payments and even some of the expenses, giving them their rent at a greatly reduced cost. They also get many of the satisfactions of ownership. For those who have a bit of a flair for it, property is an excellent investment.

Savings and loan associations. For the normal family, these have many advantages. You deposit money in them as you would in a bank, ordinarily at any time and in any amounts. The time of your deposits will affect your interest payments. In the meantime, you do not have to do janitor service or worry about getting tenants, as would be the case if you were managing your property. Everything is done for you.

They are safe. Almost all loan associations belong to a federal agency that insures their accounts up to $10,000. If you wish to invest more in the same association, each member of the family can take out one account, or you can have others held jointly, so that two persons could have three accounts, each one fully insured.

They are fluid. Ordinarily you may withdraw any or all of your account any time you want to. If you withdraw before an interest date, however, you may lose some interest.

The yield is fairly good; usually at present writing around 4 per cent. This is higher than banks pay, but lower than some other forms of investment.

Compared to other investments there are some disadvantages. The interest is not tax exempt, and there is no hedge against inflation. If your dollars invested lose in purchasing power you lose correspondingly.

On the whole, however, savings and loan associations are, for the ordinary family, among the simplest, safest, and best investments available.

Securities. A discussion of securities as a possible part of your savings program may seem remote. Yet if you have a bank account or an insurance policy, you are an indirect owner of stocks and bonds. Since you are of the socio-economic class that reads such a book as this the chances are good that you will some day own securities, if you do not now. The very considerable increase in such ownership calls for at least a brief discussion of securities as part of a total savings program.

Bonds

The bonds with which you are most familiar and are most likely to own, are United States government savings bonds. These have the advantage of being as secure as cash and safer to keep. They offer a reasonable rate of return and may be cashed in for full (not maturity) value at any time. The disadvantage is that, like all bonds, they offer no protection against inflation so that all the interest you get and more may be offset by the declining value of the dollar.

The bonds of corporations and railroads are often excellent for insurance companies, banks, and funds where tax exemption has no importance. But the ordinary investor should consider most seriously tax exempt bonds that are issued by states and smaller political units and their subsidiary corporations. Some are backed by taxes, and some by the revenues from the toll roads, parking facilities, or water and sewage systems they were sold to pay for. These pay up to 4 or more per cent of tax exempt income, depending on the bond and when it becomes due. They fluctuate in value, but far less than common stocks. Although they cannot protect against inflation, the income tax exemption feature in some measure compensates for it. Usually they are sold

only in units of $1,000. For those who have as much as this for invest-
ment, they should be carefully considered.

In 1955 about one fourth of all college graduates with incomes over $5,000 a year owned common stocks. A major advantage in owning common stocks is as protection against inflation. The hope is that as prices rise, so also will the value of the common stocks. However, the risks are great. Stocks may rise. On the other hand, even the best have sometimes dropped to half of their former value; most have at times dropped to a fifth, and many to a tenth of their former values. You can get honest advice, but no one really knows how the stock market will change, still less what any particular stock will do. There are no common stocks that you can buy and then "just forget." The rule is to invest in stocks only what you can afford to lose. Unless you would enjoy spending a lot of time studying the market and watching it constantly it is better to stay out. One exception—if the company you work for offers you a chance to buy some of their stock at an unusually favorable rate it may pay to take it.

Common stocks

The way to invest in common stocks with relative safety and a minimum of trouble is through Mutual Funds. At the present writing, for from a dollar and a half to twenty dollars each, you can buy shares in a Mutual Fund that will invest your money, usually in common stocks. With some Funds you can even pick the type of stock; autos, chemicals, rails, food, mining, steel, etc., which you prefer. The price you pay is the average worth of all the stocks held by the Fund at the time you buy, usually plus a premium of from 1 per cent to 9 per cent. Although it would hardly pay to buy shares unless you expected to keep them for some time, you can cash in your shares when you wish, at their average net worth at the time. The value of your shares may be either more or less than you paid for them. In the meantime, you will get your share of all profits and dividends received by the Fund on its holdings. You have a good chance of getting a reasonable return on your money as well as seeing it, over the long term, increase in value. For the small investor who wants the protection against inflation that common stocks offer, the advantages are obvious. You can invest as much or as little as you wish and get in or out at any time. (Hence they are called "open end" funds.) Although there is real risk, someone else who makes a full time job of it will watch the market for you and decide what and when to buy and sell. In any investment program, consider the possibilities of Mutual Funds.

Mutual funds

Many young couples rightly make the purchase of a house the start and center of their investment program. Others quite as rightly decide against this. After you have decided about a house, a good policy is to put your investment money where you can get it out quickly without loss. It may have to function as an emergency fund. After you have a sizeable saving in something like Savings and Loan, you can expand into more risky or less fluid investments, depending upon your interests and competencies. A good rule is to protect yourself with some diversification. In any case, review carefully several possibilities, develop a plan, and stick to it with reasonable persistency.

What Are Your Long Range Goals?

The basic financial problem for every family is to establish long range economic goals for itself. Until your family decides where it wants to go financially for the next few years, it cannot establish a really sound budget. Once this decision has been made progress becomes possible. Furnishings and equipment can then be bought as provided for in the long range plan. Decisions regarding a new car are made in the light of other family interests and needs. Emergency funds are built up to cushion shocks and in the meantime provide welcome additional income. Every member of the family knows what to expect and learns to adjust demands to the larger family goals. Clearly defined values do much to reduce conflict and increase family harmony.

Economic goals are in turn based upon a total philosophy of life. If your main concern is to impress others, you will put as much as possible where it will show—in a fashionable address, a flashy car, and expensive entertaining. In order to maintain this front other values may have to be sacrificed. If, on the other hand your main concern is for each other, you will have more money available for what you both genuinely want. Your economic policies will depend largely upon how you see yourself. If you measure your own worth in terms of your income and "standard of living" you take the job that pays best regardless of what it may take out of you. Or, you work long hours and perhaps hold down two jobs.

Some people are always too busy or too tired to enjoy life—leisure, culture, friends, home, or family. When we hear of a highly successful business executive who drops dead at a relatively young age we may ask, "What good will all his money do him now?" Such a question, however, misses the main point. If a large income and expensive living were his main concerns, he may have felt that it was better to have them even for a few years than to be without them twice as long. His economic behavior reflected the way he saw himself.

Your philosophy of life and its resulting economic goals will profoundly affect your choice of friends and social life. If you are socially ambitious you will choose as your friends those who "can do something for you," whether you like them or not. If you feel that friends are to be enjoyed for themselves, you will associate with those whom you like and admire—for what they are rather than for what they have.

The High Price of Daffodils [9]
by
Harriet R. Stolorow

I wander lonely as a cloud
   In subdivided Manor Hills,
Where stands my house, of which I'm proud,
   Although it's mortgaged to the gills:
Beside the lake, beneath the trees
   (A few are dying of elm disease).

Continuous as the stars that shine
   Are all the bills that I must pay;
They stretch in never-ending line
   Across my vision, night and day:
Ten thousand, see I at a glance,
   I need for patio, pool, and plants.

The waves beside me dance, but they
   Do not entrance me with their glee;
Not even poets can be gay
   Who owe a finance company:
I gaze, and gaze, with just one thought;
   The wealth it takes for what I've bought.

And oft, when on the couch I lie
   In vacant and expensive mood,
I tell my analyst that I
   Am losing all my fortitude:
And when I mention Manor Hills,
   He gives me tranquilizing pills.

If you want most of all to live a satisfying life you choose a vocation that brings you the greatest satisfaction. The amount of income, while important, is secondary. You take time to enjoy living—to be with your family and watch those you love grow and develop. The advantages that you see for them are not effortless security, but enriching relationships. Knowing that you have to "buy" your money income with

---

[9] From *The Atlantic Monthly,* March, 1959, page 81.

your life (for time and energy are the essence of life) you make sure that what you get is worth its costs. You do not "buy" more money than you need any more than you would buy more milk or automobile tires than you could use.

Important as it is to have a financial plan, it is even more important to budget your life. Many families never decide upon their goals one way or another. They just drift into them. It is important to get the most out of your expenditures of money, it is far more important to get the greatest value out of your expenditures of life. Poor judgment in the use of money may not be too serious, since its amount can be replaced. You can increase your life only by using it to its best advantage. Getting your money's worth is important, but getting your life's worth is far more so. Sound family goals help you budget your life.

READINGS

Foosaner, Samuel J., *Tax Uses of Life Insurance*. Chicago: Callaghan, 1958.

Fromme, Allan, *The Psychologist Looks at Sex and Marriage*. New York: Prentice-Hall, 1950, Chapter 8.

Institute of Life Insurance, *Life Insurance Fact Book*. 488 Madison Avenue, New York 22, annual publication.

Kiplinger Magazine, *Your Job and Your Money, 1958 Success Book*. 1729 H Street, N.W., Washington 6, D.C.

Lasser, J. K., and Sylvia Porter, *Managing Your Money*. New York: Holt, 1953.

LeMasters, E. E., *Modern Courtship and Marriage*. New York: Macmillan, 1957, Chapters 19, 20.

Lynd, Robert S. and Helen M., *Middletown*. New York: Harcourt, Brace, 1929, Chapter 8, "Why Do They Work So Hard?"

Merriam, Oreana, "How Young Families Spend Their Money," *Journal of Home Economics*, May, 1955.

Nickell, Paulena, and Jean Muir Dorsey, *Management in Family Living*. New York: Wiley, 1950, Part 3.

U.S. News and World Report, "New Ways to Use Insurance," March 28, 1958, pp. 80–91.

14 Coping with Conflict

Are differences part of being married?

Does quarreling hurt or help a marriage?

What do husbands and wives do when they differ?

How can you cope with conflict constructively?

Can marriage counseling help?

I<small>N</small> a fairy tale "they are married and live happily ever after." The assumption is that marriage is a relationship of unending bliss. The happy marriage is one in which neither partner ever raises his voice or takes issue with the other. A good family is pictured as one in which everyone always sees eye to eye with the rest of the family or, differing, keeps quiet in order to preserve the peace.

The folklore of family "harmony at all cost" goes back to the days of the patriarchal family. In those times, children were to be seen and not heard and the woman of the house was patient and long-suffering. Peace and quiet in the home were evidence of the power and authority of the father in the days when mother quieted her children with the admonition, "Hush now, here comes Father." Quarreling in the household, which meant a breakdown of patriarchal authority, was quelled without delay. Writers from Bible days onward supported the father in his position by repeating platitudes for the edification of children and their mothers. Dozens of maxims glorifying marital acquiescence are still heard today: "Forgive and forget," "Bear and forbear," "Let bygones be bygones," "Speak when spoken to," "God bless our happy home," and "Home, sweet home."

Life was rugged when the patriarchal family flourished, and a man could not be bothered with the squabbles of his wife and children.

His concerns were for their survival and nothing was allowed to distract him from his main task of protecting his home from the dangers that lurked all around it. This was not to assume thai his wife and children always saw things as he did. However, when they differed from their "Lord and Master," they were expected to bow to his judgment.

The emergence of the democratic, person-centered family has challenged these former principles of family life. Today the emphasis is on respect for personality—of wife and children as well as of the man of the house. Today the belief is that each person has the right to develop as he must, with a voice in the affairs that concern him and a chance to help make the decisions that affect his life. Democratic interaction is built upon a recognition of differences. Modern marriage flourishes as it learns to live with its differences and disagreements.

Group success is related to the willingness to disagree. Repeated research into the net effect of the expression of disagreement on groups of servicemen indicates that the greater the acceptance of disagreement, the greater the ability to adapt, the better the group judgment, and the higher degree of consensus that is reached.[1] Parallel observations have been made of the values of getting differences out into the open in family life. When all opinions are aired, the decisions are more likely to preserve the values of all the family members than in the authority-from-the-top direction that brooks no counterproposals.

Are Differences Part of Being Married?

Courtship customarily commences with the mutual discovery of similar tastes and interests. "You like sailing too? Why, how wonderful." "What a coincidence, that is what I wanted all along." "You must have been reading my mind, I was just thinking that myself." Joyful discovery of compatible preferences punctuate the dating days. Differences are glossed over as unimportant in many a courtship.

With marriage comes the challenge of shared intimacy in all areas of life. Whenever two individuals undertake a close and continuous association, some conflicts between them are inevitable. The closer the association and the freer the personalities, the more vigorous the clashes may be. Marriage, the most intimate and demanding of all adult human relationships, has conflict as an inescapable part of its nature.

No one ever marries a carbon copy of himself—fortunately. A man marries a woman, thereby precipitating both of them into the union of

---

[1] E. Paul Torrance, "Group Decision-Making and Disagreement," *Social Forces*, May, 1957, Vol. 35, No. 4, pp. 314–318.

man's world and woman's world. A woman has learned the feminine ways of meeting situations, while a man has learned the male patterns of behavior. When frustrated, she cries and he sputters; when complimented, she gushes a simulated protest and he smiles silently; she adores shopping, he loathes it; she talks on and on over the telephone, he hangs up as soon as he decently can; she wants to get out of the house after a day of housework, while he longs for nothing more than an evening at home.

Body builds and temperaments differ greatly. Some persons have a high energy output and prefer vigorous activities, while others are slow and quiet in their actions. Some individuals wake up at once in the morning, want to plan their day well ahead, get their best work done in the morning, and by evening are worn out. Others get off to a slow start, want to make few important decisions in the morning, gradually gain momentum as the day wears on and by evening are at their peak performance. There is nothing wrong in either pattern. Examinations of heartbeat, blood pressure, respiration rate, and general metabolism reveal that some persons tend to have A.M. and others P.M. peaks. The rub comes when the "A.M.'er" marries the "P.M.'er" and the two have to learn to mesh their two entirely different built-in schedules.

The struggle for autonomy within the intimacy of marriage can precipitate many a conflict situation. Two egos struggling for individual identity within the fused pair relationship may magnify differences for the sake of some breathing room. Conflict serves a useful function in setting a maximum distance and nearness that the two personalities can take in a new marriage. The struggle for privacy, for the chance to live one's own life, to make one's own decisions, and develop as one has to as a person, becomes socially acceptable in the era when fundamental human rights are guaranteed to everyone in a free society. But individual rights within marriage rarely come without a struggle. Much of the "fussing" at one another reflects the ongoing process of living intimately together while putting up a healthy resistance to self-destruction.

To some extent, every marital union is a mixed marriage. The husband and wife bring from their parents' homes different wants and wishes and different ideas of what is funny and what is serious. When a decision has to be made some of these differences are likely to come to light. Especially during the early years of marriage, the couple has to work out a common set of workable routines, a mutually acceptable way of living, a whole new set of family policies out of the two systems from which they both have come.

Studies at Harvard University [2] find that in the dimension of time, some families are oriented to the past ("Those were the good old days"), some to the present ("Let's have fun while we can"), and some to the future ("Work hard now for a bigger and better tomorrow"). In the dimension of relationships, some families are traditionally oriented toward their ancestors, some team up with their contemporaries, while others are individualistically independent persons with few ties. In the activity dimension, some families concentrate on *being* with high valuations on spontaneity, impulse, and indulging the feelings of the moment. Other families are oriented toward *being* and *becoming* with the emphasis on rounded development of the kind of person one must be. Still other families are oriented toward *doing* with accomplishment and achievement rating high. Husband and wife coming from contradictory combinations such as these inevitably face basic conflicts that must somehow be worked through. In a melting pot culture like ours some heat is to be expected as the divergent elements attempt to fuse.

Differences in marriage are found between the two partners (interpersonal). There are also role conflicts within the given individual (intrapersonal). *Interpersonal conflict* is seen in the failure of a spouse to measure up to what his mate expects of him or her. An example is seen in the present-oriented, pleasure-loving husband whose wife expects him to be a hard-working go-getter. *Intrapersonal conflict* is that in which a husband or wife fails to be what he or she wants and expects to be. Emmie for instance nags her husband. Intellectually Emmie wants to be a pleasant companion who can talk things through sensibly with her husband. Unconsciously her identification with her mother conflicts with the kind of wife she wants to be. Role conflict in marriage resulting from failure to assume the expected marital roles either in oneself or in one's spouse is not uncommon in today's marriages.[3]

Particularly pertinent to this discussion is the realization that families differ greatly in their overt expression of conflict. Some operate on a peace-at-any-price basis denying expression of difference between their members. Others openly battle for their rights and values as they see them.

---

[2] Reported by Ezra Vogel, "Value Orientations and Role Conflict in the Family," theoretical paper, Groves Conference on Marriage and the Family, April 14, 1958.

[3] A. R. Mangus of Ohio State University reports a study under way in which 27 per cent of the couples studied have extreme role conflict, 25 per cent have moderate role conflict, and 48 per cent have little or no role conflict in their marriage. A. R. Mangus and L. H. Snow, "Role Conflict in Marriage," Unpublished Study, 1958.

There is evidence that there actually are two different kinds of marriage partners—those who refuse to quarrel and those who profit from it. One research exploration of the question concludes, "The findings of this study give fairly consistent pictures of two different types of successfully or happily married persons. There is the conventional, harmony-valuing type with a tendency not to express hostility . . . and a less conventional, companionship-valuing type with a tendency to express a fairly high amount . . . a tendency to express hostility, if not excessive, is related to greater success in marriage, when marital success is judged by certain criteria of a family atmosphere conducive to personality growth of its members." [4]

Does Quarreling Hurt or Help a Marriage?

Differences are to be expected in marriage. The question is, shall you get your differences out in the open by quarreling from time to time, or should you avoid quarreling at all costs? There are two schools of thought on the place of quarreling in marriage. One denies that any good can come out of open conflict in the family. The other advocates the honest expression of real feelings between marriage partners, even when they conflict.

There are some persons who believe that quarreling inevitably involves dispute, angry feelings, fighting, and attacking one another in efforts to hurt and undermine the ability to function effectively.[5] Quarreling in marriage is feared lest it destroy love and create an unhealthy emotional climate for the husband and wife and for their children. In a quarrel both sides are seen to take extreme positions, set rigid battle lines, and fight to save face. Quarreling prevents better ways they might have found to adjust to one another. This school of thought advocates avoiding quarreling of all kinds in marriage. This point of view is frequently voiced in admonitions such as:

The dangers of quarreling

"If you can't say anything nice, don't say anything at all."

"Say something pleasant or keep quiet."

"One harsh word leads to another."

"Avoid the situations that lead to differences."

---

[4] Sylvia Turlington O'Neill, "The Relationship between Tendency to Express or Not Express Hostility and Marital Success," Ph.D. Thesis, Cornell University, June, 1955, pp. 128–129.

[5] This paragraph draws upon the statement made by Judson T. Landis on the question "Can Interpersonal Competence in a Marital Relationship Be Improved by Quarreling?" at the National Council on Family Relations Conference, at Purdue University, August 23, 1957.

"There are some things better not discussed."

"It takes two to quarrel."

"A battle ignored is a battle won."

"Better be safe than sorry."

There are several problems in the "never-a-cross-word" type of marriage. The couple who avoid quarreling at all costs may resort to substitute activity to keep their marriage on an even keel. Illness, overwork, martyrdom, daydreaming, rationalization, depreciation, and idealization are some of the mechanisms employed to escape the realities of the marriage. The conflict is handled by avoiding it. Consistently repressed tensions are hard on a relationship. They tend to circumscribe and narrow the topics of conversation in a marriage, and to delimit the areas of activity together. Unresolved tensions disturb the normal functioning of the family because they accumulate and spread and become associated with other areas of living.

Restrained discussion is advocated sometimes as a better alternative to quarreling. But the danger is that cold discussion arrives only at an *intellectual* solution which fails to do justice to the *emotional* elements in the conflict. If research and clinical evidence are valid, it is best that these emotional elements be expressed. Marriage partners can come to terms on a basis of reality only when they have *felt* the heat of each other's hostile feelings. A marriage should be organized to include the expression of both positive and negative emotions if it is to be a communicating and satisfying relationship.

The benefits of quarreling

Mental hygiene accepts a certain amount of quarreling as normal. Much conflict merely indicates the presences of differences that occur as a couple explore new areas or attempt new tasks. Gradually the friction wears the protruding parts smooth, and a consensus is reached. Thereafter conflict is less likely to occur in that specific area, but it may and should bob up again as long as the family continues to meet new and different problems.

Many of the quarrels in marriage help dispel tensions engendered by unlearning old habits and learning new ones. Some arise out of the frustrations which the discipline of marriage exacts and others arise quite naturally out of the unprepared for intimacies of marriage. Some husband-wife conflict merely reflects the growing edges of a new relationship. It denotes growth and change rather than a passive acceptance of the new tasks on the part of either party. In the early stages much conflict consists of defining the issues and finding where the other stands on the many new problems they are facing.

Quarrels in the first year serve to bring the parties face to face with the realities of their marriage. Some conflict helps to remove the blinders from their eyes and enables them to appreciate one another as persons rather than as imaginary incarnations of perfection. The reaction, "But you seemed to be so different, so much taller and romantic, when we were engaged," may bring pain of disillusionment but is a healthy experience. If romantic illusions have been built up it is a productive quarrel which brings the newlyweds down to earth. A husband can't live long in a rosy haze with an imaginary wife and remain mentally healthy.

Conflict serves a useful purpose in setting the boundaries of ego protection and ego involvement. There is a marked tendency in the ecstasy of the honeymoon and early months of marriage to establish a closeness of association which becomes burdensome, especially when erotic discoveries have ceased to suffuse the relationship with pleasure. Quarrels destroy these burdensome patterns and bring into being more tolerable customs.

Married couples learn by experience to find the optimum nearness that they can tolerate. Like porcupines who approach one another for warmth yet are repelled by the other's barbs, the married couple must achieve that distance which is optimum for warmth without being too ego-involving. Clearly this can be achieved only through conflict of a sort. Ultimately the couple must feel for themselves the reality of each other's emotional resistances and take the measure of each other's capacity for mutual accommodation.

The modern couple expect that in marriage they will have a place of security and intimacy where they are free to behave like human beings with the normal variety of emotions. The workaday world, organized as it is, does not permit the frank expression of resentment, hostility, aggression, vanity, jealousy, and selfish ambition along with the tenderness of love, all of which exist in the normal person. The individual must control his annoyances and his affections to get along in our complex industrial society. If he flies off the handle at his boss he may lose his job. There needs to be some place, however, where the individual can give vent to his annoyances and be himself, and that place seems to be in marriage. If a marriage is so fragile that it must be maintained by the same kind of artificial manners that keeps an office force functioning, it is precariously balanced. As one authority has stated: "One of the functions of marriage is to weave a rope of relationship strong enough to hold each person at his worst."

The "conflict-is-normal" point of view sees one of the functions of quarreling as releasing the tensions that arise from time to time in any relationship. The belief is that a good scrap well carried through to the end can clear the air, define the issues, let each partner know just where he stands, and stimulate the exploration of alternative ways of behaving. When open conflict becomes more socially acceptable such mottos as the following may come into vogue:

"If anything is eating you, out with it."
"Let me have it straight, I can take you as you are."
"Emotional honesty is the basis for marriage."
"So, you don't agree, well tell me why not."
"Tell me what this means to you so I can understand."
"I want you to feel this the way I do."
"I'll try to do better, but you'll have to help."
"We can take this, we can take anything."

Here then are two diametrically opposite viewpoints on the place of overt conflict in marriage. The one says that quarreling is harmful, the other that getting differences out into the open helps marriage.

The position of any individual on the question of quarreling in marriage originates in his own childhood home. The boy who grew up in a family where open quarreling was not allowed finds it hard to battle things through with his wife. The girl who was frightened by her parents' quarreling may find it hard to let her husband know how she really feels about anything that might become an issue. Children who grow up in the rough and tumble of occasional squabbling in the farmily learn how to quarrel without harm either to themselves or to others.

What a person does when he marries depends on how he was brought up as a child and what he has learned since. If each man and woman acted out his reproduction or repudiation of childhood family patterns, with no influences of later learnings, there would be little progress. Fortunately, young adults between leaving their parental homes and entering their own marriages are relatively free to evaluate alternatives and to depart from their former patterns in ways that make sense.

Differences are a part of being married. The two married partners are different persons, from different families, with their own established patterns and ways of doing things, and this means that inevitably, from time to time, there will be conflicts that have to be met in some way. The question is—what do husbands and wives do to restore their equilibrium when their differences loom up between them?

What Do Husbands and Wives Do When They Differ?

The Harvard University studies of role conflict in the family, which describe how actual families deal with their conflicts,[6] have found three basic patterns. The first and most universal is that of trying to induce the mate to change while remaining the same oneself (*role induction*). The second is that of taking the role of the other person and seeing what the situation looks like from his or her point of view (*role reversal*). In the third both members of the couple change as they work out a solution to their problem (*role modification*).

Role induction as a way of trying to resolve a conflict in marriage is essentially manipulative. One of the marriage partners puts pressure on the spouse to change. The other either agrees, submits, goes along with, or is persuaded to give in. There is seen to be a sequence of five steps in role induction techniques: (1) coercing, (2) coaxing, (3) evaluating, (4) masking, or (5) postponing.

Inducing the mate to change

Coercing ranges from overt attack or threat of attack in the future, and from verbal commands to physical force. Essentially it is the manipulation of present and future punishments. Coercion is the induction technique most used, partly because of hostile-aggressive tendencies in individuals, and partly because of culturally established ways of settling role conflicts. "It is present in every family we have studied, and it is probably safe to say that it is present in every enduring social system, no matter how much it is veiled." [7]

No induction technique guarantees success. They all can be met either by a specific neutralizing technique or by a counter induction. The specific neutralizing technique for coercing is *defying*, the counter inductions may vary from retaliatory coercion to any of the following efforts to get the partner to change.

Coaxing includes asking, promising, pleading, begging, and tempting. Coaxing may be defined as the manipulation of present and future rewards. It takes second place, not because it is less universal but because it appears to be somewhat less available as a manipulatory technique. The pressure of coaxing may be warded off by *refusing* and *withholding*, or the partner may respond by using coercion or some other induction technique.

Evaluation includes praising, blaming, shaming, approving, and disapproving. One partner responds to the other's behavior by identify-

[6] This section is drawn from John P. Spiegel, "The Resolution of Role Conflict within the Family," mimeographed memorandum from Harvard University, received May, 1958.

[7] *Ibid.,* p. 20.

ing and categorizing it, such as, "You're too big for that," or "Stop acting like a fool," or "You come alive when you're mad." The effect is a
kind of value judgment based upon manipulation of reward and punishment. The partner may accept the accusation and stop his or her
coercive activity. He or she may then substitute some other method
such as coaxing. Alternatively, *denying*, the specific neutralizing technique, may be used against evaluating, for example, "I am *not* acting
like a fool."

Masking is the withholding or altering of relevant information. It
includes such behavior as pretending, evading, censoring, distorting,
lying, hoaxing, deceiving, etc. It occurs universally. "Every culture has
its patterned ways of concealing information and its criteria for determining what information may or may not be revealed, with or without distortion." [8] The specific neutralizing technique is *unmasking*
when the two confront each other with the truth. If the masking has
been in some major area of adjustment, the unmasking can be explosive as in the revelation of true feelings or actual situations that
threaten each other's egos or the security of the marriage.

Postponing is deferring the conflict in the hope that there will be a
change of attitude. The wife sets about "feeding the brute first" before
letting a conflict situation come out. Or the husband decides to "sleep
on it" and tackle the problem again when they both are fresh. If one
of the partners has little to gain by postponing he or she may attempt
to neutralize the postponing by *provoking*—fanning the flames of the
conflict so that it appears in full force.

Each of these five forms of role induction can be met by its neutralizing technique, or by counter induction methods in which each partner tries to manipulate the other. A definite step beyond role induction
is the effort to understand the other by taking his role and trying to
see how things look from where he stands.

Taking the
role of the
other

Role reversal is the encouragement of the other to take one's role, or
the attempt to get the other's viewpoint by putting oneself in his shoes.
The wife may help her husband to see the situation from her point of
view, or the husband may initiate by saying, "If you'd only see what
this means to me you'd understand." One partner may say, "I think I am
beginning to see what you mean," thus encouraging the other to recip-
rocate by trying to understand him better. Since this is not a manipulative approach it has no specific neutralizing activity. Role reversal
does not work when one partner is unwilling to try to see the situation
from the other's viewpoint, or when he responds with some effort to

---

[8] *Ibid.*, p. 24.

manipulate the other rather than to understand him. Role reversal can be the first step toward resolving the conflict with mutual efforts to change. Then it may lead to the third approach to conflict, role modification.

In *role modification* both partners develop insight and make conscious efforts to modify their roles to fit the situation as they have come to see it. Each identifies sufficiently with the other so that the adaptation is mutual and complementary. They both voluntarily shift their former roles so that peace is restored on a new and better basis. Five steps in role modification are: (1) joking, (2) referring, (3) exploring, (4) compromising, and (5) consolidating.

Changing both roles

Joking is the first indication that role modification is under way. The two have sufficiently identified with each other so that both have developed insights into the other's feelings and values. Now both partners can disentangle themselves from their intense preoccupation with their own involvement. This allows them to back off and laugh at themselves and each other. Playfully each tries on for size a series of ridiculous solutions, a process that may lead into a reasonable one. Role reversal and joking may be enough to resolve some role conflicts. Since there is no role induction, there is no neutralizing activity. Unless one partner has "no sense of humor" or refuses to be jollied out of his pique, joking paves the way for constructive resolution of the conflict, through one or more of the following steps.

Referring to a third party or organization for help in resolving a marital conflict can help. However, if the third party takes sides, as a member of the family often does, the situation may become worse rather than improve. If the third party steers the problem back to a manipulative base, as a well-meaning friend may, the solution is delayed. When the couple goes to a qualified counselor or guidance service (as described later in this chapter) and cooperates with the worker in the interest of resolving their conflicts, the chances of their moving on to a constructive solution are improved.

Exploring each other's capacity to assume mutually satisfying roles is done by probing, testing, proposing, and rejecting possible solutions. This is basically what the marriage counselor, psychiatrist, or family case worker helps the couple do in a good counseling situation. The couple talk through possible ways of handling their conflicts and eventually come to a solution that is comfortable for both of them. They both show in their behavior that they are trying to assume the roles that the new definition of the problem calls for. Such evidence of good faith on the part of one partner elicits mutual responsiveness in the other and the relationship moves toward a new level. Of course, there are set-backs and lapses to former manipulative activities, but once exploring gets well started it tends to continue toward a mutually acceptable solution.

Compromising is based upon the willingness of the pair to settle for somewhat more complementary roles than those with which the two started. Each partner comes to see that his original goals were in terms of only part of the marriage—that which he alone perceived before he felt the other's feelings and understood the values of the total relationship. Compromise in this sense is not the same as "giving in" to the other, nor is it the same as abandoning one's values for the sake of peace in the family. It is rather the mutual commitment to a new set of joint goals that are more realistic and promising than either of the two formerly had. This brings the couple to the threshold of the last step in the process.

Consolidating is the adjustment and redistribution of the couple's joint goals. Once they have agreed upon what they have to do, they must learn to make it work in their everyday behavior with each other. Each partner now attempts to internalize the new role to which he is committed. Each learns to reward the other for his new efforts, and to find satisfaction himself from his own improvement. In time, if the role modification is successful, the new solution settles into the normal routine of the family, and the original problem disappears.

The five steps in the process of role modification lead toward the constructive resolutions of the conflict. They are based upon mutual insight and communication. They establish a new level of interaction between the pair. In contrast, role induction is essentially manipulative. One partner tries to get the other to comply with his expectations. The partner may comply, he may neutralize the thrust, or he may enter into counterattacks. Since these efforts are primarily defensive they rarely settle anything, and so are apt to crop up again and again. Thus some efforts to resolve conflict are constructive, others are not.

How Can You Cope with Conflict Constructively?

Destructive quarrels are those that leave fewer assets in the relationship than it had before. Destructive quarreling is directed at the person and succeeds in destroying the illusions and fictions by which the person lives. It is a type of conflict which concentrates on the other's ego. It is of the belittling and punishing variety. Destructive quarrels lead to alienation as the love object is transformed into a hate object, and separation is thereby made possible. Destructive quarrels have at least one value. They succeed in alienating incompatible couples so that engagements are broken, or if marriage has occurred, so that early divorce follows.

Productive quarrels are those that leave the marriage stronger through a redefinition of the situation causing the conflict. Productive quarreling is directed at an issue, and leads to more complete understanding. Issues, problems, and conditions rather than the person himself tend to be the object of productive quarrels. Ideally, the quarrels tend to become fewer and less violent as the marriage progresses and basic routines and solutions to problems are established. Gradually the couple learn the techniques for handling conflict, so that for problem-solving purposes it is not so violent nor so painful. The informed couple learn to recognize the source of their differences early and to relay to one another the message that excitement is brewing.

Most conflict situations find one party the aggressor and one the defendant. Married people need to know how to play both roles well to get the most out of a quarrel. They may have to change roles in the middle to keep things moving to a satisfying climax in which tensions are fully released. There is sometimes what appears to be a bit of perverse interdependence, the aggressive one needing the defensive and the defensive needing the aggressive, to carry the quarrel through to a satisfactory conclusion. Both would feel cheated and disappointed if either party retired from the fray too soon.

Unless the newly married couple have had a background of constructive conflict in their respective parental families, they may be devastated by their first quarrels. In time they come to recognize that conflict has a pattern and runs a course that is predictable.

The course of conflict

A typical marriage quarrel has three stages: (1) the build-up, (2) the climax, and (3) the movement toward reconciliation.

During the build-up stage there is often petulant irritability and jittery nagging on the part of the wife, if she is the aggressor. If the husband is the aggressor, the symptoms of tension express themselves in emotionally toned growling, griping, and overcritical comments on the sloppy house, the overdone steak, or the bill from the hairdresser. The aggressor is readying himself to take out his accumulated frustrations on the partner, who takes it just so long and then begins to fight back.

The privilege of initiating the conflict is available to the party who develops the irritability first. He or she has a chip on the shoulder and is looking for trouble. The aggressor role includes, therefore, the insight to recognize in oneself feelings of malaise, uneasiness, or frustration and the willingness to do something about it. The marital sparring partner who plays the defendant role has a special responsibility. If the irritability of the aggressor seems due to hunger, sickness, fatigue, pregnancy, menstrual blues, or tensions aggravated by other physiological dysfunction, the situation may call for hearing it out, for reassurance and sympathy rather than active opposition. The person who has been emotionally wounded in his workaday contacts may need the same understanding and sympathy. Humiliations and personal defeats may be offset by the understanding of the partner.

The second stage is the battle royal itself. It consists of one or more of the efforts discussed earlier to manipulate the partner around to one's own position: coercion, coaxing, name-calling, accusations, arguing, and various forms of masking and pretending. This is the time when cards are put on the table and both husband and wife clarify their values and express their feelings so that the other may get the point without question.

Constructive quarreling calls for skill on the part of both husband and wife in avoiding sensitive spots in the other. It requires skill in identifying and letting the other know the particular sore spots in one's make-up that might be hurt in the verbal jabbing. Much as fighters in the ring are expected to "fight fair," husband and wife must learn not to aim foul blows at each other in their quarreling.

For the wife to jeer at her husband's inability to make money or to become president of the firm would be for most men a blow below the belt, because she aims at the area over which he has least control. Likewise for a man to taunt his wife about her inability to have children may be such a cruel jab that she will never quite recover. In time the sparring partner learns to anticipate the hidden weaknesses and finds where to aim his blows to get the maximum release of tension with a minimum damage to the personality.

You fight fair when you—

Spell out exactly what you don't like, and how you want things changed.

Stick to the point and avoid side issues.

Stay with it until you thrash things out.

Go on to some simple next step for improvement.

Get it out, don't let it fester.

Attack the problem rather than each other.

Avoid dragging in your relatives.

Give each other cues as your tension lets up.

This second stage may be relatively short, a matter of minutes when the issue is trivial and the partners are competent in handling their conflicts. It may last in a relatively non-violent form for hours into the night, depending on the issues, the nature of the tensions, and the ability of the pair to proceed into the process of reconciliation.

The third stage of a quarrel starts as one or both of the partners recognize what the other is driving at, and communicates his understanding: "I'm beginning to see what this means to you . . ." This may elicit some mutual role reversal as each tries to feel the issues as the other does. Now comes the joking with the release of tension, and the first random efforts to find a possible solution to the problem.

If the issue is a poor meal or an evening's disappointment the quarrel may end here. If something of greater value and permanence is involved the process of making-up has to continue through further exploration of causes and possible ways out of the situation. This may include an agreement to seek help through marriage counseling, the local family service bureau, or mental health clinic. This plan for further action mutually agreed upon is usually enough to bring peace for the time being.

It is important that the conflict be brought to a genuine conclusion. "It does not suffice merely to abandon an attitude of hostility and resume an attitude of tenderness. The whole episode must be given an artistic consummation. The dispute which ends when one person slams the door and walks out, to return when the storm is blown over, is probably not ended at all. Even if they kiss and go to bed they may be leaving their quarrel half done, like a play which does not go beyond the second act. When it is said that the quarrel must be brought to a conclusion, this does not mean that the substance of the dispute must be settled one way or the other, once and for all, but only that the episode of the dispute must be so stage-managed that it will become, in retrospect, a pleasant memory." [9]

If the quarrel has been a good one, both husband and wife are purged of their earlier tensions, resentments, fears, and anxieties. Suddenly the world seems bright again, and each, a little sheepishly at first, grins with satisfaction upon the other. Now the marriage seems sturdier than ever with the realization that "If we can take this, we can take anything!"

Skillful couples realize that conflict is not something to fear, but something to utilize to strengthen their relationship when tensions and misunderstandings arise. One of the benefits of productive quarrels is that they reveal to the married couple how strong their relationship really is. Some men and women, deluded by the romantic notion that

[9] Robert C. Binkley and Frances Williams Binkley, *What Is Right with Marriage*, New York: Appleton, 1929, pp. 227–228.

love must have left when monotony came in, are surprised at the force of love emotions that arise as a result of a quarrel. Quarreling thus helps to stabilize the marriage by reminding the couple, as they kiss and make up, of the depth of their love.

Skillful handling of conflict

Opposition in marriage is universal and normal, but skillful handling of marital conflict must be learned. The channels of communication between husband and wife can be kept open during conflict only if they each use gestures of acceptance of the other as they differ. In the old West there was a saying "Smile when you say that, pardner; them's fighting words!" In marriage, opposition is less likely to arouse animosity if the partner prefaces his assertions with a family gesture of acceptance. Heat in an argument, and animosity directed against the person are joined in some conflicts, but they need not be threatening if the combatant is secure, knows he is loved, and realizes that the love is not conditionally dependent upon his agreeing with the spouse.

Two people can afford to be genuinely honest with each other, and share fully their feelings as well as their ideas when their relationship is based upon unswerving loyalty. "You are a thoughtless brute. You walk all over my feelings. But, mean as you are, I love you and always will," suggests the kind of basic security that allows for differences and for the expression of hurt and hostility without threatening the marriage.

The handling of conflicts in marriage is helped by previous experience with conflict in one's parental family or with one's peers. There needs to be a deeply held conviction that problems can be solved and that consensus is possible. A happy by-product of observation of successful quarreling in one's parental family is the absence of fear when conflict looms in later marriage. People who are afraid of combat are often the first to get hurt.

There are other ways of handling tensions than the forthright methods described above. In the film *Who's Boss*, the husband warns his wife upon arrival home that he has had a hard day and may prove irritable during the evening by *twirling his hat*, and his wife has a signal just as voiceless; she *wears her apron astern*. With this advance notice, the partner less fatigued can take some responsibility for providing a sounding board for the day's tensions. The wife may give her husband a snack, if supper is going to be late, knowing that hunger complicates any tensions which may have arisen. The husband may whisk out the children from under foot, knowing that preparing a hot meal requires coordination that demanding children can upset.

Some married partners who perceive conflict brewing attempt to drain out their tensions first on the woodpile, or with a golf club, or in bowling. The wife may scrub the floors or pound Sibelius out on the piano. When they return to face each other the original conflict is probably still unresolved but they are better prepared to deal with it, now that the most intense feelings of unpleasantness have subsided. The widespread interest in baseball, wrestling, murder mysteries, and western stories suggests the almost universal need in our culture to drain off excessive aggressions before they become explosive.

In time, the two marriage partners get well enough acquainted so that they can recognize trouble brewing between them, and dissipate the tensions without the intensity of their earlier quarrels. Short cuts to understanding, to communication, and to coping with conflict are learned so that the earlier struggles to get through to each other are no longer necessary.

One immeasurably helpful attitude toward conflict of all kinds is to see its roots and its meanings within the person. "See him as the child he was. Behind the pomp or the rudeness, beneath the crust of meanness or coldness, begin to perceive the wistful little boy (or girl) who is hurt and disappointed and determined to strike back at the world. Or the little boy who is frightened, and tightens his jaw and clenches his fist to ward off some overwhelming fear that hovers deep in the dark past . . . Only in this way can we guard ourselves against responding in kind, against returning pettiness to the petty and cruelty to the cruel." [10]

An attitude of humility within onself as an individual is similarly helpful. The person who realizes that he is not always right, that he has been profoundly influenced by forces over which he had little control, that he has to live with himself in the best way he can, such a person can seek professional help without shame, and start on a program of self-improvement with pride.

Can Marriage Counseling Help?

Before conflicts become either too critical or too chronic, competent marriage counseling may help re-establish harmony in the relationship. As quarreling begins to depart from issues and to concentrate on attacking the persons, the process of destructive quarreling is under way. This may get out of hand in progressively more severe attacks and counterattacks. The chain reaction of released hostility may be halted only by recourse to a competent marriage counselor, psychiatrist, or other qualified specialist.

[10] Sidney J. Harris, "See Him as the Child He Was" in *Strictly Personal,* syndicated feature, September 17, 1956.

The chronically petulant nagging, fussing, feuding that can gnaw away at a marriage, never quite reaching the explosive point but constantly precluding mutual enjoyment, may continue for years unless effective help is brought in to get the marriage off the dead center of its impasse.

Marriage counseling services, mental health clinics, family service bureaus, and practicing therapists accept just such cases. They do not take over or run the couple's marriage for them. Rather they help the couple find out just what their problems are, define the issues, decide what they want to do about them, and explore various courses of action until one emerges that is mutually satisfying. Then, if necessary, further help may be given to help each of the pair with a program that must be assimilated and lived with in action. Thus the competent marriage counselor helps the married couple accomplish what, unaided, they could not do for themselves.

Counseling services are available in a number of large cities for couples whose marriage conflicts prove too much for them. The case of Charlie and Edna demonstrates the possibilities of professional counseling services for cases of progressive domestic discord.

Charlie is a young physician just getting a good start in building up a practice in a small Midwestern city. Three years ago he married Edna, who sang in the choir of the Methodist church. In their courtship and engagement period they did all the things young lovers do, from discussing the kind of furniture they liked to deciding on the number of children they would like to have. Their marriage had been a happy one on the whole. Their year-and-a-half-old son was a darling whom they both adored. The practice was building up so well that they were making regular payments on a little bungalow at the edge of town. Everything should have been wonderful. They loved each other, had their little home, their baby, and the promise of the kind of future they both looked forward to all their lives.

The one problem that disturbed them greatly was their frequent and heated quarreling. Spats seemed to start over nothing. But once they were started, Edna found herself getting so mad she just couldn't contain herself, while Charlie shut up like a clam, and after he had stood just so much left, slamming the door, not to return for several hours. Edna felt that if Charlie loved her he would be willing to stay and talk it out and make some rules so that they wouldn't fight over the same thing again. He felt that she was being unreasonable most of the time and that she should be able to control her temper better.

The situation became so acute that several months ago they went to see their minister about it. He was an up-and-coming young pastor with a good training in helping people in trouble, and after listening to both sides of the case suggested that they go to the city and visit the marriage and family counseling agency there. He told the couple what they might expect from such a service and said that he was suggesting that they go to such a center in much the same way as he would recommend a good hospital or doctor if some troublesome physical difficulty didn't respond to home remedies.

Two week ends later the couple were meeting with the counselor. She assured them that she was not going to pry into anything that either of them did not want to tell her, but that sometimes it helped to talk out bothersome problems with a person who was not tied up emotionally in the situation. She helped them both to see that she could not unravel human mysteries in the first twenty minutes, but that her training might help her to suggest to both of them just where to look for the real reasons for their trouble. The counselor indicated that by working together some suggestions for meeting the situation might emerge. The couple seemed relieved that the counselor was not assuming a "know-it-all" attitude and that she appeared to be the sort of friendly person who could be trusted to like them, whatever they told her. She looked as if she would hear their story without being shocked or making too much of it.

Each described the situation as he saw it. Edna got so excited as she relived the last quarrel that she started to cry. Then feeling better, she leaned toward the counselor, saying earnestly, "You see how much this matters to me. If only we could get to the bottom of it all, I'd be the happiest girl alive." She was encouraged by the counselor's reflection that it was just that motivation to do something about it that was the most important step toward an effective solution.

After several individual interviews and a personality study of each, the couple came in again for a joint conference. At that time they were each helped to share with the other the insights they had gained concerning their problems, and to look at them together. It was slow going the first time, a new way of approaching the problem for both of them. By the third and fourth session with the counselor they were much more at ease and had begun to talk in terms of what they would do now that they were returning home.

Within three months they were both more comfortable with the whole idea of their quarreling and neither of them became panicky when one started. As time went on, the quarrels grew less frequent and lasted for shorter periods. Each developed some understanding of what it was in their early experiences which made them feel so differently when a conflict situation emerged. Both began to develop some skill in handling themselves and in understanding the other when the fur began to bristle. Of course they still squabble, and they probably always will. But they can take it now, and are comforted by the recognition that there is less of it to have to take.

The baby daughter who recently arrived has added to their sense of being a family and to the growing satisfactions of their life together. As young Doc put it himself, "No one could have told me a year ago that marriage could be like this. Why, with all the education I had, I never had the foggiest idea that you could be as scientific about your feelings as you can about a tonsillectomy. I want some books to read. This has all been an eye opener for me."

It's an eye opener to many people. Reading the advice columns in the daily papers gives many people the idea that asking for help on a personal or family tangle is maudlin. Many are afraid that the problem will be taken out of their hands and that they will be told what to do without having a part in the decision. Others are skeptical about the type of person who acts as a counselor. Still others hesitate to tell their personal problems to a stranger who may not keep their confidences. All of these fears and reluctances are perfectly natural. There is a certain sanctity about your emotional and married lives; you do not want things spread all over the town. It is this respect for the persons and for their confidences that is characteristic of a good counseling service and of the well-trained counselor. This is the big difference between the quackery that you are afraid of and the reliable, modest, helpful counseling service that is becoming more widely available.

Criteria for judging a good counseling service are fairly simple to enumerate. Briefly summarized they are as follows:

A Good Marriage Counseling Service

1. Does not advertise or make exaggerated claims.
2. Establishes a genuinely professional relationship.
3. Does not promise quick results or make snap judgments.
4. Does not diagnose until after a careful study has been made.
5. Does not rely on trick devices or gimmicks.
6. Keeps all information confidential.
7. May charge nominal fees which are frankly discussed.
8. May call in other competent specialists to help.
9. Uses only trained professional workers from reputable colleges specializing in such fields as social work, human development, psychiatry, and related areas. (At least a Master's degree in the specialized area is the usual professional standard.)
10. Is affiliated with such reliable bodies as local councils of social agencies, and nationally with such professional organizations as the National Conference of Social Work, and the National Council on Family Relations.
11. Builds up a clientele through referrals from satisfied users, other agencies, and professional persons.

12. May have a membership and a board of directors of reliable citizens who take the responsibility for supporting and interpreting the program to the community.

Conflict is normal; it performs a valuable function in maintaining emotional balance through the release of tensions accumulated in a workaday world. Conflict in early marriage is understandable as the outcome of merging two different sets of family habits into a new pattern—a painful process which is speeded up by overt conflict and definition of the issues. This type of conflict tends to be progressively delimiting in the area it covers as the marriage continues and serves a valuable problem-solving function. Productive quarreling is directed at issues, problems, and conditions rather than at persons. Destructive quarreling concentrates on the ego of the participants and destroys the fundamentals on which the marriage is based.

In line with modern research concerning the nature of personality needs, more honesty in the husband and wife relationship is advocated. This involves facing issues squarely and mastering the arts of 'constructive conflict. It is not so much the conflict in marriage which is to be deplored as the inability to face the issues and work them through. Conflict has a dual function: the solution of issues, and the release of the resentment and tensions which arise in every relationship.

Every couple needs to learn the techniques of effectively handling conflict situations. Mature married couples report the feasibility of direct aproaches to conflict. The inexperienced, the immature, and the progressively discordant couples who are unable to handle the complexities of normal conflict in marriage are fortunate in the increasing number of reputable marriage counseling services that may help them cope constructively with their conflicts.

READINGS

Bernard, Jessie, Helen E. Buchanan, and William M. Smith, Jr., *Dating, Mating, and Marriage.* Cleveland: Howard Allen, 1958, Chapter 8.

Blood, Robert O., Jr., *Anticipating Your Marriage.* Glencoe, Illinois: Free Press, 1955, Chapters 10 and 11.

Burgess, Ernest W., and Harvey J. Locke, *The Family: From Institution to Companionship.* New York: American Book, 1945, Chapter 18, "Family Conflicts and Accommodations."

Folsom, Joseph K., *The Family in Democratic Society.* New York: Wiley, 1943, Chapter 13, "Marriage Interaction."

Hollis, Florence, *Women in Marital Conflict.* New York: Family Service Association of America, 1949.

Kirkpatrick, Clifford, *The Family as Process and Institution.* New York: Ronald Press, 1955, Chapter 18, "Marriage Adjustments."

Landis, Judson T. and Mary G., *Building a Successful Marriage*. New York: Prentice-Hall, 1958, Chapter 15, "Achieving Adjustment in Marriage."

Levy, John, and Ruth Munroe, *The Happy Family*. New York: Knopf, 1938, Chapter 5, "Living Together."

Magoun, F. Alexander, *Love and Marriage*. New York: Harper, 1956, Chapter 11, "Emotional Adjustments."

Mowrer, Harriet, in Howard Becker and Reuben Hill (eds.), *Family Marriage and Parenthood*. Boston: Heath, 1948, Chapter 12, "Discords in Marriage."

Mudd, Emily H., *The Practice of Marriage Counseling*. New York: Association Press, 1951.

Nimkoff, Meyer, *Marriage and the Family*. Boston: Houghton, Mifflin, 1957, Chapter 15, "Marital Adjustment."

Rutledge, Aaron L., *Responsible Marriage and Family Living: A Text with Adapted Readings*. New York: Harcourt, Brace, 1960, chapters 10, "Marital Adjustment and Conflict," and 18, "Marriage and Family Counseling."

Travis, Lee E., and Dorothy W. Baruch, *Personal Problems of Everyday Life*. New York: Appleton-Century, 1941, Chapters 13–14.

Waller, Willard, and Reuben Hill, *The Family: A Dynamic Interpretation*. New York: Dryden Press, 1951, Chapters 14–15.

15 Facing Crises

Are family troubles inevitable?

What happens when you are down on your luck?

How serious is infidelity?

Can you take death in the family?

What are ways of meeting family crises?

WHEN the family meets a situation for which there is no ready solution from past experience and no immediate answer forthcoming from family members, then the family is said to face a *crisis.* Sudden poverty, infidelity, divorce, and bereavement are good examples of disruptions which throw most families into temporary confusion. Some families may be permanently disabled, particularly if the remaining members are unable to absorb the duties of the persons incapacitated by the crisis. Other families are drawn closer together by the threat to their unity and survive the crisis stronger than ever.[1]

Are Family Troubles Inevitable?

Death, the crisis least talked about of all, normally hits the average family not once but several times. Sudden poverty hovers constantly over all but the wealthiest of families under an industrial economy which has produced cycles of inflation, depression, and widespread unemployment every five years or so since 1790. These are hard blows to take, but they are part of living. Families must be prepared not so

---

[1] It appears that middle-class families may have more troubles but weather them more successfully than working class families, according to Earl L. Koos, "Class Differences in Family Reactions to Crises," *Marriage and Family Living,* Summer, 1950, pp. 77–78.

much to avoid them as to regard them as challenges. The question that should be raised is not "How can I avoid family crises?" but "How can I learn to take them?"

○The first step in learning to take trouble in stride is to realize that other people the world over are facing similar problems—not "Why does all this have to happen to us?" but "I guess we're having our turn now." Another step in learning to take trouble is to recognize the normality of problems and conflict. Much of the anguish which follows a crisis arises from the shock of the unexpected and the fear that no recovery is possible. The shock of the blow is easier to absorb if one is relaxed and unafraid of the pain which is bound to follow. Some families are so well prepared for trouble they grow under it. Their preparation for crises began back in courtship and early marriage, and even before.

In the early years of marriage the husband-wife relation stabilizes, with each taking roles with prescribed duties, many of which continue after children arrive. Later, with the children, husband and wife work out solutions to the problems of daily living. Members learn the answers to most questions, and they express it neatly—"This is the way we do it at our house," or, "I was brought up to think this way." Conflicts are settled and decisions made regarding vacations, birthday parties, and school difficulties. Well-organized families have the resources for meeting these problems without too much distress and readjustment.

This chapter will discuss crises that produce both demoralization (loss of morale and family unity) and dismemberment (loss of family member): sudden impoverishment, infidelity, and bereavement. Divorce will be discussed in some detail in the next chapter.

A Classification of Family Breakdowns [2]

Dismemberment only	Demoralization only
Loss of child	Nonsupport
Loss of spouse	Progressive dissension
Orphanhood	Infidelity
Hospitalization	Delinquency and events bringing disgrace—
War separation	reputation loss
	Alcoholism
	Drug addiction

---

[2] Expanded by Reuben Hill in *Families Under Stress,* New York: Harper, 1949, p. 10, from a classification originally suggested by Thomas D. Eliot, "Handling Family Strains and Shocks," in Howard Becker and Reuben Hill (eds.), *Family, Marriage and Parenthood,* Boston: Heath, 1948, p. 617, n.

Accession only	Demoralization plus dismemberment or accession
Unwanted pregnancy	Illegitimacy
Deserter returns	Runaway situations
Stepmother, stepfather additions	Desertion
Some war reunions	Divorce
Some adoptions, aged grandparents	Imprisonment
	Suicide or homicide
	Institutionalization for mental illness or alcoholism

What conditions must a family maintain to withstand the buffeting of circumstances in this turbulent country of ours? The family members must be physically fit and healthy; they must have adequate mental and emotional resources to cope with complexities and unpredictables; they must be adaptable and flexible; they must have achieved a workable adjustment to one another and must be proud of their family membership; and they need to have an income from some source adequate to maintain a normal standard of living. In addition, the family needs the support of neighbors and friends and of community agencies like the church and the school. Lacking these attributes, a family may muddle through for a period of years without breaking up. But in the face of a crippling crisis, such a family will become badly disorganized, and dismemberment or demoralization will take place.

What Happens When You Are Down on Your Luck?

Impoverishment is one of the crises which has been studied most completely, and there is considerable agreement concerning its effects on the family. One of the surprising findings from the depression of 1929–36 was the ability of many families to absorb the shock of impoverishment without demoralization or great personal disorganization.[3] The reactions of the family when the breadwinner is laid off and the income ceases must be seen against the backdrop of associations within the family and the family's earlier reactions to crises. As children are added to the family, methods of adjustment develop and become habitual. Father traditionally earns the money and spends most of his day away from home. Mother runs the domestic end of the household, supplying services and supervision of the children, who are

---

[3] Ruth S. Cavan and Katherine H. Ranck, *The Family and the Depression,* Chicago: University of Chicago Press, 1938, pp. vii–ix.

primarily consumers with minimum responsibilities and who are accustomed to depend on parents for the satisfaction of their major wants. There comes a crash on the market—people are thrown out of work. The loss of father's job and the subsequent loss of income disrupt this habitual arrangement. It leaves father at home, exercising unaccustomed supervision of children, and it places other members of the family in situations for which they have no accustomed responses.

One of the best descriptions of the nature of the crisis of impoverishment is drawn from a study of one hundred Chicago families:

The development of a crisis often involves disorganization, that is, a breakdown in the organization of the family or person. The depression, as a crisis, may effect wide-spread disorganization, for the influence of the economic aspect of the family is so pervasive that lowered income may affect every realm of family life. The family may have to abandon certain objectives, such as buying a home or educating the children; it may be unable to conform to certain social and community standards in which it has always taken pride, such as the prompt payment of rent and bills or the maintenance of a certain type of home; it may be disturbed by the shifting of the dominant role, perhaps from the father to the mother or to a son or daughter. Not only is the family organization shaken, but the members of the family most affected also may become personally disorganized over the loss of accustomed activities, a lowering of status, or a failure to meet responsibilities. This disorganization may be evidenced by worry, "nervous breakdowns," excessive fears, or demoralization.

A crisis and the disorganization that accompanies it are highly charged with emotion, a reaction to be expected when habits become ineffective and new modes of response must be found and adopted. In the case of the depression the emotion tends to be fear—fear of loss of status, of loss of money reserves, of failure to have needed food and clothing, of the necessity to go on relief. When re-employment is not found, worry, discouragement, and depression follow. Some people become resentful or angry, but most of them are simply afraid of a moneyless existence for which they have no habitual conduct and no philosophy. For many people the condition of unemployment continues over many months, even over several years. It is almost impossible, however, for a highly charged emotional state to continue over a long period of time. Therefore, the period of unemployment cannot be considered as a static period. The situation, as it appears during the first shock of unemployment, is not the situation as it would be described six months or a year later. The unemployment may still exist, the income may still be low; but the experience of a person who has been unemployed for a year is not the experience of a person who has just been told that he has no job. At some point the disorganization reaches a climax and the extreme tension lessens. This turning point is psychological; it may not coincide with the time at which employment is last. Self-confidence and financial resources may postpone the peak of the crisis until an indefinite number of months after the time when unemployment begins. Perhaps the disorganization may be said to culminate when the family accepts the fact that it can no longer continue its old mode of life, when it admits that it can no longer control the situation by its old procedures. Such a realization usually brings with it severe emotional reactions which have perhaps been manifesting themselves in minor form during the period when the disorganization was developing. This period of acute emotional stress is usually terminated either by an adjustment to the situation or by the development of pathological reactions. If an adjustment to the new circumstances occurs, new roles are assigned, new functions defined, a new status accepted. This adjustment may take the same form as the old family organization, so that after the period or disorganization the old roles, functions, and status are readily resumed; or the adjustment may involve roles of a lower status, curtailed functions, and lowered community status. In the case of a break or failure to adjust, the family may disintegrate through separation of its members or the person may escape through mental illness or suicide. In any case, there is a tendency for the period of extreme disorganization to reach an end, either through reorganization or disintegration of the group or personality.

. . . another factor must be considered: the habitual ways in which families and members of families have met earlier changes and crises. A crisis, because it sweeps away the customary ways of living, tends to expose the resources or deficiencies of the family or person. The family that, in the past, has faced a difficult situation squarely, evaluated it, and made adjustments to it may be expected to react in this way to the depression, even though there may be an initial period of disorganization. The family that, in the past, has refused to face issues or has evaded difficult situations may be expected to evade facing the changes in family life brought by unemployment or decreased income. It seems clear from the present study that only rarely did the crisis cause the development of any totally new reactions. Rather, the crisis caused an exaggeration of previously existing family and personal habits. The man who occasionally drank began to drink to excess. The family that was harmoniously organized became more unified and the members more loyal. Reactions to the depression therefore cannot be stated categorically; the depression as a family and personal crisis must be viewed in the light of previous methods of meeting difficulties used by the family or its members.[4]

Although no studies have been undertaken on the reactions of families to sudden prosperity, it would not be surprising to find that the impact of rapid fluctuations of income upward in war-boom prosperity was fully as disorganizing for some families as the sudden impoverishment experienced by millions in the depression times. In both instances the family is faced with a disruptive occurrence in which the

---

[4] Cavan and Ranck, *op. cit.*, pp. 5–8.

old customs of the group and the old attitudes and habits of the family members are no longer consistent with the new situation brought about by the crisis.

How Serious Is Infidelity?

One of the least understood yet most discussed crises in family life is marital infidelity. It is a type of crisis which represents a possible solution of a personal problem for one member while creating a family crisis for the others. From the Kinsey reports we learn that one fourth of the wives and one half the husbands in his sample had had at least one extramarital sexual relationship at some time during their marriage. These are probably underestimates of the actual incidence of infidelity. For women the incidence is relatively low until age thirty, after which the percentages increase sharply due possibly to sexual boredom and disillusionment with the marriage partner as a sex mate.[5]

Few crises are filled with more insecurity and sense of loss in a marriage than that involved when "the other woman" or her male counterpart breaks the sense of unity so important to marital solidarity. The fear of faithlessness haunts many married people and is especially understandable when the members of a pair are separated for long periods of time. The triangle rarely fits into a family circle. Even when popular opinion tended to be lenient in allowing a man to sow his wild oats, to have his fling, to go gaily through his dangerous forties and his treacherous fifties, his "poor little wife" was pitied as deeply as though she had been bereaved. Friends and neighbors watched to see how she was taking it. Her loss was accentuated by a keen sense of inadequacy and shame, for hadn't she failed to hold her man?

With the explosion of the myth that "men are built that way," constancy has tended to be more widely expected of husbands. But the emancipation of women has been misinterpreted by some wives as license and has made infidelity a double-edged sword that cuts both ways. Acceptance of woman's new freedom requires a whole new definition of our sex mores so that free interchange between people of both sexes may be possible socially, industrially, professionally, politically, intellectually, and financially without threatening the unique emotional sphere of the marriage relationship. This transition involves redefining what is "right" and what is "wrong" in many areas of common experience.

---

[5] See Alfred C. Kinsey, and others, *Sexual Behavior in the Human Female*, Philadelphia: Saunders, 1953, pp. 416–417.

For instance, the situations listed below would be judged as provocative of infidelity by our forefathers. They are worth scanning because they highlight the types of compromising situations men and women face in carrying out professional tasks in an urban society. It requires the exercise of the competence of interpersonal relations which we earlier identified as *judgment* to ascertain which of these would be most likely and which least likely to lead toward infidelity:

1. A married secretary works late to get out some important letters for her boss. He sends out for sandwiches which they eat together at her desk. No one else is in the office at the time.

2. A married woman doctor spends one night a week at a clinic in a poor section of town. It has been customary for some time for one of her colleagues (a married man physician) to drive her home when they are both through at the clinic.

3. A woman whose husband spends weeks at a time in Washington on business has taken in an older man as a roomer. No one else lives in the home except her one-year-old child.

4. A woman whose husband is overseas met one of his old friends recently while lunching downtown. He accepted her invitation to stay and have lunch with her as they talked of her husband's work and interest. As he left her at the conclusion of the luncheon, he invited her to come out and see his family soon.

5. A man and a woman (both married but not to each other) have jobs as inspectors that involve their traveling together a great deal by car. Frequently they are gone from home for days at a time. When away from home, they stay in hotels near the plant they are visiting. She registers under her own married name and occupies a separate room.

6. A singer whose home is in Connecticut must spend two or three nights a week in town at her work. It is often necessary for her to work with her agent (a married man) and her accompanist (an attractive young bachelor) at her New York apartment in the evening. It is not always possible for her husband to be present on the nights she must remain in town.

7. A farmer's wife is alone with the hired man in the house every month while her husband takes stock to market (an all-night job).

8. An unusually talented nurse is unable to continue her professional work now that she is married, because her husband does not trust her with "all those good-looking young doctors."

9. A woman whose husband handles legal cases for a large feminine clientele insists that there always be a third person present when her husband is on a case. She threatens to divorce him if she ever finds that he has been with a woman alone anywhere at any time.

If you interpret fidelity narrowly, as many people do, to make the appearance of evil equivalent to the thing itself, any situation which looks as though it might be compromising could be interpreted as infidelity. Chaperons once were provided to supply complete surveillance when infidelity was suspected in any situation in which premarital or extramarital sex experience might take place. If you were to brand as evidence of infidelity all expressions of affection for anyone other than the spouse, you would also run into a dilemma. The normal person becomes genuinely fond of a great many friends and associates of both sexes. Is a person faithless who feels genuine affection for other fine people?

However, when you interpret loyalty as mutual trust in each other and as faith in the marriage itself, neither the detective role called forth by the first definition nor the uncertainty inspired by the second is involved. The blow falls only if you find that your faith and trust have not been justified. It is only then that a crisis is said to occur. There is no crisis if there is no problem, or if the family members are equipped to meet whatever problem arises with their present resources.

Infidelity may almost always be seen as a system of unmet affectional need. The nature of the unmet need varies from couple to couple. Infidelity on the part of the husband may be an attempt to prove his manliness, or it may be a revolt against his conscience, or perhaps a method of working out little-understood impulses stemming from childhood experiences. The other woman may represent a refuge from an overprotecting wife, or she may be a means of attacking the wife. Extramarital affairs grow out of the same attraction a forbidden piece of candy has for a hungry, undisciplined child—further proof of the importance of emotional maturity in marriage. Monogamous marriage requires that the participants be sufficiently mature to find in their relationship the satisfaction of their basic needs.

The crisis of infidelity

The act of infidelity by itself may be relatively unimportant to the stability of the marriage. Among 221 cases of infidelity by wives in the Kinsey study where the husbands knew of the affair, only 42 per cent created any serious difficulty in the marriage. In 58 per cent the husbands were apparently able to tolerate and forgive the infidelity of their wives. Wives were even more tolerant of their husbands' trespasses.[6] It is the interpretation of the infidelity which the couple make that introduces panic into the relation; what the participants see as the motive behind the defection is more important than the act itself. To some couples the slightest flirtation may prove calamitous, because it

---

[6] See Kinsey, *op. cit.*, pp. 434–436.

symbolizes much more than that to them. Others may tolerate without anxiety considerable promiscuity of partners.

A complicating factor in the interpretation of flirtations and unorthodox behavior with others is the health of the spouse. When he is bedridden, a man eyes his wife's recreational activities much more narrowly than when he is on his feet. Pregnant women are frequently susceptible to jealousy and read infidelity into situations where none exists. Jealousy is the product of insecurity and fear—the anxiety produced when one senses the possible loss of a love object. Unfortunately for the aggrieved person, jealousy may drive the mate into acts of infidelity that originally he may not have intended.

Meeting the crisis of infidelity with the necessary understanding leads couples so threatened to marriage counselors and similar professional advisers. A good counselor can relieve the pain of the moment and can often deal with the underlying causes of the infidelity, the unmet needs and frustrations of the couple. The view that infidelity is a symptom needing treatment gives a more scientific answer to the question of what shall be done about it than has heretofore been given. A platitude such as "give and forgive" or the self-righteous assumption that evidence of infidelity should always be promptly punished with separation and divorce fails to meet the issues and introduces no satisfactory readjustment or reorganization to the marriage. Even when the affair has gone so far that the salvage of the marriage is impossible, the abandoned mate may be helped by counseling to understand what has happened so that his or her resources may be mobilized for building a stronger life.

Can You Take Death in the Family?

Of all the crises which afflict a family, none is more sure to occur and none receives less advance preparation than death. Its discussion is discouraged in our society and anyone who mentions seriously the possibility of death entering his family is silenced as morbid. Death as a subject of conversation is almost as taboo today as was sex fifty years ago. Today we prepare our children for the shock of the birth of a brother or sister, for the newness of the first day at school, and, in the case of a girl, for her first menstruation, but to prepare children for death in the family is almost unheard of.

There is no program of death education to cushion the shock of this universal crisis. Not only children, but adults as well, are shielded from the realities—mothers are not told when their children are dying—patients afflicted fatally are not prepared for the event that is a certainty.

Until recently it was bad taste for picture magazines to show pictures of actual battle dead. In sum, there is virtually no preparation for the emotional shock that accompanies the death of a dear one. For that reason death is frequently a personal as well as a family crisis.

The importance of death as a personal crisis lies not primarily in the fact of dying or ceasing to exist biologically, but in the emotional shock which follows the break in the unity of the family. Two things happen to the member who is closely identified with his family: 1. He senses that the circle is broken and that the family is threatened with dissolution (What will ever happen to us, now that mother has gone?). 2. He senses that a part of himself as a person has been cut off, amputated, so to speak. The closer the identification with the deceased, the more distressing is the sense of personal loss.

The shock varies

The situation is eased considerably for family members who have left the parental home and have established families of their own. The emotional dependence which existed before their departure from their childhood home has been replaced by relative independence, and the sense of loss is diminished accordingly. The passing away of relatives, even brothers and sisters, brings less grief than the loss of parents with whom one is emotionally more closely identified. To make one further comparison, it might be safe to say that the mature independent adult normally senses greater pangs of grief at the loss of husband or wife or child than at the loss of a parent from whom he has won independence.

In general, death following a long, drawn-out illness brings less shock than sudden death for which no preparation can be made. Much of the mourning occurs in the period of illness as the relatives vacillate between acceptance of the loss of the loved one and wishful thinking that a cure can be found. Gradually, as the medical evidence piles up, the negative prognosis is accepted, and the parties assimilate the idea of permanently losing the afflicted one. As accommodation to the idea of losing part of oneself takes place, the afflicted one becomes an object of pity rather than a symbol of personal loss. It is at that point that the expression may be heard, "I hope his suffering will soon be over."

In time of war, bereavement is lightened to some extent by the public recognition achieved and by the realization that others face equal or worse crises. Although the hole that any one person leaves can never be completely filled, there is less of a break in family unity, because the other members have already made some adjustment to the absence of the member at the time he entered the armed services. The shock is lessened by the presence of neighbors and friends who offer understanding and genuine comfort. Moreover, death in wartime is given purpose and made meaningful both at home and in the war zones. In their adjustment, family members plunge into the common task with renewed determination to bring to fulfillment the goals for which *he* died.

On the other hand, bereavement in time of war is the less bearable because the victims are taken in the prime of life. The uncertainty of death in a "missing in action" notice leads family members to disbelieve later notices of death. For some people, only the rites of death serve as corroborators of fact, and the overseas death is hard to realize. When the body is not in evidence, it is easier to convert grief into disbelief.[7]

To the person away from home the loss of a member of his family may be very difficult. He may feel for a time that the bottom has fallen out of life. He misses the relief which comes in joining with relatives and friends in mourning. He finds that a part of himself as a person may no longer be responded to and that there is all too little help in healing the wound. Every opportunity should be taken to talk about the loved one with ministers, counselors, and others who are professionally trained to listen and understand. Letters home can draw off the overflow of emotions if one can express himself on paper and has the courage to let himself cry during the process whenever he feels like it. Weeping is an effective tension-dispelling device. A person in mourning should allow himself the same privileges in the interest of recovery.

Even when anticipated, the actual death of a beloved person comes as a shock, and the first reaction is usually one of disbelief. A numbness comes over the bereaved and acts as a buffer to protect him from a shock that is too devastating to absorb all at once. It is quite common for persons to feel that the entire experience is a dream and that they will awake to find things as they were.

First reactions to bereavement

The apparent calmness of the bereaved mourners immediately after receipt of the news is often a detachment cultivated to protect the self from the total reality. It may represent a repression of the news into the nether depths of the mind, where conflict may rage at great emotional expense to the individual. As realization intrudes upon consciousness, periods of uncontrolled abandon may appear, with weeping, cursing, self-blame, even self-injury. Accompanying these reactions is the longing for that part of the self which has been amputated. The beloved, now irrevocably departed, is relinquished with the greatest reluctance.

The mind will play strange tricks on the bereaved—he will hear the

---

[7] Thomas D. Eliot, "—of the Shadow of Death," *The Annals of the American Academy of Political and Social Science*, Vol. 229, September, 1943, p. 94.

voice of the departed, sense the presence of the other, and dream that they are together again. Clothing, mementos, locks of hair of the deceased, will be preserved as symbols to summon the presence of the departed. In extremity, the mourner may in his despondence be impelled to commit suicide to rejoin the other. These first reactions carry on after the rites of the funeral period are over. The routines of the mortuary, of funeral and burial, serve to dispel the illusions of disbelief and to channel the emotions into approved lines. The rituals of funeral and burial are performed by professionals who take the responsibilities off the hands of the bereaved, yet give them the maximum opportunity for undisturbed grief.

In contrast to the well-defined routines of the funeral is the lack of definition for readjustment afterward. The professional undertaker retires from the scene, and no other professional person enters to aid the members of the family in the next phase of their readjustment. Each family is left more or less to shift for itself, with occasional help and advice from well-meaning relatives and friends. The family members are urged to resume normal activities as soon as possible—no time is allowed in our society for unnecessary show of grief, although it is not considered good taste for a widow or widower to remarry in less than a year's time after the funeral. Three days' sick leave is allowed the worker in civil service positions for funeral and mourning. He is expected back at work after that. Life must go on!

Trial-and-error adjustments

The first reactions to death are largely protective, designed to save the personality from serious damage. Eventually the bereaved seeks to assimilate the realities and makes trial-and-error attempts to pick up the threads of normal living. There are alternate periods of plunging into work and activity and of lassitude and depression. As time passes, periods of activity become longer and the periods of depression become shorter and less frequent. During the person's attempts to arrive at some pattern of stabilized behavior, he finds it necessary to force himself to respond to people, to children, and to his work. He resumes his duties with great effort at first, but gradually the routines are assumed and he rejoins the workaday world. There are also during this period frequent attempts to secure attention through wearing mourning symbols—the desire to tell of troubles to others is evident. There is much sharing of the vagaries of fate with children and friends.

Back in life's channel

As a reward for the many trial-and-error attempts at resuming normal activities, a new life organization will develop, and the bereaved will achieve the permanence and stability of settled living. The bereaved has accepted the death of the beloved and has made the experience a part of his personality instead of walling it off and struggling against it. He is now able to resume relationships with others and may even substitute these relationships for those he had with the deceased. Religion is often a major source of support at this time, as you will see in Chapter 21.

◯ One of the characteristics of the recovery is the emphasis upon participation in activities, upon entering into community services and other socially approved endeavors. If the deceased was active in any of these, there is often an identification by the mourner in carrying on the work the other had started.[8]

. . . successful recovery from bereavement means gradual relaxation of its tensions and frustrations in favor of some more satisfactory or at least tolerable patterns of behavior. The bereaved find someone else through whom they can satisfy their affectional needs; or they find religious beliefs which fully reconcile them; or they reabsorb their energies and redevote their affections in some life work as an alternate channel; or they assume the role of the deceased or project his personality by some conspicuous service in his name, or through creation of some appropriate and constructive memorial. Even gradual relaxing through "forgetting" . . . may produce "successful" recovery.

. . . One may never feel a "decision" to take up life again; it is, in a sense, life which takes one up again. Mourning may never be absolutely finished, but it gradually approaches zero as a limit.[9]

What Are Ways of Meeting Family Crises?

The family may be said to face a crisis when it meets a situation for which there is neither a ready solution from past experience nor an immediate answer forthcoming from family members. Individual families face the crises of sudden poverty, infidelity, and bereavement in many ways. In greatly telescoped form, the steps which family members take in the tedious process of adjustment to a major crisis may be summarized:

First, comes the news of the event, followed by: —
Second, prompt recognition of the facts or refusal to believe their actuality, —
    failure to face facts; and
Third, prompt, realistic action in the emergency or escape mechanisms such —
    as fainting, suicide, running away, drinking, tantrums, or violence;
Fourth, a period of rationalization, of fixing the blame, of clearing the self —

---

[8] Adapted from David Martin Fulcomer, "The Adjustive Behavior of Some Recently Bereaved Spouses," doctoral dissertation, Northwestern University, 1942, quoted in Eliot, "—of the Shadow of Death," pp. 88–92.

[9] Thomas D. Eliot, "Bereavement: Inevitable but Not Insurmountable," in Becker and Hill (eds.), op. cit., pp. 664–665.

of responsibility, after the immediate situation has been met in some way, to protect the ego;

Fifth, a struggle to attain a livable balance, a trial-and-error search for solutions; depending on the previous ways of meeting crises, the person will follow one or another of the major patterns of readjustment below:

a. Escape: e.g., desertion, divorce, suicide, enlistment, dependency, delusions, drink, drugs, distractions, vice.

b. Submission or defense: e.g., apathy, resignation, religion.

c. Compensatory efforts within the existing and accessible resources of the family's members:

1. Redoubled work.
2. Substitution of new channels of income, affection, energy.
3. Persuasion.
4. Appeal to others for help: relatives, church, charity, clinics, relief, etc.

Sixth, attainment of a final adjustment and solution of problems by the intelligent use of new resources and the renewal of routines consistent with the new situation, enabling a new life organization to emerge—a re-establishment of stable habits, self-control, reorganized economic life, and normal social life—for those who do not find permanent adjustment in one of the phases of stage five.

READINGS

Bernard, Jessie, Helen E. Buchanan, and William M. Smith, Jr., *Dating, Mating, and Marriage.* Cleveland: Howard Allen, 1958, Chapter 11.

Cavan, Ruth S., *American Marriage, A Way of Life.* New York: Crowell, 1959, Chapter 17.

Duvall, Evelyn Millis, *Facts of Life and Love for Teen-Agers.* New York: Association Press, 1956, Chapter 14.

Duvall, Sylvanus M., *Men, Women, and Morals.* New York: Association Press, 1952, Chapters 7 and 8.

———, *Before You Marry.* New York: Association Press, 1959 revision, Chapter 11, "Emergencies and Crises."

Hill, Reuben, *Families Under Stress.* New York: Harper, 1949, Chapters I and II.

Koos, E. L., *Families in Trouble.* New York: King's Crown Press, 1946.

Levy, John, and Ruth Munroe, *The Happy Family.* New York: Knopf, 1938, Chapter 3.

Osborne, Ernest G., *When You Lose a Loved One.* New York: Public Affairs Pamphlets, 1958.

Waller, Willard, and Reuben Hill, *The Family: A Dynamic Interpretation.* New York: Dryden Press, 1951, Part VI.

16 What about Divorce?

How does parents' divorce affect attitudes about marriage?

Does divorce run in families?

Are people who divorce different?

What causes divorce?

Why do divorcing people take so long to make up their minds?

Do second marriages work?

Are divorce courts in need of reform?

CHILDREN of divorced parents approach the issue of readiness for marriage with mixed feelings and many questions. What has been the impact of divorce on their own chances of a happy marriage? Would they be more likely to succeed in marriage if their parents had remained together, though unhappy, "for the sake of the children"? They also ask often, "What causes divorce?" "Do people who divorce have anything in common?" "What are the chances of success of the divorced who marry a second time?"

The research findings on some of these issues are either scanty or ambiguous. Still, a scanning of the readings will reveal that there is much more known today about divorce and what leads to divorce than was true thirty years ago when the first marriage texts were written.

How Does Parents' Divorce Affect Attitudes about Marriage?

Landis [1] asked 3,000 young people in California how frequently they had experienced doubts about their chances of achieving a successful marriage. The answers proved overwhelmingly that children from hap-

---

[1] Unpublished data from Judson T. Landis, June, 1958.

py marriages had fewer doubts that those from unhappy or divorced homes. Girls from unhappy homes had experienced doubts more frequently about their chances of a successful marriage (22 per cent frequently, 42 per cent occasionally, and only 11 per cent never) than girls from divorced homes (12 per cent frequently, 37 per cent occasionally, and 17 per cent never). Boys were almost equally influenced in their attitudes about future successful marriage whether they came from unhappy homes or divorced homes (47 per cent rarely or never having doubts from unhappy homes compared with 49 per cent rarely or never having doubts from divorced parents). There can be little doubt that a background of unhappy parental marriage, whether or not it eventuates in a divorce, creates doubts and mixed feelings about one's future marital career.

Does Divorce Run in Families?

From a study of divorce in three generations, based on responses from college students, Landis finds support for the thesis that divorce runs in families. The divorce rate among the parents and aunts and uncles of 1,977 single children increased in proportion to the incidence of divorce among the grandparents of the students from a ratio of one to 6.8 for those marriages in which neither grandparent family had divorced, to one to 4.2 if one grandparent family had divorced, to one to 2.6 if both sets of grandparents had divorced or separated.[2] However, Landis found no support for the theory that a major reason for marriage failure of children from divorced marriages is that they go steady with, become engaged to, and marry children from divorced marriages.

Other studies of marital adjustment provide less evidence of the carry-over of divorce proneness by generations. Burgess and Cottrell failed to find significant differences in the marital adjustment of couples by marital status of their parents, although sons of maritally intact families did have slightly higher marriage adjustment scores than sons of divorced parents.[3] Locke, likewise, found no relationship between divorce among parents and marriage adjustment scores of children.[4] Ter-

---

[2] Judson T. Landis, "The Pattern of Divorce in Three Generations," *Social Forces*, Vol. 34, No. 3, March, 1956, pp. 213–216. Locke's earlier findings had also pointed in this same direction. He found significantly more divorces among the parents and relatives of the divorced men in his study population than among the happily married. See Harvey J. Locke, *Predicting Adjustment in Marriage,* New York: Holt, 1951, pp. 111–112.

[3] Ernest W. Burgess and Leonard S. Cottrell, *Predicting Success or Failure in Marriage,* New York: Prentice-Hall, 1939, p. 383, Table 64.

[4] Harvey J. Locke, *op. cit.,* p. 351.

man and Oden found a significant relationship only if the divorce occurred after the child reached the age of eight.[5] All of these studies, however, found that the parents' marital happiness was closely related to their children's marital happiness. This suggests that whereas the divorced status by itself has a modest impact, at most, on future marital adjustments of children, the meaning of the experience to the child may be quite important for his marital future. At worst parental divorce is a handicap to carry into marriage which can be counterbalanced by other favorable experiences subsequent to the divorce.

Are People Who Divorce Different?

There are marriages which never see a divorce court in which the atmosphere is much more hostile than in homes about to be broken. Conflict is not unique to unhappy marriages but is present in all homes. Much of the contention is normal and understandable, indeed almost inevitable, if marriage is to function as a release from tensions. Only perfectionists would consider the bickering of family members resulting from the inevitable collision of wishes as evidence of intolerably unhappy marriage.

Many divorces occur between ostensibly congenial couples who may have needed help at only one point to work out misunderstandings which they were emotionally incapable of handling alone. (See the case of the doctor and his wife who profited from marital counseling, Chap. 14.) It is also true that many marriages which are chronically unhappy don't break up. These marriages produce psychologically, if not legally, broken homes which are quite as devastating to the personality of children. There are marriages that might better be dissolved by divorce and there are marriages broken by divorce that might have been salvaged by a marital counselor.

What Causes Divorce?

The most popular explanation of divorce by the general public is the moralistic one in which the unpardonable sin is adultery which is seen as the only bona fide grounds for divorce. A major shortcoming of the moralistic theory is that relatively few divorces occur as a result of adultery. Kinsey's reports on extramarital intercourse for American males places adultery in the vicinity of 50 per cent of married men interviewed, whereas the reporting of adultery as grounds for divorce in

---

[5] Lewis M. Terman and Melita H. Oden, *The Gifted Child Grows Up*, Stanford: Stanford University Press, 1947.

1956 was only 1.3 per cent of all divorces recorded in the twenty-three states reporting divorce statistics to the National Office of Vital Statistics.[6] Even when the well-known discrepancy between legal grounds reported and actual grounds estimated by divorce attorneys is compared, the proportion of divorces due to adultery increases to no more than 19 per cent of cases known to lawyers.[7]

Economic factors and divorce

A number of studies have established the close relationship between low income and high divorce rates. Divorces are disproportionately found in areas of high mobility, dense population, low home ownership, high juvenile delinquency, and high proportion on relief, which are also areas of low income.[8] Similarly, divorce varies sharply by occupational groupings. "Proneness to divorce" increases from an index 67.7 for professional groups to 180.3 for non-farm laborers and 254.7 for service workers, according to a sample survey of the U.S. Census Bureau in 1949.[9] Very much the same pattern was found true in Iowa in 1953, where unskilled laborers provided three times their fair share of the number of divorces.[10]

The relationship between economic factors and divorce is more subtle than the juxtaposition of income and divorce rates can possibly depict. In a society in which the living is not *made* by family members working together, but is *earned* by the breadwinner, the symbolic character of income is magnified. Conflict rages on the economic front when the interpersonal relations in other areas of life are strained. The "theme of complaints" from research on family difficulties places "money matters" in the top position in Terman's list of husband-wife complaints.[11]

Economic strain is possibly greater in the lower strata and more likely to be expressed in noneconomic situations such as sex and repudiation of marital responsibilities. Whereas the wife may withdraw sexual favors and affectional response, the husband withdraws economic

---

[6] See *Divorces and Annulments: Detailed Statistics for Reporting Areas, 1956*, Vol. 48, No. 2, March 25, 1958, p. 34.

[7] See Harry C. Harmsworth and Mhyra S. Minnis, "Non-Statutory Causes of Divorce: The Lawyer's Point of View," *Marriage and Family Living*, Vol. XVII, No. 4, November, 1955, pp. 316–321.

[8] See summary of studies by Bossard, Schroeder, Weeks, Kephart, and Glick in W. J. Goode, *After Divorce*, Glencoe: Free Press, 1956, pp. 43–55.

[9] *Current Population Reports*, Labor Force Series, No. 22, April 19, 1950, p. 50, Table 5.

[10] Thomas P. Monahan, "Divorce by Occupational Level," *Marriage and Family Living*, November, 1955, pp. 322–324.

[11] Lewis M. Terman, *Psychological Factors in Marital Happiness*, New York: McGraw-Hill, 1938, p. 105, cited in W. J. Goode, "Economic Factors and Marital Stability," *American Sociological Review*, Vol. 16, No. 6, December, 1951, p. 807.

support as the spiral of interpersonal conflict reaches a climax. Goode points out that this withdrawal of economic support is laden with less guilt at the lower-class levels because the lower-class father tends to feel his children belong more to the mother than to himself. They are primarily her task and responsibility and her waning loyalty relieves him of at least some of his guilt concerning the children. If she no longer "deserves" his support, then neither do they.[12] These generalizations provide ample evidence of the complexities of the interrelationships of economic factors and the phenomenon of divorce.

Another theory of the cause of divorce is that it has increased with the growth of stress and strain in modern society. Wherever the family finds itself cut off from the props of social control and social pressure, divorce increases. The shifting of population from the influences of stable, controlled rural life to the anonymity of the city accounts in part for the weakening of millions of family groupings in America.

Social change

One expression of social change has been the improved opportunities for women both in education and in employment. Marriage for the educated woman capable of earning her living ceases to involve merely a meal ticket and becomes a more companionable, although a more precarious, arrangement. Women today are economically more independent and enjoy increased equality in the courts. These factors explain in part the greater ease with which they obtain divorces in our time.

One way to test the theory that divorce is a function of social change is to observe the divorce rate during periods, such as war or revolution, when social change reaches its zenith. Inventions pour in, new ways of life are devised and accepted, populations are on the move, expediency is the watchword.

Figure 18, depicting the ratio of divorces to average annual marriages ten years previous, shows marked variation over the decades since 1910. A sharp increase is observed immediately following World War I, with a decline during the depression of 1930–1933. Thereafter the ratio of divorces to marriages in the preceding ten-year period rose steadily in the prosperity in preparing for World War II and during the war itself, to reach a high point of 450 divorces per 1,000 marriages in 1946. Since that peak the divorce ratio has declined, except for the Korean War, to a point lower than it has been in twenty years. It must be remembered that the divorce ratio follows closely on the marriage rate, since a high proportion of divorces occur in the first years of mar-

---

[12] *Ibid.*, p. 809.

riage. Therefore, whatever stimulates marriages to occur will automatically affect divorces too. The greater the proportion of the population married, the higher the likelihood of divorces being high. Divorces de-

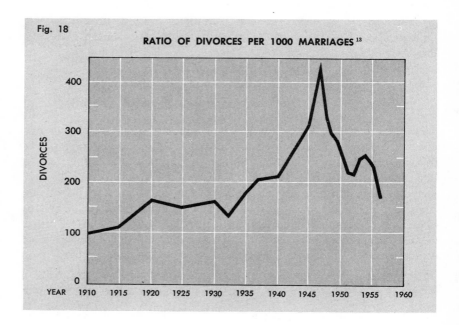

Fig. 18

RATIO OF DIVORCES PER 1000 MARRIAGES [13]

cline during depressions both because it is expensive to get a divorce and because fewer people are marrying.

The social change theory explains in part why there are more frequent divorces than there used to be, and why we have more divorces at certain points in our history than at other times, but it fails to pinpoint why particular marriages are broken. The breakdown of neighborhood controls, the declining size of the family, the decline in the number of hours spent together, and the increasing mobility of people have operated to make individual families more susceptible to disorganization, but these changes operate on most American marriages without producing equally divisive effects.

Incompatible personalities

Another explanation for the cause of divorce is offered by marriage counselors, psychoanalysts, and psychotherapists. In the early childhood experiences in the parental family, preferences are formed which

[13] *Vital Statistics, National Summaries*, Vol. 48, No. 3, April, 1958, Table 1, "Population, Marriages and Divorces and Rates: United States, 1920–56," p. 58.

make it easier to get along with some persons than with others. In a happy marriage the partner must meet some of the preferred childhood specifications, which often include resemblance to the father, the mother, or the favorite brother or sister.

Unfortunately, we not only form preferences in childhood, but we also develop pet hates—for Jim Mallory who struck you when you cut across his lawn or that old witch Cissy Perkins who peevishly threw sticks at your dog. While childhood memories continue to influence us as adults we may come to forget the source of our hates. Marriage to an otherwise charming person who faintly reminds one of a pet hate may soon, for no other reason, prove intolerable.[14]

Patterns of protection and dependency also appear to be important in achieving cohesion in marriage. Burgess and Wallin in their experiments in marital prediction find the factor of interdependence important.[15] Certain combinations of roles work out well. For example, a girl raised to be dependent on her father makes a good partner for a man raised to assert himself in a family in which the father was dominant. On the other hand, a man who is raised to be dependent on a strong female character may, if married to a dependent feminine type of woman, find himself in trouble. The marriage may eventually end in divorce as they struggle over who is to be dependent upon whom.

These illustrations may sound extreme, but they reveal quite clearly the personality twists which make one person bad company for another. Because certain personalities are what they are, there must be conflict between them as they live together in marriage. The irritations go deeper than the conscious mental states and date back to patterns fixed in early childhood, and for that reason do not lend themselves to self-doctoring. The quarrels are of the sort which never become resolved and never stop, because they are due to blockings or repressions out of the control of the conscious mind. They concern little things which become so much a part of a couple that they can no longer stop quarreling long enough to talk them out.

---

[14] In order to identify himself with the problem, the reader should think back over his experiences since childhood and see what situations produced the following feelings, common to the members of a divorcing pair: (1) feelings of revulsion in the presence of another person with whom you were forced to associate continuously; (2) desire to escape an intolerable situation which you were unable to handle with the resources you had at hand; (3) impulses to argue with certain types of personalities no matter which side of the fence they were on, impulses to show them up and reveal their stupidities.

[15] E. W. Burgess and Paul Wallin, *Engagement and Marriage*, Chicago, Lippincott, 1953.

What are the differences between couples whose quarrels are chronic and couples whose quarrels become progressively more bitter and destructive? The latter furnish a great number of our cases of divorce and separation, and an examination of their make-up may give us a clue to the causes of individual divorces.

One difference is the presence in one partner of the desire to escape, a desire strong enough to involve willingness to pay the penalties of divorce. This desire to escape may be traced to infantile techniques of handling situations by running away, but is more often the result of the shifting of love from the spouse back upon himself. From a normal heterosexual attachment, a narcissistic self-love is produced in which the spouse becomes a source of bitterness, a thwarting agent from which escape is imperative. The whole marriage comes to be looked upon as a frustration. The desire to escape becomes even stronger if another more suitable love object comes into view. The love will be transferred to the new object in what is known as "a rebound," and the desire to escape from the original marriage is accelerated. He is falling out of love with one as he falls in love with another! The desire to escape, then, is one of the observable differences between couples who are fighting in order to separate and those who fight but don't separate.

To answer the question of why one marriage ends in divorce and another persists requires investigation of the individual marriage. Aside from the social changes which have made marriage precarious for all couples, the following are helpful explanations of divorce in individual marriages: the unfortunate combination of personalities, the carry-over of childhood infantilisms, and the presence in one of the partners of the desire to escape. All these factors seem to explain in individual cases the progressive conflict and alienation which precede separation and divorce.

Why Do Divorcing People Take So Long to Make Up Their Minds?

The transition from single to married life is relatively easy because all our previous training leads to marriage and our own inner motivations prompt us to accept it. The whole procedure is not unlike canoeing downstream with well-wishers on shore waving us along. Our progress is accomplished more or less without effort because it all seems natural and right.

---

[16] We are indebted to Willard Waller for many of the ideas expressed in this and the next subsection. See *The Family: A Dynamic Interpretation*, New York: Dryden Press, 1951, pp. 509–527.

In the stages preceding the actual divorce many of the events of the courtship are experienced in reverse. The differences lie in the reluctance with which each step is taken and the regret apparent as the inevitable separation approaches. Neither partner likes to admit he has failed in this life project which started with so much promise and expectation of success. Even after the divorce, marriage exerts a strong back-pull, and the number of reconciliations of divorced couples attests to the strength of the desire to make marriage a success.

In our discussion of courtship we showed how each step in the process was a further commitment and how obligations were built up until a summatory effect was produced. The process by which the couple became permanently involved developed a movement of its own which carried the couple along. Alienation too is a similar development, which moves step by step from married life to separation and readjustment to life without the partner.

The accompanying table shows the typical stages of both processes. Alienation, like courtship involvement, proceeds to its conclusion in a series of commitments which are not easily renounced. Each response leads to the next in line, and the motive for each new step is furnished by the experiences up to that point—alienation cannot easily be arrested. After each crisis the relationship is redefined on a level of greater alienation. The destructive quarrels which are so characteristic of the marriages ending in divorce are often followed by intervals of comparative peace in which the couple make a determined attempt to adjust to life with each other. The conflict picks up again, however, around another sore point and continues until the couple can bear the

Typical Critical Points in Courtship Involvement Compared with Alienation Crises Leading to Divorce

Boy meets girl	First mutually destructive
Going together	quarrel
Eye-opener quarrel	Affectional responses withheld
Declaration of love	Mention possibility of divorce
Public begins talking	Others find out
Mutual understanding	Move into separate bedrooms
Mention possibility of engagement	Break up housekeeping
Engagement announcement	Divorce agreed upon
MARRIAGE	DIVORCE

pain of separation more comfortably than continued opposition. This concept of alienation will be clearer as we describe the critical points in the movement from early marriage to separation.

Alienation crises

Quarrels occur in any marriage, as we have shown in the chapter on conflict. It is the mutually destructive type of quarrel which is most difficult to handle and which characterizes the progressive alienation of couples heading for divorce. If the process can be said to begin anywhere, it probably starts with the first brutal truth session in which both partners frankly expose their real feelings about the other. We have defined quarrels of this type as destructive because they concentrate on the person rather than on issues or conditions. They leave the relation with fewer assets than it had before. They attack the ego and reduce the self-respect by which persons live. Constructive quarrels, in contrast, make the marriage stronger through a redefinition of the situation causing the conflict. The destructive quarrels are progressive and succeed eventually in alienating couples to the point where separation is inevitable.

Affectional responses withheld

Disturbance shows up relatively early in the affectional response area. "Don't come near me until you're ready to say you're sorry," was Jane's response to Jim after their first explosive upset. The withholding of affectional response quite naturally broadens to include the sex life of the couple, in which antagonism is quickly reflected. There could well have been excellent sex adjustment to begin with, but through loss of understanding neither feels right about continuing intimate relations. Some people withhold affection to punish the mate just as they do to punish a child. Withholding of affection in marriage always evokes insecurity and anxiety, particularly for those individuals who have identified the good marriage entirely with continuous love intimacies. The familiar Hollywood pattern of early divorce is the only remedy that the over-romantic have devised to meet this situation. For most marriages the withholding of affection and sex intimacies is merely a first symptom of difficulty, to be followed by many more severe crises before divorce takes place.

Mention of the possibility of divorce

In the course of conflict there comes a great moment when mention is made of the possibility of divorce, the stage roughly equivalent to the declaration of love in the courtship process. Each member of the pair has thought of separation but neither has mentioned it, not knowing what the response would be.[17] One should differentiate between the banter of husband and wife in which the threat of divorce is used playfully and the more critical use of the threat among couples in seri-

---

[17] Waller and Hill, *op. cit.*, p. 514.

ous conflict. The blow falls hardest on the one who is told. He is the one who must take the role of opposing the divorce and usually holds that role to the end. But there is an interdependence, which may seem to some perverted, each needing the other to continue the conflict, to work out the hostility. Both persons are really alienated, but one presses the fighting and one opposes the divorce. Each requires the continued participation of the other; indeed, each would be disappointed if the other stopped struggling. The passive one suffers more intensely, but has the virtuous feeling of being right, while unconsciously desiring to break the relation.[18] The immediate effect of the mention of the possibility of divorce, then, is one of restraint from strife, but when the hostilities begin again the couple have become used to the idea of divorce, and definite steps are taken in that direction.

At some point the fiction of solidarity is broken as the public is let in on the couple's troubles. The relationship changes and goes on a different basis. The expectation of success which was so important in holding the marriage together originally is replaced with the admission of failure. For many sensitive couples this is the master symptom of alienation: "People are talking about us." The couple have lost face and are no longer a pair in the eyes of the public. Invitations which include them both will decrease as friends refuse to take the risk of a row.

Others find out

The public divides into two camps, friends who are for the wife and friends who are for the husband. They act as a wedge to divide the two. The more sympathy expressed to members of the pair separately, the more committed the couple becomes to separation. Take the following case:

I was first conscious of the fact that I did not want to go back to my wife, or that a part of me did not want to go back about two months after our break. I analyzed this, and thought that traced to the fact that I had introduced myself into this new community on a single-man basis, and people had sort of come to think of me as a separate individual, rather than as a married man. Then later I had talked to several people and I had wondered what they would think if I went back to this woman who had caused me so much trouble. They sympathized, of course, and that made it all the harder. Then later, people insinuated to me that I was such a fine fellow that it must have been my wife's fault. In telling the story of our break I had always been careful not to say anything against my wife, for two reasons: one that she is really a very nice person and the other that she might come to this new place and I didn't want people prejudiced against her when she did. But the very fact that I tried to be fair with her and take the blame myself made my

---

[18] *Ibid.*, p. 520.

friends all the more certain that whatever had happened had been her fault rather than mine.[19]

This case exemplifies well the role of the public in bringing about commitment to a permanent separation. The man's failure to identify himself as a married man further complicated the situation and accelerated the movement toward a complete break.

Breaking up housekeeping

The crisis of separation is one of the most severe because of the associations tied up with the home. Every piece of furniture symbolizes something, every piece brings back memories of common experiences. These belongings which must now be parcelled out and divided are reminders of days when. . . . The phase of separation which is probably most poignant is that of leaving the home to take up separate quarters. This act seems to signify more than anything else the lengths to which alienation has gone.

The severance of such a meaningful relationship is usually extremely painful. Although quarrels and conflict are useful in bringing out a decision that will stick, the couple should be able to say they tried hard to make their marriage go and to live up to the expectations of friends and well-wishers. Reconciliations which fail show the uselessness of continued compromises and force the conclusion that the marriage won't work and can't be made to work. The separation which comes with taking up separate quarters is a signal to friends and the public that the rift is serious. Usually both parties become committed permanently to the break, and they finally agree to divorce. The interval between separation and divorce is sometimes short, sometimes long, depending on the readiness and preparation of the parties.

Divorce

Divorce is a final severance for which some preparation has to be made. It may take months before the actual work of reconstructing one's life can begin. The decree doesn't close the case, however; one doesn't divorce and live happily ever after. Indeed, the divorce court experience is described by some participants as being the most trying shock of the entire alienation process. Both members of the couple suffer through the procedure, with a feeling of numbness, of unreality, as if they were not really themselves but someone else looking on at the crazy scene.

After the divorce there is a period of mental conflict in which the individual attempts to reconstruct his world, often a period of depression, melancholia, and even suicidal attempts. Tensions build up which can be handled only with careful and skilled guidance. The divorced

[19] Willard Waller, *The Old Love and the New: Divorce and Readjustment,* New York: Liveright, 1930, pp. 131–132.

person should be watched for any evidence of depression and encouraged to seek counseling if symptoms appear.

Already during the alienation period preceding the divorce, personality adjustments are taking place. The many habits which hold marriages together—sex habits, response habits, food habits, work habits— all of these have to be broken and reoriented for the parties to face single life healthily. Everyone who has tried breaking a habit knows how painful the process is and how easy it is to fall back into the old routine again. Those who have gone on diets to keep a certain weight remember how insistently appetites cry out for foods to which they have become accustomed. The divorcing person faces the frustration of not one but several fundamental habits, and the separation is doubly painful if he must make that adjustment quickly. The habits of married living are much more fundamental than dancing or smoking or eating, and as they are broken, living loses its savor.

Post-divorce adjustments

As the person is forced to turn within himself for satisfaction, the results are often curious. He becomes capable, or so he thinks, of doing grandiose things. A man revives dreams of boyhood and believes that in a short period he will become a great banker or writer. A woman after thirty years of being hemmed in by housewifely duties sees possibilities of attaining startling personal success. Now that the routines of married life no longer exist as hampering bonds, the person sees no bounds to his possible accomplishments.

Sour-grapes rationalizations work overtime to convince the person he has done the right thing. Pleasant memories are repressed, and the illusions which supported the marriage are gradually replaced by cold, cruel reality. There is a certain grim conviction that the marriage could never have worked and that it was foolish to prolong it as long as it was prolonged.

Some helpful suggestions in reconstructing and readjusting the everyday life of the divorced warrant at least brief attention:

1. Talking the whole business out with someone who listens without praise or blame, who understands and helps but doesn't become involved; in sum, spending hours of counseling until the memories no longer bring numbing pain and can be faced with some objectivity.
2. Developing new skills which have no associations with the marriage and which can show progress quickly, such as singing, painting, working at certain types of crafts; doing "something you have always wanted to do," in order to balance the accounts with something positive and satisfying.
3. Plunging into professional work with renewed vigor, but not to the exclusion of all social contacts.

4. Picking up social contacts; the person is his own best judge of the number and depth of new contacts he is emotionally able to take.

5. Reorienting oneself in terms of the rest of the universe, and working out a philosophy of life which gives purpose and zest to living.

Do Second Marriages Work?

The remarriage of divorced persons is a phenomenon of marked significance in our society. Divorced persons remarry at a high rate, only about one fourth in recent years remaining in the divorced status for as long as five years. We have much less information, unfortunately, concerning the success or failure of second marriages. It is argued by those studies which find second marriages more successful than the first that divorced persons have learned a great deal from their experiences and that this can be seen in their second marriages. For example:

. . . There is no question now that second marriages are happier than first marriages. I believe that this is not only true when one compares the second marriage with the first unhappy marriage but that the percentage of failures is less among all second marriages than among all first marriages. . . . My sample is not large enough to include the number of "repeaters" which would be necessary for good analysis. There are several bizarre cases of this kind in my group, but most people seem to be couples who simply couldn't adjust to each other at their particular level of growth and experience. Unless you agree that a substantial proportion of the population is emotionally defective, you can't accept the neurosis and personality explanations of divorce. I suspect that most of these people could, after the divorce, adjust happily to their changed spouse—if they could really meet him for the first time, with the unhappy memories expunged.[20]

When viewed statistically in terms of "proneness to divorce," the findings support the view that the probability of divorce is greater in a second or subsequent marriage than it is in the first; indeed, one analyst of census data computes the probability as fifty per cent higher for second than for first marriages.[21] Yet the stubborn facts of high proportions of happy second marriages argue that remarriage is well worth the risk. Bernard has completed the first serious study of second marriages of divorced and widowed people and has evaluated this is-

[20] Personal communication to one of the authors from William J. Goode, Columbia University, clarifying generalizations from his Detroit study of 425 divorced women reported for the *Saturday Evening Post* by David G. Wittels, "The Post Reports on Divorce," *Saturday Evening Post*, January 21, 28, and February 4, 11, and 18, 1950.

[21] Paul Landis, "Sequential Marriage," *Journal of Home Economics*, Vol. 42, October, 1950.

sue very carefully. She points out that there is a selective process at work which brings a superior breed of individuals to a second marriage. The first sieve is quite coarse since almost anyone can get married a first time, but it does eliminate some unmarriageable individuals. The second sieve is more rigorous, and she finds that those who divorce are superior in many respects to those who remain unhappily married. Finally, the last sieve, involving selection of those who marry the second time, brings individuals more attractive and more mature than those "hard core" 14 per cent who remain unattached. It is therefore no wonder, she asserts, that second marriages do very nearly as well as first marriages in the four studies reporting.[22]

As divorce is more generally accepted, it is possible that the divorced group will include more and more essentially well-adjusted individuals who failed largely because of poor matching or other extraneous circumstances related to their early dating experiences. These individuals in second marriages would have high probabilities of success.

Are Divorce Courts in Need of Reform?

Divorce is not something to fear, but to understand and to make less painful if we can. Prejudice in the past has made the adjustment to divorce doubly hard and painful, because the divorced person has been set in a class apart when he needs most of all to be accepted and assimilated back into social life.

The divorce decree is a perfunctory ceremony which merely signifies the lack of unity in a marriage, just as the wedding ceremony solemnizes the pair unity which existed before marriage. Judge Paul W. Alexander has termed the divorce court judge a "public mortician" who buries dead marriages.

There is little justification for the emotional reaction to divorce as divorce. It is only a confirmation of the fact that the couple have separated and are no longer performing the required functions of matrimony, and it merely serves to regularize the matter for the protection of all concerned.

The big problem is not to keep people who want divorce badly from getting relief but to keep more people from wanting divorce. This will

---

[22] She reports findings from Terman, *op. cit.*, p. 418; Harvey J. Locke and W. J. Klausner, "Marital Adjustment of Divorced Persons in Subsequent Marriages," *Sociology and Social Research*, Vol. 33, November–December, 1948, pp. 97–101; Paul Popenoe, "Remarriages of Divorcees to Each Other," *American Sociological Review*, Vol. 3, October, 1938, p. 696; and her own reports on Utopolis, see Jessie L. Bernard, *Remarriage*, New York: Dryden Press, 1956, pp. 108–113.

EASY MARRIAGES,
No health training or residence requirements

**DIVORCE action can be started
as SOON after marriage as desired**

DIVORCE can be applied for ANYWHERE—
after setting up temporary residence

GENERAL COURT hears cases
in many fields: criminal, equity,
divorce, civil suits

FORMAL QUASI–CRIMINAL ACTION
bent on proving guilt in open court

LAWYERS' ROLE
To win case

**ROTATION
OF JUDGES—**
Each judge hard
pressed to keep up
with legal aspects
of the fields he
presides over

SPOUSE'S ROLE—
Antagonist trying to prove
guilt of mate

GOAL

DIVORCE

NEW A.B.A. PROPOSAL Based on Diagnosis and Treatment

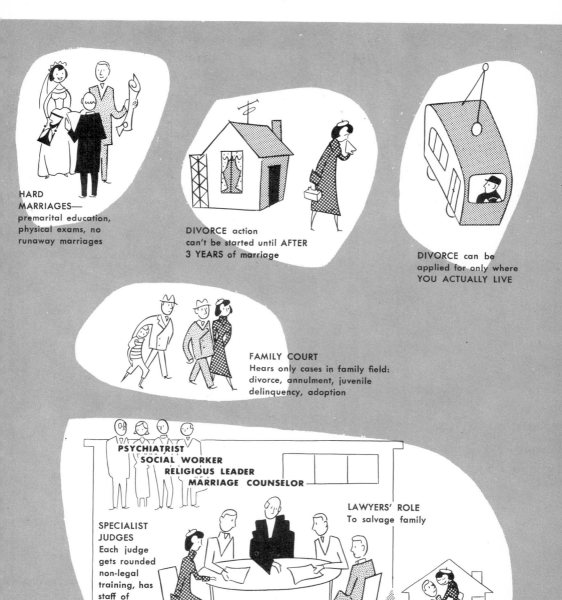

HARD MARRIAGES— premarital education, physical exams, no runaway marriages

DIVORCE action can't be started until AFTER 3 YEARS of marriage

DIVORCE can be applied for only where YOU ACTUALLY LIVE

FAMILY COURT Hears only cases in family field: divorce, annulment, juvenile delinquency, adoption

PSYCHIATRIST
SOCIAL WORKER
RELIGIOUS LEADER
MARRIAGE COUNSELOR

SPECIALIST JUDGES Each judge gets rounded non-legal training, has staff of specialists to help

LAWYERS' ROLE To salvage family

SPOUSES' ROLE Patients being treated for an illness

GOAL

INFORMAL ADMINISTRATIVE PROCEDURE looking for cause and cure of trouble in private sessions

WHAT'S BEST FOR THE FAMILY

Redrawn from chart by GRAPHICS INSTITUTE, N. Y. C., for *Pageant Magazine*

PRESENT METHOD OF SECURING A DIVORCE

Application for divorce is made

Public trial—damaging to both parties and their children

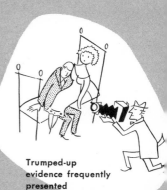

Trumped-up evidence frequently presented

Divorce possible only if one is "proved" guilty of grounds for divorce

DIVORCE IS NOT GRANTED IF

Both parties are proved guilty of charge

It comes out that both parties have cooperated to arrange grounds for divorce

Alimony settlement based on bargaining power

An attempt—even though non-lasting—at reconciliation has been made

A.B.A. PROPOSAL FOR DIVORCE REFORM

Application
for help is made

Private diagnostic investigation
made by court's specialists

Psychological aid to
try to solve personality-
emotional problems

Welfare counseling
to try to solve social-
economic problems

Treatment efforts may
last from 2 months to 2 years

Report on results made to judge. Will show
treatment has succeeded, in some cases

Divorce granted only if treatments fail
and judge is convinced case is hopeless

Alimony settlement based on
real needs and resources

Redrawn from chart by GRAPHICS INSTITUTE, N. Y. C., for *Pageant Magazine*

involve a complete reversal of policy with respect to the granting of legal separations. Our divorce system has developed out of the importance played by property rights in the marriage contract. In order to protect the respective rights of each party, the law provides a means by which one member might complain of the offenses of the other and, by fixing guilt, obtain a legal release from the contract. Marriage has long since changed in emphasis from property contracts to companionship and affection giving.

Since the National Conference on Family Life in 1948, a committee headed by Judge Paul W. Alexander which has been actively formulating a new approach to marriage and divorce laws, in 1956 formed a permanent section on The Family and The Law with the American Bar Association. Their proposals, shown in the charts on the preceding four pages, start from a new premise, that divorce is an effect rather than a cause of broken homes. They propose a new kind of court based on a new philosophy sweeping away the "archaic legal philosophy" of punishment for guilt and substituting for it a positive, constructive approach which would ask "What is best for the family?" and hence best for society. The case would no longer be titled "Jane Doe vs. John Doe," but "In the Interest of the John Doe Family." Trained personnel of the court would be used to diagnose, and if possible heal, the breach. Divorces would not be easier, but more difficult to obtain. The final decree would be issued, Judge Alexander has written, "only if the investigation plus proper judicial inquiry compelled the conclusion that the marriage could no longer be useful to the spouses, the children, or the state; that the partners could not or would not permit it to fulfill the functions imposed by the natural law and the civil law; that perpetuation of the bare legal bond would be more harmful than beneficial to all concerned." [23]

The proposals of the American Bar Association's committee are being debated in conferences not only of the legal profession but of many interprofessional groups. An Interprofessional Commission on Marriage and Divorce Laws sponsored by the American Bar Association and representative of all the major professions dealing with marriage and divorce is conducting research and evaluating the many varied proposals for divorce reform likely to come before legislative committees. A model marriage and divorce act is in the making which will be presented to one of the fifty-two jurisdictions in the United States for debate and action.

---

[23] New York *Times,* September 17, 1950.

In concluding this chapter on divorce, some account should be taken of the possibilities of rebuilding unhappy marriages into more satisfactory patterns through marital guidance. The increasing availability of family counseling through marriage and family counseling agencies suggests that counseling should be sought as an alternative to divorce. Rebuilding broken marriages

Persons of their own will can't successfully arrest the process of alienation, but a third party often can, if well trained and if he gets the marriage early enough. The work of the family consultant is to rebuild the discordant family, if the matter has gone so far as to need remedial rather than preventive treatment.

The marital guidance clinic serves in many ways as a guard against divorce. As a premarital guidance center it assures couples that they are prepared emotionally and physically for marriage. Premarital guidance utilizes careful premarital examination (discussed in Chapter Six, "Getting Engaged") and instruction given in conferences and class work in preparation for marriage. Later the center enters the picture to aid the couple in understanding the normality and inevitability of conflict, and encourages the development of techniques for resolving their difficulties (see Chapter 14, "Coping with Conflict"). Finally, the couple that has failed to use these resources until they are well along in the alienation process may turn to the counseling services for help in rebuilding the marriage in a more satisfactory pattern. Thus the work of counseling agencies is in line with our earlier statement of principle with respect to divorce: "The big problem is not to keep people who want divorce from getting it but to keep more people from wanting divorce."

READINGS

Alexander, Paul, "Our Legal Horror—Divorce," *Ladies' Home Journal*, October, 1949.

Barnett, James H., *Divorce and the American Divorce Novel, 1858–1937*. Philadelphia: Privately printed, 1939.

Bernard, Jessie, *Remarriage*. New York: Holt, 1956.

"Children of the Divorced," *Law and Contemporary Problems*, Vol. 10, Summer, 1944. A symposium.

Davis, Kingsley, "Statistical Perspective on Marriage and Divorce," *Annals*, November, 1950.

Despert, J. Louise, *Children of Divorce*. Garden City, New York: Doubleday, 1953.

Glick, Paul C., "First Marriages and Remarriages," *American Sociological Review*, Vol. 14, December, 1949.

Goode, William J., *After Divorce*. Glencoe: Free Press, 1956.

Groves, Ernest R., *Conserving Marriage and the Family: A Realistic Discussion of the Divorce Problem*. New York: Macmillan, 1945.

Landis, Paul, "Sequential Marriage," *Journal of Home Economics,* October, 1950.

Locke, Harvey J., *Predicting Adjustment in Marriage: A Comparison of a Divorced and a Happily Married Group.* New York: Holt, 1951.

Mead, Margaret, *Male and Female.* New York: Morrow, 1949, Chapter 17.

Rosenthal, Herbert C., "Painless Divorce," *Pageant,* April, 1952.

"Toward Family Stability," *The Annals,* Vol. 272, November, 1950. A symposium, see especially articles by Hollingshead, Murdock, and Goode.

Waller, Willard, *The Old Love and the New.* New York: Liveright, 1930.

———— and Reuben Hill, *The Family: A Dynamic Interpretation.* New York: Dryden Press, 1951, Chapters 23–24.

Wittels, David G., "The Post Reports on Divorce," *Saturday Evening Post,* January 21, 28, and February 4, 11, and 18, 1950.

17 Strengthening Marriage Ties

What binds a new marriage together?

How are basic adult needs satisfied in marriage?

Where does love fit in?

What does sex symbolize for the marriage?

How does understanding grow?

What tension dispellers are there?

Why do people stay married?

W_{HY} people stay married deserves as much attention as the sources of alienation which crack and dissolve families. In this discussion the bonds that hold marriages together are stressed. Successful marriages don't just happen. Indeed, a happy union takes working at, and its accomplishment is the product of much sweat and toil in the art of getting along.

What Binds a New Marriage Together?

"We expect our marriage to work" is one of the strongest bonds tying a marriage together at the outset. This conviction supplies the motivation to stick together when the going is rough rather than to run home to Mother. It impels the couple to work out the solutions to problems so they won't recur. Honeymooners with the expectation of success are already consciously addressing themselves to the task of building their marriage so that it will work. They are saying, "We want to be good for one another and we want to be good parents. Show us how."

In spite of the high divorce rate in America, the standard held up for every couple is successful marriage. If a person can't make a success of marriage he is made to feel inadequate, and his failure is pointed out by members of society to young people about to be married. Along with the personal expectation of success goes the public's expectation of success. The individual couple may feel strongly the necessity of not letting down the friends who have wished them well. Making marriage work is often easier than facing the public with the admission of failure. One of the real forces in tying marriages together, then, is the expectation of success, the ideal of a happy marriage as the only possible outcome of the marriage, and the feeling that the public can't be let down by a breakup.

Friends are admonished in the "whom God hath joined together" formula to keep hands off the marriage and stay out of the sphere of marital interaction.[1] It is not good form to ask how the marriage is going or to inquire as to its health. The assumption in our society is that all marriages are happy until proved otherwise by appearance in a divorce court. It is doubtful if the net effect of this assumption of marital bliss is good, since it makes for hypocrisy and implies that conflict is abnormal and unusual, but the assumption is an additional force in holding many marriages together.

Society for married pairs

A second reason for sticking together is the system of pairing young people off for social purposes. Most social life is organized around married couples or couples about to be married. The development of pair unity in the engagement period was furthered by the public's recognition that the couple did belong together, shown by inviting them to social occasions as a pair. This acknowledgment caused the boy and girl to regard themselves differently and thus gave stability to the relationship. The years of married life add to this sense of "we" and further unify the couple. Together they explore the social circles (and are explored by them); together they make friends and choose the sets which they wish to join. Early in the marriage, if not in the engagement, a person learns to accept invitations tentatively until he can find out whether or not the other member of the pair is able to go. The public understands because it expects the couple to act as a unit.

The marital relationships are strengthened because society in America is not organized for sexes separately as are some societies. Most of the entertaining in a community centers within the married set and is motivated by the "you invite us and we'll return the invitation later on" phenomenon, leaving almost no social activities for bachelors and spinsters and other non-married people. Moreover, to invite one member of a married pair and not the other is something of a breach of

[1] Willard Waller and Reuben Hill, *The Family: A Dynamic Interpretation*, New York: Dryden Press, 1951, p. 324.

etiquette. The cards are stacked in favor of married couples sticking together if they want any social life.

The positive social pressures just described do hold couples together. In addition, the fear of public disapproval, of neighborhood gossip, and the fear of scandal are negative forces of which many couples are conscious. These socially imposed forces, however, are essentially *adhesive*, inasmuch as they are applied externally. They are most effective in a simple agrarian society where everybody knows everybody else and are less effective within the social sets of the metropolitan centers. Of more importance today are the forces within the couples as individuals, forces which might be termed *cohesive*, since they are based on the inner needs of the participants themselves. It is because marriage is welded together by both adhesive and cohesive forces, by external societal pressures and by internal desires and needs, that it is surviving the buffeting of social change in our day.

How Are Basic Adult Needs Satisfied in Marriage?

One of the cohesive forces holding American marriages together is the power of the marital relationship to meet the basic affectional needs of its members. The American family is built around the husband-wife relationship, and the power of that relation to satisfy the needs of the couple flavors the whole of family life. Children become accustomed to having their needs for affection, companionship, recognition, and response met in the parental family. Moreover, they are conditioned to expect that the phenomenon of love and affection will carry over into a family of their own making. With that expectation, the early courtship activities are surrounded by questions such as "Does he love me?" "Is she good for me?" "Does he do anything for me?" or in sum, "Will he satisfy my hunger for affection and security permanently?" The history of the courtship is one of finding in the growing relation reciprocal satisfactions and increasing interdependence of one on the other to satisfy these imperious needs.

The adult is, after all, basically the child older grown. In marriage the child, now grown older, has transferred from the parent to the marriage partner his need to give and receive affection and security. The transfer takes place piecemeal, beginning with the first recognition of the capacity to love someone other than the parent and continuing until the marriage is stabilized as the main source of affection and appreciation.[2]

To be wanted, to be understood, to be appreciated, to be loved, and

---

[2] See Chapter 3.

to belong to someone are fundamental needs which parallel the needs to possess, to love, and to respond to someone. Uniquely met in the intimacies of the marriage relation, these needs should be listed among the main sources of cohesion holding marriages together in America today.

Where Does Love Fit In?

Love is not the only force at work stabilizing a marriage. Public approval, the meeting of basic needs for affection and security, co-joint habits of living together, interests and intimate jokes in common, experiences in working toward a common goal, interdependence because of duties performed, and inertia to change, all have a part in maintaining the integrity of a marriage.

The romantic dogma has been a major source of premature breakups through its brittle philosophy, "If you really loved me, you wouldn't do this." Not helpful to marriage solidarity are the following romantic notions: that a marriage will ride through on love alone, that it doesn't take working at, and that true love always runs smoothly. Every marriage faces bumps and jolts—to pretend otherwise is fantastic. The all-too-frequent example of the woman who runs out on a marriage before it really gets started just because her husband acts like a human being instead of a Prince Charming derives support from the romantic love philosophy. Marriages based mainly on romantic love are precariously balanced because they weaken as the emotion itself changes.

Conjugal love is quite another emotion. It grows as the marriage progresses, thrives on companionship, common experiences, and the number of happy episodes which are scattered through a rich marriage. Conjugal love builds on the familiar, the mementos, the souvenirs, and waxes stronger with each additional year of marriage. Unlike romantic love, conjugal love is impossible for newly acquainted young people, since it requires time to form and grows from continuous association. Romantic love is greatest where each party knows least about the other—reality gets in the way of romance. This is the love that is blind.

As conjugal love comes to the fore in marriage, the relationship is strengthened. Few marriages in America persist over any length of time without developing conjugal love sentiments, because they are based on companionship and common interests which intertwine the experiences of established marriages. In contrast, romantic love gradually disappears in the partnership marriage except for the lip service paid it in the exaggerated moments of bliss which occasionally occur throughout married life. Romantic love as a solidifying factor in marriage gives way to conjugal love, which is more mature and more compatible with the companionable features of contemporary marriages.

What Does Sex Symbolize for the Marriage?

Married love, which we have called conjugal love, finds expression in many day-by-day experiences. None of these is more effective as a unifying force than regular, satisfying sexual intercourse. Sex is potentially solidifying because it requires a complement of two in order to function. The regular release of tension in coitus is extremely satisfying in the purely physical sense, and in addition it serves as an expression of fulfillment for the entire relationship. Thomason has found greater evidence of communication and agreement between spouses in the sexual areas of marriage adjustment than in the non-sexual realms. There appears to be willingness to talk and thereby to secure greater satisfaction in this hitherto tabooed area of marriage.[3]

Take a really satisfying day from the life of Fred and Mabel, who have been married long enough to have achieved a satisfactory sex adjustment. Fred comes home from a busy day at the plant full of the doings of his day. He tells Mabel about how grouchy the boss is, how green his new assistant is, how much progress he is making on his new machine, what he had for lunch, and what a funny duck he got to talking to on the way home on the bus. This conversation takes up most of the dinner hour; it leaves Fred relaxed at having spilled his day's experiences and gives Mabel the feeling that she has been a part of Fred's day.

Mabel too has things to relate. She wants to share excerpts of the letter she has just received from her folks. She is eager to discuss with Fred what they will do with her mother when her father goes (this last letter tells of another heart attack, and both Fred and Mabel know that some day soon there will be one too many of them). Although they don't reach a final decision, Mabel senses that Fred is back of her, whatever happens, and she feels a sudden burst of affection for her good old dependable Fred right there while they are finishing dessert. She gets confidence to confess that she has been running over her budget for the month, which they talk over with some heat. They end up with an understanding of the financial situation, and the atmosphere is cleared, leaving them both relieved.

After supper they do the dishes together. Fred drops and breaks the jelly dish. Mabel starts to fuss and then admits that she hated the thing anyway. They got it last Christmas from Aunt Harriet, whom she always has dis-

---

[3] Bruce Thomason, "Extent of Spousal Agreement on Certain Non-Sexual and Sexual Aspects of Marital Adjustment," *Marriage and Family Living*, Vol. XVII, No. 4, November, 1955, pp. 332–337.

liked. Fred grins and says he can't stand her either, as he kisses the back of Mabel's neck. She leans against him for a moment and observes that this is one thing she likes about him: they both dislike the same people.

Aunt Harriet gets a going over by both of them as they move into the living room. Fred puts on some records that they both enjoy and goes over his paper once more, and Mabel sews in front of the fire. The clock strikes ten as the symphony hour comes on. They are both tired but agree to stay up until the program is over. Mabel puts up her sewing and stretches out on the sofa. Fred drops his paper and comes over to sit beside her. As a favorite passage of music flows into the room, Fred squeezes Mabel's hand and smiles into her eyes.

By bedtime there has developed a strong sense of belonging to each other, a feeling of true unity. Sex intercourse then becomes not just a physical release, but a symbol of the whole relationship. Into it flow the meanings and the feeling tones of the broken jelly dish and the music and Fred's boss and Mabel's mother and all the security that has come from working it all through together.

Next morning Fred gets up feeling like a million, and leaves for work with the conviction that it would take a dozen bosses to get him down today. Mabel goes out to shop with a tune on her lips, and in her mind a resolution to economize. Both face the new day with more poise, more peace, more strength and courage, because the two are more than ever one.

The accompanying diagram shows roughly what the sex relationship has meant to Fred and Mabel in symbolizing their sense of unity.

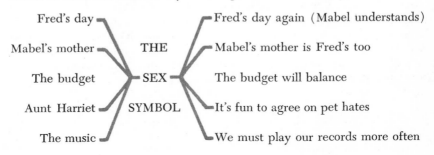

Fred's day		Fred's day again (Mabel understands)
Mabel's mother	THE	Mabel's mother is Fred's too
The budget	SEX	The budget will balance
Aunt Harriet	SYMBOL	It's fun to agree on pet hates
The music		We must play our records more often

How Does Understanding Grow?

As the marriage wears on and the couple come to take for granted the unreserved intimacies of wedded life, there is a growth of understanding between the mates. The newlywed is all too often downcast when his wife is slightly displeased with him, but the experienced husband knows that she will get over it after a while. He has been all through this before and can predict the method of bringing the affair to a satisfactory conclusion. It is disillusioning to a man to see his wife having breakfast in a housecoat with her hair in pins, and unpleasant for a wife to see her husband's unshaved face, but it is comforting to both to realize that such liberties do not seriously threaten the relationship. These are the jolly little coarsenesses which give to the marriage relation its unique strength. Shady little sallies between them, the vulgarities which they alone think funny and which before marriage might have shocked them both, these indiscretions also hold a marriage together.

Gradually each member of a pair comes to share the mental states of the other, to live vicariously in the other, and to learn to predict the other. They are becoming competent in exercising their skills in empathy (see pages 104–105). In this state of complete intimacy, the members of the pair develop similar tastes and similar aspirations. The wife hears her husband's jokes hundreds of times but enjoys them because they are her jokes, and prods him to "Tell that one about when we were in Chicago, dear."

In the growth of understanding, the sharing of ideas often results in the sharing of depressions and predicting when they will come. Husband and wife learn to handle one another's blues as well as one another's temper tantrums. Each knows if he's put in the doghouse the other will soon let him out.

Marriage solidarity develops immensely as members of the pair perceive the strength of the relationship. It is seen as they recognize, while fighting, that they care more about the marriage than they do about winning. It comes forcibly to their attention when a crisis like infidelity is met without the wife's running home to her parents as she would have done earlier in the marriage. It is seen in the willingness of the husband to tolerate shoddy household management or sterility of the wife with nary a hint at separation. The relationship has come to have a value in itself. All such incidents may not seem very romantic; indeed, some romantic-minded people would say such marriages had gone to seed. But family unity is built on just such foundations as these: "We have come to take each other for granted; we know we can count on one another"; "She'll see me through thick and thin. What a lucky man I am!"

The married pair bring to marriage two separate systems of habits formed during life in their respective parental families as well as during the years away from the family. Consciously, at first, they must go about the task of adjusting the differences in the two systems. The wife must find out how strong her husband wants his coffee and when he must arise in the morning in order to get to work on time. The husband must learn that to his wife permanent waves are more important than golf equipment and that ashes on the rug are not to be tolerated.

Family habits are solidifying

After a time the two systems are modified and become an interlocking habit system which is a great deal more stable than that of the single person could ever be; they rest upon the habit of adjusting to the situation created by the real or imaginary demands and expectations of others.

Consider the following illustration of habits at work in a typical urban home:

> . . . the husband used to laugh when the wife referred to anthills as ants' houses, but now he does not laugh any more; in fact, he sometimes uses the expression himself. Each individual member of a family has made certain habit adjustments to the physical setting in which the family lives; each knows at just what height to insert the key in the lock of the front door and each has acquired the knack of giving a little twist to the key which makes the door open easily; each one is able to enter any of the rooms in the darkness and to find the switches for the lights without any difficulty; each knows where to sit on hot afternoons in August, and how to descend the rickety cellar stairs. And each one, likewise, has made a multitude of adjustments to the presence of others in the house. In the morning the father of the family gets up and starts the furnace. He walks carefully in order not to disturb the others, but there is no need of this, for the others have adjusted to his early morning noise and do not hear him. A little later the mother gets up and calls the children, perhaps a number of times, for they may have made an adjustment to her habitual technique and have shifted the responsibility entirely upon her; they have, perhaps, developed "mother deafness." She then gets breakfast, sets the table, and calls the family. Father has been reading the paper, which is now split into sections. Each one eats his breakfast in his customary way; there is the usual interchange of pleasantries and the usual grumbling and complaining. Then ensues the morning crisis of getting the children off to school and helping father to catch the eight-thirty train: the struggle over the bathroom, the effort to find things, the examination of shirts to see whether they will do for another day, and all the myriad adjustments which arise from a civilization which demands neatness and promptness. Then all the members of the family but one leave the home, pausing a moment to say good-by to mother and to pet the dog.[4]

This is just a small part of the family day and misses many of the habits of family living reflected in conversation and gestures. It does serve to illustrate, however, the intermeshing of social habits of family members. Once you become a part of a cooperative enterprise in which your behavior is habitually determined by the responses and helps of others, it is highly inconvenient to separate yourself.

As the pair become accustomed to each other and dependent upon

---

[4] Waller and Hill, *op. cit.*, pp. 328–329.

one another for the sharing of family habits, they cease to operate in the family as individuals and come to take on a family personality. This is the reason married people in time come to talk alike, think alike, plan alike, and in some instances even to look alike. Back of the common gestures and facial expressions are common attitudes and beliefs. These habits serve as an additional source of solidarity in marriage.

Couples find that one of the techniques for making marriage work is to enter wholeheartedly into the business of building common habits. They may lose some of their premarriage individuality and independence, but they gain a more satisfying joint personality in the process.

In any marriage, after the initial adjustments to personal idiosyncrasies have been made and routines established, a level is reached at which the married pair feels comfortable. Decisions have been reached concerning the division of duties, and the time schedule for each day has been committed to memory. The routines are fast becoming habits through repetition and the achievement of satisfying results. The major needs are being met, the major drives satisfied. The fact that habits are established makes experimentation less and less necessary. The couple are finding the grooves and married life is gradually reaching an optimum level of interaction. **Habits and resistance to change**

These routines act for the marriage as a gyroscope acts for a ship, pulling it back on an even keel when it is about to go over. It sometimes seems inevitable that a particular marriage should break up in divorce or desertion. Conflicts arise which seem impossible to resolve, but somehow equilibrium is restored and things go on very much as before. Sometimes, too, a series of fortunate events makes it look as if a marriage were going to reach a level of impossible happiness—but that also passes.

An illustration may help to explain the tendency to stabilize marriage at a given level. When there is a "blowup," each person is conscious of the cultural standards (that is, what is right in the situation) and of the fact that friends and families would disapprove if the truth were known. To add to their sense of guilt, the couple may hear a sermon, or read a story, or hear a bit of gossip about a recently divorced couple which reminds them of the cultural norm. Discussion and reconciliation follow, and the marriage is restored to its normal level. Thereafter the couple is tempted to let sleeping dogs lie. Ways are found for settling conflicts with a minimum of disturbance.

Another explanation of marriage stabilization lies in an understandable reluctance to change a mutually satisfying relation in favor of something new or unknown. The collective habits of a married pair are solidly based on the needs and motives of both parties—or at least they were originally built up to satisfy the couple's needs. As long as these needs are satisfied, there is reluctance to change. Another kind of reluctance to change arises from the inability of either partner to know the mind of the other and the consequent difficulty of getting together on any ground other than that they now share.

One of the forces holding marriages together is the reluctance to give up "a good thing." The marriage may not be perfect, but breaking habits is painful. They become vested interests, active in their own perpetuation, as anyone knows who has tried to stop smoking.

Working towards common objectives

Dick is a medical student just beginning his four-year course and would like to get married, but he is afraid it is impossible for about six years. He has his M.D. to get first, followed by an internship and residence work. Marie suggests that there are things a girl would dislike more than working jointly with a man for an M.D. It would be *their* M.D., and they would share the experiences and sacrifices together, if they were married.

In the struggle to reach a common goal, a new feeling arises, a sense of having fought and bled together. Pride in common achievement, the sense of superiority which common accomplishments bring, or the feeling of struggling together against misfortune—such experiences are basic to marriage solidarity. They form a backlog to hold the marriage together in the crises which follow later in family life. The reference to "leaner" days, the technique of reminiscing together, reminders of the history of the relation, these can be called up when trouble arises on the home front.

Many regret that the family appears to have lost many of the old-time economic functions which made it a partnership. In the old-style family, making a living was a common enterprise which tied the family members together. Today it is more typical that the man earns and the woman spends. In the modern family, mutual interdependence arises largely out of husband's and wife's sharing the budgeting and planning of expenditures, the joint consumption rather than the joint production of economic goods. In addition, it must be admitted that the modern division of familial duties between man and wife makes for interdependence, as any husband will find who is forced by circumstances to take over the task of managing the home while his wife is gone. One harried husband found, thanks to his parental family training, that he had been given some background for all except one of the wifely homemaking duties. Can you guess what it was? Braiding his daughter's hair! Even so, this husband's life was immeasurably brighter when his wife returned and the balance of duties was established once again.

Another phase of partnership centers around buying furniture and setting up a home. The things you buy are often bought after much deliberation. You scrimped and saved for each stick of furniture. Each item brings to memory a multitude of associations which solidify marriage. In the divorce process, the most painful step of all is breaking up housekeeping and distributing the furniture. The converse of breaking up housekeeping is the solidifying function of building a home by self-sacrifice and hard work. The good family person comes to talk about his accomplishments and his possessions as "ours": "our degree," "This is our chance," "When we bought this, Jane was just a baby," "We saved for six months for our television set."

Another evidence of partnership as a binding force in marriage is seen in the unselfish goals which a pair will set for themselves. Many marriages are initiated and grow as the participants strive to serve humanity in specific ways. The ideal of alleviating the lot of the sick and the lame, of leaving society the better for their marriage, unifies many modern couples. An age-old ideal is that of rearing healthy, useful children, and this appears to be positively related to marital happiness. Couples are drawn together and their marriage is given meaning as a partnership by the wider interests and services which they care about.

What Tension Dispellers Are There?

When the peace of the household has been broken and the offending party finds himself in the doghouse, he may utilize any number of devices to restore the *status quo*, one of the most effective being the use of humor. There is something funny about almost every marital crisis if the participants don't take themselves too seriously. A mate with a sense of humor is an asset to any partnership and has saved many a marriage from cracking up.[5]

Conciliatory devices become extremely handy to "save face" in a tense situation and are most often learned in the parental family in the process of growing up. In our culture we have developed a repertoire of techniques which most of us recognize when they are used on us but which enable us to save face and make up if we really want to. These devices are no cure for fundamental alienation, but they tide over many a marriage in the early stages of conflict to the point where a workable balance is attainable. Every couple should be familiar with these techniques and should learn to use them to advantage. They are:

---

[5] See Chapter 14, "Coping with Conflict."

(1) humor twists, such as punning, kidding, baby talk; (2) storytelling; (3) compliments and flattery; (4) verbal and physical outlets, such as swearing, crying, walking, chopping wood, or even playing it out on the golf course; (5) appeals to the past history of the relationship; (6) displacing hostility onto a pet peeve common to both; (7) apologies and resolutions to improve.

Closely allied to the devices for dispelling tension are the mechanisms of escape and rationalization by which couples make up for the deficiencies of their marriages by creating beliefs that the deficiencies don't really matter. "My husband is hard to get along with and not a very good breadwinner, but he's a great artist and has a heart of gold." "My wife's not beautiful, but after all, she is a good mother to the children." Were it not for the wide use of rationalizations and the face-saving devices listed above, married life would be much less bearable to many who now remain wedded permanently.

Weathering the storms

No marriage can be called a strong marriage at the outset. It is untried, untested; only after experiences with normal conflict and only after meeting such crises as war separations, depressions, unemployment, or serious illness can we be assured of the fundamental solidarity of a marriage. This is to say that a marriage is both tested and strengthened by the crises it has overcome. We have heard people say, "If we get through this crisis we know we can face anything together," and, "We got married during the depression when there weren't any jobs, and we lived on $50 a month for two years and it brought us together as nothing else could. We depended on ourselves for moral support, and our recreation consisted of walks to all the free museums and factories in the city and attendance at all the free concerts of the city symphony orchestra. We shall never be afraid of facing impoverishment, because we know from experience we can take it."

Some of the forces we usually think of as making for breakups also make for solidarity. It is a source of security to a married couple to have been through enough conflicts to learn how to handle them. The pair need no longer be afraid if tensions build up to a high pitch; a blowup might clear the air. A good fight defines the issues and leaves the combatants knowing that they are still loved and can get away with airing their differences. Over a period of time, grievances accumulate and tension arises. There is a quarrel, and the grievances are expressed. Both persons experience a purging of their souls and then settle back into the accustomed level of routine interaction. Crises, conflict, and illnesses, mastered and assimilated, act as forces to hold marriage together.

Why Do People Stay Married?

Much has been written about marital conflict but relatively little about marital solidarity. The happily married pair have until recently kept their secrets locked up—only the alienated and the divorced have spilled for research workers. This discussion of marital solidarity draws largely from materials on well-adjusted families obtained from shrewd observers of family life and from the files of marital guidance clinics, which deal with both marital failures and marital successes.

What are the factors which stabilize marriages in America today?

1. Couples begin marriage with the expectation of success, and this ideal of solidarity holds them together.
2. Social life is organized around married pairs—there is no satisfactory provision for the single person, unmarried, widowed, or divorced.
3. Couples find in marriage the satisfaction of many basic adult needs: the desire for affection, companionship, security, recognition, response, and understanding.
4. Conjugal love is a tying factor which grows as marriage progresses, thrives on companionship, common experiences, and the memory of things familiar.
5. The meeting of sexual needs comes to symbolize for the couple the sense of growing unity in the marriage relationship.
6. Joint interests, family jokes, and common experiences hold marriage together.
7. Marriage becomes a habit that is painful to break; the interdependence which develops because of duties performed solidifies marriage.
8. In the struggle for a common goal, a new feeling of unity arises, a sense of having fought and bled together.
9. The use of tension-dispelling devices tides over many marriages in the early stages of conflict to the point where a workable balance is attainable.

READINGS

Baber, Ray E., *Marriage and the Family*. New York: McGraw-Hill, 1953, Chapter VI, "The Husband-Wife Relationship."

Bowman, Henry A., *Marriage for Moderns*. New York: McGraw-Hill, 1954, Chapters X and XI, "Personality Adjustment in Marriage."

Burgess, Ernest W., and Harvey Locke, *The Family: From Institution to Companionship*. New York: American Book, 1953, Chapter 11, "Family Unity."

Cavan, Ruth S., *American Marriage, A Way of Life*. New York: Crowell, 1959, Chapter 12, "Learning to Live Together."

Duvall, Sylvanus M., *Before You Marry*. New York: Association Press, 1959 revision, Chapter 12, "What Can Bind Your Marriage Together?"

LeMasters, E. E., *Modern Courtship and Marriage*. New York: Macmillan, 1957, Chapter XI, "Marital Adjustment."

Levy, John, and Ruth Munroe, *The Happy Family*. New York: Knopf, 1938, Chapter 5, "Living Together."

Mace, David R., *Marriage*. Garden City, N.Y.: Doubleday, 1952, Parts 3 and 4, "Finding Fulfillment in Each Other" and "Meeting Those Problem Situations."

Peterson, James A., *Education for Marriage*. New York: Scribner, 1956, Chapter XII, "Achieving Individuation and Togetherness."

Waller, Willard, and Reuben Hill, *The Family: A Dynamic Interpretation*. New York: Dryden Press, 1951, Chapter 16, "Bases for Marriage Solidarity."

PART THREE

BECOMING A FAMILY

18 Where Babies Come From

Why won't your children be just like you?

What happens before birth?

Why can't some couples have children?

What about adopting a child?

The miracle of life starts with the wonder of each individual's unique inheritance. There are so many old wives' tales and superstitions about heredity that you probably often have asked questions that begin with the phrase "Is it true that . . . ?" Just what do you really know about heredity? Try taking the test on pages 354–355.

Why Won't Your Children Be Just Like You?

There isn't one chance in 300,000,000,000,000 of there ever being another person just like you! Yet you were not a haphazard accident that could happen only once in the history of mankind. You were rather the result of a complete new deal of human characteristics. Every one of your children, and your grandchildren, and their children will be quite as unique—yet they will be your progeny and draw from the same general pool of inheritance that produced you. The fact that your father chose your mother (or the other way around) brought together two streams of heredity that had been branching out in similar twosomes since the beginning of time. Out of the hundreds of eggs produced by your mother and the hundreds of millions of sperm available from your father, the fusion of the particular egg with the particular sperm that started you off was something that could never happen twice the same way.

WHAT DO YOU KNOW ABOUT HEREDITY? [1]

Mark each statement true or false. Check your answers with those which follow immediately after the test. Give yourself ten points for each right answer. Then add up your score and see how you stand; 80 to 100 is excellent, 60 to 80 is good, 40 to 60 is average, 20 to 40 means that you will learn a lot from this chapter that you never knew before.

_____ 1. A child's sex is determined by the father.

_____ 2. A son born to a man of seventy will be weaker than one he fathers at thirty.

_____ 3. A pregnant mother can in no way improve the future character of her child by keeping her thoughts pure, listening to good music, reading inspiring books, and so on.

_____ 4. The mother contributes more to her son's heredity than does the father.

_____ 5. Redheads are by nature more passionate than blondes.

_____ 6. In a blood transfusion, a mother's blood is safest for her child.

_____ 7. A Negro child may be born to an apparently white couple if one of them had a Negro ancestor.

_____ 8. Members of certain human races cannot reproduce if mated with members of a widely different race.

_____ 9. Women have just as much native intelligence as men.

_____ 10. There are no human "thoroughbred" families.

Here are the facts:

1. (*True.*) The human male produces two kinds of sperm which differ in a minute degree with respect to sex-determining properties. The egg produced by the mother is "neutral." Thus if one type of sperm (containing an "X" chromosome) fertilizes the egg, the result will be a girl; if the other type (containing a "Y" chromosome), a boy results.

2. (*False.*) Neither the age nor the condition of the father can change the nature of the chromosomes (hereditary factors) which he transmits to a child.

3. (*True.*) Any hereditary factors bearing on the child's character are in it the moment it is conceived. Not until after it is born can the mother influence the child's character for the better.

4. (*True.*) While their contributions to a child's heredity are in all other respects equal, the sex chromosomes ("X") contributed by mother to son contains many additional "genes" not present in the sex chromosome ("Y") from the father.

---

[1] Reprinted by special permission of the Curtis Publishing Company from Amram Scheinfeld, "How Much Do You Know about Heredity?" *Ladies' Home Journal*, November, 1941, pp. 121–123.

Thus, certain defects—such as hemophilia—are passed on to sons only by their mothers, because the genes for them occur only in the sex chromosomes they get from her.

5. (*False.*) The hereditary factors producing hair coloring (and eye coloring as well) are not linked with those making for any specific type of personality. Any kind of coloring may go with any kind of temperament.

6. (*False.*) A mother's blood may often be as different from her child's and as dangerous to transfuse as that of some total stranger. Blood types are inherited through a combination of factors from both parents, and it is just as possible for a child and parent to have different blood types as to have different-colored eyes.

7. (*False.*) Only if both parents have Negro blood, and in a considerable degree, can a Negro baby appear. Stories to the contrary are either myths or cases of doubtful paternity.

8. (*False.*) All human beings belong to the same species, Homo sapiens, and are fertile with one another.

9. (*True.*) All intelligence tests now indicate that women have as much mental capacity as men, but that any intellectual inferiority on their part is due to less opportunity to develop themselves.

10. (*True.*) To produce human thoroughbreds, as in domestic animals, would have required the closest inbreeding between mothers and sons, fathers and daughters, brothers and sisters. As matters stand, all humans, even members of royalty, are biologically mongrels.

You began with the union of one of your mother's eggs which, though no bigger than a fraction of a dot on this paper, carried to you the full deal of her side of the family, and the microscopic sperm which brought you everything that had been dealt out for you from your father's side of the house. The microscopic miracle that carried all your characteristics and inherent tendencies in this union of egg and sperm was an elaborate and highly exact arrangement of ultra-minute packets of hereditary determiners called *genes*. For each characteristic that was inherited there was a pair of genes (one from father, one from mother). The color of your eyes, the shape of your nose, the set-up of your body, the length of your fingers, the tendency to freckle or not, to sing on key or not, and to have twins or not, these and all of your other characteristics were to be found in potential form in the genes somewhere in the fertilized ovum. These genes are strung like beads on a string, each one exactly matching in position the parallel gene of every other germ cell, and separated at convenient lengths in tiny bodies called *chromosomes*.

Deep in your reproductive organs is a cluster of cells that exist for the sole purpose of transmitting your particular line-up of genes and chromosomes to your children. These *germ cells* (produced in the ovaries of the girl and in the testes of the boy) coast along through childhood without much activity. At adolescence the ovaries and the testes begin their business of turning out at regular intervals the germ cells that have the capacity of making a parent of you—an ovum every month in the girl, hundreds of millions of sperm every few days in the boy. Whether you marry or not, these germ cells are produced with a faithful regularity throughout your active adulthood. In germ cell production, instead of each chromosome splitting to form 48 new ones for each cell, the members of each *pair of chromosomes* separate and one member goes into each new cell, so that the final germ cell has just half the original twenty-four pairs, twenty-four singles. Twenty-four singles from the father plus twenty-four singles from the mother equal twenty-four new pairs when they unite to form the beginnings of a new baby.

Twenty-four pairs of chromosomes, each with its own gene deter-miners, now struggle for dominance. Some characteristics cover up others, in the same way that darker colors cover up lighter ones on a canvas. A gene for dark hair, for instance, finding itself paired off with a gene for blond locks, has the right of way and wins the race for ex-pression in the new individual. This tendency for some genes to win over others in the expression of characteristics is called *dominance* and works according to the well-known laws of heredity. The characteristic that is there but doesn't show in the new individual is said to be *re-cessive*. A monk by the name of Mendel, studying many generations of flowers in his garden during the last century, discovered this tend-ency of some genes to cover the expression of others, and worked out the mathematical expectancy in each succeeding generation. The prin-ciples of Mendelian heredity are found to work in the inheritance of some human characteristics, but like most rules there are exceptions, so not even experts can reliably predict what their children will be like.[2]

Sex determination   Figure 19 shows that the father is responsible for determining the sex of his child. There are two kinds of sperm cells and the sex of the child is determined by the type that penetrates the egg. There are hundreds of millions of sperm in each ejaculation of semen and it is pretty much a matter of chance which variety it is. Since a few more boys than girls are conceived, there would seem to be a slight ad-

[2] Amram Scheinfeld, *The New You and Heredity,* Philadelphia: Lippincott, 1950.

This is what makes all the differences there are
between a woman and a man:

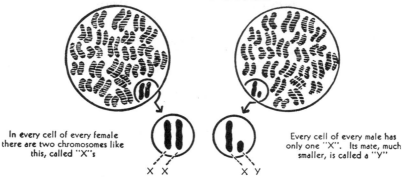

In every cell of every female
there are two chromosomes like
this, called "X"s

Every cell of every male has
only one "X". Its mate, much
smaller, is called a "Y"

X X   X Y

For reproduction, a female forms eggs, a male sperms,
to each of which they contribute only HALF their quota
of chromosomes, or just one from every pair

Since a female has TWO "X"s, each egg gets one
"X", so in this respect every egg is the same:

But as the male has only ONE "X", paired with
a "Y", he forms TWO kinds of sperms:

HALF WITH
AN "X"

HALF WITH
A "Y"

Thus: If an "X"-bearing sperm enters the egg,
the result is an individual with TWO "X"s

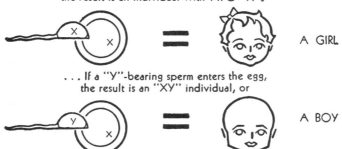

A GIRL

... If a "Y"-bearing sperm enters the egg,
the result is an "XY" individual, or

A BOY

From Amram Scheinfeld, *You and Heredity* (Lippincott)

Fig. 19 HOW SEX IS DETERMINED

vantage in favor of the male-determining sperm. The normal ratio of 105 boy babies to 100 girls at birth in the U.S.A. varies slightly with race and age of mothers,[3] but no one has been able to explain satisfactorily just why. Nor is there any method by which the variety can be selected, so the sex of the child-to-be remains a mystery until the baby is born.

Twinning

Twinning seems to run in families, and there has been a great deal of speculation on just how the tendency is inherited. Like almost all of the other products of gene shuffling there is a new deal for each new child, and prediction of twins is difficult.

Figure 20 points to the following generalizations concerning twins: (1) there are two kinds of twins, identical and fraternal; (2) identical twins come from the *same* fertilized egg; (3) identical twins are always of the same sex and share the same heredity; (4) fraternal twins come from two different fertilized eggs, that is, two eggs and two sperm; (5) fraternal twins have no more in common in their heredity than other brothers and sisters, except that they have shared the mother's uterus; and (6) fraternal twins may be of the same sex or of different sexes.

Triplets, quadruplets, and quintuplets are formed by extensions of these two basic processes. For instance, triplets may be all fraternal (three fertilized ova), or all identical (one fertilized ovum with two divisions and separations), or partially identical and partially fraternal (one pair of identical twins and a fraternal third individual conceived and delivered together). The famous Dionne quintuplets were apparently identical. Often it is difficult without scientific assistance to tell which type of twinning has occurred.

How skin color is inherited

The facts about skin color are not widely known. Especially is there confusion about the inheritance of skin color in interracial unions. The materials presented in Figure 21 cover only two types of skin-color genes, but there are probably more. Some of the facts of skin-color inheritance implied from this chart are worthy of restatement: (1) two full-blooded Negroes could not have a white child; (2) two pure whites could not have a Negro baby; (3) two parents from mixed Negro-white stock *might have* a white child; (4) two parents from mixed Negro-white stock *could have* a dark-skinned child, even though they were relatively light-skinned themselves; (5) in respect to skin color, the mulatto is always of mixed heredity, Negro and white; and (6) a

---

[3] C. A. McMahan, "An Empirical Test of Three Hypotheses concerning the Human Sex Ratio at Birth in the United States, 1915–1948," *Milbank Memorial Fund Quarterly*, July, 1951, pp. 273–293.

IDENTICAL TWINS
Are products of

A single
sperm

and

A single
egg

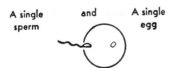

In an early stage
the embryo divides

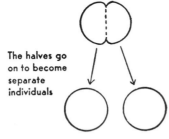

The halves go
on to become
separate
individuals

Usually — but not always — identical twins share the same placenta and fetal sac

But regardless of how they develop, they carry the same genes and are therefore

Always of the same sex — two boys
or two girls

FRATERNAL TWINS
Are products of TWO different eggs fertilized by TWO different sperms

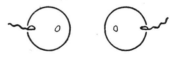

They have different genes and may develop in different ways, usually— but not always — having separate placentas and separate fetal sacs

Also, as they are totally different individuals, they may be

Both
of the
same sex

Two boys

—or two girls

—Or a
mixed
pair

One
boy

One
girl

From Amram Scheinfeld, *You and Heredity* (Lippincott)

Fig. 20 HOW TWINS ARE PRODUCED

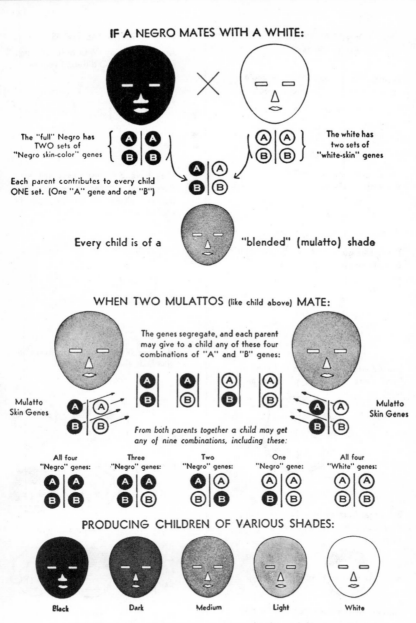

IF A NEGRO MATES WITH A WHITE:

The "full" Negro has TWO sets of "Negro skin-color" genes

The white has two sets of "white-skin" genes

Each parent contributes to every child ONE set. (One "A" gene and one "B")

Every child is of a "blended" (mulatto) shade

WHEN TWO MULATTOS (like child above) **MATE:**

The genes segregate, and each parent may give to a child any of these four combinations of "A" and "B" genes:

Mulatto Skin Genes

Mulatto Skin Genes

From both parents together a child may get any of nine combinations, including these:

All four "Negro" genes:

Three "Negro" genes:

Two "Negro" genes:

One "Negro" gene:

All four "White" genes:

PRODUCING CHILDREN OF VARIOUS SHADES:

Black   Dark   Medium   Light   White

[NOTE: Only two types of skin color genes are shown, but there probably are more]

From Amram Scheinfeld, *You and Heredity* (Lippincott)

Fig. 21 SKIN COLOR

truly black-skinned child can occur only if *both* parents carry some Negro skin-color genes.

What Happens before Birth?

That period between the moment when the egg is fertilized and the time when the baby is born is characterized by the most rapid growth and the greatest differentiation of the whole life span. The accompanying pictorial presentations show the development of the baby from conception through birth. At the top of Figure 22 you can see the relative positions of the reproductive organs in the female body in a sagittal section of the lower pelvis. The pictures just below show the relative size and position of the uterus flanked on either side by the two ovaries, as seen from the front. At the bottom of Figure 22 you find a cross section of a uterus, a Fallopian tube, and the ovary at the right side of the figure.

You recall that the egg released from a ruptured Graafian follicle enters the tube, normally is fertilized there (if at all), and journeys down the tube into the uterus. The journey from follicle to uterus takes from three to five days. The elements shown in Figure 23 are greatly magnified in size so that you may see them better. Each egg is several times larger than in life. This picture shows the egg leaving the follicle, being fertilized, and developing as it moves down the tube to implant in the wall of the uterus. Remember that there is but one egg in the tube at a time. What this figure shows is the progression of a single egg from Graafian follicle to uterine implantation in a series of thirteen steps, each illustrated by a separate picture. Can you see at which stage fertilization is taking place in this illustration?

The fertilized egg plants itself in the wall of the uterus. The placenta forms and the baby's circulation is established in such a way that the fetus receives its nourishment from the mother's blood stream without coming in direct contact with it. The amniotic sac (membrane) forms, in which the baby floats in fluid (nature's own shock absorber), and the fetus itself develops at a rapid rate.

The illustrations in Figure 24 show the pregnant uterus and the fetus at six weeks. By this time the fetus already has a definite shape, although it cannot be said to look very human as yet. Even so, you can detect the head with its prominent eye, the curved back (at the right), and the arm and leg buds that are to become limbs.

At the top of Figure 25, the 2½-months-old fetus shows marked development beyond the six-weeks-old fetus of Figure 24, while the fetus at 3½ months (at the bottom of Figure 7) is beginning to look like a

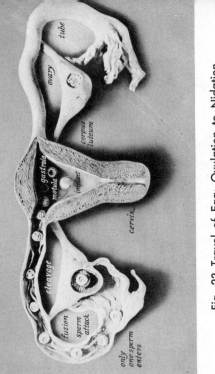

Fig. 23 Travel of Egg: Ovulation to Nidation

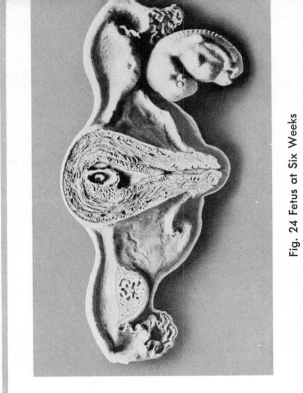

Fig. 24 Fetus at Six Weeks

Photographs by Dickinson-Belskie

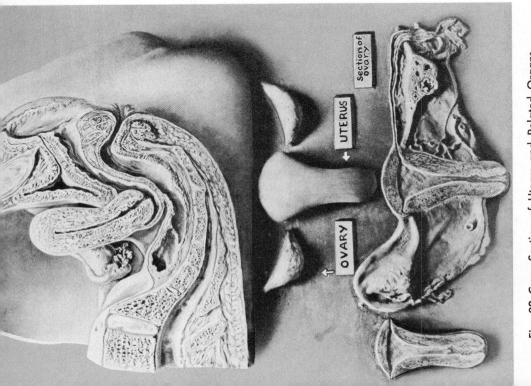

UTERUS

OVARY

Section of ovary

Fig. 22 Cross Section of Uterus and Related Organs

Below: Before and After Pregnancy

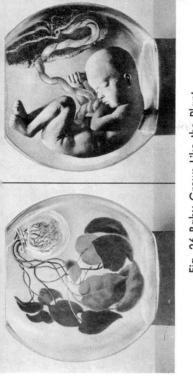

Fig. 26 Baby Grows Like the Plant

Fig. 27 Before Labor

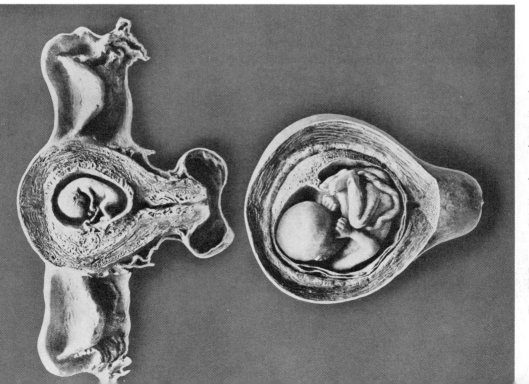

Fig. 25 Fetus at 2½ Months and 3½ Months

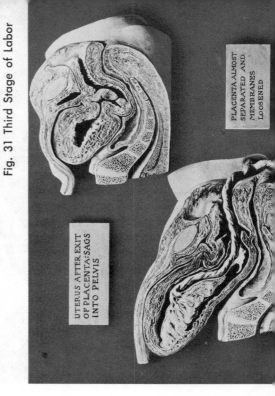

Fig. 30 Birth of Shoulders Rotation

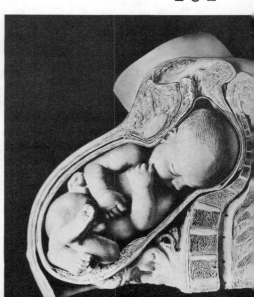

Fig. 31 Third Stage of Labor

PLACENTA ALMOST SEPARATED AND MEMBRANES LOOSENED

UTERUS AFTER EXIT OF PLACENTA: SAGS INTO PELVIS

Fig. 28 Labor: Cervix Dilating and Bag of Waters

Fig. 29 Full Dilation, Cervix High, Head Deep in Pelvis

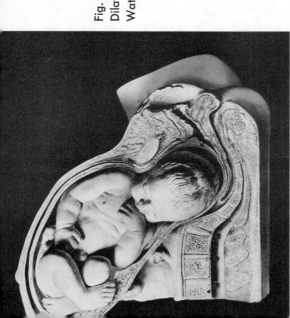

real baby. Although it weighs only about two ounces, this 3½-months-old fetus is already complete with fingers and toes and a very shapely ear. Clearly seen in this figure are the amnion and chorion, the double membrane that surrounds the fetus. Wound around the little right thigh is the umbilical cord, leading into the placenta seen just above and to the right of the tiny feet.

The two pictures in Figure 26 are designed to show how the fetus is fed through the umbilical cord and the placenta in much the same way as a plant is nourished through its stem and root system. In the case of the fetus, the blood vessels of the baby are surrounded by maternal blood within the placenta, and the exchange of food (from the mother's blood to the baby's) and waste (from the baby to the mother) takes place through the walls of the blood vessels. The mother's blood does *not* enter the baby. Blood from the placenta is conveyed by blood vessels in the cord to the baby.

Figure 27 shows the baby in the uterus just before labor begins. The baby is full term and is ready to be born. Now it weighs seven and one half pounds, more or less, and is about twenty inches long. The baby is in the best position for birth with the head against the cervix.

Figure 28 shows the cervix dilating (notice how much thinner it is than in Figure 27). The mother is now in labor. The *first stage of labor,* in which the cervix dilates enough to let the baby through, usually lasts about sixteen hours for the first baby (less for subsequent children) and is characterized by rhythmic contractions that increase in intensity and frequency until the cervix is completely open. It is early in the first stage that the woman usually notifies her physician of labor pains. She generally will be told to go to the hospital when the interval between contractions is from ten to fifteen minutes.

Figure 29 shows the cervix completely open. One thin portion of the cervix shows just at the baby's right ear lobe, the other high on the forehead. The mother is now in the *second stage of labor,* in which the pains come frequently and with great intensity. The contractions now have a bearing-down quality as the uterine muscles attempt to expel the baby. This stage of labor ordinarily lasts only a few minutes and is usually made endurable for the woman by anesthetic or analgesic.

In Figure 30 we see the baby's head already born and the doctor assisting in the birth of the shoulders. The uterine and abdominal muscles are contracting vigorously now. Note how the baby's shoulders turn to fit the size of the birth passage. Not all babies are born with head and shoulders first, although that is the most frequent position. The so-called breech presentation, buttocks first, is the other normal position.

In Figure 31 we see the *third stage of labor*. During this stage the placenta separates from the uterine wall; it, together with the membranes by which the fetus was enclosed and the umbilical cord, is then expelled. These structures are often known as the afterbirth because they come after the birth of the baby. Their expulsion ordinarily takes only a few more uterine contractions and is over in a very short time.

The doctor examines the materials carefully to make sure that the placenta has been completely expelled after the birth of the baby, because of complications which might otherwise arise.

Abortions and miscarriages

The emptying of the uterus before *full term* (nine months) is not uncommon and may occur as often as one out of every five pregnancies. The popular term *miscarriage* refers to the unintentional or spontaneous emptying of the pregnant uterus, while an *abortion* is generally understood to mean the intentional emptying of the pregnant uterus. In medical language an abortion is the expulsion or removal of the fetus and placenta from the uterus for any cause between the time of conception and the twenty-eighth week of pregnancy. Between this period and full term, expulsion of the baby is called *premature labor*.

The cause of most miscarriages is unknown. Some may be due to defective germ plasm (bad eggs or sperms). Other causes are glandular disturbances, maternal diseases, and abnormalities of the uterus. Injuries and shock to the mother are not usually sufficient in themselves to precipitate a miscarriage.

Occasionally it is necessary for a physician to terminate a pregnancy to save a mother's life. This is called a *therapeutic abortion* [4] and is done only under the most favorable conditions. It must be medically justified and agreed upon by at least two physicians.

Unless carried out in a recognized hospital by a competent physician under the conditions just specified, interrupting a pregnancy by destroying the fetus is legally forbidden in this country and is known as *criminal abortion*. The dangers of *infection* and *hemorrhage* are great, since criminal abortions are usually performed under the most unfortunate conditions by practitioners of questionable skill and training. Since there is no known medication which when taken by mouth will empty the uterus of its contents without grave danger to the woman, the abortionist must resort to surgical procedures. These are usually performed without aseptic safeguards and they exact a heavy toll of maternal well-being.

---

[4] For a good recent symposium on this topic see Harold Rosen (ed.), *Therapeutic Abortion: Medical, Psychiatric, Legal, Anthropological, and Religious Considerations,* New York: Julian Press, 1954.

The study made at Indiana University by the Institute for Sex Research finds [5] that physical complications are reported by 17 per cent of the women acknowledging abortions. Of these, 3 per cent report mild bleeding or cramps, temporary menstrual difficulties, or the necessity of going to a hospital for a day or two; 7 per cent report more severe bleeding, cramps, or menstrual difficulties lasting a longer period, some amount of infection or the necessity of going to a hospital for several days; while still another 7 per cent report blood poisoning, peritonitis or other serious infections, or a long hospital stay, invalidism, or almost fatal illness. Actual fatalities do not appear in these reports, since they come from interviews with women who were alive at the time of the study.

Unpleasant emotional results of abortions are even more frequent. Feelings of depression, guilt, being emotionally upset, nervous, feeling ruined mentally, and having seriously contemplated suicide are some of the psychological results of abortion reported by 9 per cent of the women surveyed.

Legal, religious, and ethical considerations deter many women from having abortions. The general attitude is that having an abortion is a serious step with many unfortunate consequences, all of which cannot be fully foreseen. Therefore, the intelligent woman does not panic when she finds herself unwillingly pregnant. She first considers all the possibilities open to her. She talks with her doctor. She seeks psychiatric, psychological, and social guidance as well. She confides in a trusted counselor. She realizes that having children is a privilege not to be lightly cast aside.

Since 1941, when it was first discovered, there have been hundreds of articles on the Rh factor in the blood. Too few have properly interpreted the material so that non-medical people could understand and much needless alarm has resulted. Although difficulty sometimes arises, as described below, it does so infrequently. Only about 1 in 20 Rh-negative women ever have an abnormal pregnancy because of this fact.   *The Rh factor*

Approximately 85 per cent of the white population of the United States have Rh-positive blood. The remainder have Rh-negative blood. When both father and mother have the same Rh blood type there is no difficulty. When the mother is Rh-positive, all goes well. But when an Rh-positive man and an Rh-negative woman have an Rh-positive child, then there may be trouble if Rh-positive cells from the fetal circulation escape into the mother's blood stream. There they may stimulate

---

[5] Ernest Havemann, "The New Kinsey Institute Report: Pregnancy, Birth and Abortion," *McCall's*, March, 1958, p. 100.

the mother's blood to produce antibodies capable of destroying the Rh-positive blood cells. These antibodies may enter the fetal circulation and attack the baby's blood cells and destroy them, producing *erythroblastosis fetalis*,[6] or *hemolytic disease*. The principal symptoms are anemia and jaundice. Such babies may die during pregnancy but if born alive and properly treated immediately after birth the majority will survive and be perfectly normal children.

In spite of all the public concern, erythroblastosis is not very common. Although 15 per cent of all white women are Rh-negative, only about 1 in 250 babies is born with this disease. The incidence is lower than might be expected because other conditions besides the Rh factor must be present in order for the disease to develop. There must be some leakage of the fetal blood cells into the maternal circulation in the placenta or the mother must have received a transfusion of Rh-positive blood at some earlier date. Except when the mother has had a transfusion, erythroblastosis practically never affects the first-born. It is only after antibodies have been built up in the mother's blood by previous pregnancies or earlier transfusion that the baby may be affected. Nineteen out of twenty Rh-negative women will *never* have an erythroblastotic child.

Why Can't Some Couples Have Children?

Roughly one tenth of all couples who want children are unable to have them. This inability to conceive is called *infertility* when it is treatable, or *sterility* when the inability is permanent, and may be due to many causes. Sometimes the male sperms are not numerous enough or sufficiently active to reach and fertilize the egg. Rest, improved health, and medical treatment may correct the condition sufficiently for conception to take place. In the woman the cause may be (1) immature or abnormal sex organs, (2) obstructions of the cervix, (3) unfavorable vaginal secretions which affect the sperms' motility, (4) glandular deficiencies, or (5) closed tubes which make it impossible for the sperm and the egg to meet. *Infertility clinics* in our larger maternity hospitals are successfully treating many couples who desire their own children, with many responding favorably to treatment.

Artificial
insemination

When the treatment of the physician or of the infertility clinic still cannot assure a couple of conception, the wife may become pregnant through *artificial insemination*. This is a procedure by which live

---

[6] Fred H. Allen, Jr. and Louis K. Diamond, *Erythroblastosis Fetalis*, Boston: Little, Brown, 1958.

sperms are introduced into the woman's genital tract under optimum conditions. The physician determines the time most favorable to conception, usually by having the woman record her morning temperature immediately upon waking for several months to determine her ovulatory cycle. Then on a day when ovulation is most likely, using a syringe, the physician deposits the semen donation in the upper end of the vagina, in the cervix, or directly into the uterus. This is repeated monthly until conception occurs.

The semen donation may be either that of the husband, or in case he is completely sterile, that of an anonymous donor. Semen donors are carefully selected by the doctor performing the insemination from among men whose health and heredity are acceptable and compatible. Psychological factors are discussed with the couple to make sure that any baby that eventuates will be completely acceptable as a full-fledged member of the family.

Since the baby resulting from artificial insemination using a donor's semen is technically not the husband's child, legal, social, emotional, and religious aspects of the child's status can become problems. Reluctance on the part of some couples to consider such a step, scarcity of doctors skilled in the practice, and the strong resistance of certain church groups keep artificial insemination from becoming widely accepted. It has promise, however, for many couples who would otherwise be childless.

What about Adopting a Child?

For marriages in which couples cannot have children, adoption is a possibility if the couple are emotionally mature and ready to accept the "chosen child" as their own.[7]

Where to find a child available for adoption is a big question in many localities. It is not that there are not enough children needing homes. One child out of every seven in the United States is not living with both parents. In 1955, about seven million children under eighteen years of age were living with neither parent, or with only one parent.[8] Of these, approximately three million children are orphans, with an increasing number of them the children of young unmarried mothers.[9]

---

[7] Lee and Evelyn Brooks, *Adventuring in Adoption*, Chapel Hill: University of North Carolina Press, 1939.

[8] *Statistical Bulletin*, Metropolitan Life Insurance Company, February, 1955, pp. 3–5.

[9] National Office of Vital Statistics, as quoted in *A Chart Book, op. cit.,* Chart 14.

Without proper controls these babies form a potential black market in adoption. The "baby farm" offering babies for a price, or a "contribution" of several hundred to more than a thousand dollars, should be assiduously avoided. Such unscrupulous outfits rarely offer the vital records, birth certificates, and other controls that should come with adoption. The well-staffed, state-licensed agency, public or private, places a child for adoption only after a thorough study has been made to safeguard the future of the child and the foster parents. Such an agency can be located through the state or local welfare department. *Adoption laws* are built upon three important objectives.[10]

1. To protect the child from unnecessary separation from parents who might give him a good home and loving care if sufficient help and guidance were available to them; from adoption by persons unfit to have responsibility for rearing a child; and from interference after he has been happily established in his adoptive home by his natural parents, who may have some legal claim because of defects in the adoptive procedure.

2. To protect the natural parents from hurried decisions to give up the child, made under strain and anxiety.

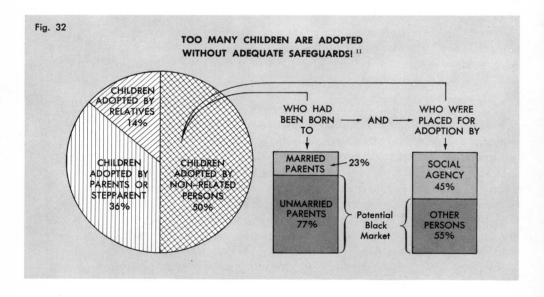

Fig. 32

TOO MANY CHILDREN ARE ADOPTED WITHOUT ADEQUATE SAFEGUARDS! [11]

CHILDREN ADOPTED BY RELATIVES 14%

CHILDREN ADOPTED BY PARENTS OR STEPPARENT 36%

CHILDREN ADOPTED BY NON-RELATED PERSONS 50%

WHO HAD BEEN BORN TO —→ AND —→ WHO WERE PLACED FOR ADOPTION BY

MARRIED PARENTS ◄— 23%

UNMARRIED PARENTS 77%

} Potential Black Market {

SOCIAL AGENCY 45%

OTHER PERSONS 55%

[10] Adapted from *Essentials of Adoption Law and Procedure,* Children's Bureau Publication Number 331, Federal Security Agency, Washington, D.C., 1949, pp. 2, 3.

[11] From *Children and Youth at the Midcentury—A Chart Book,* Health Publications Institute, Inc., Raleigh, N.C.

3. To protect the adopting parents from taking responsibility for children about whose heredity or capacity for physical and mental development they know nothing; and from later disturbance of their relationship to the child by natural parents whose legal rights had not been given full consideration.

Once the approved procedures for adoption have been followed, the parents may relax and bring up their chosen children as their own. Not all the answers in the heredity-environment controversy are in, but there is evidence that children tend to resemble their adoptive parents in many characteristics more closely than they do their biological parents.[12] From what we know of personality development we would expect this to be generally true. Usually one's "own baby" is not as carefully selected from the grab bag of genes as is the chosen baby at adoption! Parents mature enough to be ready to adopt a child take it as a privilege and a challenge, very much as emotionally mature parents have welcomed their babies from time immemorial.

You are not guaranteed perfectly normal children; there are unfortunate conditions that crop up from time to time in the finest families. Ever since the Eugenics Society was established in London in 1908, men and women have been interested in doing what they could to protect the unborn generations from known difficulties. Denmark now has a complete register of all cases of known hereditary disease, such as hemophilia and achondroplasia. Similar registers are being compiled for certain districts in the British Isles.[13] In the United States, genetics clinics and counselors are beginning to be available.[14]

There are some hereditary tendencies that, detected early enough, can be ameliorated. "For example, it is known that a particular abnor-

Genetic counseling and eugenics

---

[12] See especially F. N. Freeman, K. J. Holzinger, and B. C. Mitchell, "The Influence of Environment on the Intelligence, School Achievement, and Conduct of Foster Children," *27th Yearbook of the Society for the Study of Education,* 1928, Part I, pp. 103–217; H. H. Newman, F. N. Freeman, and K. J. Holzinger, *Twins: A Study of Heredity and Environment,* University of Chicago Press, 1937; Anne Roe and Barbara Burks, *Adult Adjustment of Foster Children of Alcoholic and Psychotic Parentage and the Influence of the Foster Home,* Yale University Section on Alcohol Studies, 1945; Harold Skeels, "Mental Development of Children in Foster Homes," *Journal of Consulting Psychology,* Vol. 2, 1938, pp. 33–43; Marie Skodak, "Intellectual Development of Children in Foster Homes," in *Child Behavior and Development* by Barker, Kounin, and Wright (eds.), McGraw-Hill, 1943, Chap. 16; and R. S. Woodworth, "Heredity and Environment: A Critical Survey of Recently Published Material on Twins and Foster Children," *Social Science Research Council Bulletin,* 1941.

[13] Reported in an editorial in *Biological and Human Affairs,* London, October, 1957.

[14] See Appendix A.

mal gene, when found in both parents, can produce a disease called *phenylketonuria.* This accounts for 2 to 5 per cent of all cases of mental retardation. It is now known that this type of mental retardation can be prevented by giving the child a special diet early in life." [15]

Even more familiar is the routine testing of Rh blood types of prospective parents. When the mother-to-be is Rh-negative and the prospective father is Rh-positive, the mother's blood is checked throughout the pregnancy for the presence of possible antibodies that might result in *erythroblastosis fetalis* in the baby. When the condition is suspected to exist, preparations are made before delivery to transfuse the new-born's blood if indicated, thus greatly increasing the baby's chance for healthy survival.

You concern yourself with eugenics when you honestly face the strengths and weaknesses in your family background, when you choose as wisely as you can the marriage partner who will be your children's other parent, and when you tap those resources near you, through your physician or hospital, where questions of your child's heredity may be explored.

Healthy babies born of good stock to couples who sincerely want them and intelligently plan for their arrival are the hope of the nation and the joy of their parents.

READINGS

Boss, Helen and Carl, *If You Adopt a Child.* New York: Holt, 1957.

Children's Bureau, *Essentials of Adoption Law and Procedure.* Washington, D.C.: Federal Security Agency, 1949, Publication #331.

Davis, M. Edward, *Natural Child Spacing: The Body Temperature Method for Having Children When You Want Them.* Garden City, N.Y.: Hanover House, 1953.

Fishbein, Morris, and Ruby Jo Reeves Kennedy (eds.), *Modern Marriage and Family Living.* New York: Oxford University Press, 1957, Part Four, "Conception, Pregnancy, and Childbirth."

Goodrich, Frederick W., Jr., *Natural Childbirth, a Manual for Expectant Parents.* New York: Prentice-Hall, 1950.

Guttmacher, Alan, *The Story of Human Birth.* New York: Pelican, 1947.

Hammons, Helen G., *Heredity Counseling.* American Eugenics Society, 230 Park Avenue, New York 17, N.Y., 1959.

Kinsey, Alfred C., Paul Gebhard, Wardell Pomeroy, Clyde Martin, and Cornelia Christenson, *Pregnancy, Birth and Abortion.* New York: Harper, 1958.

Maternity Center Association, *A Baby Is Born.* Maternity Center Association, 48 East 92nd Street, New York 28, N.Y., 1957.

---

[15] "New Clinic Guides Parents Wary of Hereditary Flaws," *Chicago Daily News,* October 24, 1957.

Museum of Science and Industry, *The Miracle of Growth*. Urbana: University of Illinois Press, 1950.

Osborn, Frederick, *Preface to Eugenics* (Rev. Ed.). New York: Harper, 1951.

Potter, Edith, *Fundamentals of Human Reproduction*. New York: McGraw-Hill, 1948.

————, *Rh*. Chicago: Yearbook Publishers, 1947.

Raymond, Louise, *Adoption and After*. New York: Harper, 1955.

Scheinfeld, Amram, *The New You and Heredity*. Philadelphia: Lippincott, 1950.

19 Having Children

Why have children?

When should you have a baby?

How much do children cost?

What do you need to know about pregnancy?

How is pregnancy a family affair?

How does it feel to become parents?

Can grandparents be assets?

WANTING children is as natural as wanting a mate and is a normal manifestation of your growth as a person. For the couple ready for this step, having a baby is a supremely satisfying experience. There is more to having a child than just wanting it, however. This chapter is concerned with the preparations and adjustments couples make in readying themselves for parenthood.

Why Have Children?

Powerful physical, psychological, and social forces drive us into the experience of parenthood. No substitute has been devised to return satisfactions equal to those received from bearing and rearing children. One expert summarizes the fundamental gratification of pregnancy, childbirth, and child rearing for women when he writes: "The bearing and rearing of children is woman's greatest achievement and the climax of her erotic expression . . . not only her greatest joy, but the source of her greatest power."[1] Having a family is a fulfillment of a couple's desire to establish a home of their own.

---

[1] Karl Menninger, *Love against Hate*, New York: Harcourt, Brace, 1942, p. 52.

Studies of both college and noncollege young people indicate that they are looking forward eagerly to parenthood. Increasingly, both boys and girls are signing up for courses in child care and are becoming intellectually interested in parenthood long before they are ready chronologically to become parents.

How do you explain such interest in having babies? One explanation is that each one of us has played the role of parent in childhood play groups and in his daydreams for years. When we marry it seems only right and natural that we should have children in our family. This expectation is derived from having been reared in a family and having learned so satisfyingly the parental roles.

Social pressures add their weight to bring couples around to starting a family. It is the thing to do after a few months of marriage. Other couples married about the same time blossom forth with baby carriages and beaming smiles, leaving laggards feeling strangely empty and fruitless. Bridge table and back-yard discussion among women, and golf and office conversation among men, center on first teeth, bright sayings, and recent accomplishments of babies. Parents of the newly married are reminded of their desire to become grandparents and may exert their influence in that direction. Attractive advertisements in magazines and daily papers are another insidious force in stimulating interest—picture after picture shows winsome cherubs clothed in beguiling infant-wear, eating healthful cereal, and sleeping under downy quilts. No wonder the childless couple conclude that "all the world is having babies and we should have one too."

More than one half of divorcing couples (55 per cent) have no children according to most recent official figures.[2] There is little question but what the relative frequency of divorce is greater for families without children than for families with children. Yet, the presence of children is not necessarily a deterrent to divorce. Monahan reminds us that research studies of the relationship between marital adjustment and childlessness are at odds with one another, and concludes after a careful study of existing figures, "A more complete answer to the question of the relationship between marital instability and children must await the compilation of more refined data on divorce, desertion, and domestic discord, and the characteristics of stable families in the population as a whole."[3] It is possible that in most cases both divorce and

---

[2] Paul C. Glick, *American Families*, New York: Wiley, 1957, p. 140. See also Paul H. Jacobson, "Differentials in Divorce by Duration of Marriage and Size of Family," *American Sociological Review*, April, 1950, Vol. 15, pp. 235–244.

[3] Thomas P. Monahan, "Is Childlessness Related to Family Stability?" *American Sociological Review*, August, 1955, Vol. 20, No. 4, pp. 446–456.

childlessness result from more fundamental factors in the marital relationship. Children may be seen as symbolic of both the permanence of the marriage relationship and a high valuation of family life.

Informal polls of college students on a number of campuses in recent years find that today's young men and women want to have larger families than those from which they come. When asked how many children they plan to have, present-day college students typically reply "three or four," with a considerable percentage saying they want even larger families.

Reviewing the number of recent surveys of goals and values among business and professional people, as well as college students, David Riesman [4] finds that home and family life top the list of what Americans want out of life. This high valuation on domesticity means, among other things, that children are important both in themselves, and as fulfilling the American man's and woman's dreams of living in the private world of a home of their own surrounded by their children.

This may somewhat account for the phenomenal increase in the birth

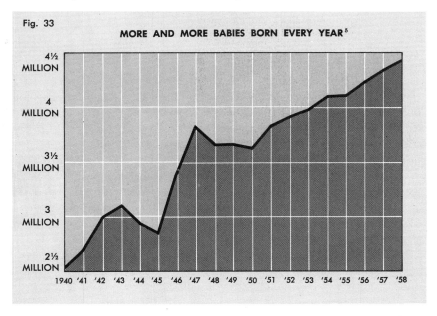

Fig. 33

MORE AND MORE BABIES BORN EVERY YEAR [5]

---

[4] David Riesman, Mandel Hall lecture series, University of Chicago, January–February, 1958.

[5] 1940–1957 U.S. Office of Vital Statistics, estimates by *U.S. News and World Report* Economic Unit, from "More and More Babies Born Every Year," *U.S. News and World Report*, January 3, 1958, p. 49.

rate that began with World War II. From around 2.6 million in 1940, births rose to more than 3 million by 1943. There was a slight decline in the birth rate in 1944 and 1945 when approximately 8 million American men were overseas. Then, with the war's end, the baby boom grew and grew. In 1954 the United States counted more than 4 million new babies for the first time. In 1957 some 4.3 million babies arrived and in 1958 the number of new babies was even greater.

Why so many babies? (1) There are more women in the childbearing ages of 15 to 44 (one third more than in the early 1930's); (2) A larger proportion of women are having children (1 out of every 6 now, in contrast to 1 in 8 in a typical year in the '30's); (3) An increase in the number of families having two or more children (second and third children have been at the highest rate since the 1920's); (4) Economic prosperity with jobs available for both men and women; (5) Spiraling growth in population as bumper crops of children mature, marry, and have babies of their own. It is estimated that in the 1970's the babies of the 1950's will begin to marry at the rate of about 3 million a year. Births then will rise to above 6 million a year, bringing the total population to around 240 million (see Fig. 33).

When Should You Have a Baby?

Many couples need time to work out the adjustments of a new marriage before adding pregnancy and its complications. First, the couple needs to adjust to living as two, to work out the routines of marriage and establish firmly the unity of the relation. All told, this process may take several months.

There are dangers in postponing the first baby too long. Better and more costly furniture, automobiles, travel, can easily become so established a part of the budget that children may never find a place. The young wife who works to save money for a family may find that her earnings serve only to advance the couple to a plane of living which they are reluctant to relinquish in favor of a baby.

Studies of Dr. Nicholson Eastman at Johns Hopkins University indicate that the age of the mother is of great importance in the bearing and delivering of babies. The decade between twenty and thirty in the woman's life is the optimum period for childbearing. The older the mother above thirty, the more dangerous is childbearing both for her and for the child.

Another important factor to consider is the readiness of the mother for a baby. A teen-age girl is rarely sufficiently grown up herself to sincerely want a baby and be able to love it and care for it properly. The older woman likewise faces emotional difficulties in relating herself to her first baby. If she has wanted one for years, her final joy in having it may make for more possessive attachment than is good for the child. If she has been long postponing the baby's arrival, she may not really want one when it does arrive. Her ways may be fixed and her life routinized along other channels which may make it difficult to accept a child fully into the household.

The time of year may be a factor to consider in deciding when to have a baby. Since babies are especially susceptible to respiratory diseases and food infections during the early months of life, the autumn is a more desirable season than midsummer or winter. The Children's Bureau finds that the death rate of tiny babies is highest during July and August, especially in those parts of the country where refrigeration is not universally available. When the couple is prepared to provide adequate care for the infant, the seasonal factor may be of less importance than other matters of personal and family convenience.

The time to have a baby is when you want it! More important than all external factors is the genuine desire of both husband and wife for the baby. Child development studies have shown without doubt that being wanted is of primary importance in the well-being of the child. When a couple is ready and eager for children, then is the time to have them.

How Much Do Children Cost?

Children are expensive. They may have been an economic asset back on the farm where "a kid could earn his keep around the place." Today children are an economic liability in most families. Yet, they are not "luxury goods" that only the rich can afford. On the contrary, families with the most children are in low and moderate income brackets.[6]

The cost of rearing a child in higher income families is proportionately higher than in more modest brackets. The Metropolitan Life Insurance Company, using data for the most part issued by the National Resources Planning Board and the Bureau of Labor Statistics, has carefully compared the item-by-item costs of rearing a child to the age of eighteen in two types of American families: those having an income of $2,500 a year, and those with an income of from $5,000 to $10,000 a year. Every item but food shows a considerable proportionate increase at higher income levels, while expenditures for education, medical care, transportation, and recreation show the greatest increases. If interest on the investment and cost of burial are added, this study con-

---

[6] Eleanor H. Bernert, *America's Children*, New York: Wiley, 1958, p. 40.

cludes, "the total cost of bringing up a child to the age of eighteen in families with an income of $5,000 to $10,000 a year averages $20,785. This figure does not, however, include the cost of public education and other services furnished by the community, nor the value of the personal services of the mothers." [7]

In addition to costing money, babies make drastic changes in the pattern of daily living, especially for those young people who heretofore have been relatively footloose and fancy free. If the couple wish to rationalize postponement, they can find reasons aplenty for dodging the restrictions and responsibilities that babies inevitably bring. Husbands accustomed to the undivided attention of a wife will be unwilling to share with the newcomer. Wives who enjoy the role of "just keeping my husband happy" will rebel at the prospects of long lines of diapers. Moreover, city dwellers find it especially difficult to find apartment space when they have little children.

Discouraging as all these factors of cost and disrupted routines and housing would seem to be, the fact remains that a great many people do still have children. Children may be expensive, but it looks as though they are here to stay—a vital part of the American way of life.

What Do You Need to Know about Pregnancy?

Not every sex intercourse ends in pregnancy. A couple may be married for some time before conditions are just right for conception to take place. Both live sperm and egg must be present. The pathways that bring them together must be clear. And the timing of copulation must be such that the sperm reaches the egg while it is still in the tube (less than one full day's acceptance each month) in order for impregnation to take place.

Presumptive signs

The woman may diagnose pregnancy herself by the appearance of a certain combination of symptoms. No symptom is conclusive by itself, but taken together they give her the basis for seeking definite confirmation in a medical examination.

The cessation of menstruation is usually the earliest and most im-

---

[7] *Statistical Bulletin* (New York: Metropolitan Life Insurance Company), January, 1944. NOTE: Since these figures, the most recent available according to a personal communication from Louis Dublin, former Statistician, the Metropolitan Life Insurance Company, are for 1935–36 price levels, and so markedly below those at midcentury, we read with interest from the same authority that, with a fixed income in a period of rising costs, the cost of bringing up a child will be raised by only a relatively small amount. Louis I. Dublin and Alfred Lotka, *The Money Value of a Man*, New York: Ronald Press, 1946, p. 57, footnote.

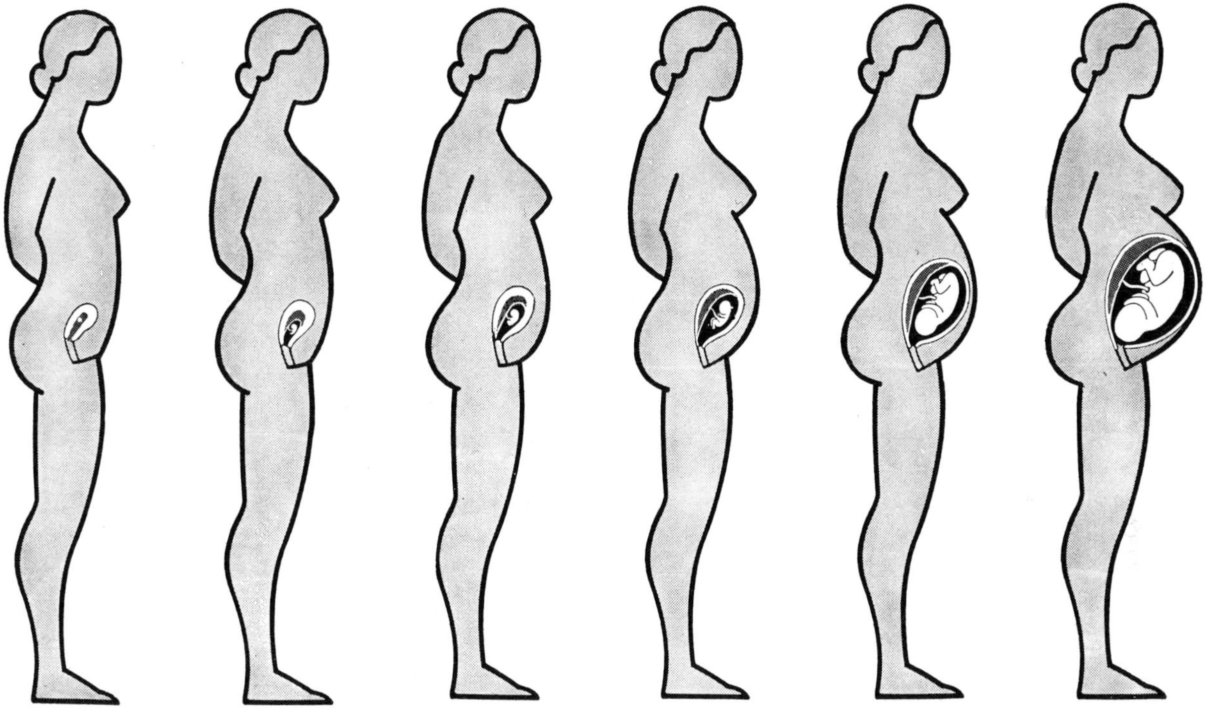

From *Life and Growth* by Alice V. Keliher (Appleton-Century)

Fig. 34 PREGNANCY

portant sign of pregnancy. When a healthy married woman who has been menstruating regularly suddenly misses a period, it is a good indication that pregnancy may have occurred. Occasionally a woman has one or two scanty menstrual periods after conception has taken place. More frequently, the menstrual period may be delayed by a variety of causes—change in climate, certain diseases, nervous tension, fear of or extreme desire for pregnancy.

Another symptom which appears in about two thirds of all women in early pregnancy is morning sickness. The pregnant woman will experience waves of nausea for a few hours in the morning, but even this symptom may be caused by other conditions and is only a presumptive sign of pregnancy.

A third symptom is a change in the breasts of the woman. Many women sense a fullness and tenderness of the breasts early in pregnancy, accompanied by a change in pigmentation of the nipple.

Frequency of urination is also an early presumptive sign of pregnancy. The tendency diminishes as the uterus rises in the pelvis and the bladder is no longer so closely associated with the enlarging uterus.

The married woman who experiences a missed menstrual period, who feels nauseated for a while in the morning, who is aware of changes in her breasts, and who feels the urge to urinate frequently may well presume that she is pregnant.

Pregnancy tests

The woman may receive definite confirmation or denial of her condition from her physician, who will conduct certain tests before making a diagnosis. He will note changes in the uterus and changes in the coloring of the vaginal lining, and he may use one of several standard urine tests to establish the fact of pregnancy. These tests are based upon the changes in hormonal secretions in the urine of the pregnant woman which affect noticeably the development of the sex structures or function in small animals, such as frogs, rats, mice, or rabbits. The great advantage of these tests is that they are remarkably reliable very early in pregnancy. They are well worth the extra cost if the wife needs to be sure of her condition early in pregnancy. In most cases the urine tests are unnecessary for diagnosis; the experienced physician can usually detect pregnancy reliably by the other signs.

Positive signs

As the pregnancy continues, many other confirming signs appear. Changes in the abdomen, the cervix, the vagina, and the uterus become apparent. By the middle of the pregnancy the fetal heart sounds may be heard. Fetal movements within the uterus may be felt from the fifth month on. X-ray pictures show the outlines of the fetal skeleton after the twentieth week and are positive proof of pregnancy.

As soon as the fact of pregnancy is established, the question inevita-

bly arises as to just when the baby can be expected. Labor usually occurs about 280 days from the first day of the last menstruation. The
rule in most frequent use is the following: determine the first day of
the last menstruation, add seven days, and count ahead nine months.
The date arrived at, however, is only approximate. There may be a
leeway of two weeks either way. As one obstetrician put it, "If I could
know exactly when babies would arrive, I could take my vacations like
a normal man, and I could catch up on my sleep. An obstetrician leads
the life of a fire chief, constantly on call."

Since maternal care became universal in America, having a baby is *Maternal care*
no longer the dangerous experience that it once was. The chief causes
of maternal death are infection, hemorrhage, and toxemia, and can be
avoided today by early diagnosis and regular supervision of the pregnancy and birth as well as of the *post partum* period. That is why
there is such a striking decrease in maternal mortality associated with
births in hospitals (see Fig. 35).

Ideally the couple should have gone to a physician for a thorough
physical examination before marriage. The physician would note at
that time any remedial operation which might need to be performed
before children should be conceived. If some time elapses between

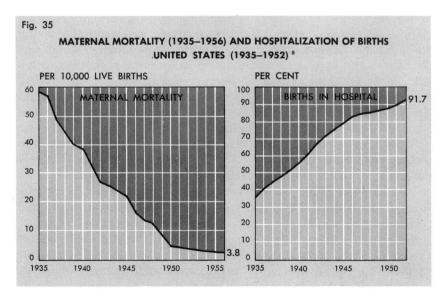

Fig. 35

MATERNAL MORTALITY (1935–1956) AND HOSPITALIZATION OF BIRTHS
UNITED STATES (1935–1952) [8]

[8] From Metropolitan Life Insurance Company *Statistical Bulletin,* July, 1951,
p. 2; Sept., 1957, p. 9; Aug., 1955, p. 8.

marriage and the time the couple is ready to conceive, another visit should be arranged with the physician. His go-ahead sign is based on careful check-up paralleling the investigations which took place in the premarital examination. As soon as the woman suspects that she may be pregnant she should again put herself under the care of a reliable physician. After making a thorough physical examination from head to foot, he will take pelvic measurements to see if normal delivery or Caesarian section may be indicated by the position and size of the opening between the pelvic bones. Periodically through the pregnancy he will check the patient's blood, urine, rate of gain in weight, heart rate, and blood pressure. He will note the progress of the baby's growth, even though his major concern is to keep track of the mother's health. These are factors which are all-important for the well-being of the mother and the baby. Maternal care starts, then, before conception takes place and ends after the baby has been delivered and checked over and the mother is back on her feet again.

You and your doctor

Selecting a doctor whose education, training, and experience will assure both mother and baby the kind of care they need is not easy for the couple newly established in a strange town. Neighbors' recommendations over the back fence are not reliable. Far more adequate help may be secured by calling the best hospital in the community and getting its list of physicians who deliver babies. Cities that have family welfare agencies, maternal health societies, and medical societies will offer other sources of information. The couple unable to tap any of these local resources may write to the American Board of Obstetrics and Gynecology, 1015 Highland Boulevard, Pittsburgh, Pennsylvania, for a listing of doctors in or near their community that have been certified by the Board. From such a list a choice may be made on the basis of convenience and personal preference.

Many smaller towns and most rural communities do not have obstetricians. A well-trained general practitioner can meet the obstetrical needs of most families successfully if he or she has the full cooperation of the couple. Pregnancy is a normal function requiring only regular supervision to keep the mother well.

The couple's confidence in the doctor is very important. If he performs his function well, he will need to know many intimate details of the couple's life together and will want to advise them about many of their daily habits, including eating, resting, recreation, vacations, sexual relations, etc. The wife will need to trust her doctor implicitly so that she will eagerly follow his directions as her pregnancy progresses. It is helpful, however, to understand the reasons for the advice given by the physician. The husband must recognize that this relationship between his wife and the doctor does not exist to deprive him of his wife's full companionship, but to insure her health. Whenever possible, it is helpful for the husband to go with his wife on the first visit to the doctor, so that he may have a part in the general arrangements. At that time he may ask the doctor what the cost will be and agree on the payments to be made. The couple may want to ask about such things as:

1. The general condition of the wife and the prognosis for the pregnancy.
2. The time when the baby may be expected.
3. Advice about diet, exercise, clothing, sex intercourse, bathing, rest, trips, etc.
4. Frequency of the wife's visits to the doctor during her pregnancy.
5. The hospital the physician takes his patients to, and how arrangements there are made.
6. Anesthetics that the doctor uses to relieve pain at birth.

One obstetrician gives his expectant mothers a little manual of directions in which he specifies the conditions under which he is to be called:

Notify Your Physician at Once in Case of:
1. Bleeding or brownish discharge from the vagina
2. Cramps
3. Excessive vomiting
4. Severe pain in lower abdomen
5. Headaches
6. Disturbances of vision
7. Swelling of feet and, particularly, of face and hands
8. Scanty urine or bloody urine
9. Persistent constipation
10. Sore throat or cough
11. Marked shortness of breath
12. Chills and fever
13. Sudden escape of fluid from vagina

Your personal questions about the nature of pregnancy and childbirth may be discussed with your physician. The doctor will be glad to explain why a mother's experiences cannot affect her unborn child, why certain infrequent abnormalities and markings are unavoidable, and why no one can accurately predict the sex of the child before its birth or determine its sex before conception, and why the mother's attitude and feelings are important for her health and well-being.

Pain in childbirth

Childbirth is usually painful. The pains which result from the contractions that open the cervix are sharp and increase in intensity and duration for several hours. The pains which mark the expulsive contractions of the uterus are intense, probably the most excruciating pain women ever experience. The knowledge that the pains are helping her bring forth her own baby helps the woman bear the suffering and to forget its agony soon after delivery. Although through the years ways of relieving the pain of childbirth have been sought, no completely satisfactory, safe, and universally applicable method has yet been found. Some of the newer methods such as caudal anesthesia, hypnosis, twilight sleep, etc., may present hazards to mother or child under certain conditions. The wise couple discusses the question with their doctor who makes the final decision.

Natural Childbirth

Childbirth is a normal, natural process. Some doctors [9] believe that much of the mother's labor pain is the result of muscular tension associated with fear. The expectant mother is trained for "natural childbirth" by instruction in what to expect (thus relieving unfounded anxieties), and by supervised exercise in the relaxation and control of pertinent muscle groups so that she may cooperate in the birth process more effectively.

How Is Pregnancy a Family Affair?

The man who said, "We are pregnant at our house," expressed the "we" feeling that is so important for both husband and wife during their period of expectancy. Pregnancy is a social condition quite as much as a biological state. It involves the adjustment of both the husband and the wife, their relatives, their children already born as well as those yet to come. Yes, even more, pregnancy is of importance to the community and to the state. We find more and more laws introduced to assert the interest of the commonwealth in healthy, robust families.

Pregnancy and childbirth can be a strain on immature young folk, but the experience can be and usually is a happy adventure for emotionally and socially mature people. They will show it in many ways. The husband who learns early how he may help will find that his role is not the anxious one portrayed in the cartoons of fathers nervously pacing waiting rooms. He may assume certain responsibilities of helping with the housework, plan recreational jaunts that are possible for his wife, make furniture for the new arrival, cooperate in maintaining the diet that the doctor has prescribed, and provide many other per-

---

[9] Grantly Dick Read, *Children without Fear*, New York: Harper, 1944.

sonal attentions that do much to ease the wife's burdens and to help him share more fully the experience.

More important than anything that the husband does is how he feels about the pregnancy and his expectant wife. If he is happy about it and proud of his wife, if he treats her as a real person and not as an invalid, he will be giving her the support that she needs from him. The pregnant woman may become self-conscious about her figure and general awkwardness as the pregnancy continues and may need her husband's reassurance of his continuing love and admiration. Jealousies and oversensitiveness about her husband's activities outside the family are frequent and may be recognized as resulting from the restrictions imposed by her pregnancy. Even though his wife is not able to participate freely in the activities he enjoys, the mature man will show that he values her companionship. Her silhouette may not be what it once was, but their pride and pleasure in being "in the family way" compensate both for some of the temporary cumbersomeness of the pregnancy.

Many couples openly enjoy their expectancy and take pleasure in thinking of themselves as parents-to-be. Men as well as women are eager to learn how babies are born and reared and cared for today. Classes for expectant parents are proving popular in many communities. Books on the subject of parenthood are read with new interest. Expectant parents are most receptive to teaching and find that study adds to their enjoyment of anticipation.

How Does It Feel to Become Parents?

Every time a first baby is born there is a new mother and a new father. Each must learn his or her new role in the family. Each now has new privileges and new responsibilities. Previous relationships change as each member of the family adapts and adjusts to the newcomer. Even the family of many children realigns itself every time another baby enters the circle. This stretching of the family ties is satisfying and challenging. But it is strenuous too.

There are at least three stages in getting used to a new baby. The first is the "flower and pink ribbons" stage. Mother is in her glory, bedecked in her best bed jacket, with roses on her table and solicitous friends and family asking after her little newcomer. Father, who has felt like a fifth wheel during the long days of the pregnancy and the interminable hours of labor and birth, now comes into his own as exuberant herald to all the world of the miracle that has happened. He

When the first baby comes

passes cigars to all the boys and showers this wonderful woman of his with tokens of his undying affection.

Not long after mother and baby have returned from the hospital, the second stage of parent-child relations is apparent. The exuberance of the first flush of parenthood gives way under the weight of daily diapers, lusty cries at 2:00 A.M., and the cleaning woman who didn't come. The insistent demands of a hungry baby break into the tenderest of moments of husband and wife. The mother's preoccupation with feedings and daily baths often seems to take precedence over diversions previously enjoyed by the couple. Let a friend suggest a movie or an evening out, and the chorus sounds from new mother and father alike, "What will we do with the baby?" Babies bring new responsibilities thick and fast, sometimes so fast that it takes quite a bit of readapting before things run smoothly around the little newcomer and his family.

Before very long the family has a helper or two. Aunt Molly is willing to come in and stay with the baby occasionally. Or a trustworthy baby sitter has been found who allows the new mother and father an occasional evening out to themselves. The routines which at first seemed so exacting settle down into comfortable schedules. Baby gets used to its food and sleeps straight through the night without whimper. Mother begins to feel more like herself now that she is around the house and doing her own work without getting too tired. It is fun wheeling baby to the store and back. Bath time has become a frolic for both mother and baby. Life is good again. The new family is really under way.

This characteristic cycle reappears in various forms again and again in the lifetime of the family. Enthusiasm and the sense of being in on a wonderful miracle of life occurs many times as parents take pride in their children. But the heavy weight of responsibility is constantly present; children *are* a responsibility. It takes many years to work through the ways and means of handling these obligations effectively and comfortably, but time is a great educator. And then comes the quiet satisfaction of being a family, the happy contentment so characteristic of parenthood.

When the husband is absent

It is sometimes necessary for the husband to be away from home during his wife's pregnancy. Unfortunate as this situation is, the mature couple can find much satisfaction in letters. Sharing the eagerness of anticipation, expressing the dreams of family reunion and the baby's future, choosing the baby's name, discussing detailed plans for the confinement and care of the baby for the first few weeks until the mother is able to undertake its full care herself—all these things bring a sense of partnership to the couple even though they are separated.

The prospective mother can reassure her husband about her condition by relaying accounts of her trips to the doctor, telling him what the prognosis is, how she is spending her time, and how she looks forward to her husband's return and the baby's arrival so that they can all be a real family.

One way to become a parent is to marry one. In these days when remarriage is common, it is not unusual for a man to find himself with not only a wife, but with a child or more as well, when he marries their mother. The stepmother so cruel and heartless in the fairy tale often turns out today to be a lovely person trying her best to win a place in the lives of the children of the man she married.

Marrying a ready-made family

Being a stepparent is not easy. After all, the others were there first. The children may be expected to cling to their original parent and to accept the new parent in a full-fledged parental status only after he or she has proven worthy. Jealousy and sibling rivalry that in other homes are but irksome interludes are apt in the stepparent's eyes to be insurmountable obstacles, green-eyed monsters that will not be tamed. Discipline administered with a casual hand by the "real parent" may seem like a threatening form of hostility or rejection in the hand of the stepmother or stepfather.

"Time is on your side" was never more true. Patience, understanding, and a willingness to wait and not force affection bring rewards of new family ties and renewed solidarity. Even teen-aged young people grow up and learn to love their stepparents; in fact that may be a good index of their growing maturity. As soon as parents and children seem ready, steps may be taken to adopt the stepchildren legally so that "your children" may be "our children" in the fullest, final sense.

Can Grandparents Be Assets?

Family solidarity at this time is often enhanced by the attention of the other relatives. Grandparents-to-be are especially interested in the newcomer. There is a sense of fulfillment in anticipating one's grandchildren that even parenthood is said to miss. It is fortunate that the American trend toward exclusion of members of the extended family from the intimate father-mother-child constellation has been reversed with the increase in births in recent years. Wisely managed, grandparents are real assets to the new family. When help is hard to hire, a visiting grandmother who sees the new family through the birth and confinement is a godsend. When new habits must be established around the new little family member, the going will be rough for the inexperienced parents. The perspective and the practical help of a grandmother who knows the way through the routine of bathing and feeding schedules is a real boon. When the new father and mother feel swamped with their new responsibilities, it is comforting to be able to lean for a bit on parents and to take advantage of their presence to slip out for an evening's fun as a couple once again.

THE WAY OUT [10]

If baby-sitters charge a lot,
For services they render,
Call Grandma in to mind the tot,
For she's the legal tender.
M. M. PARRISH

To be sure, grandparents have limitations and should be used sparingly. Child-training methods do change. But if Grandma rocks the baby there are some child care specialists who will support her. The couple do want to feel that they are on their own and that they can manage their own family in their own way. But there are few in-law problems if the family members are well-adjusted persons.[11] Modern grandmothers are as eager as their daughters and daughters-in-law to follow modern methods of child care. Together the two generations can greet the newcomer with a united front that promises well for his future.

Having children is just about the most exciting and satisfying thing that can happen to a family. The more it is shared and enjoyed and enhanced by intelligent planning, the more satisfying it becomes.

READINGS

Becker, Howard, and Reuben Hill (eds.), *Family, Marriage and Parenthood.* Boston: Heath, 1955, Chapter 15.

Blood, Robert O., Jr., *Anticipating Your Marriage.* Glencoe, Illinois: Free Press, 1955, Chapters 15 and 16.

Davis, M. Edward, *Natural Child Spacing.* Garden City, New York: Hanover House, 1953.

Duvall, Evelyn Millis, *Family Development.* Chicago: Lippincott, 1957, Chapter 7.

Fishbein, Morris, and Ruby Jo Reeves Kennedy (eds.), *Modern Marriage and Family Living.* New York: Oxford University Press, 1957, Part Four.

Genné, William, *Husbands and Pregnancy: The Handbook for Expectant Fathers.* New York: Association Press, 1956.

Grinstein, Alexander, and Editha Sterba, *Understanding Your Family.* New York: Random House, 1957, Chapter 7.

---

[10] From *The Saturday Evening Post,* April 28, 1951.

[11] Evelyn Millis Duvall, *In-Laws: Pro and Con,* New York: Association Press, 1954.

Himes, Norman, and Donald Taylor, *Your Marriage*. New York: Rinehart, 1955. Chapters 20, 21, and 22.

Jackson, Edith B., and Genevieve Trainham (eds.), *Family Centered Maternity and Infant Care*. New York: Josiah Macy, Jr., Foundation, 1950.

Koos, Earl Lemon, *Marriage*. New York: Holt, 1953, Chapter 10.

Landis, Judson, Thomas Poffenberger, and Shirley Poffenberger, "The Effects of First Pregnancy upon the Sexual Adjustment of 212 Couples," *American Sociological Review*, Vol. 15, December, 1950, pp. 767–772.

———, ———, and ———, "Intent toward Conception and the Pregnancy Experience," *American Sociological Review*, Vol. 17, No. 5, October, 1952, pp. 616–620.

Lewis, Abigail, *An Interesting Condition: The Diary of a Pregnant Woman*. Garden City, New York: Doubleday, 1950.

Newton, Niles, *Maternal Emotions*. New York: Paul Hoeber, 1955.

Rowland, Loyd W., *Pierre the Pelican, Prenatal Series*. New Orleans: Louisiana Association for Mental Health, 1528 Jackson Avenue, New Orleans 13, Louisiana.

20 Bringing Up Your Children

How do you feel about having children?

Will your child be a brat?

What kind of discipline works?

What are children after?

What kind of sex education?

What helps a child feel secure?

Y ou have already thought about what it will be like to have children. Quite possibly you have argued with your friends about various methods of child rearing. You may have reacted strongly to the way in which you see children being raised and have said in no uncertain terms, "Believe me, when I have children, I'll bring them up differently." In your heart-to-heart talks, the question of children is bound to come up as you find out how you each feel about them.

How Do You Feel about Having Children?

The chances are you want children of your own. You very possibly have dreamed for years about how fine it will be to be settled in a home of your own with your children around you. You have grown up at a time when children are highly valued. The birth rate in this country since 1940 has outdistanced all expectations. Most young people of college age plan to have several children and look forward to parenthood with eagerness.

Your own personal experience with children determines your feelings about them. Your family relationships as a child may have prepared you for parenthood with a warm sense of security with children. Your education and special training may have helped you develop effective

393

skills for getting along well with children. Or you may approach the experience of having your own children with fear and trembling.

Parenthood as a crisis

The arrival of children makes a family of a marriage. When the first child comes, marriage undergoes a drastic shift from that of a couple living in an adult world to that of a family unit organized around meeting the needs of a completely dependent baby. Interviews with young couples reveal that four out of five (83 per cent) report extensive or severe crisis in adjusting to their first child. The interpretation is that these couples have so romanticized parenthood that they are completely unprepared for the realities of living with an infant. One young mother in the study put it neatly when she said, "We knew where babies came from, but we didn't know *what they were like.*"[1]

Shifting scenes in parenthood

As children grow, so do the parents in rapid succession as stage follows stage in family development. By the time you master the intricacies of caring for a tiny infant, he is a toddler with a world of his own to conquer that requires a whole new set of skills for the parents. When you have finally baby-proofed the house to safeguard the child and protect your things from his explorations, he is out in the yard with the other children. Before you know it he is in school and you as a parent are caught in a round of new activities with the P.T.A., scouts, Sunday school, trips to the zoo, and helping with homework. Puberty and adolescence come along before you are quite ready for their turmoil, and then before you get the house in order the youngster is off to college or marriage or the first job, leaving you with an entirely new role to perfect.

Child-rearing practices have changed so rapidly in recent decades that few adults today feel comfortable rearing children as they were brought up. Within the memory of most of us the pendulum has swung from the rigid spare-the-rod-and-spoil-the-child philosophy to child-centered permissiveness. In the 1920's parents were told to treat their children like young adults, to always be completely objective, and to never hug, kiss, or indulge them.[2] By the 1950's, parents were told that children need love, and lots of it. Expert opinion on methods of handling children have undergone such drastic shifts[3] that a great many of us do not know what to think.

---

[1] E. E. LeMasters, "Parenthood as Crisis," *Marriage and Family Living*, Vol. 19, No. 4, November, 1957, pp. 352–355.

[2] John B. Watson, *Psychological Care of Infant and Child.* New York: Norton, 1928, pp. 81–82.

[3] See the documented review of the changing trends in discipline in Grace Langdon and Irving Stout, *The Discipline of Well-Adjusted Children.* New York: Day, 1952, pp. 3–47.

The conflicting philosophies of child rearing have caused some people to act as though bringing up children is all a matter of opinion, and that one man's ideas are as good as another's. As a matter of fact, a great deal is known about why children act the way they do and what kind of rearing works best in helping children grow up effectively.

Will Your Child Be a Brat?

As much as anything else, you probably want to avoid having one of your children become a little brat. You look around you and see disagreeable children who are so obviously spoiled that you grit your teeth and vow that no child of yours will get away with such behavior. Take Jimmy as a case in point.

Jimmy was described by his mother as having become the "brat" of the neighborhood. At home, he was the center of the family and in one way or another got what he wanted. He was unable to accept any kind of disagreement or criticism, and distorted situations to fit his own purposes and interests. His mother stated that he often blamed others for his mistakes. He refused entirely to admit his responsibility for numerous accidents which occurred at home, like breakage of glasses and china. He accused his mother of giving his baby sister more and better toys than she got for him, made constant demands and plagued his mother until she gave in to his wishes. He refused to cooperate when his parents tried to teach him how to skate, ride a bicycle, and play baseball, insisting that he already knew enough to do these things, though he was never able to demonstrate his skill.

He often yelled at other children in the neighborhood until he got his way. Gradually, they avoided him and refused his invitations. When he approached them, they would run in the opposite direction. Sometimes he came home crying. He would insist that his mother defend him against other children, and when his mother did not respond immediately he would have a temper tantrum. When he was frustrated he often sucked his thumb and masturbated. He refused to eat most foods that were cooked for the family and "suffered" during the meal until some special treat was offered. He was always slow in getting ready for school, so tardy that his mother usually drove him, though the school was only a short distance. He made so many demands at bedtime that getting him settled was always a long and involved procedure. The mother felt that she had to do something about him as he was controlling everyone in the family.

For the father, the sun rose and set with Jimmy. He was happy to give him anything he wished. He would beg Jimmy's permission to go on an errand, read the newspaper, write a letter, or watch a particular program on television. In short, his father always gave in to him.

The teacher's note to the parents stated that Jimmy was the major disrupting influence in her classroom. He was described as a lazy and irresponsible boy. To the therapist the teacher reported that Jimmy was failing in school. He rarely completed an assignment, talked whenever he wished, and got out of his seat at inappropriate times, in the middle of special announcements or when the teacher was presenting new skills. . . .[4]

The children that you know may or may not be as spoiled as Jimmy obviously is, but chances are you find their disrespect annoying, their irresponsibility exasperating, and their unwillingness to cooperate frustrating. Beyond the unpleasantness of the "spoiled brat's" behavior lies our concern for his welfare as a person. We see a child like Jimmy as unhappy—with himself and with his world. We feel that he is not growing up wholesomely and well. We fear for his future and the kind of person he is developing into. What will he become? A truant later on, a juvenile delinquent, perhaps?

Back to the woodshed

There are loud voices raised against the "coddling" of children. The advocates of the "get-tough-with-them" school of thought say in effect, "I was never allowed to act the way these modern kids do. One step out of line when I was a kid, and I was marched out to the woodshed. I obeyed, or else." They imply that the only way to bring up children is to "break their will" early so that they "will know who's boss." They point to our rising rates of juvenile delinquency as an alarmingly clear indication that modern methods of child guidance just do not work.

Yet, those who know children best do not agree. An experienced children's judge, Justice of the Domestic Relations Court in New York City since 1935, says,

I have read literally scores of studies of the effect of punishment on children. Not a single one gives comfort to the "get tough" approach. Over and over, they show just the opposite. One such study clearly proves, for instance, that where parents constantly resort to corporal punishment or other violence, the incidence of delinquency is higher. Another, covering adolescents in a criminal court, disclosed that "their behavior was generally hostile and whatever adjustment they had achieved was based on fear of punishment rather than awareness of responsibility." [5]

A review of the history of child-rearing practices in the United States over the past two centuries or more finds two main attitudes vying for support. The first, originating in Calvinism, appeared in European in-

---

[4] Clark E. Moustakas, "Spoiled Behavior in a School-Age Child," *Child Study*, Vol. 35, No. 1, Winter, 1957–1958, pp. 18–20.

[5] Justine Wise Polier, *Back to What Woodshed?* Public Affairs Pamphlets No. 232, 1956, p. 14.

fluences toward strictness at the end of the nineteenth century and still later in this country in Watson's *behaviorism*. The second is the "gentle nurture" attitude advocated by Rousseau, Froebel, G. Stanley Hall, and recent authorities in child development who see children as developing persons with tremendous capacities for growth that are best realized in friendly, encouraging situations. The first approach calls upon parents to see to it that their children conform. The second sees parents as loving and lovable models of good living with whom the child will identify.

Rearing children is not simple. It requires a great deal of study. Being an extremist can get you, and your child, into a great deal of trouble. But just what middle road to follow must be learned—in action. You do not need to fear that your children will be brats if you treat them kindly. The issue is not whether to be "tough" or "soft," but rather what kind of discipline is effective.

What Kind of Discipline Works?

None but the most rabid extremist believes that children can be reared without any discipline. The only question is what kind of discipline works. How, for instance, have particularly well-adjusted, healthy, happy children been disciplined? This was the question two workers set themselves to answer in a study of 261 school-age children, selected by their teachers and principals as well-adjusted. Any child might qualify if the answer to each of the following eight questions was "Yes":

1. Does he play well with other children?
2. Does he appear to be a happy child?
3. Does he have reasonable control over his emotions?
4. Can he be depended upon?
5. Is he achieving somewhere near his capacity?
6. Is he able to think for himself?
7. Is he kind and helpful to teachers and classmates?
8. Is he liked and respected by his peers?

The children selected by their teachers and principals as well-adjusted were distributed from kindergarten through college. They came from all kinds of families in all types of neighborhoods. Their parents' ideas about child rearing varied greatly, although they all agreed that children need discipline and responsibility, "but most important of all is loving them and letting them know it, thinking of them as people and treating them so, appreciating what they do and trusting them and telling them so, and above all letting them know they are wanted." [6]

In a later volume summarizing the kind of discipline these well-adjusted children had had, the researchers conclude:

The discipline suggested by what the parents said has to do with outward actions, but first of all with inner thoughts, feelings, and motives since these govern actions. Finding out what is right and what is not is a part of it, with emphasis on wanting to do what is right. Being obedient is included, being obedient first to the parents' word, then to the basic laws of living with others, and finally to the underlying principles upon which those laws are founded. Building on strength is emphasized, with the premise that children want to be good. Rebuke, correction, punishment, and control are in the picture, but only as a means for accomplishing the discipline, not as the discipline itself, as they are often taken to be. The approach is from an understanding of the youngster, his characteristics and abilities, and the learning he needs and is ready for. The adult has a very important part, bringing as needed direction, counsel, help, correction, understanding, commendation, companionship, interest, confidence, and always a love that never needs to be questioned. [7]

Intensive interviewing of 379 American mothers of children from birth to kindergarten age was done by the staff of the Laboratory of Human Development of the Graduate School of Education of Harvard University to discover how mothers are bringing up their children. There was great variability in child-rearing patterns, making generalization difficult. It was clear that maternal warmth was beneficial. It was even more apparent that punishment was not effective in child rearing. The workers report,

The unhappy effects of punishment have run like a dismal thread through our findings. Mothers who punished toilet accidents severely ended up with bed-wetting children. Mothers who punished dependency to get rid of it had more dependent children than mothers who did not punish. Mothers who punished aggressive behavior severely had more aggressive children than mothers who punished lightly. They also had more dependent children. Harsh physical punishment was associated with high childhood aggressiveness and with the development of feeding problems.

Our evaluation of punishment is that *it is ineffectual over the long term as a technique for eliminating the kind of behavior toward which it is directed.* [8]

---

[6] Grace Langdon and Irving Stout, *These Well-Adjusted Children*, New York: Day, 1951, p. 157.

[7] Grace Langdon and Irving Stout, *The Discipline of Well-Adjusted Children*, New York: Day, 1952, pp. 209–210.

[8] Robert R. Sears, Eleanor Maccoby, Harry Levin, et al., *Patterns of Child Rearing*, Evanston, Illinois: Row, Peterson, 1957, p. 484.

But if you don't punish a child, what else can you do? If punishment does not work in controlling unfortunate behavior, what approaches are left to the parent?

In recent years there has been general recognition that all children at times feel hostile, rebellious, and mean. When they feel bad, they act bad, *unless*. . . . Understanding and implementing this "unless" provides the basis for a constructive approach to children's destructive tendencies. The rationale goes something like this: Feeling left out, frustrated, inadequate, or unloved makes a child feel mean. When a child feels mean, he wants to hurt something or someone. When he hurts with his aggression he feels worse than ever, because now his mean feelings are compounded with feelings of guilt and being still further on the "outs with his world."

Accept feelings, control behavior

The sensitive parent or teacher listens to what the child is saying with his words or actions and does not confuse him with its denial—"Of course you love the baby," "You know you'll get it right," "You should love your mother," "You're not afraid of such a little dog." Rather what the youngster is feeling is put into words—"Sometimes you don't like the baby," "You are cross because it won't come right," "Right now you are mad at Mother," "You are afraid of the puppy." By so mirroring his feelings the adult helps the youngster clarify his own honest emotions.

Putting the child's actual feelings into words helps him see that you accept him as he really is, and gives him the courage to see what it is that is troubling him. The next step is giving him some constructive channel for his feelings. When he has a "head of steam up" some safety valve must be provided or he'll "blow his top." Depending upon his age and interests, you hand him modeling clay, or you suggest he hammer his pegboard, or act out his problem, or talk it through, or have a round with his punching bag—to "get it out of his system" in active play or work. As Dorothy Baruch, the most articulate advocate of this approach, puts it, "When unwanted negative feelings have been emptied out sufficiently then warm and good positive feelings flow in." [9]

Destructive behavior is controlled so that the child is not allowed to hurt others, or himself, or to wantonly damage property. Even severely disturbed children are restrained during their tantrums so they will not compound their problems with violence.[10] The child is not allowed

---

[9] Dorothy Walter Baruch, *New Ways in Discipline*, New York: Whittlesey House, 1949, p. 45.

[10] Charles Seib and Alan Otten, "The Case of the Furious Children," *Harper's*, January, 1958, pp. 56–61. (Reporting on Fritz Redl's work at the National Institutes of Health Clinical Center, Bethesda, Maryland.)

to "run wild." His behavior is checked before it gets to a hurtful, destructive level. At the same time he is given the assurance of the desire to help on the part of the adult. He is accepted, even while what he is doing or is about to do is kept within acceptable bounds.

Diversion is better than restraint

It is far easier and much more pleasant to avoid a run-in with a child than to have a battle of wills with him. A ready example is found in the toddler's need to become acquainted with his world by getting into things around the house. With thoughtful preparation for his explorations, he can be protected from harm, and the house and its furnishings can be safeguarded during the period of child rearing. Such "child-proofing"[11] makes it possible to protect the little child and the more fragile things in the house without having to resort to continual punishment, restraint, and "No-No." A child can learn to respect those hazards that cannot be removed if they are not in too confusing array around him.

Restraining a youngster in trouble, or at the threshold of misbehavior, may be necessary if the adults in charge have not anticipated his problem. In everyday situations with normal children, parents can spot trouble brewing and ward it off before it strikes. The child's attention may be diverted from the hurtful to a harmless situation. Before he gets into a tantrum he can be bundled into his outdoor clothing for a romp in the park. He can be given a cooky while the baby gets his bottle. A thousand and one ingenious diversions are part of the methods an alert mother uses, almost without thinking, to keep her children within the boundaries of reasonable behavior.

There have to be many approaches. Some will work with one child, and not with another. Some children are compliant and tractable, others are stubborn and single-minded, some are energetic and "into everything," and others are more quiet and self-contained.

Every child is different

Research in child development has proven what every mother of several children has always known—that "no two children are alike." Prescott puts his finger on four factors that contribute to the uniqueness of each individual.

1. *Physical processes that affect the body and its operation.* The individual's inherited pattern of growth and the rate at which he matures physically, his rate of energy output and normal rhythm of activity and rest, his health history and habits, his physical handicaps and limitations, his skills in managing his body, his physical attractiveness and his grooming. Each

---

[11] For detailed listing of suggestions for child-proofing the house during the childbearing stage of the family life cycle, see Evelyn Millis Duvall, *Family Development,* Chicago: Lippincott, 1957, pp. 203–206.

of these affects the way others feel about him, and influences his own perception of himself and what he can do.

2. *Love relationships and the emotional climate in which he lives.* The individual's relationship to his mother, father, siblings, pets, and other adults, the emotional climate in which he lives are determined by all the interrelationships of his home. Given the full feeling of being loved, a child feels "emotionally secure" and can face the vicissitudes of life with courage and equanimity. Given doubt as to whether he is loved, he becomes emotionally insecure and his behavior is characterized by a continuing and pervasive anxiety about his own worth . . . A child's security or insecurity profoundly influences his concept of himself, his feelings about himself, and his capacity to accept and love others. The behavior he shows as a result of his "security" and his anxiety about himself influences the way other people think and feel about him and the kind of relationships others are willing to have with him.

3. *Cultural elements that the child internalizes from family, neighborhood, and community.* The culture he is raised in shapes his concepts of the world and of society. His language skills, his daily living habits influence his attitudes toward everything he experiences, his codes of conduct, his values and his goal definition. They give him his initial orientation in the universe. They influence his conceptions of himself and of others and his feelings about himself and his relationships to others. They form his concepts of right and wrong and shape his appreciation of what is beautiful. They establish his initial loyalties and teach him what he should strive toward. When the cultural elements that he internalizes are inconsistent, they generate mental and emotional conflicts. When cultural demands and expectancies are incompatible with his capacities or maturity level, they result in a sense of failure and inadequacy and engender doubts about himself. .

4. *Roles and status in the child society of his peers.* All children do not possess the knowledge, skills and personal characteristics necessary to win full and satisfying status among others. Some children become high-prestige persons and leaders; others become full belongers; others can be only "fringers," admitted to some roles but excluded from others to which they aspire. Some are isolated and have little or no significance to their fellows; still others are actively rejected by their ineffective or objectionable characteristics. The roles and status a child has in the group influence his feelings about himself and shape others' feelings about him.[12]

These four factors, complex as each is, operate each within the presence of the others in a dynamic constellation of interacting forces that give rise to a steady flow of motivations and feelings within the growing person. As the self develops it takes a hand in shaping its own des-

---

[12] Adapted from Daniel A. Prescott, *The Child in the Educative Process,* New York: McGraw-Hill, 1957, pp. 377–378.

tiny in characteristic ways that further make and keep each child a unique individual. Every gene in the hereditary make-up, every situation in the person's experience, every aspect of the emotional climate within which the child lives, every ambition and goal he sets for himself tends to make and maintain him as a person who is and must be different from all others.

Bossard and his staff find that no matter how large the family, each child finds and fits to himself a uniquely appropriate role that no one in the family has appropriated. This specialization of role is seen in the children of large families in eight main types: the responsible one, the popular one, the socially ambitious one, the studious one, the family isolate, the irresponsible one, the sickly one, and the spoiled one.[13] Such evidence suggests strongly that children are not only born different and grow differently, but that they literally *have to be different*. A

TABLE 24. *Children's Responses to Questions about Their Involvement in Family Activities* [14]

Questions	Responses				
	Always	Often	Sometimes	Seldom	Never
1. How much do your parents discuss with you what your family is going to do?	21%	35%	30%	10%	4%
2. Does your family talk over plans together?	25	24	37	10	4
3. How much do you help in choosing things to eat when you go to the grocery store with your parents?	9	22	40	20	9
4. Do you help decide what clothes to buy for yourself?	18	26	40	10	6
5. Are you praised when you do a job well at home?	25	25	35	10	5
6. Are you thanked for doing little extra jobs at home?	48	25	19	5	3
7. Do you have regular jobs to do at home?	Yes (72)		Usually (18)		No (10)
8. Do you think that you have too many jobs?	6		5		89

[13] James H. S. Bossard and Eleanor S. Boll, *The Large Family System*, Philadelphia: University of Pennsylvania Press, 1956, p. 221.

[14] Glenn R. Hawkes, Lee G. Burchinal, and Bruce Gardner, "Pre-Adolescents' Views of Some of Their Relations with Their Parents," *Child Development*, Vol. 28, No. 4, December, 1957, p. 394.

younger brother of the boy who was doing well in his music was heard to say, "No music lessons for me, I'm the ball-player of the family." The third daughter in another family could muster little enthusiasm for cooking in which her older sisters already excelled. In still another home, the parents report success in pointing out to their several children the ways in which each one is "best" in something.

The folly of unfavorably comparing one child with another is evident. Yet, how easy it is to say to a youngster, "Why don't you play nicely as your brother does?" or "If only you would cooperate and help the way the others do." If such adult proddings are ineffective, how can children's work and play be guided?

When Junior comes home from kindergarten to report that he knows what "cooperate" means—"It means you gotta do it," he has discovered a general adult desire for children to participate in group activities and work together rather than at cross-purposes. Parents often regret that when little children want to help with chores around the house they are too small to be of any assistance, and when they get big enough to be of service, they are no longer interested. One of the reasons for the loss of interest may be that when the child was ready to help, he was not permitted to and so missed the satisfaction of participating when he was ready.

Guiding children's work and play

Studies at Iowa State University have explored the extent to which 730 fifth-grade boys and girls are involved in family activities. Practically nine out of every ten (89 per cent) of these children replied "No" to the question, "Do you think you have too many jobs (at home)?" and only 6 per cent responded in the affirmative (see Table 24).

Most of these fifth-grade youngsters were thanked for doing things at home and praised for doing jobs well there, and the great majority had some voice in family plans and purchases at least some of the time. Only 10 per cent had no regular jobs to do at home. Such relatively high participation of children in family activities might be expected to contribute to the development of responsibility if the parents exploited the situation rather than the child in getting family chores done. Special studies on children's work attitudes indicate that moralizing about the glories of work is not effective, but that involving children in family activities, sharing tasks that challenge children's ability, interests, and imagination, and helping children get satisfaction from their work are recommended.[15]

Current studies of 1,027 teen-agers' participation in various family

---

[15] Jerome Count, *When Your Child Dislikes Work.* Pittsfield, Massachusetts: Work Education Foundation, 1955, 24 pp.

activities lead Johannis to conclude that most of the families he studied were still so traditional in their family task assignments that the adolescents were not getting enough experience to adequately prepare for their own marriage.[16] Senn reflects authoritative opinion on uncooperative teen-agers in the home when he answers a mother's question about how she can get her adolescent daughter to help her in the kitchen,

> Perhaps your daughter is so uncooperative because you delegate only the monotonous kitchen chores to her. She might be more willing to help if you let her join you in the pleasanter and more creative kitchen jobs and gave her a sense of accomplishment by encouraging her to plan or make some of the family meals herself.[17]

The conclusion is that children work when they are a part of the project, when the tasks are at the level of their abilities, and are challenging and satisfying, and when they feel that they are doing a real job and not just being "used."

Play for a child is work too. Watch how hard a group of children at any age level work. When you can see what they are doing from their point of view, you realize that play to them is not frittering away time, but that it usually involves vigorous practice of activities they are readying for, such as "playing school," or implementing some creative fantasy, such as being "space men," or working at some skill development that preoccupies them at the moment (practicing standing, walking, running, skipping, throwing and catching a ball, riding a bike, skills in elaborate games).

Guiding children's play is more than "chasing the children" to keep them out of danger or "Go see what Johnny's doing and tell him to stop." It is a positive assistance of the child in the task he is undertaking by providing stimulating materials and equipment, being available with help as needed, encouraging him by recognition and praise when he has earned it, and most of all by recognizing his play as important and granting him the freedom to use it fully for his purposes.

The word "discipline" comes from the same root as "disciple." It suggests becoming the kind of persons children want to follow and it calls for the development of their self-control and self-discipline. It in-

---

[16] Theodore B. Johannis, Jr., "Participation by Fathers, Mothers, and Teenage Sons and Daughters in Selected Family Economic Activity," *The Coordinator,* Vol. 6, No. 1, September, 1957, pp. 15–16; and "Participation by Fathers, Mothers, and Teenage Sons and Daughters in Selected Child Care and Control Activity," *The Coordinator,* Vol. 6, No. 2, December, 1957, pp. 31 and 32.

[17] Milton J. E. Senn, "Can You *Make* Your Child Be Helpful?" *McCall's,* September, 1957, p. 84.

volves encouraging them to mature and it implies growth from within rather than forcing from without. Ultimately, we find that we can do only a few things *for* our children, we do very little *to* them, but we have unlimited opportunities for doing things *with* them to our mutual advantage.

What Are Children After?

As soon as you observe children from their point of view, rather than that of an exasperated or bewildered adult, you see that children normally are after three things. They have powerful drives (1) to grow, (2) to know, and (3) to belong. These urgent aims of children are so insistent that they take precedence over many other pressures, such for instance as adult scolding or nagging.

Recent decades have seen a great deal of research in child development which emphasizes that, although each child is first of all himself, and different from all other children, there is a certain developmental timetable that all children follow. The Yale Clinic of Child Development for the past twenty years has been investigating the stages children normally go through from birth to maturity.[18] Other research centers have also been engaged in longitudinal studies of human growth and development with results that corroborate, check, and elaborate one another. One of the most helpful fruits of these labors is in a system of concepts that help us see and understand human nature more perceptively than we could before we had these "tools to think with." Such a concept is the developmental task.

Every individual throughout his lifetime is involved in accomplishing the growth responsibilities of his particular stage of development. As originally defined at the University of Chicago, "A developmental task is a task which arises at or about a certain period in the life of an individual, successful accomplishment of which leads to his happiness and to success with later tasks, while failure leads to unhappiness in the individual, disapproval by the society, and difficulty with later tasks."[19] These developmental tasks change as the individual grows, and can be seen in a sequence throughout the lifetime of the individual or the family.[20] In much abbreviated form some of the major de-

Developmental tasks

18 Arnold Gesell, Frances Ilg, Louise Ames, et al., *Infant and Child in the Culture of Today* (1943); *The Child from Five to Ten* (1946); and *Youth, the Years from Ten to Sixteen* (1956): New York: Harper.

19 Robert J. Havighurst, *Human Development and Education*, New York: Longmans, Green, 1953, p. 2.

20 As elaborated in Evelyn Millis Duvall, *Family Development*, Chicago: Lippincott, 1957, 533 pp.

velopmental tasks are outlined below for five stages of childhood and youth.

Developmental Tasks of Children and Youth [21]

Developmental Tasks of Infancy and Early Childhood (Birth to thirty months)

1. Achieving physiological equilibrium following birth
2. Learning to take food satisfactorily
3. Learning the know-how and where-when of elimination
4. Learning to manage one's body effectively
5. Learning to adjust to other people
6. Learning to love and be loved
7. Developing systems of communication
8. Learning to express and control feelings
9. Laying foundations for self-awareness

Developmental Tasks of Preschool Children (2½ to 5 years)

1. Settling into healthful daily routines of rest and activity
2. Mastering good eating habits
3. Mastering the basics of toilet training
4. Developing the physical skills appropriate to his stage of motor development
5. Becoming a participating member of his family
6. Beginning to master his impulses and to conform to others' expectations
7. Developing healthy emotional expressions for a wide variety of experiences
8. Learning to communicate effectively with an increasing number of others
9. Developing the ability to handle potentially dangerous situations
10. Learning to be an autonomous person with initiative and a conscience of his own
11. Laying foundations for understanding the meanings of life

Developmental Tasks of School-Age Boys and Girls (6 to 12 years of age)

1. Learning the basic skills required of school children
2. Mastering the physical skills appropriate to his development
3. Developing meaningful understandings of the use of money
4. Becoming an active, cooperative member of his family

---

[21] Adapted and excerpted from *ibid.*, pp. 190–192, 229–232, 261–264, 294–297, 338–372.

5. Extending his abilities to relate effectively to others, both peers and adults
6. Continuing the learnings involved in handling his feelings and impulses
7. Coming to terms with his or her own sex role both now and as it will become
8. Continuing to find himself as a worthy person
9. Relating himself to loyalties beyond the moment and outside himself

Developmental Tasks of Teen-Agers (13 to 20 years of age)

1. Accepting one's changing body and learning to use it effectively
2. Achieving a satisfying and socially accepted masculine or feminine role
3. Finding oneself as a member of one's own generation in more mature relations with one's age mates
4. Achieving emotional independence from parents and other adults
5. Selecting and preparing for an occupation and economic independence
6. Preparing for marriage and family life
7. Developing intellectual skills and social sensitivities necessary for civic competence
8. Developing a workable philosophy of life that makes sense in today's world

Developmental Tasks of Young Adults (Early 20's)

1. Choosing a vocation and getting established in a job
2. Getting an education
3. Satisfying military service requirements
4. Becoming marriageable
5. Learning to appraise and to express love feelings appropriately
6. Choosing a marriage partner
7. Getting engaged
8. Being married and starting a family

Essentially, developmental tasks are thrusts from within the individual in his effort to grow up and to become what appears to be possible for him. As he matures physically to the place where new horizons and statuses appear attainable, he is motivated to achieve the new roles implied. When others around him expect new levels of performance of him, he is encouraged to meet their expectations if he can. Cultural demands may pattern the task but the urge to accomplish it comes from within the individual:

The individual's assumption of a given developmental task consists of at least four interrelated operations: (1) perceiving new possibilities for his behavior in what is expected of him or in what he sees others, more mature than he, accomplishing, (2) forming new conceptions of himself (identity formation), (3) coping effectively with conflicting demands upon him, and (4) wanting to achieve the next step in his development enough to work toward it (motivation). To illustrate: a small boy sees somewhat bigger boys riding their bicycles (operation 1—perception); he conceives of himself as a potential bicycle rider (operation 2—identity formation); he resolves the conflicts between his mother's protests that he might get hurt and his own fears of failure with the expectancies of his peers, and the demands of his father that he become "a big boy" (operation 3—coping with conflicting demands); and finally, he wants to learn to ride a bike enough to practice what it takes to become proficient in it (operation 4—motivation).[22]

Looking at the dynamics of development from the point of view of a culturally oriented psychoanalyst, Erikson sees the individual maturing through a series of stages in which his ego "is strong enough to integrate the timetable of the organism with the structure of social institutions."[23] The stages through childhood and youth are seen as steps in the sense that one must follow them in a certain order to get upstairs; and when one slips, he falls down in reverse order. For each step achieved, there is an opposite negative condition that marks the individual's failure to make that stage effectively.[24]

Stage 1—*Trust* (vs. basic mistrust). The baby must develop a sense of trust in himself, in his parents, in his world, in life itself if he is to have a sturdy foundation for further development. What trust is to the infant becomes a mixture of faith and realism to the adult.

Stage 2—*Autonomy* (vs. shame and doubt). The little child in his second and third years must literally stand on his own feet and fight for his right to be an individual for all he is worth. He is autonomous among others and so cooperates with others that each has a maximum autonomy. Laughed at or exploited as "cute" the child may lose a valuable sense of dignity as a person and slip into a state of shame and doubt.

Stage 3—*Initiative* (vs. guilt). The preschooler having attained a degree of autonomy focuses on certain goals and goes after them. He learns how to set goals for himself in fact or fantasy and works hard (in his play) to achieve them. His mother reports that he "plays by himself without asking what to do." He is finding out that he can take initiative for his actions and make things happen.

---

[22] Evelyn Millis Duvall, *Family Development*, Chicago: Lippincott, 1957, p. 105.

[23] Erikson, *Childhood and Society*. New York: Norton, 1950, p. 218.

[24] Paraphrased freely from Erik Erikson's contribution to *Healthy Personality Development in Children* (Report of the Interagency Conference), Josiah Macy, Jr., Foundation, New York, 1952, pp. 84–93.

Stage 4—*Industry* (vs. inferiority). The school-age child goes to school where he is helped to learn techniques and skills for getting things done. He discovers the pleasures of work completion by steady attention and persevering diligence. His danger at this stage lies in a sense of inadequacy and inferiority.

Stage 5—*Identity* (vs. role diffusion). The adolescent strives to find out who he is. Out of all the meaningful frustrations and satisfactions he has thus far experienced, he must discover his own best answer to the perplexing question "Who am I?" If he does not know where he is going, he faces difficulty settling in any kind of life, and may drift into delinquent behavior. His sense of identity emerges out of his accrued confidence in himself as the person he sees himself becoming.

Stage 6—*Intimacy* (vs. isolation). The young adult, having found his own identity, is not afraid to fuse with others and become fully intimate, in sexuality, love, and interdependence. Only then is he ready for marriage. For, until the individual has a well-established sense of identity he cannot complete the stage of intimacy with meaningful sexual union, readiness for parenthood, and close personal relationships with others in intimate ways.

Children are after a chance to develop, to find out about life and find themselves in it. They ask questions because they need to know the "what" and the "how" and the "why" of things. Many of our children's questions can be answered easily and directly with a certain pride that the child is smart enough to ask. There are other questions and situations that adults find hard to handle. One of these involves the inevitable, universal one of sex education.

What Kind of Sex Education?

Sex guidance is something like the weather in that everyone agrees that it is important but few are able to do anything effective about it. All too often it is subjected to "buck passing," with home, school, and church each feeling that the others ought to "do something about it." It is a sad commentary that recent youth polls show few more adolescent boys and girls getting their sex information from home, school, or church than was true in 1938 at the time of the first extensive youth survey conducted by the American Council on Education.

In interviews with 13,528 young people between 16 and 24 years of age, selected as typical of American youth prior to 1938, the American Youth Commission found 66 per cent of the boys and 40 per cent of the girls reporting that what they knew about sex was limited to what friends of their own age had told them. Only three out of every ten young people reported most of their sex education from parents or relatives, and fewer than one in ten (8 per cent) from school.[25]

The poll of a nation-wide sample of 10,000 9th through 12th grade boys and girls in 1950 found 35 per cent of both sexes reporting their parents or guardians and 12 per cent their teachers or school counselors as the source of most of their sex education (an increase of less than 5 per cent over the years intervening between the two studies).[26]

More recently a study focusing on what college freshmen find hard to discuss with their parents found that sex headed the list of difficult topics. "More boys said they had trouble discussing sex than any other subject; 80 per cent had some degree of difficulty with the subject with their fathers and 84 per cent had some trouble in talking to mothers about it. Likewise, more girls had difficulty with sex than any other subject: 90 per cent in talk with fathers, 64 per cent in talk with mothers." [27]

This is not to suggest that sex education properly belongs at the high school and college years. Quite the contrary. Some kind of education in the nature of sex, reproduction, and intimate interaction has been going on through the years, whether or not it is consciously guided. The question is not, "Shall there be sex education?" but rather, "What kind of sex education will it be?" Properly, all students of the question agree, sex education begins early in the life of the child and is a continuous process through to his maturity.

Sex education begins early   Little children learn by watching, imitating, and exploring. This is as true in learning about how their bodies are made and function as in any other area. To get the facts they need about themselves and others, little children explore (1) by asking questions and talking about how their bodies work, (2) by watching and imitating adults, (3) by looking at the bodies of others, and (4) by feeling and rubbing genitalia. In our culture all four of these activities are considered taboo by some adults. Parents are sometimes uncomfortable at seeing little girls running about in abbreviated sunsuits and are shocked to see nursery school children looking at each other at toilet time. A great many parents and teachers have been so frightened by false stories of the evils of masturbation that they severely punish and shame little children who touch their genitalia. Too many adults still are embarrassed by the

[25] Howard M. Bell, *Youth Tell Their Story*. Washington, D.C.: American Council on Education, 1938, p. 40.

[26] Purdue Opinion Panel, *Courtship Conduct as Viewed by High School Youth*, Poll No. 27, Lafayette, Indiana: Division of Educational Reference, December, 1950, p. 36.

[27] Marvin C. Dubbé, "What Teen-Agers Can't Tell Their Parents and Why," *The Coordinator*, Vol. IV, No. 3, March, 1956, pp. 3–7.

searching questions and interest of intelligent children naturally concerned about their origin, the functions of their bodies, and the hap-
penings in human and animal families around them. Consequently
many children are left at an early age with the impression that there
is something dirty and shameful about the sex organs, and something
wrong about sexual sensations. Adult embarrassment, uneasiness, and
fear are transferred to the child almost without his being aware of it.
As he grows older, sex references continue to bring feelings of guilt
and shame. Dirty stories, giggles, and other indirect outlets are found
to take the place of the more normal, complete responses of sex love.
Feelings of personal unworthiness make it difficult to fall in love with
desirable love objects, and control of the powerful sex urge becomes
difficult.

Parents who are more wholesomely conditioned and more aware of
their own limitations clamor for guidance in the sex education of their
children. Few topics are more popular in child study, parent education,
and teacher-training classes. Books like the following are basic.

Selected Starter Library in Sex Education

Books for Children

Child Study Association of America, *Facts of Life for Children* (Indianapo-
lis: Bobbs-Merrill, 1954).

Faegre, Marion, *Your Own Story* (Minneapolis: University of Minnesota
Press, 1943).

Gruenberg, Sidonie M., *The Wonderful Story of How You Were Born*
(Garden City, N. Y.: Hanover House, 1952).

Levine, Milton, and Seligmann, J. H., *The Wonder of Life* (New York:
Simon and Schuster, 1940).

Strain, Frances Bruce, *Being Born* (New York: Appleton-Century, 1938).

Books for Young People

Beck, Lester, *Human Growth* (New York: Harcourt, Brace, 1949).

Dickerson, Roy, *So Youth May Know* (New York: Association Press, Revised
Edition).

Duvall, Evelyn Millis, *Facts of Life and Love for Teen-Agers* (New York:
Association Press, Revised Edition, 1956).

Museum of Science and Industry, *The Miracle of Growth* (Urbana: University of Illinois Press, 1950).

Books for Parents and Teachers

Biester, Lillian; Griffiths, William; and Pearce, N. O., *Units in Personal
Health and Human Relations* (Minneapolis: University of Minnesota
Press, 1947).

Eckert, Ralph G., *Sex Attitudes in the Home* (New York: Association Press, 1956).

Kirkendall, Lester, *Sex Education as Human Relations* (New York: Inor Publishing, 1950).

Strain, Frances Bruce, *New Patterns in Sex Teaching* (New York: Appleton-Century-Crofts, Revised Edition, 1951).

———, *The Normal Sex Interests of Children* (New York: Appleton-Century-Crofts, 1948).

———, *Sex Guidance in Family Life Education* (New York: Macmillan, 1948).

What Helps a Child Feel Secure?

These are times when even strongest hearts may falter. With man-made moons spinning in outer space, with destructive designs at dizzying heights, some anxiety is inevitable. Disasters strike continents, communities, and families from time to time. Change is ever present in every aspect of life. How then, can children be brought up safe, secure, and free from scarring anxieties?

Studies of children in London in the air raids of World War II, of other children caught in the catastrophes of fire, hurricane, floods, and earthquake, and in the crisis of rapid urbanization, show that if the adults they depend on do not panic, the children do not either. Nothing can take the place of a child's confidence in a beloved adult who remains unshaken through a crisis. Further, specific procedures can be recommended to help children find security in the midst of some of the inevitable crises of life.

When a child must move

Families with little children move more often than any other age group. Two out of every three families who changed residence during a recent year were those in which the man of the house was under 35 years of age.[28] There are several reasons for such high mobility in young families: (1) taking a job, (2) moving to a more promising position, (3) satisfying housing needs of the expanding family, (4) going where there are better schools for the children, (5) getting into the suburbs, and (6) having fewer roots and vested interests in one place than is true of longer established families. Even though the move may be necessary for vocational advancement and family well-being, it may come as a jolt to the children.[29] How can the youngsters be given maximum security when the family must move?

---

[28] Paul C. Glick, *American Families*. New York: Wiley, 1957, p. 89.
[29] See Robert Sheehan, "We've Been Transferred," *Fortune*, July, 1957, pp. 116–118, 198, and 200.

Allied Van Lines, in cooperation with the Child Study Association of America, has prepared an excellent folder of specific suggestions for families who move.[30] These recommendations are in three phases—before, during, and after you move.

Before you move . . . talk it over with the children, and include them in your plans; if the child is old enough encourage him to plan his new room arrangement and what he will take of his old things; help the children send change-of-address cards to the friends they must leave behind; and make the moving an adventure in change.

During the move . . . keep the baby as close to his familiar things and schedule as feasible, send the toddler off to Grandma's if possible, and enlist the full participation of the teen-ager in the moving details; pack a basket of things you'll need to travel with you, including food and drink and toilet articles; and keep calm, patient, and loving; enjoy it with the children if you can.

After you move . . . sit down and catch your breath, have something to eat, and give the youngsters a chance to plan what should be done and how; if there has had to be a change of schools, encourage the children to bring their new friends home, even if the house isn't in apple-pie order; do what you can to help them get into community and school activities, projects, and clubs as soon as they can; above all help them to see the possibilities and promise of the new location in your own positive adjustment to it.

Living in the modern world is full of potential harm to a child. Accidents cause 39 per cent of all deaths of school-age children in the United States.[31] From the time a toddler tries to stick his finger into the fire, a strange dog's mouth, or the electric mixer, to the traffic dangers he meets as a school child crossing the street, to the thousand and one hazards he meets daily as a teen-ager, a child must learn to cope effectively with potential danger. Adults help this essential learning by instilling caution instead of fear. Fear immobilizes and promotes panic while caution teaches the child what might happen and what to do about it if it does. Until a child is old enough to listen to reason, harm must be put out of his way. As soon as he can understand he is taught what is all right and what is to be avoided, with no exceptions. This includes such everyday things as the use of knives and matches, gas and electric outlets, learning to cross the street safely, and learning to handle oneself in the water. Children should be taught never to accept rides from strangers, nor go with them on any pretext, nor take

Safeguarding children from danger

---

30 *When Families Move,* 1957.
31 "Some Important Causes of Deaths in the U.S. at School Age, 1955," *Safety Education,* May, 1957.

candy, money, gifts, or jobs from them. School children should explicitly be told to report any stranger who hangs around or accosts them to the nearest police officer, teacher, mailman, or parent. They should be brought up to see the policeman as their friend and to go to him with anything that disturbs them or distresses them away from home.

But won't these teachings make the child fearful and distrustful of others? The answer is in the negative if the directions are explicit, simple, and interpreted as necessary because "Some people are mixed up and do things that are wrong." Most youngsters have seen enough TV shows to be aware of the crime detection process and are quite probably less emotional about such problems than the adults who caution them.

Security from within

The only real security is from within the personality. All the teaching in the world will not rid the severely disturbed child of his anxieties. The child who grows up in a happy home, where "Mama loves Papa" and lets him know it, where the youngster is accepted for himself and does not have to keep testing or earning his parents' love all the time, has a heritage of emotional security that cannot be shattered.

As the child grows he finds and builds strengths within himself that become his inner citadel of security. His home may not have been the best, he may lack the warmth, or the freedom, or the controls that he might have had. But if he has the courage to find life's goodness for himself and to strive toward living the good life with whatever of himself he can give to the quest, he will be secure. Peace of mind comes not just from growing up in a favorable emotional climate. It is ultimately the triumph of the human spirit in becoming a finer person within a nobler way of life than he ever dreamed was possible—as a child.

READINGS

Baruch, Dorothy Walter, *New Ways in Discipline*. New York: Whittlesey House, 1949.

Brim, Orville G., Jr., *Education for Child Rearing*. New York: Russell Sage Foundation, 1959.

Bro, Marguerite Harmon, *When Children Ask* (Rev. Ed.). New York: Harper, 1956.

Duvall, Evelyn Millis, *Family Development*. Chicago: Lippincott, 1957.

English, O. Spurgeon, and Constance Foster, *Fathers Are Parents Too*. New York: Putnam, 1951.

Erikson, Erik H., *Childhood and Society*. New York: Norton, 1950.

Frank, Lawrence K. and Mary, *How to Help Your Child in School*. New York: Viking Press, 1950.

Gesell, Arnold, Frances Ilg, and Louise Ames, *Child Behavior*. New York: Dell, 1955.

Langdon, Grace, and Irving Stout, *The Discipline of Well-Adjusted Children.* New York: Day, 1952.

Pierre the Pelican Series: 28 pamphlets for parents of children, birth to six years, from Louisiana Association for Mental Health, 1528 Jackson Avenue, New Orleans 13, La., New Revision, 1958.

Polier, Justine Wise, *Back to What Woodshed?* New York: Public Affairs Pamphlets, 1956.

Prescott, Daniel A., *The Child in the Educative Process.* New York: McGraw-Hill, 1957.

Sears, Robert R., Eleanor E. Maccoby, Harry Levin, et al., *Patterns of Child Rearing.* Evanston, Illinois: Row, Peterson, 1957.

Spock, Benjamin, *Baby and Child Care* (Rev. Ed.). New York: Pocket Books, 1957.

Stone, L. Joseph, and Joseph Church, *Childhood and Adolescence.* New York: Random House, 1957.

21 Finding Religious Roots

What part does religion play in family living?

What should you teach your children?

How can you deal with religious differences?

How does a religious family differ from one that "has" religion?

How can religion contribute to your family life?

What spiritual resources has a religious family?

When you seek the blessing of your church on your marriage, you are doing more than following tradition. You are recognizing the importance of planting your marriage firmly in the spiritual soil where it may thrive. You are attempting to find the religious roots for your life together.

There are important reasons why you want your union to have religious significance. Marriage is a very special step in life. Tied into it are your hopes, your dreams, your most tender sentiments, your central values, and to a considerable extent your future. Trying to find roots for this vital relationship puts you right in the middle of religious issues, whatever your theology. The better you understand these issues and spiritual resources, the more they can contribute to the richness, the worth, and the success of your marriage.

What Part Does Religion Play in Family Living?

All American families, whether related to churches or not, live in a society in which religious ideas, practices, and institutions are influential. Sunday is not always devoted to religious purposes, but it is a religious holiday. So also are Thanksgiving, Christmas, and Easter. Such family ceremonies as baptisms and funerals are usually performed by clergy. In a wedding ceremony the clergyman acts as both a representative of his church and an official of the state.

The traditions and ideals of the American people have important religious roots. Identifying capitalism and its "rugged individualism" with the "Protestant ethic" is open to considerable historical question and qualification,[1] but the relationship implied is certainly valid. The extraordinary generosity of the American people in everything ranging from collections for impoverished neighbors to world-wide foreign aid programs can be attributed in part to the generosity of nature on the American continent and the productive energies and genius of our people. But it roots also in the humanitarian ideals of our Jewish and Christian traditions. The form and conduct of our families themselves, and the related sex codes designed to protect them, stem from historic religious roots.

The continuing influence of religious principles is apparent in the moral conduct of both Christians and Jews. For instance, the incidence of premarital sex intercourse is markedly less for both men and women who are closely identified with church groups than for those who are not.[2]

As religion profoundly affects family life, so families influence religion. Theologies make extensive use of family terms in such doctrines as the "Fatherhood of God" and the "Brotherhood of Man." Christian and Jewish groups are vitally concerned with the soundness of family life. The relationship between religion and family life for many centuries has been central.

The church needs the family

With few exceptions, people belong to and support churches because they have been taught to do so by their parents. Some parents contribute considerably to the religious education of their children by reading them Bible stories or drilling them in the catechism. In Judaism the main responsibility for the teaching of religion belongs to the family, not to the synagogue. In Poland, despite the killing of rabbis the Jewish religion continues strong because it is being carried on by the family. In America most Christians depend upon churches to teach religion to their children, but it is the parents who largely support these

---

[1] For discussion of this issue, see Kemper Fullerton, "Calvinism and Capitalism," *Harvard Theological Review*, Vol. XXI, #3, July, 1928; R. H. Tawney, *Religion and the Rise of Capitalism*, Penguin Edition, 1947; William H. Whyte, *The Organization Man*, New York: Simon and Schuster, 1956.

[2] Alfred C. Kinsey, Wardell B. Pomeroy, Clyde E. Martin, and Paul H. Gebhard, *Sex Behavior in the Human Female*, Philadelphia: Saunders, 1953, pp. 331, 342.

churches and develop loyalties in their children for them. Without such family support no church could long continue without crippling losses.

Religion has vital emotional or feeling aspects. The knowledges of religion can probably be taught better by specially trained teachers than by most parents. But for some teachings (including some of the knowledges) experience in family living is essential. A church may teach that "God is Love," but "love" can have meaning only for those who have experienced it. How can a child understand about trust and faith in God, unless he has had experiences with people whom he could trust, and in whom he had faith? Many teachings of religion can be understood only by those who have had a background of appropriate experiences in their own families.

Families lay the basis for religious teaching

So it is with religious loyalties. Religion is important for most children only as they see that it is important to their parents. Parents can see that their children get some knowledge about religion by sending them to church school, but religious attitudes and loyalties are first learned from the parents.

Family life is becoming a central interest of the church.[3] Clergymen have always counseled with, and provided special services for, families as a regular part of their duties. Specific training for these functions now is given in many seminaries and professional workshops. In recent years, the major religious bodies have established extensive family life programs. The National Council of Churches of Christ in America has a full department on family life. The Roman Catholic Church has extensive programs in family life education in its Pre-Cana and Cana Conferences, designed to strengthen family life. The Methodist Church offers a number of courses on marriage and family life for both young people and adults, and regularly holds national and area conferences attended by thousands. Departments of Christian Family Life are now part of many denominations. Jewish groups, historically outstanding in their concern for families, steadily increase their interest and effectiveness.

Even more influential than these special efforts is the stability that religious fellowship encourages within its members. In study after study, church-related families have been shown to be more stable than non-religiously oriented families. One of the first studies of representative American youth in the late 1930's [4] found a striking correlation between religious affiliation and family stability. Of the 13,000 young

---

[3] For the sake of brevity, the term "church" is used here to mean any religious organization, whether Christian, Jewish, or other.

[4] Howard M. Bell, *Youth Tell Their Story*, American Council on Education, Washington, D.C., 1938.

people studied, less than 7 per cent of those from religious backgrounds came from broken homes (Jewish 4.6 per cent, Catholic 6.4 per cent, Protestant 6.8 per cent) in contrast to 16.7 per cent of those who came from non-church families. Substantially parallel findings came from the study of 4,108 families of students of Michigan State University ten years later.[5] (These findings are summarized in Chapter 4, see especially Fig. 6). Practically three times as many non-church marriages (17.9 per cent) had ended in divorce or separation as had the Catholic, Jewish, or Protestant marriages (4.4 per cent, 5.2 per cent, 6.0 per cent respectively).[6] Only the mixed Catholic-Protestant marriage comes close to the high rate of dissolution of the non-church family (14.1 per cent and 17.9 per cent respectively).

Goode's intensive study of divorce finds a positive relationship between the frequency of church attendance of Roman Catholic married partners and the duration of their marriages (see Table 25).

TABLE 25. Duration of Marriage by Frequency of Church Attendance [7]

Frequency of Church Attendance	Median Duration of the Marriage
Once a week or more	11.0 years
Less than once a week but sometimes	9.8 years
Never	7.2 years

When he compared duration of marriage with religious affiliation, he found, as had others before him, that both Catholic and Protestant families lasted longer than did those who had no religion. Apparently, regularity of church attendance is a better indicator of the person's acceptance of church attitudes and policies than the particular religion to which he or she belongs.

Comparing happily married with divorced couples, Locke found that happily married pairs attended church much more frequently than did the divorced. "Never going to church" was without question associated with marital maladjustment, and "going four or more times a month" was unquestionably associated with marriage success in this study.[8]

---

[5] Judson T. Landis, "Marriages of Mixed and Non-Mixed Religious Faith," *American Sociological Review*, June, 1949, Vol. 14, No. 3, pp. 401–407.

[6] *Ibid.*, p. 403.

[7] William J. Goode, *After Divorce*, Glencoe, Illinois: Free Press, 1956, p. 105.

[8] Harvey J. Locke, *Predicting Adjustment in Marriage: A Comparison of a Divorced and a Happily Married Group*, New York: Holt, 1951, pp. 240–241.

What Should You Teach Your Children?

If you are a Roman Catholic, a Lutheran, or a member of any similar orthodox Christian group this question will present few problems. Your church will tell you what should be taught through its catechisms, schools, and ritualistic ceremonies. If you belong to a "non-creedal" orthodox group your problem is somewhat more difficult. But the general outlines of your theology are definitely defined and the songs sung may prove quite as effective as a catechism in Christian instruction.

If you are Jewish your theology is less clearly defined. But this may be more than compensated for by your vital family rituals and the intense family and group loyalties that your culture engenders.

If you do not accept any specific religious teachings, it might seem that your problem is even simpler; you need only do nothing. Yet inaction can hardly solve the problem. For whether you like it or not, your children will be growing up in a religious culture. In Christmas carols and celebrations, in the Easter festivals, and in numerous other ways your children will learn the Christian story and be exposed to Christian influences. If they are to be intelligent members of such a culture, they should know something of the Bible and about various Christian and Jewish groups. Some instruction about religion is part of general education for all children.

Liberals, who comprise a large proportion if not a majority of the Protestants in this country, face a difficult problem because they lack a generally accepted system of beliefs. Liberals do have beliefs; any liberal can make a list of them. But these are *his* beliefs, many of which other liberals do not agree with. Therefore, liberals have no common body of organized religious teaching, backed by cohesive group support, to impart to their children.

Another problem lies in the liberal's attitudes toward his beliefs. Essential tolerance and humility keep him from feeling that the eternal salvation of man depends upon an acceptance of his views. Therefore he cannot feel the intensity of conviction that the more orthodox often have.

What you teach your children depends on what you believe. In areas where your convictions are strong, your teachings will be specific and definite. When you and your mate are less certain, your interpretation of life to your children will reflect your tolerance. You will teach your children the religious elements that are meaningful to you not only in what you tell them, but in what you are. Beyond this you face the challenge of all Americans in dealing in some way with the problem of religious difference.

How Can You Deal with Religious Differences?

We Americans live in a multicultured society in which we must live with a variety of different groups and sub-groups, racial, national, and religious. We have prided ourselves not only on a legal tolerance of all religious groups but on the tolerance of our attitudes of mind. Therefore, Americans have been quite unprepared for religious conflicts that have broken out with increasing frequency and intensity in community after community, especially since World War II.[9] The handling of religious differences is becoming an increasingly important and difficult problem for all families.

It would be simple if we could say that this conflict is due to a revival of bigotry, possibly based upon Communist propaganda, and that the way to combat bigotry is to bring about better understanding among different religious groups. However, a careful study of the problem by social scientists [10] has come to a different conclusion. Bigotry is unquestionably present, but the major conflict is over differences in basic values and convictions that make serious conflict inevitable. A better understanding will at first intensify this conflict of fundamental differences. If this is the case, what can you do?

The first essential is to take a sound position toward the nature of conflict. In Chapter 14, "Coping with Conflict," you saw that conflict in the family is not inherently an evil, but is a normal part of human relations that can be faced constructively. So it is in the larger family that is America. Conflict is present in all areas of life—between labor and management, between the two major political parties, and between all kinds of pressure groups. In these conflicts people sometimes say harsh things about each other, or the party, union, or business organization that they oppose. Is this "bigotry," or is the right to fight for one's convictions the essence of democracy? The only certain way to abolish religious conflict would be to abolish religious convictions. The problem is not to abolish conflict but to conduct conflict honestly, fairly, and with a minimum of harm to others.

Once you accept conflict and the fact that you must live in the same country and community with those with whom you differ intensely, you have a solid groundwork for adjustment of religious conflicts. Here are some further suggestions:

---

[9] See, for example, the article by Henry M. Christman in the May, 1958, issue of *Coronet*, "Church, State—and Strife."

[10] "Religious Conflict in the United States," in the *Journal of Social Issues*, Vol. XII, #3, 1956. The Journal is the official publication of the Society for the Psychological Study of Social Issues, a division of the American Psychological Association.

1. Differences and the feelings people have about these differences can be brought out in the open. The old "hush-hush" policies and attempts to promote "good will" by glossing over differences are ineffective.

2. On the positive side, you can build as many bridges as possible. You can emphasize the beliefs held in common with others, such as the Fatherhood of God and the Brotherhood of Man. You can work together in common projects and toward the solution of common problems.

3. You can recognize the essential humanness of all men. All groups have their bigots, including your own; and all groups have their people of honor and integrity, including those whom you may oppose.

4. The strongest bridge is between religious families who share the same basic spiritual attitudes, regardless of differences in church affiliation.

How Does a Religious Family Differ from One That "Has" Religion?

Some "religious" families are only ordinary, respectable families that have a religious "plus." This "plus" usually includes certain beliefs—as about God, Christ, the head of the church, and certain practices, such as church-going, prayer, and Bible reading. Religion at its best, however, is not an addition to life, but a transformation of life. A religious family does not merely add a religious "plus." It is a family organized around religious ideals. This religious core relates all aspects of life meaningfully to each other, and transfuses them with religious ideals. As a result, life is unified and takes on new meaning and basic worth. For the religious family, religion is not a set of often burdensome obli-

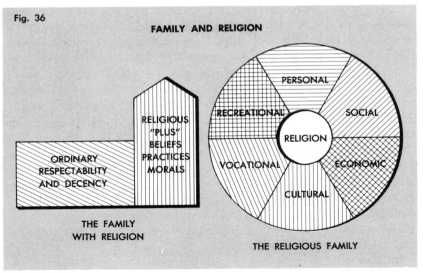

Fig. 36

FAMILY AND RELIGION

RELIGIOUS "PLUS" BELIEFS PRACTICES MORALS

ORDINARY RESPECTABILITY AND DECENCY

PERSONAL

RECREATIONAL

SOCIAL

RELIGION

VOCATIONAL

ECONOMIC

CULTURAL

THE FAMILY WITH RELIGION

THE RELIGIOUS FAMILY

gations. It gives to family life meaning and purpose, and is a source of wisdom, insight, and power.

Living religion in the family

The religious quality of a family is not to be judged by the fidelity with which parents teach their religious views to their children. Neither is it to be determined by the forms and ceremonies observed. Some will find prayers, especially at mealtime, to be a natural and helpful expression of religious faith. But whatever the form, you may expect considerable variation.

In the development of religion within the family, the important consideration is the spirit which dominates all relationships. If religious teaching is to be effective, it must be inculcated into children as a normal result of the processes of living. In the final analysis the problem is not the teaching of religion in the family; it is rather to make the family religious.

How Can Religion Contribute to Your Family Life?

It would be wrong to imply that only a religious family can get along well, or even that it can necessarily get along better than other families. However, religion can make significant contributions to families, among which are the following:

Religion can strengthen and support love

"God is love; and the love of husband and wife brings us nearer to the heart of reality, the knowledge of God, than any other experience," says Dean Inge. A religious family knows that love is the greatest thing in the world.

One important contribution of religion is to help you to identify genuine love. Like anything precious, love has many counterfeits that often look like the real thing. The façade of sentimentalism, by which one hopes to get the rewards of love without the risks of its commitments; the romantic "falling in love" that is so often essentially neurotic need; exploitative lust—these are counterfeits. In the coddling of the "devoted" mother who wishes to retain the child as a possession, in the excessive demands of "if you really loved me you would do as I wish," counterfeit love is a mask for neurotic greed.

Religion helps protect against the counterfeits of love in two ways. It encourages a divine skepticism regarding the "goodness" of the well-intentioned. Positively, it defines love in terms of desiring, not the possessing of or satisfactions from the other, but his welfare. The welfare of others is interpreted, not as material advantage but as character development and personality growth. You love when you desire the spiritual development of others.

Religion strengthens love in a family by making it an unearned gift.

In some families, love is given or withheld as a reward, as a punishment, or as a means of control. "Mother loves you when you are good" can signify a damaging relationship. In a religious home, while conditions are often placed upon privileges and favors, no conditions are placed on loving and being loved.

Religion helps to make love an achievement. Some people see love only as giving to, or serving, others. Religion helps people see love in terms of the growth of others. Children need, not only to be loved, but to love as well. In a religious family care is taken that love circulates in a two-way flow.

Religion can contribute to the handling of conflicts, partly by helping you to know what to expect. Historic Christianity maintains that all men are sinners. An awareness of this truth makes the discovery of defects in others less surprising and threatening. It helps each party to a dispute to be saved from the illusion that he is necessarily right. In short, religious families should find it easier to understand and to accept the normality of conflict.

Religion can help in handling conflicts

Secondly, religion provides a moral code upon the basis of which conflicts can more readily be adjusted. However short of the ideal they may fall, a religious couple in conflict have the common basis of love for and acceptance of each other. They both have reconciliation as their goal. Their conflicts, therefore, tend to be less damaging and irreconcilable. In some cases, clearly defined moral standards greatly simplify the problems of. adjustment. For example, many couples are actually uncertain about sex morality in marriage. In religious families, adultery is far less common. When infidelity does arise, a common moral standard limits the area and the complexity of the conflicts. In many other areas, including honesty, cheating, and the value systems that encourage these, the religious family has real advantages.

Religion aids the resolving of conflict through the therapeutic functions of love. Love in family life, like blood in the body, not only feeds but cleanses. As each one is fed, so he also discharges into its stream his fears and resentments, that he may be renewed in purity as well as in strength. Conflict is part of the cleansing and healing function of family living. There is admittedly risk that the more docile members shall absorb an undue proportion of this burden, and not be fed as they should be. But when love is real, a person does not allow himself always to be the "goat."

Finally, religion provides that basic essential for the adjustment of conflict—forgiveness. The major problems of conflict arise, not so much out of what people do as out of what they are. "I'll forgive you this time if you promise never to do it again" is often an impossible condition.

You do what you do because of what you are. No one can change himself by merely promising, however sincerely, to be or to do differently. Forgiveness is not primarily a tow truck to pull you out of a mud hole in which you happen to have been stuck. It is rather like the oil in the crankcase, which must always be available in constant flow.

Religion can be a sound basis for child training

Religion cannot be a substitute for a basic knowledge of sound psychological principles. However, it can help you understand valid goals. Religion helps you to see your objectives, not in terms of the "good child who never causes me any trouble" or as an extension of yourself. Rather you are concerned about such goals as character, personality development, and the stature-stretching growth of maturing responsibilities. At this point the best insights of religion and child psychology join hands.

Religion can be a sound basis for self-respect

If your feelings of personal worth and self-respect depend upon your having a higher income than you can comfortably earn, you are in trouble. At best you will go through life, struggling and straining, putting on a "front," and all the time feeling frustrated and ashamed. If yours is a religious family you know that income is in no sense a valid measure of worth. It is far more important to be a good person of honesty, love, and integrity than to drive a fine car. Your family need never feel ashamed or embarrassed because they cannot afford as much as their neighbors and friends. This gives you three advantages:

1. *Tensions are reduced.* Real peace of mind comes, not from tranquilizers, either chemical or theological, but from self-acceptance based upon a sense of Divine Acceptance. The ability to see yourself as you really are, with all your limitations and defects, without threat to the structure of your personality concepts, is the basis of freedom from fear.

2. *Progress becomes easier.* You cannot make headway against a defect until you dare admit that it is there. Divine Acceptance makes it easier to admit a fault, so that you can drag it out in the open and work on it.

3. *Success becomes possible.* Not everyone can be a good earner but everyone can become a good person. Not many can become "Big Shots," but everyone can stand for big things. Religion can help you to quit knocking yourself out struggling for what is beyond your capacities. It can encourage you to start working on what is possible for you. Such a shift cannot guarantee success, but it does make it possible. The rewards of dignity and self-respect come with doing what you can do.

Religion can help with the budget

Financial troubles often result, not from the high cost of living but from the high cost of impressing others. Since a religious family does not try to buy friendship, respect of others, and a position in the community, all its income is available for economic satisfactions and needs. Conflicts within the family are handled by facing them and making adjustments, not by trying to hide them behind expensive gifts. As a result, a religious family has important economic advantages.

What is true for the money budget is also true for the time budget. Religious people do not have to spend day and night working to earn enough money to impress others. They do not have to attend social events and programs merely for the sake of appearances and to keep their "fences mended." They have time for their real friends, their family, and for the growth-promoting, soul-satisfying experiences that mean most. In a religious family you have a better chance to become a better person with a richer and more satisfying family life together, with other growing persons.

Religion can give more time for real living

As you can accept yourself as you are, you do not have to blame others for your failures or to be "touchy" when they are exposed. You will have neither to dominate nor to crawl before others. Knowing your own limitations better, you can feel more kindly toward the limitations of others. The result can be humility without humiliation, dignity without snobbery, confidence without arrogance. As you become a better person, others will like you better.

Religion can help in getting along with others

Despite all recent gains, both in modern medicine and in economic security, this remains a difficult and, in many respects, an insecure world. Old age and death have been postponed, but remain as inevitable as ever. In several respects, we have lost ground. The physical death rate has dropped but the marriage death rate has increased. Physical diseases have declined but social diseases, such as delinquency and crime, have spurted. Life has become more comfortable, yet many people face problems of personal adjustment quite as serious and difficult as did their ancestors. Finally, we live in a world that may at any time be destroyed by super bombs. It is a world such as this that families must live and bring up children in.

Religious families in an insecure world

The problem of living successfully in today's world presents some of the same problems faced by our ancestors, living in a rough and perilous wilderness. Men had to learn both to surmount its dangers and to utilize its resources. The task of parents was not to make life pleasant and happy for their children, it was rather to teach them as rapidly as possible the essentials for survival. Any undue delay in giving them experience in grappling directly with the often harsh realities of their world would have been regarded, not as a kindness but as a dangerous disservice.

Today we face a world that is both dangerous and abundant in resources—material, intellectual, and spiritual. Undue sheltering of children that prevents them from getting first-hand understanding of both its risks and its rewards has become highly dangerous. Children must be protected from life's disasters, but not from its bruises. There is one important difference between our world and that of our ancestors. In an earlier time, personal adequacy was essential for the survival of a man and his family. In our day, personal adequacy has become essential to the survival of civilization itself.

What Spiritual Resources Has a Religious Family?

In developing adequacy in themselves and in their children religious families have important spiritual resources. First, they know that the goal of life is not to avoid suffering, pain, or disaster, but to overcome them.[11] Some infantile people may expect that because of their piety God will (or should) protect them and theirs from tragedy. Truly religious people see as the end of life not the avoidance of suffering but the attainment of righteousness. Far from expecting divine protection, they know that those who stand for ideals often arouse opposition that brings upon them even more suffering. Even greater is the anguish that results when they see the noblest ideals nailed to human iniquity. Religion helps mainly, not by protection from suffering but by providing strength to overcome it. Religion in its essence means, not shelter from, but triumph over, tragedy.

A second advantage of the religious family is the realization that the most important things of life cannot be lost. When some families have lost their money they have lost "everything." Financial loss can be serious in a religious family, but the most valuable things of life remain untouched. In some families the death of a loved one may mean the loss of the very center of their lives. For a religious family the loss and the grief are quite as great, but love remains and can be redirected to others who may need it. Such spiritual values do not protect from tragedy. But when tragedy does strike, a religious family meets it with built-in resources. It is these spiritual stabilizers that provide the peace and the joy that the world cannot give, and the world cannot take away.

A third resource is worthy commitments. Stated in a more familiar terminology these commitments include love, concern for the common good, respect for the individual, sound personal integration, and the abundant life interpreted in terms of personality development and spiritual needs. A religious family seeks not only to live its commit-

---

[11] For an excellent statement of this aspect of religion, see Peter Bertocci, *Religion as Creative Insecurity*, Association Press, 1958.

ments but also to build them into the culture of which it is a part. Religious commitments mean primarily, not shelter and protection, but getting out into the stream of life with all its crosscurrents of evil and good, and learning about it from first-hand contacts. Children are not to be sheltered and coddled, but enlisted—an enlistment that includes a careful training that is often arduous and painful. People who are at home in a world of evils and goods no longer have to "solve" problems by concealing them, nor do they panic when serious dangers emerge. An awareness of positive resources gives substance to their faith, and experienced understanding gives effectiveness to their efforts. The survival of civilization may well depend upon religious families who see the need and do their job.

Finally, a religious family, although it lives by spiritual insights and draws upon divine resources, also lives intimately in the world. It can nourish itself only as it shares its strengths with others. As the church is a center of religion in the community, so a religious family is a center of spiritual power among its neighbors and friends. Religious families are the arteries and veins of society that derive their sustenance from the spiritual nourishment that they channel to others. As such they are the bulwarks of society and the means for its nourishment and strength.

READINGS

Beach, Waldo, *Conscience on Campus: an Interpretation of Christian Ethics for Campus Life*. New York: Association Press, 1958.

Bertocci, Peter A., *Religion as Creative Insecurity*. New York: Association Press, 1958.

Bonthius, Robert H., *Christian Paths to Self-Acceptance*. New York: King's Crown Press, 1948.

Brav, Stanley R. (ed.), *Marriage and the Jewish Tradition*. New York: Philosophical Library, 1951.

Chaplin, Dora P., *Children and Religion*. New York: Scribner, 1948.

Clark, Kenneth B., *Prejudice and Your Child*. Boston: Beacon Press, 1955.

Fahs, Sophia L., *Today's Children and Yesterday's Heritage: A Philosophy of Creative Religious Development*. Boston: Beacon Press, 1952.

Fallaw, Wesner, *The Modern Parent and the Teaching Church*. New York: Macmillan, 1946.

Fosdick, Harry Emerson, *On Being a Real Person*. New York: Harper, 1943.

Harrington, John B., *Essentials in Christian Faith*. New York: Harper, 1958.

Herberg, Will, *Protestant-Catholic-Jew*. New York: Doubleday, 1955.

Liebman, Joshua Loth, *Peace of Mind*. New York: Simon and Schuster, 1946.

Life, the editors of, *The World's Great Religions*. New York: Time, 1957.

Rosen, Leo, *Religion in America*. New York: Simon and Schuster, 1955.

Rutledge, Aaron L., *Responsible Marriage and Family Living: A Text with Adapted Readings.* New York: Harcourt, Brace, 1960, Chapter 15, "Religion and the Family."

Sorokin, Pitirim A., *Altruistic Love: A Study of American "Good Neighbors" and Christian Saints.* Boston: Beacon Press, 1950.

———— (ed.), *Explorations in Altruistic Love and Behavior: A Symposium.* Boston: Beacon Press, 1950.

Spurrier, William A., *A Guide to the Christian Faith.* New York: Scribner, 1953.

Thomas, John L., *The American Catholic Family.* Englewood Cliffs, N. J.: Prentice-Hall, 1956.

Tillich, Paul, *The Courage to Be.* New Haven: Yale University Press, 1952.

Williams, J. Paul, *What Americans Believe and How They Worship.* New York: Harper, 1952.

Appendix A

HEREDITY CLINICS [1]

State	Institution	City	Chief Counselor
California	Department of Zoology University of California	Berkeley	Curt Stern
Canada	Department of Genetics McGill University	Montreal	F. C. Fraser
	Hospital for Sick Children	Toronto	N. F. Walker
Illinois	Department of Zoology University of Chicago	Chicago	H. H. Strandskov
Louisiana	The Medical School Tulane University	New Orleans	H. W. Kloepfer
Michigan	Department of Medical Genetics University of Michigan	Ann Arbor	J. V. Neel
Minnesota	Dight Institute University of Minnesota	Minneapolis	S. C. Reed
	The Mayo Clinic	Rochester	J. S. Pearson
New York	New York State Psychiatric Institute	New York	F. J. Kallmann
North Carolina	Department of Preventive Medicine Bowman Gray School of Medicine	Winston-Salem	C. N. Herndon
Ohio	Department of Zoology Western Reserve University	Cleveland	A. G. Steinberg
	Starling Loving Hall The Ohio State University	Columbus	M. T. Macklin
Oklahoma	Department of Zoology University of Oklahoma	Norman	P. R. David
Rhode Island	Institute for Research in Health Services Brown University	Providence	G. W. Hagy
Texas	The Genetics Foundation University of Texas	Austin	C. P. Oliver
Utah	Laboratory of Human Genetics University of Utah	Salt Lake City	C. M. Woolf
Virginia	Department of Biology and Genetics Medical College of Virginia	Richmond	B. L. Hanna
Washington	School of Medicine University of Washington	Seattle	A. G. Motulsky
Wisconsin	Department of Medical Genetics The Medical School	Madison	N. E. Morton

[1] Adapted from Sheldon C. Reed, *Counseling in Medical Genetics*. Philadelphia: Saunders. From a revised listing by Dr. Sheldon Reed in a personal communication, 1958.

Appendix B

PREMARITAL, MARRIAGE, AND FAMILY
COUNSELING RESOURCES

Counseling facilities in your community may be recommended by your physician, your pastor, your lawyer, social agency, or community organization. In general, it is wise not to consult persons who advertise their services as marriage counselors without first checking their standing with your local welfare council or County Medical Society. If your own community seems to lack the resources you seek, you may find adequate facilities near you by writing one of the national organizations able to recommend competent counseling resources in your area:

American Association of Marriage Counselors, Inc., 104 East 40th Street, New York 16, N.Y. Has more than one hundred registered members who come up to established standards for competent marriage counselors. One or more may be not too far from you.

American Institute of Family Relations, 5287 Sunset Boulevard, Los Angeles 27, Cal. Maintains a full complement of services at the Los Angeles headquarters, and has regional consultants across the country available for marriage and family counseling.

American Social Health Association, 1790 Broadway, New York 19, N.Y. This agency with central interests in marriage and family life has a field and professional headquarters staff, in contact with many qualified counseling resources across the United States.

Council of Jewish Federations and Welfare Funds, 729 Seventh Avenue, New York 19, N.Y. Local Jewish organizations may consult with the national staff on special problems and facilities for counseling and family service in the area.

Family Service Association of America, 215 Fourth Avenue, New York 3, N.Y. There are 267 authorized member agencies listed by states in the *Directory of Member Agencies* published from time to time by the Family Service Association, to whom you might write for their recommended counseling resource nearest you.

National Association for Mental Health, Inc., 10 Columbus Circle, New York 19, N.Y. Maintains contact with mental health and guidance resources throughout the United States; publishes at intervals *Outpatient Psychiatric Clinics;* and refers inquirers to nearest counseling or guidance facility.

National Catholic Welfare Conference, Family Life Bureau, 1312 Massachusetts Avenue, N.W., Washington 5, D.C. Your parish priest may be able to direct you either to a Pre-Cana Conference (for about-to-be-married couples), Cana Conference (for young married couples), or to a special individual counseling resource recommended by the Family Life Bureau.

National Council of Churches of Christ in the U.S.A., Department of Family Life, 475 Riverside Drive, New York 17, N.Y. Your pastor may want to confer with the national staff on counseling resources in your area to supplement what he can do for you in premarital, marriage, and family counseling.

Planned Parenthood Federation of America, Inc., 501 Madison Avenue, New York 22, N.Y. The national headquarters of the planned parenthood movement can direct you to the nearest clinic, where premarital, marriage, and family counseling, as well as specific birth control and infertility services, is available.

INDEX